FORMATIONS OF MODERNITY

UNDERSTANDING MODERN SOCIETIES: AN INTRODUCTION

Series editor: Stuart Hall

Book 1 *Formations of Modernity*
edited by Stuart Hall and Bram Gieben

Book 2 *Political and Economic Forms of Modernity*
edited by John Allen, Peter Braham and Paul Lewis

Book 3 *Social and Cultural Forms of Modernity*
edited by Robert Bocock and Kenneth Thompson

Book 4 *Modernity and its Futures*
edited by Stuart Hall, David Held and Anthony McGrew

For general availability of all the books in the series, please contact your regular supplier or, in case of difficulty, Polity Press.

This book forms part of the Open University course D213 *Understanding Modern Societies*. Details of this and other Open University courses can be obtained from the Central Enquiry Service, The Open University, P.O. Box 200, Milton Keynes, MK7 2YZ; Tel: 0908 653078.

Cover illustration: John Tandy *Abstract composition* (*c.* 1930) Private Collection, London. Reproduced by courtesy of the Redfern Gallery, London, and by kind permission of Mrs Suzanne Tandy. Photo: A.C. Cooper.

FORMATIONS OF MODERNITY

EDITED BY STUART HALL AND BRAM GIEBEN

POLITY PRESS IN ASSOCIATION WITH THE OPEN UNIVERSITY

Copyright © The Open University 1992

First published 1992 by Polity Press in association with Basil Blackwell and The Open University

Editorial office:
Polity Press,
65 Bridge Street,
Cambridge CB2 1UR, UK

Marketing and production:
Blackwell Publishers Ltd,
108 Cowley Road,
Oxford OX4 1JF, UK

ISBN 0 7456 0959 7

ISBN 0 7456 0960 0 (paperback)

British Library Cataloguing in Publication Data
A CIP catalogue record for this book is available from the British Library.

Library of Congress Cataloguing in Publication Data
A CIP catalogue record for this book is available from the Library of Congress.

Edited, designed and typeset by The Open University

Printed in Great Britain by Butler & Tanner Ltd, Frome

CONTENTS

Understanding Modern Societies Course Team

Stuart Hall	Professor of Sociology and Course Team Chair
Maureen Adams	Secretary
John Allen	Senior Lecturer in Economic Geography
Margaret Allot	Discipline Secretary, Sociology
Robert Bocock	Senior Lecturer in Sociology
David Boswell	Senior Lecturer in Sociology
Peter Braham	Lecturer in Sociology
Vivienne Brown	Lecturer in Economics
Dianne Cook	Secretary
Robert Cookson	Senior Editor, Social Sciences
Helen Crowley	Lecturer in Women's Studies, North London Polytechnic
Molly Freeman	Discipline Secretary, Sociology
Bram Gieben	Staff Tutor, Social Sciences
Peter Hamilton	Lecturer in Sociology
David Held	Professor in Politics and Sociology
Paul Lewis	Senior Lecturer in Politics
Vic Lockwood	Senior Producer, BBC
Anthony McGrew	Senior Lecturer in Politics
Gregor McLennan	Professor of Sociology, Massey University, New Zealand
David Scott-Macnab	Editor, Social Sciences
Graeme Salaman	Senior Lecturer in Sociology
Jane Sheppard	Graphic Designer
Paul Smith	Media Librarian
Keith Stribley	Course Manager
Kenneth Thompson	Professor in Sociology
Alison Tucker	Producer, BBC
Pauline Turner	Secretary
Diane Watson	Staff Tutor, Social Sciences
David Wilson	Editor, Book Trade
Chris Wooldridge	Editor, Social Sciences

Consultants

Harriet Bradley	Senior Lecturer, Sunderland Polytechnic
Tom Burden	Tutor Panel
Tony Darkes	Tutor Panel
Celia Lury	Lecturer in Sociology, University of Lancaster
Denise Riley	Researcher in political philosophy
Alan Scott	Lecturer in Politics, University of East Anglia
Jeffrey Weeks	Professor in Social Relations, Bristol Polytechnic
Geoffrey Whitty	Professor of Education, Goldsmith's College
Steven Yearley	Professor of Politics, Queens University, Belfast

External Assessor

Bryan Turner	Professor of Sociology, University of Essex

PREFACE

Formations of Modernity is the first book in a new series of sociology textbooks which aims to provide a comprehensive, innovative and stimulating introduction to sociology. The four books in the series, which is entitled *Understanding Modern Societies: An Introduction*, are listed on page ii. They have been written to suit students and readers who have no prior knowledge of sociology and are designed to be used on a variety of social science courses in universities and colleges. Although part of a series, each book is self-contained to facilitate use with students studying different aspects of the history, sociology and ideas of modern society and its international context.

The four books form the central part of an Open University course, also called *Understanding Modern Societies*. Open University courses are produced by an extensive course team consisting of academic authors and consultants, a panel of experienced tutors, an external academic assessor, editors and designers, BBC producers, academic administrators and secretaries. (The full course team responsible for this course is listed on the opposite page.) Every chapter has been subjected to wide-ranging discussion and improvement at each of several draft stages. The result is a unique series of textbooks which draw on the cumulative academic research and teaching experience of the Open University and the wider academic community.

All four books have three distinctive features. First, each chapter provides not only a descriptive, historical account of the key social processes which shaped modern industrial societies, and which are now, once again, rapidly transforming them, but also analysis of the key concepts, issues and current debates in the related academic literature. Secondly, each chapter includes a number of extracts from classic and contemporary books and articles, all of them pertinent to the chapter. These are printed conveniently at the end of the chapter in which they are discussed. They can be distinguished from the main text (and can thus be found easily) by the continuous line down the left-hand margin. The third important feature of the text is that it is *interactive*: every chapter contains specially designed exercises, questions and activities to help readers understand, reflect upon and retain the main teaching points at issue. From the long experience of Open University course writing, we have found that all readers will benefit from such a package of materials carefully designed for students working with a fair degree of independence.

While each book is free-standing, there are some cross-references to the other books in the series to aid readers using all the books. These take the following form: 'see Book 1 (Hall and Gieben, 1992), Chapter 4'. For further information on a writer or concept, the reader is sometimes referred to the *Penguin Dictionary of Sociology*. Full bibliographic details of this dictionary are provided where relevant at the end of each chapter, together with other references which suggest further reading which can be undertaken in each area.

In the long collaborative process by which Open University materials are made, the editors of such a volume are only the most obvious of those who have helped to shape its chapters. There are many others with responsibilities for the detailed and painstaking work of bringing a book with so many parts to completion. Our external assessor, Professor Bryan Turner, provided invaluable intellectual guidance, comment, advice, stimulus and encouragement at every stage of the production of these books. We owe special thanks to Molly Freeman, Maureen Adams, Pauline Turner, Dianne Cook and Margaret Allott for really marvellous secretarial support. Rarely in the history of word-processing can so many drafts have been produced so swiftly by so few. Our Open University editors, Chris Wooldridge, David Scott-Macnab, David Wilson and Robert Cookson, have improved each chapter with their insight and professionalism, usually under quite unreasonable pressures of time, and with unfailing good nature. Thanks also to Paul Smith, our media librarian, for his creative work in finding so many of the illustrations. Debbie Seymour, of Polity Press, has been a constant source of encouragement and good sense.

Finally, the chapter authors have borne stoically our innumerable criticisms and suggestions, and have managed to preserve the essence of their original creations through successive rounds of amendments and cuts. Their scholarship and commitment have made this book what it is.

Bram Gieben and Stuart Hall

INTRODUCTION

Stuart Hall

Formations of Modernity, as the title suggests, is concerned with the process of formation which led to the emergence of modern societies, and which stamped them with their distinctive character. The book addresses a number of questions which have proved to be of fundamental importance throughout the history of the social sciences. When, how and why did modern societies first emerge? Why did they assume the forms and structures which they did? What were the key processes which shaped their development? Traditionally, modern societies have been identified with the onset of industrialization in the nineteenth century. *Formations* breaks with this tradition, tracing modern societies back to their origins in the rapid and extensive social and economic development which followed the decline of feudalism in Western Europe. It sees modern societies now as a global phenomenon and the modern world as the unexpected and unpredicted outcome of, not one, but a series of major historical transitions.

The six chapters which comprise this volume not only map this historical process of formation, but attempt to provide an explanatory framework for this development. The commonsense term 'modern' — meaning recent, up-to-date — is useful in locating these societies chronologically, but it lacks a theoretical or analytic rationale. This book, however, analyses the passage to modernity in terms of a theoretical model based on the interaction of a number of 'deeply structured processes of change taking place over long periods', as David Held puts it in Chapter 2. The book does not collapse these into a single process (e.g. 'modernization'), but treats them as different processes, working according to different historical time-scales, whose interaction led to variable and contingent outcomes. As Held observes, 'the stress is on *processes*, *factors* and *causal patterns* ... there is no mono-causal explanation — no single phenomenon or set of phenomena — which fully explains [their] rise ... It is in a combination of factors that the beginnings of an explanation ... can be found'. We return to the implications of this multi-causal approach later in this Introduction.

The four major social processes which the book identifies are: the political, the economic, the social and the cultural. They form the basis of the four central chapters in this volume, and organize the narrative or 'story-line' of the other books in the series. In the next two volumes, *Political and Economic Forms of Modernity* and *Social and Cultural Forms of Modernity*, these processes provide the framework for an analysis of what developed industrial societies look like and how they work. In the final volume in the series, *Modernity and its Futures*, they provide the basis for identifying the emergent social forces and contradictory processes which are radically re-shaping modern societies today.

Formations of Modernity is divided into six chapters. In Chapter 1, 'The Enlightenment and the birth of social science', Peter Hamilton examines the explosion of intellectual energy in eighteenth-century Western Europe which became known as 'the Enlightenment'. This movement gave definition to the very idea of 'modernity' and is often described as the original matrix of the modern social sciences. Of course, in one sense, the study of society was not new. Writers had been making observations about social life for millennia. But the idea of 'the social' as a separate and distinct form of reality, which could be analysed in entirely 'this-worldly', material terms and laid out for rational investigation and explanation, is a distinctly modern idea which only finally crystallized in the discourses of the Enlightenment. The 'birth of the social' as an object of knowledge made possible for the first time the systematic analysis and the practices of investigation we call 'the social sciences'.

Chapter 1 examines the historical and geographical context of the European Enlightenment, and the vision of intellectual emancipation which seized its principal figures — the *philosophes* — including such major precursors of modern social theory as Montesquieu, Diderot, Voltaire, Rousseau, and the luminaries of the 'Scottish Enlightenment' such as David Hume, Adam Smith, and Adam Ferguson. It discusses the Enlightenment critique of traditional authority and examines some of its leading ideas — progress, science, reason, and nature. These gave shape to the 'promise' of the Enlightenment — the prospect which it opened up of an unending era of material progress and prosperity, the abolition of prejudice and superstition and the mastery of the forces of nature based on the expansion of human knowledge and understanding. The chapter takes the story forward, through the Romantic movement and the French Revolution to those major theorists of nineteenth-century social science — Saint-Simon and Comte. It looks forward to that later moment, at the end of the nineteenth century, when the social sciences were once again reorganized.

This second moment in the development of the social sciences — between 1890 and 1920 — was the time of what are now known as the 'founding figures' of sociology: Durkheim, Weber, Simmel and Tönnies. Thereafter the social sciences became more compartmentalized into their separate disciplines, more specialized and empirical, more 'scientific' (positivistic) and more closely engaged with application to the 'real world' through social engineering. Nevertheless, these classical figures of modern sociology also undertook a major examination of the formation of the modern world and its 'laws of development', not unlike that which the Enlightenment *philosophes* had inaugurated. These Enlightenment concerns continue to underpin the social sciences today. Indeed, in recent years, there has been a remarkable revival in historical sociology, which is concerned with these questions of long-term transformation and development; and, interestingly, they are being pursued in a more interdisciplinary way, drawing together the researches of sociologists, economic and social historians, political theorists and philosophers. It is as if these profound questions about the origin and destiny of the modern world are surfacing again at the very moment when modernity itself — its promise and its vicissitudes — is being put in question. This book draws on much of that new work in historical sociology and reflects these emerging concerns and debates.

The second chapter 'The development of the modern state' opens by examining the formation of the modern state. David Held sees the modern state emerging at the intersection of the national and international systems. He traces the state's development through a variety of historical forms — from the classical European empires, the divided authority of the feudal states (Papacy and Holy Roman Empire), the estates system and the absolutisms of the early modern period, to the emergence of the forms of political authority, secular power, legitimacy and sovereignty characteristic of the modern *nation-state*. The chapter considers the roles of warfare, militarism and capitalism in underpinning the supremacy of this nation-state form. It discusses the system of nation-states as the foundation of the modern international order. Into this story are woven the changing conceptions of politics elaborated in western political philosophy by writers such as Hobbes, Locke, Rousseau, Mill, Marx and Weber. The chapter looks forward to the emergence of liberal democracy as the privileged twentieth-century state form of modern societies in the West.

In Chapter 3, 'The emergence of the economy', Vivienne Brown examines the formation of a distinct sphere of economic life, governed by new economic relations, and regulated and represented by new economic ideas. She describes the spread of commerce and trade, the expansion of markets, the new division of labour and the growth of material wealth and consumption — 'opulence' — in eighteenth-century British society, consequent upon the rise of capitalism in Europe and the gradual transformation of the traditional economy. European economic development began early — some date it as early as the fifteenth century — and the expansion of trade and the market was at the centre of the process. But for a long time, capitalism developed under the protective shadow of state monopolies at home and mercantilism overseas. By the eighteenth century, however, *laissez-faire* and the market forces of the private economy were beginning to unleash the productive energies of the capitalist system. Vivienne Brown reminds us that the engines of this development were the commercial and agrarian revolutions. The economic model in the mind of Adam Smith when he wrote *The Wealth of Nations* — that bible of capitalist development — was agrarian and commercial capitalism, not the industrial smokestacks and factory-hands of Marx and Engels. The chapter weaves together an account of the formation of the modern economy and the new ways of speaking and thinking about economic life — the new economic discourse — which emerged in the eighteenth century. It provides a re-reading of Adam Smith's classic work, which became such a landmark text of the modern age, and sets its ideas in their proper historical and moral contexts.

In Chapter 4, 'Changing social structures: class and gender', Harriet Bradley takes the story forwards from the agrarian and commercial revolutions of the eighteenth century to the upheavals of the Industrial

Revolution of the nineteenth. She also shifts the focus from economic processes to the changing social relations and the new type of social structure characteristic of industrial capitalist society. Her chapter is concerned with the emergence of new social and sexual divisions of labour. She contrasts the class and gender formations of pre-industrial, rural society with the rise of the new social classes, organized around capital and waged labour; the work patterns associated with the new forms of industrial production; and the new relations between men and women, organized around the shifting distinctions between the public and the private, work and home, the public world and the family and household.

The chapter discusses some of the major sociological theories and models of class formation. It also deploys the concepts of gender, patriarchy, and family which feminist social theorists have advanced in the social science agenda and which are increasingly problematizing 'class' as the master (sic) explanatory category. Harriet Bradley analyses the social structure of industrial society in terms of the deep interpenetration of class *and* gender. The chapter points forward to how these class and gender structures evolved and were complicated by questions of race and ethnicity in the twentieth century.

In Chapter 5, 'The cultural formations of modern society', Robert Bocock looks at the increasing importance given to the analysis of culture, meaning, language and the symbolic structures of social life in contemporary social theory — what the anthropologist, Lévi-Strauss, identified as 'the study of the life of signs at the heart of social life'. The chapter then turns to a discussion of three key cultural themes in the transition to modernity. First, the shift from a religious to a secular world-view, and from a 'sacred' to a 'profane' foundation for social and moral values, which characterizes the passage from traditional society to modern society. Second, the role which religion played in the formation of the 'spirit of capitalism' — a discussion of Max Weber's thesis about 'the Protestant ethic'. Third, the growing awareness among western philosophers and social theorists of the costs of modern culture — what Freud called civilization's 'discontents', and Weber saw as the consequences of the increasing rationalization and disenchantment of the modern world. This final theme points forward to recent critiques of the 'promise' of the Enlightenment, which are taken up in subsequent volumes in the series. It shows that a pessimistic assessment of enlightenment and modernity has in fact been part of Enlightenment reason — its 'dark shadow' — from its very inception.

Finally, in Chapter 6, 'The West and the Rest: discourse and power', Stuart Hall places the early Europe-centred — and Euro-centric — account of the evolution of modern societies and modernity in the West, in a wider global context. The gradual integration of Western Europe, its take-off into sustained economic growth, the emergence of the system of powerful nation-states, and other features of the formation of modern societies is often told as a purely *internal* story — as if Europe provided all the conditions, materials and dynamic necessary for its own development from within itself. This view is challenged at several places in this book and Chapter 6 reminds us, once again, that the process also had *external* and global conditions of existence. The particular form of 'globalization' which is undermining and transforming modernity today (the internationalization of production, consumption, markets and investment), is only the latest phase in a very long story; it is not a new phenomenon. The early expansion of the European maritime empires in the fifteenth century, the exploration of new worlds, the encounter with new peoples and civilizations very different from that of Europe, and the harnessing of them to the dynamic development of Europe through commerce, conquest and colonization are *key* episodes (but often neglected ones) in the formation of modern societies and the modern age.

Chapter 6 argues that the integration of Western Europe also involved the construction of a new sense of cultural identity. Europe only discovered and produced this new identity in the course of representing itself as a distinct, unique and triumphant civilization, and at the same time marking its difference from other cultures, peoples, and civilizations. These 'Others' were incorporated into the West's image of itself — into its language, its systems of representation, its forms of knowledge, its visual imagery, even its conception of what sorts of people did and did not have access to reason itself. This encounter with difference and the construction of 'otherness' is sketched in relation to the European exploration and conquest of the Americas, Asia, Africa and the Pacific between the fifteenth and nineteenth centuries. The chapter analyses the formation of these discourses of 'self' and 'otherness', through which the West came to represent itself and imagine its *difference* from 'the Rest'. It looks forward, across the centuries, to the way these images of the West and 'the Rest' resurface in contemporary discourses of race and ethnicity, at a time when 'the Other' is beginning to question and contest the 'centredness' of the West, which western civilization (and western social science) has for so long taken for granted.

We can now turn to consider in greater detail some of the themes and approaches in this book. As noted earlier, the account of the formation of modern societies is organized principally in terms of four major processes — the political, the economic, the social and the cultural. The transition to modernity is explained in terms of the interaction between these four processes. It could not have occurred without them. No one process, on its own, provides an adequate explanation of the formation of modern societies. Consequently, no one process is accorded explanatory priority in the analysis. Analytically, we treat each process as distinct — an approach which has certain consequences to which we shall return in a moment. However, it must be borne in mind that, in 'real' historical time, they interacted with one another. The evolution of the modern state, for example, has a different history from that of the modern economy. Nevertheless the nation-state provided the institutional framework and shared legal and political norms which facilitated the expansion of the national economy. Modernity, then, was the outcome, not of a single process, but of the condensation of a number of different processes and histories.

How does this relate to the definition of a society as 'modern'? What characteristics must it have to merit that description?

What we mean by 'modern' is that each process led to the emergence of certain distinctive features or social characteristics, and it is these features which, taken together, provide us with our definition of 'modernity'. In this sense, the term 'modern' does not mean simply that the phenomenon is of recent origin. It carries a certain analytic and theoretical value, because it is related to a conceptual model. What are these defining features or characteristics of modern societies?

1   The dominance of secular forms of political power and authority and conceptions of sovereignty and legitimacy, operating within defined territorial boundaries, which are characteristic of the large, complex structures of the modern nation-state.

2   A monetarized exchange economy, based on the large-scale production and consumption of commodities for the market, extensive ownership of private property and the accumulation of capital on a systematic, long-term basis. (The economies of eastern European communist states were an exception to some of these features, though they were based on the large-scale industrial production and consumption of goods.)

3   The decline of the traditional social order, with its fixed social hierarchies and overlapping allegiances, and the appearance of a dynamic social and sexual division of labour. In modern capitalist societies, this was characterized by new class formations, and distinctive patriarchal relations between men and women.

4   The decline of the religious world view typical of traditional societies and the rise of a secular and materialist culture, exhibiting those individualistic, rationalist, and instrumental impulses now so familiar to us.

There are two other aspects to our definition of modernity, which should be loosely included under the rubric of 'the cultural'. The first refers to ways of producing and classifying knowledge. The emergence of modern societies was marked by the birth of a new intellectual and cognitive world, which gradually emerged with the Reformation, the Renaissance, the scientific revolution of the seventeenth century and the Enlightenment of the eighteenth century. This shift in Europe's intellectual and moral universe was dramatic, and as constitutive for the formation of modern societies as early capitalism or the rise of the nation-state. Second, the book follows modern social analysis in the emphasis it gives to the construction of cultural and social identities as part of the formation process. By this we mean the construction of a sense of belonging which draws people together into an 'imagined community' and the construction of symbolic boundaries which define who does *not* belong or is excluded from it. For many centuries, being

'Christian' or 'Catholic' was the only common identity shared by the peoples of Western Europe. 'European' was an identity which only slowly emerged. So the formation of modern societies in Europe had to include the construction of the language, the images, and symbols which defined these societies as 'communities' and set them apart, in their represented differences, from others.

The importance given to major historical processes helps to explain the significance of the term 'formations' in our title. The political, economic, social, and cultural processes were the 'motors' of the formation process. They worked on and transformed traditional societies into modern ones. They shaped modern society across a long historical time-span. We speak of processes, rather than practices because, although processes are made up of the activities of individual and collective social agents, they operate across extended time-scales, and seem at times to work on their own, in performing the work of social transformation. One effect of the operation of these processes is to give modern societies a distinctive shape and form, making them not simply 'societies' (a loose ensemble of social activities) but *social formations* (societies with a definite structure and a well-defined set of social relations). One particular feature of modern social formations is that they became articulated into distinct, clearly demarcated zones of activity or social practice. We call these domains — corresponding to the processes which produced them — the polity, the economy, the social structure and the cultural sphere. These spheres are the 'formations' of modern societies. *Formations,* then, in our title refers to *both* the activities of emergence, and their outcomes or results: both process *and* structure.

The next aspect which deserves discussion is the role of history in the book. As we noted earlier, *Formations of Modernity* adopts a historical perspective on the emergence of modern societies. The relation between history and the social sciences has often been a troubled one. Our aim is to map long-term historical trends and changing social patterns. There is an extensive use of historical evidence; a number of summary histories are embedded in the chapters, which provide a historical context and chronological framework for different aspects of the formation process; and there are several comparative historical case studies. We also use simple contrasts (e.g. feudalism vs capitalism), summarizing concepts (e.g. traditional vs modern society) and rough-and-ready chronologies (e.g. towards the end of the fifteenth century).

However, there is no attempt to match the detail and specificity which is the hallmark of modern historical scholarship. By contrast, these accounts make extensive use of *historical generalizations*. Generalizations always abstract from the rich detail of complex events — that is their function. There is nothing wrong with this: all serious intellectual work involves abstraction. The point, however, is always to bear in mind the *level of abstraction* at which the generalizations are working. Each level has its strengths (i.e. it is good for highlighting some aspects) and its limitations (it is obliged to leave out much of importance).

Formations of Modernity works with historical generalizations, because its purpose is not only to describe when and how modern society developed, but to explain *why* it happened. However, describing a process and providing an explanation are more closely related that is sometimes assumed. The sociologist Michael Mann has remarked that 'the greatest contribution of the historian to the methodology of the social sciences is the date', by which he meant that careful periodization is an essential part of explaining the development of any social phenomenon. As he went on to say, '... when things happened is essential to establishing causality' (Mann, 1988, p.6). In *Formations*, care is taken to establish, as far as possible, when things happened. This includes simple things like giving the dates of major figures, key events or important texts. The point is not to oblige readers to memorize dates but to help them develop a sense of historical time, context and sequence. However, readers will notice that there is no attempt to provide a precise date when modern societies began. There are at least several reasons for this reluctance.

First, the formation processes operated across several centuries and in a slow, uneven way, so it is difficult to identify a clear starting point. For example, when exactly does trade and commerce cease to be the economic basis of a few European cities — Venice, Florence, Bruges — and become the dominant economic form of western societies as a whole? Another reason is that there is no convenient cut-off point between what emerged and what went before. The processes we have identified as necessary to modern formation worked on and transformed already-existing societies. Those 'traditional' societies were the 'raw materials', the preconditions of modernity — the cloth out of which its shapes were cut. Modern capitalism sprang up in the interstices of the feudal economy. The modern nation-state was carved out of the old feudal and absolutist systems. So where does modern history really start — since it seems to have been always-already in process? This is an old problem in historical explanation — what is sometimes known as the danger of infinite regress, which, if we aren't careful, will transport us back to the beginning of time! Of course, this does not mean that history just seamlessly unfolded. That would be to hold an evolutionary model of historical development. In fact, as we show, as well as continuities connecting one historical phase or period to another, history is also full of *discontinuities* — breaks, ruptures, reversals. The focus on 'transitions' in this book is designed precisely to emphasize these significant breaks in historical development.

Another reason for avoiding a simple date when modern societies began is that, as we noted earlier, the processes which form the main explanatory framework of the book had different time-scales. They began at different times, followed different trajectories, had different turning-points and seem to exhibit different tempos of development. This is reflected in the different periodizations used in each chapter. Chapter 2 takes the history of the modern state back to the Greek and Roman empires. Chapter 3 on the economy is mainly an eighteenth-century story. Chapter 4, on the industrial social structure, focuses on the nineteenth century. Chapter 5 begins with the Protestant Reformation in the sixteenth century. And the last chapter begins with Portuguese explorations in the fifteenth century.

Therefore, it does not make much sense to say that modern societies started at the same moment and developed uniformly within a single historical 'time'. The modern state, for example, has a very different 'history' and 'time' from the capitalist economy. Thus you will find that, although the various chapters cross-refer to different processes, they do not chart the formation of modern societies as a single historical process. The book has been written in the aftermath of the break-up of a more uniform conception of history which tended to dominate nineteenth-century evolutionary social theories; that is to say, in the wake of a certain relativization of historical time. The use of the plural — histories, societies, formations, conditions, causes, etc. — is one way of recognizing and marking these differential times of 'history', avoiding what some theorists have called 'homogeneous time' (Benjamin, 1970; Anderson, 1986).

Closely related to this idea of a single historical time-scale is the view that modernity is really *one* thing, towards which every society is inevitably moving, though at different rates of development. Some social scientists not only conceptualized history as one process, working to a unified time-scale, but saw it as unfolding according to some necessary law or logic towards a prescribed and inevitable end. This was true, not only of certain kinds of classical Marxist historical analysis but also of those theorists who, while not accepting the Marxist model, did assume some form of western-style modernity to be the inevitable destiny of all societies. This assumption of an inevitable progress along a single path of development may have made it easier to read the meaning of history, since — despite much evidence to the contrary — it seemed to give it direction and we knew in advance the end of the story. But it did not square very easily with the great diversity of actual forms of historical development. Critics now call this one-track view a 'teleological' conception of history — moving towards a preordained end or goal. Modern social theorists have become increasingly aware of the limitations of this position in all its variants. It seems more and more implausible to see history as unfolding according to one logic. Increasingly, different temporalities, different outcomes seem to be involved. Many events seem to follow no rational logic but to be more the contingent effects of unintended consequences — outcomes no one ever intended, which are contrary to, and often the direct opposite of, what seemed to be the dominant thrust of events. Of course, the processes of formation were not autonomous and separate from one another. There were connections between them — they were articulated with one another. But they weren't inevitably harnessed together, all moving or changing in tandem.

One major weakness of the teleological view of history is that it tended to assume that there is only one path of social development — the one taken by western societies — and that this is a universal model which all societies must follow and which leads sooner or later, through a fixed series of stages to the same end. Thus, tribal society would inevitably lead to the nation-state, feudalism to capitalism, rural society to industrialization, and so on. In one version, this was called 'modernization theory', a perspective which became very popular in the 1950s particularly in the writings of Walter Rostow (Rostow, 1971). This formed the basis of much western policy in the Third World, which was directed at bringing into existence as rapidly as possible what modernization theorists identified as the necessary conditions for western-style development and growth. Modernization theory also assumed that there *was* one, principal motor propelling societies up this ladder of development — the economy. The laws of capitalist industrialism — capital accumulation, supply and demand, rapid industrialization, market forces — were the principal engines of growth. Paradoxically, though they took a very different view of the nature and consequences of capitalism, modernization theorists tended to agree with Marxists in attributing social development ultimately to one, principal cause: the economic. This belief that all societies could be laid out at different points along the same evolutionary scale (with, of course, the West at the top!) was a very Enlightenment conception and one can see why many non-European societies now regard both these versions as very Euro-centric stories.

Few would now deny the link between capitalism and modernity. But in general this book breaks with this kind of one-track modernization theory and with the economic reductionism which was a key feature of it. In general, it adopts a more multi-causal explanation of how modern development in Western Europe occurred. It notes that few modern societies are or even look the same. Think of the US, the UK, France and Japan. Each took a radically different path to modernity. In each, that evolution depended on, not one, but a number of determining conditions. In general, though economic organization is a massive, shaping historical force, the economy alone cannot function outside of specific social, political and cultural conditions, let alone produce sustainable development. Modern societies certainly display no singular logic of development. The formation processes combine, in each instance, in very different ways. Japan, for example, combines a fiercely modern, high-tech economy with a strikingly traditional culture. Dictatorship was as much the engine of industrialization in Germany, Japan and the Soviet Union as democracy. Force, violence and coercion have played as decisive a historical role in the evolution of capitalism as peaceful economic competition. One of the purposes of comparative analysis, which is a feature of this book, is to highlight differences as well as similarities, and thus to underline the necessity of a break with mono-causal or reductionist explanations of social development.

In fact, even the idea of a necessary forward movement or progressive impetus towards 'development' built into history may be open to question. Development has indeed become the goal of many societies.

But not all societies are in fact 'developing'. And the under-development of some appears to be systematically linked to the over-development of others. So the 'law' of historical development keeps missing its way or failing to deliver. Development itself turns out, on inspection, to be a highly contradictory phenomenon, a two-edged sword.

Many social theorists now see unevenness and difference as an even more powerful historical logic than evenness, similarity and uniformity. Gradually, therefore, a more plural conception of the historical process of formation has emerged in the social sciences. It lays more stress on varied paths to development, diverse outcomes, ideas of difference, unevenness, contradiction, contingency (rather than necessity), and so on. However, it should be noted that giving greater weight to contingency in the accounts of social development does not mean that history is simply the outcome of a series of purely random events. But it does imply that in history everything does not seamlessly unfold according to some internal logic or inevitable law.

These are contentious issues in social science, and the questions they raise are far from settled. The six chapters in this book, for instance, take different positions on these questions. But the critique briefly outlined above is now widely accepted. Contributors to this volume still hold to the view that there *are* processes of formation which have shaped western societies, that these can be identified, mapped and analysed, and that explanations for some of their directions can be provided. That is to say, the book remains committed to what may be described as a qualified version of the Enlightenment belief that social development *is* amenable to rational analysis and explanation. But unlike many earlier sociological accounts, which tended to privilege class as the 'master' category, it does not adopt a clear hierarchy or priority of causes, and is generally critical of economic reductionism, in which the economic base is assumed to be the determining force in history 'in the last instance', as Frederick Engels once put it. As one social theorist, the French philosopher Louis Althusser, remarked, the trouble is that 'the last instance never comes'. Instead, this book analyses different, interdependent 'organizational clusters' — the polity, the economy, the social and the cultural — whose 'original association in western Europe', as Perry Anderson puts it, 'was fortuitous' (Anderson, 1990, p.53). In general, its contributors adopt a weaker notion of formation and causality and a pluralization of key concepts, as we noted earlier.

We have suggested why the history of modern societies had no absolute beginning or predetermined goal. However, it is almost impossible to describe the process of formation without using the language of 'origins', 'development' and, at least implicitly, 'ends'. Organizing the account of the formation of modern societies as a 'story' seems to carry its own narrative logic. A story-line imposes a form on what may be otherwise a formless and chaotic series of events. Narrative gives a chapter a certain impetus, flow and coherence, moving it smoothly from a 'beginning' to 'the sense of an ending' (as all good stories do). This imposes a certain order or meaning on events which they may have lacked at the time. Increasingly, historians and philosophers have been puzzling over this impact of language, narrative and the literary devices which we use when constructing accounts, on the content and logic of an argument (White, 1987; Derrida, 1981). Some 'deconstructive' philosophers, for example, go so far as to argue that the persuasiveness of philosophical argument often depends more on its rhetorical form and its metaphors, than its rational logic. And they point to the fact that, in addition to imposing one meaning on events, narrative lends an account a certain unchallengeable authority or 'truth'.

Contributors to this volume have tried to build up the accounts they offer on the basis of a careful sifting of evidence and arguments which make their underlying theoretical assumptions clear. Nevertheless, you may also notice the impact of a greater reflexivity and self-consciousness about language, writing, and the forms which explanations take in the way the chapters in this book are written. Authors are constantly aware that it is *they* who impose a shape on events; that all accounts, however carefully tested and supported, are in the end 'authored'. All social science explanations reflect to some degree the point of view of the author who is trying to make sense of things. They do not carry the impersonal guarantee of inevitability and truth. Consequently, arguments and positions are advanced here in a more tentative and provisional way. It is more a choice between convincing accounts, which deal persuasively with all the evidence, even the part which does not fit the theory, than a simple choice between 'right' and 'wrong' explanations. Readers should recognize that arguments advanced in the book are open to debate, not variants of the Authorized Version.

Of course, being sensitive to language, meaning and the effect of narrative does not imply that social science simply produces a series of 'good stories', none better than the other. This would be an extreme form of relativism which would undermine the whole project of social science. There are criteria of assessment which help us to judge between the relative weight and explanatory power of different accounts. Most social analysts are still committed to providing systematic, rigorous, coherent, comprehensive, conceptually clear, well-evidenced accounts, which makes their underlying theoretical structure and value assumptions clear to readers, and thus accessible to argument and criticism. But the greater degree of awareness of one's own practices of producing meaning, of writing, even while doing it, means that we cannot deny the ultimately interpretive character of the social science enterprise.

This greater reflexivity — the attention to language, and the plural character of 'meanings' — is not, of course, entirely novel. Many earlier traditions which have influenced social science practice have raised similar issues — for example, linguistic philosophy, hermeneutics, phenomenology, interpretive sociology — though they pointed to different philosophical conclusions. However, the return of these issues to the centre of social theory in recent years reflects what some social theorists now call the 'discursive turn' in social theory (Norris, 1983; Young, 1990). This implies a new — or renewed — awareness in theory and analysis of the importance of language (discourse) and how it is used (what is sometimes called 'discursive practice') to produce meaning. Meaning is recognized to be *contextual* — dependent upon specific historical contexts, rather than valid for all time. You will find this 'discursive turn' reflected, to different degrees, in this book and the other books in the series. The 'discursive turn' in modern philosophy is more fully debated in Gregor McLennan's final chapter in the last book in the series, *Modernity and Its Futures*.

The 'discursive turn' affects not only how some chapters in the volume are written but what they are about. The processes of economic, political and social development seem to have a clear, objective, material character. They altered material and social organization in the 'real world' — how people actually behaved — in ways which can be clearly identified and described. But cultural processes are rather different. They deal with less tangible things — meanings, values, symbols, ideas, knowledge, language, ideology: what cultural theorists call the symbolic dimensions of social life. Hitherto (and not only in Marxist types of analysis), these have been accorded a somewhat secondary status in the explanatory hierarchy of the social sciences. The cultural or ideological dimensions of social life were considered by some to be 'superstructural', dependent on and merely reflecting the primary status of the material base.

This book gives much greater prominence and weight to cultural and symbolic processes in the formation of modern societies. Chapters 1, 5 and 6 all deal directly with broadly cultural aspects. More significantly, culture is accorded a higher explanatory status than is customary. It is considered to be, not reflective of, but *constitutive* in the formation of the modern world: as constitutive as economic, political or social processes of change. What is more, economic, political and social processes do not operate outside of cultural and ideological conditions. The distinction between 'material' and 'ideational' factors in sociological analysis is thus considerably weakened, if not invalidated altogether. Language is seen to be 'material' because it is the result of social practice and has real effects in shaping and regulating social behaviour. Similarly, material processes — like the economy or politics — depend on 'meaning' for their effects and have cultural or ideological conditions of existence. The modern market economy, for example, requires new conceptions of economic life, a new economic discourse, as well as new organizational forms. It may not be helpful to draw hard and fast distinctions between these two aspects of social development — the material and the discursive.

Max Weber argued that social practices are always 'meaningful practices' and that this is what distinguishes them from mere biological reflexes, like an involuntary jerk following a tap on the knee. What Weber meant was not that practices have only one, true meaning, but that all social practices are embedded in meaning and are in that sense cultural. In order to conduct a social practice, human beings must give it a certain meaning, have a conception of it, be able to think meaningfully about it. Marx (to many people's surprise) said something rather similar when he observed that 'the worst of architects is better than the best of bees'. What he meant was that bees build hives by instinct whereas even the worst architects are obliged to use a conceptual model of the buildings they are constructing. The production of social meanings is therefore a necessary condition for the functioning of all social practices. And since meanings cannot be fixed but constantly change and are always contested, an account of the discursive conditions of social practices must form part of the sociological explanation of how they work. This explains why, in general, *Formations of Modernity* gives greater weight to the discursive aspect of social processes than is conventional.

Nothing demonstrates better the importance of social meanings than the word which both features in the title of the book and occurs regularly throughout its argument: the term, 'modern'. Is it as innocently descriptive a concept as it seems, or it is more 'loaded'? Raymond Williams argues that the word 'modern' first appeared in English in the sixteenth century, referring to the argument between two schools of thought — the Ancients and the Moderns (a long-running dispute between those following classical literary models and those wanting to up-date them). 'The majority of pre-nineteenth century uses', he notes, 'were unfavourable'. Claiming things to be 'modern' — up-to-date, breaking with tradition — was, on the whole, held to be a bad thing, a dangerous idea, which required justification. It is only in the nineteenth century and 'very markedly in the twentieth century' that there is a strong movement the other way, 'until "modern" becomes virtually equivalent to "improved"' (Williams, 1976, p.174).

This suggests that the discourse of 'the modern', which we slip into without thinking, has never been purely descriptive, but has a more contested discursive history. Historians sometimes call the period of European history which begins in the late fifteenth century the 'early modern' period. They are using the term to mark the break with the old, the collapse of older structures, models, ways of life and the rise of new conceptions, new structures. As Harold Laski wrote:

> By 1600 we may say definitely that men [sic] are living and working in a new moral world. … There is a new social discipline which finds its sanctions independently of the religious ideal. There is a self-sufficient state. There is an intellectual temper aware … that a limitation to the right of speculation is also a limitation to the right to material power. There is a new physical world, both in the geographical sense and the ideological. The content of experience being new also, new postulates are needed for its interpretation. Their character is already defined in the realm of social theory no less than in those of science and

philosophy. This content is material and of this world, instead of being spiritual and of the next. It is expansive, utilitarian, self-confident. It sets before itself the ideal of power over nature for the sake of the ease and comfort this power will confer. In its essence, it is the outlook of a new class which, given authority, is convinced that it can remould more adequately than in the past, the destinies of man.
(Laski, 1962, pp.57–8)

This is the moment of 'the modern', albeit in its very early stages. This book begins with this moment and what follows from it. But, as we noted, 'modernity' has a long and complex history. Each succeeding age — the Renaissance, the Enlightenment, the nineteenth century (the age of revolutions), the twentieth century — has a sense of itself as representing the culminating point of history, and each has tried to clinch this capture of history by claiming the epithet 'modern' for itself. Yet in each age the claim has proved illusory. Each age succumbed to the fantasy that *it* was the last word in advanced living, in material development, in knowledge and enlightenment. Each time that 'modern' was superseded by something even more up to date! The whole idea of modernity received an enormous impetus towards the end of the nineteenth century, when industrialization was rapidly transforming social and economic life, not only in Western Europe but elsewhere, and the globalization of the world economy and of western ways of life rapidly reshaped world history. This is the period of the new avant-garde intellectual and artistic movements in the arts, literature, architecture, science and philosophy, sometimes called 'Modernism', which aggressively embraced 'the new' — novelty for its own sake — and revelled in challenging and overthrowing the old forms, traditions, theories, institutions and authorities.

Today, 'post-modernism' is challenging the old 'modernisms'. The closure of history keeps advancing into the future. It sometimes seems that what is quintessentially 'modern' is not so much any one period or any particular form of social organization so much as the fact that a society becomes seized with and pervaded by this idea of ceaseless development, progress and dynamic change; by the restless forward movement of time and history; by what some theorists call the compression of time and space (Giddens, 1984; Harvey, 1989). Essential to the idea of modernity is the belief that everything is destined to be speeded up, dissolved, displaced, transformed, reshaped. It is the shift — materially and culturally — into this new conception of social life which is the real transition to modernity. Marx caught this spirit of modernity in his prophetic epigram — 'All that is solid melts into air'.

However, this idea of 'the modern' as a roller coaster of change and progress contains a paradox. At the very moment when 'the modern' comes into its own, its ambiguities also become evident. Modernity becomes more troubled the more heroic, unstoppable and Promethean it seems. The more it assumes itself to be the summit of human achievement, the more its dark side appears. The pollution of the environment and wastage of the earth's resources turns out to be the reverse side of 'development'. As many recent writers have noted, the Holocaust, which ravaged European Jewry, was perpetrated by a society which regarded itself as the summit of civilization and culture. The troubled thought surfaces that modernity's triumphs and successes are rooted, not simply in progress and enlightenment, but also in violence, oppression and exclusion, in the archaic, the violent, the untransformed, the repressed aspects of social life. Its restlessness — a key feature of the modern experience — becomes increasingly unsettling. Time and change, which propel it forward, threaten to engulf it. It is little wonder that modern societies are increasingly haunted by what Bryan Turner calls a pervasive nostalgia for past times — for lost community, for the 'good old days': always day-before-yesterday, always just over the horizon in an ever-receding image (Turner, 1990). The logic of modernity turns out to be a deeply contradictory logic — both constructive and destructive: its victims are as numerous as its beneficiaries. This Janus-face of modernity was inscribed in its earliest moments, and many of its subsequent twists and turns are laid out for inspection and analysis in this first volume of the modern story.

References

Anderson, B. (1986) *Imagined Communities*, London, Verso.

Anderson , P.A. (1990) 'A culture in contraflow', *New Left Review*, no.180, March/April.

Benjamin, W. (1970) 'Theses on the philosophy of history', in *Illuminations,* London, Cape.

Derrida, J. (1981) *Writing and Difference*, London, Routledge.

Giddens, A. (1984) *The Constitution of Society*, Cambridge, Polity Press.

Harvey, D. (1989) T*he Condition of Post-Modernity,* Oxford, Blackwell.

Laski, H. (1962) *The Rise of European Liberalism*, London, Unwin.

Mann, M. (1988) 'European development: approaching a historical explanation', in Baechler, J. *et al.* (eds) *Europe and the Rise of Capitalism*, London, Blackwell.

Norris, C. (1983) *The Deconstructive Turn*, London, Methuen.

Rostow, W. (1971) *The Stages of Economic Growth*, London, Cambridge University Press.

Turner, B. (1990) *Theories of Modernity and Post-modernity,* London, Sage.

White, H. (1987) *The Content of the Form: Narrative, Discourse and Historical Representation*, Baltimore, John Hopkins University Press.

Williams, R. (1976) *Keywords*, London, Fontana.

Young, R. (1990) *White Mythologies: Writing, History and the West*, London, Routledge.

CHAPTER 1   THE ENLIGHTENMENT AND THE BIRTH OF SOCIAL SCIENCE

Peter Hamilton

CONTENTS

1   INTRODUCTION

> Know then thyself, presume not God to scan,
> The proper study of Mankind is Man.
> (Alexander Pope, Epistle ii, *An Essay on Man*)

This chapter sets out to do the following:

- provide a critical, analytical introduction to the key ideas of the body of writers and writings known as the Enlightenment;
- demonstrate the centrality of *the social* in Enlightenment thought, and to indicate the relative lack of intellectual boundaries between disciplinary domains;
- analyse and present the key ideas of Enlightenment sociology and social science;
- indicate how some key ideas of Enlightenment sociology and social science were incorporated within the characteristic features of nineteenth-century sociology and social thought;
- present and contextualize the thesis that the Enlightenment represents a watershed in human thought about society — that it produced a qualitatively new way of thinking concerned with the application of reason, experience and experiment to the natural and the social world.

In the chapter I set out to examine critically the emergence of sociology — and the social sciences generally — as a distinctive form of thought about modern society. My argument is that one of the formative moments in this process came about in the eighteenth century, in the work of a key group of thinkers: the Enlightenment philosophers and their successors.

My main task is to trace the development of distinctively 'modern' forms of thought about society and the realm of the social. Although their roots are evident as early as the sixteenth and seventeenth century in the works of such figures as Bacon, Hobbes and Locke, these ideas received their most effective expression in the mid-eighteenth century, in the writings of a number of Enlightenment thinkers. These thinkers include men (there are almost no prominent women amongst them, for reasons to which we shall return) such as the Baron de Montesquieu (1689–1755), whose *De l'Esprit des Lois* (The Spirit of the Laws) is the starting point for a modern understanding of the relationship between the sociology of politics and the structure of society; Voltaire (1694–1788), whose writings on science, freedom of thought and justice express so well the excitement generated by the critical rationalism and secularism which characterizes the Enlightenment; David Hume (1711–76), who formulated a theory of human nature which sets the tone for modern empirical research in psychology and sociology; and Adam Ferguson (1723–1816), whose writings on 'civil society' prefigure modern comparative sociology.

Montesquieu (1689–1755)

David Hume (1711–76)

My task is also to trace how certain elements of the central mode of thinking about modern society established by the Enlightenment are carried into nineteenth-century 'classical sociology' in the writings of Henri de Saint-Simon (1760–1825) and Auguste Comte (1798–1857), and underpin the emergence of a distinctively modern sociology.

In a special sense, *Understanding Modern Societies* is all about the formation — the *invention* and the *reproduction* — of a *modern* way of thinking about society. This theme finds its way into all the chapters in a more or less explicit way. And this form of reflection upon *society* — which is after all a less than tangible entity — is one of the characteristic features of *modern* in contrast with earlier forms of thought. Such a reflection allows us to conceive of society itself as something over and above the individual — as the early sociologist, Émile Durkheim (1858–1917), said, as something unique, society as a social fact, '*sui generis*'. We are concerned with the emergence of a *new group of ideas* about society and the realm of the social. These ideas provided a reflection of a changing and evolving society, and in turn helped people to think about society in a different way, as something open to change and transformation. This new way of thinking about society appeared shortly before certain very significant changes began in the ways in which western societies were organized — symbolized by the American and French Revolutions on the one hand, and the Agrarian and Industrial Revolutions on the other.

Before going further I should point out one difficulty with the attempt to present — even in outline — a history of the sources of sociology. No history is innocent of the purposes of its author. So you should always bear in mind that, in trying to make connections between a discipline as it is practised in the last decade of the nineteenth century and the writings of a group of European intellectuals of the eighteenth century, I shall be looking to make exactly those connections which allow me to present a coherent history; that is, an account which does indeed draw connections between the ideas of now and then. I attempt to control the distorting possibilities of this approach by relating my account as accurately as I can to the context of the time, and connecting what was written then to the environment in which it was written and the audiences to whom it was directed. As you will see when you come to Chapter 3, the use of the writings of Adam Smith as a precursor of modern economics is a particularly apt example of how distorting it can be to treat an eighteenth-century text in the intellectual context of contemporary issues in political economy.

When the American historian Crane Brinton said that 'There seem to be good reasons for believing that in the latter part of the eighteenth century more intellectual energy was spent on the problems of man in society, in proportion to other possible concerns of the human mind, than at any other time in history' (Brinton, 1930, p.129), he may have been exaggerating a little: but the argument that this period of intense concentration on the social produced an emergent 'science of society' seems incontrovertible. Indeed, Crane Brinton even argued, quite convincingly, that the term '*philosophe*', which was used to describe the main figures of the Enlightenment, would nowadays be rendered as 'sociologist', given the term's usage at the time. I shall use this term to refer to the central figures of the Enlightenment throughout the chapter; its meaning will be explored in more detail in Section 2.1.

In order to understand the impact of the Enlightenment on modern sociology and the emergent social sciences, my thesis is that we must also examine the carry through of Enlightenment ideas into the nineteenth century. Perhaps the most significant example of this is the project originally undertaken by Henri de Saint-Simon, and later more fully extended by his follower, Auguste Comte, to construct a 'positive science' of society, or in other words a *sociology* — the very word Comte coined to name this entirely new science. The sociology of Comte and Saint-Simon is not, as some have argued (e.g. Robert Nisbet, 1967), just a mirror image of the Enlightenment programme — a sort of nineteenth-century conservative inversion of what the *philosophes* tried to do. It is similarly hard to see it as a radical break or jump from one mode of thinking about society to another. In a very real sense, the Comtean project of a positive sociology is the Enlightenment's *continuation*. It prepared the way for the emergence of a professionalized discipline of sociology in France, Germany and America at the end of the nineteenth century. But that is to anticipate my account, which returns to this issue in Section 6.

The concerns and interests of Saint-Simon and Comte prefigure those of modern sociology, principally (though not exclusively) via Émile Durkheim; but they are also deeply rooted in the Enlightenment's preoccupations with a particular mode of thought. It is convenient to call this mode of thought *critical rationalism*, for it combines the application of reason to social, political and economic issues with a concern with progress, emancipation and improvement, and is consequently *critical* of the status quo. The critical rationalism of the Enlightenment is the precursor of the 'positivism' of Saint-Simon and Comte, understood as the striving for a *universal* science which, through the application of a reason tempered by experience and experiment, would eliminate prejudice, ignorance, superstition, and intolerance. At the same time it would be hard to understand the work of Marx, particularly in what is called his Young Hegelian period up to about 1850 (and one so important for certain central concepts of sociology, such as alienation and ideology), without drawing a connection between his version of critical rationalism and that of the Enlightenment *philosophes*, for the latter informs and underpins his early writings too. We shall not examine Marx's work in this chapter, but it is important to bear in mind that many of the ideas that he developed as a young student and philosopher in Germany prior to 1845 were directly influenced by the central ideas of the Enlightenment.

Before looking at the content and context of the key ideas of the Enlightenment, let us set them out in a concise form here. They make up what sociologists call a 'paradigm', a set of interconnected ideas, values, principles, and facts which provide both an image of the natural and social world, and a way of thinking about it. The 'paradigm' of the Enlightenment — its 'philosophy' and approach to key questions — is a combination of a number of ideas, bound together in a tight cluster. It includes some elements which may even appear to be inconsistent — probably because, like many intellectual movements, it united people whose ideas had many threads in common but differed on questions of detail. As a minimum, however, all the *philosophes* would have agreed on the following list:

1   *Reason* — the *philosophes* stressed the primacy of *reason* and rationality as ways of organizing knowledge, tempered by experience and experiment. In this they took over the 'rationalist' concept of reason as the process of rational thought, based upon clear, innate ideas independent of experience, which can be demonstrated to any thinking person, and which had been set out by Descartes and Pascal in the seventeenth century. However, the *philosophes* allied their version of rationalism with *empiricism.*

2   *Empiricism* — the idea that all thought and knowledge about the natural and social world is based upon empirical facts, things that all human beings can apprehend through their sense organs.

3   *Science* — the notion that scientific knowledge, based upon the experimental method as developed in the scientific revolution of the seventeenth century, was the key to expanding *all* human knowledge.

4   *Universalism* — the concept that reason and science could be applied to any and every situation, and that their principles were the same in every situation. Science in particular produces general laws which govern the entire universe, without exception.

5   *Progress* — the idea that the natural and social condition of human beings could be improved, by the application of science and reason, and would result in an ever-increasing level of happiness and well-being.

6   *Individualism* — the concept that the individual is the starting point for all knowledge and action, and that individual reason cannot be subjected to a higher authority. Society is thus the sum or product of the thought and action of a large number of individuals.

7   *Toleration* — the notion that all human beings are essentially the same, despite their religious or moral convictions, and that the beliefs of other races or civilizations are not inherently inferior to those of European Christianity.

8   *Freedom* — an opposition to feudal and traditional constraints on beliefs, trade, communication, social interaction, sexuality, and ownership of property (although as we shall see the extension of freedom to women and the lower classes was problematic for the *philosophes*).

9   *Uniformity of human nature* — the belief that the principal characteristics of human nature were always and everywhere the same.

10   *Secularism* — an ethic most frequently seen in the form of virulent anti-clericalism. The *philosophes'* opposition to traditional religious authority stressed the need for secular knowledge free of religious orthodoxies.

It would be possible to add other ideas to this list or to discuss the relative importance of each. However, the above list provides a good starting point for understanding this complex movement, and for making connections between its characteristic concerns and the emergence of sociology. Each of these central ideas weaves its way through the account that follows, and all form part of the new social sciences which emerged in the nineteenth century.

2   WHAT WAS THE ENLIGHTENMENT?

A simple answer to this question would separate out at least eight meanings of the Enlightenment:

1   A characteristic bundle of ideas (as in the list at the end of Section 1).

2   An intellectual movement.

3   A communicating group or network of intellectuals.

4   A set of institutional centres where intellectuals clustered — Paris, Edinburgh, Glasgow, London, etc.

5   A publishing industry, and an audience for its output.

6   An intellectual fashion.

7   A belief-system, world-view, or *Zeitgeist* (spirit of the age).

8   A history and a geography.

All of these are overlapping aspects of the same general phenomenon, and they remind us that it is ultimately futile to try to pin down a single definitive group, set of ideas, or cluster of outcomes and consequences, which can serve as *the* Enlightenment. There were many aspects to the Enlightenment, and many *philosophes*, so what you will find here is an attempt to map out some broad outlines, to set some central ideas in their context, and to indicate some important consequences.

In its simplest sense the Enlightenment was the creation of a new framework of ideas about man, society and nature, which challenged existing conceptions rooted in a traditional world-view, dominated by Christianity. The key domain in which Enlightenment intellectuals challenged the clergy, who were the main group involved in supporting existing conceptions of the world, concerned the traditional view of nature, man and society which was sustained by the Church's authority and its monopoly over the information media of the time.

A traditional world-view

These new ideas were accompanied by and influenced in their turn many cultural innovations in writing, printing, painting, music, sculpture, architecture and gardening, as well as the other arts. Technological innovations in agriculture and manufactures, as well as in ways of making war, also frame the social theories of the Enlightenment. We have no space to explore such matters here, except to point out that the whole idea of a professionalized discipline based on any of these intellectual or cultural pursuits was only slowly emerging, and that as a consequence an educated man or woman of the eighteenth-century Enlightenment saw him or herself as able to take up any or all of them which caught his or her interest. The notion that Enlightenment knowledge could be strictly compartmentalized into bounded domains, each the province of certificated 'experts', would have been completely foreign to Enlightenment thinkers. The 'universalism' which thus characterized the emergence of these ideas and their cultural counterparts assumed that any educated person could in principle know everything. This was in fact a mistaken belief. Paradoxically, the Enlightenment heralded the very process — the creation of specialized disciplines presided over by certificated experts — which appears to negate its aim of universalized human knowledge. Such a 'closing-off' of knowledge by disciplinary boundaries occurred earlier than anywhere else in the natural sciences, those models of enlightened knowledge so beloved of the *philosophes*. The main reason for this was that science produced specialist languages and terminologies, and relied in particular upon an increasingly complex mathematical language, inaccessible to even the enlightened gentleman-*philosophe*. Denis Diderot (1713–84), a key figure in the movement, noted perceptively in 1756 that the mathematical language of Newton's *Principia Mathematica* is 'the veil' which scientists 'are pleased to draw between the people and nature' (quoted in Gay, 1973b, p.158).

However much they might have wanted to extend the benefits of enlightened knowledge, the *philosophes* helped the process by which secular intellectual life became the province of a socially and economically defined group. They were the first people in western society outside of the Church to make a living (or more properly a *vocation*) out of knowledge and writing. As Roy Porter has put it, 'the Enlightenment was the era which saw the emergence of a secular intelligentsia large enough and powerful enough for the first time to challenge the clergy' (Porter, 1990, p.73).

In the next section, I want to locate the Enlightenment in its social, historical, and geographical context.

2.1   THE SOCIAL, HISTORICAL AND GEOGRAPHICAL LOCATION OF THE ENLIGHTENMENT

When we use the term 'the Enlightenment' it is generally accepted that we refer to a period in European intellectual history which spans the time from roughly the first quarter to the last quarter of the eighteenth century. Geographically centred in France, but with important outposts in most of the major European states, 'the Enlightenment' is composed of the ideas and writings of a fairly heterogeneous group, who are often called by their French name *philosophes*. It does not exactly correspond to our modern 'philosopher', and is perhaps best translated as 'a man of letters who is also a freethinker'. The *philosophes* saw themselves as cosmopolitans, citizens of an enlightened intellectual world who valued the interest of mankind above that of country or clan. As the French *philosophe* Diderot wrote to Hume in 1768: 'My dear David, you belong to all nations, and you'll never ask an unhappy man for his birth-certificate. I flatter myself that I am, like you, citizen of the great city of the world' (quoted in Gay, 1973a, p.13). The historian Edward Gibbon (1737–94) stressed the strongly European or 'Euro-centric' nature of this *universalistic* cosmopolitanism: 'it is the duty of a patriot to prefer and promote the exclusive interest and glory of his native country; but a philosopher may be permitted to enlarge his views, and to consider Europe as a great republic, whose various inhabitants have attained almost the same level of politeness and cultivation' (quoted in Gay, 1973a, p.13). Gibbon even composed some of his writings in French, because he felt that the ideas with which he wanted to work were better expressed in that language than in his own.

The Enlightenment was the work of three overlapping and closely linked generations of *philosophes*. The first, typified by Voltaire (1694–1778) and Charles de Secondat, known as Montesquieu (1689–1755), were born in the last quarter of the seventeenth century: their ideas were strongly influenced by the writings of the English political philosopher John Locke (1632–1704) and the scientist Isaac Newton (1642–1727), whose work was fresh and controversial whilst both *philosophes* were still young men. The second generation includes men like David Hume (1711–76), Jean-Jacques Rousseau (1712–78), Denis Diderot (1713–84), and Jean d'Alembert (1717–83), who combined the fashionable anti-clericalism and the interest in scientific method of their predecessors into what Gay calls 'a coherent modern view of the world'. The third generation is represented by Immanuel Kant (1724–1804), Adam Smith (1723–90), Anne Robert Turgot (1727–81), the Marquis de Condorcet (1743–94), and Adam Ferguson (1723–1816), and its achievement is the further development of the Enlightenment world-view into a series of more specialized proto-disciplines: epistemology, economics, sociology, political economy, legal reform. It is to Kant that we owe the slogan of the Enlightenment — *sapere aude* ('dare to know') — which sums up its essentially secular intellectual character.

Of course there is a danger in applying the term 'the Enlightenment' too loosely or broadly, to the whole of intellectual life in eighteenth-century Europe, as if the movement was one which touched every society and every intellectual élite of this period equally. As Roy Porter emphasizes in an excellent short study of recent work on the Enlightenment, the Enlightenment is an amorphous, hard-to-pin-down and constantly shifting entity (Porter, 1990). It is commonplace for the whole period to be referred to as an 'Age of Enlightenment', a term which implies a general process of society awakening from the dark slumbers of superstition and ignorance, and a notion certainly encouraged by the *philosophes* themselves, although it is one which perhaps poses more questions than it resolves. Kant wrote an essay *'Was ist Aufklärung?'* (What is Enlightenment?), which actually says 'if someone says "are we living in an enlightened age today?" the answer would be, "No: but …

we *are* living in an Age of Enlightenment" '. The French *philosophes* referred to their time as '*le siècle des lumières*' (the century of the enlightened), and both Scottish and English writers of the time talked about 'Enlightened' thinking.

Certainly the metaphor of the 'light of reason', shining brightly into all the dark recesses of ignorance and superstition, was a powerful one at the time: but did the process of Enlightenment always and everywhere have the same meaning? One recent historical study of Europe in the eighteenth century has suggested that the Enlightenment is more 'a tendency towards critical inquiry and the application of reason' than a coherent intellectual movement (Black, 1990, p.208).

In fact, if we look at such indicators as the production and consumption of books and journals, the Enlightenment was a largely French and British (or more properly Scottish) intellectual vogue, although one whose fashionable ripples extended out to Germany, Italy, the Habsburg Empire, Russia, the Low Countries and the Americas. But its centre was very clearly Paris, and it emerged in the France of Louis XV (1710–74), during the first quarter of the eighteenth century.

By the last quarter of the eighteenth century, Enlightenment ideas were close to having become a sort of new intellectual orthodoxy amongst the cultivated élites of Europe. This orthodoxy was also starting to give way to an emergent 'pre-Romanticism' which placed greater emphasis on sentiment and feeling, as opposed to reason and scepticism. However, the spirit of enlightened and critical rationalism was quite an influential factor in the increasing disquiet about how *ancien régime* France was being run, which began to set in after about 1770 (Doyle, 1989, p.58). It helped to encourage a mood of impending disaster which led inexorably towards the French Revolution of 1789, a topic to which we shall return in Section 5. If we need to find a historical end to the Enlightenment, it could be said to be the French Revolution — but even that is a controversial notion.

Although the Enlightenment was in reality a sort of intellectual fashion which took hold of the minds of intellectuals throughout Europe, rather than a consciously conceived project with any institutionalized form, there is one classic example of a cooperative endeavour among the *philosophes*: the great publishing enterprise called the *Encyclopédie*.

2.2   THE *ENCYCLOPÉDIE*

In order to explain the influence of this massive publication, it is worth reminding ourselves that by the mid-eighteenth century French was the language of all of educated Europe, except for England and Spain (and even in those two countries any self-respecting member of the educated élite would have had a good knowledge of the language). As a Viennese countess put it, '… in those days the greater part of high society in Vienna would say: I speak French like Diderot, and German … like my nurse' (Doyle, 1989, p.58).

The universality of French as the language of reason and ideas explains in part the Europe-wide popularity of the *Encyclopédie*, where the intellectual fashion for treating all aspects of human life and the natural world as open to rational study is displayed in astonishing depth.

The cooperative endeavour which produced the *Encyclopédie* parallels another distinctive feature of the Enlightenment — the learned society committed to the pursuit of knowledge, whose prototypes were the Académie française (est. 1635) and the Royal Society of London (est. 1645). Such organizations were the first modern social institutions devoted to the study of the arts and sciences. The most distinctive break with the past came about because the members of such academies believed in the grounding of knowledge in experience as opposed to secular authority, religious dogma, or mysticism.

Science was the supreme form of knowledge for the *philosophes* because it seemed to create secure truths based on observation and experiment. Their confidence in scientific method was such that they believed it was a force for enlightenment and progress: there was in principle no domain of life to which it could not be applied. They believed that a new man was being created by this scientific method, one who understands, and by his understanding masters nature.

The *Encyclopédie* represented this belief in the beneficial effects of science put into practice. It was also the product of an intellectual society — 'a society of men of letters and artisans' as Denis Diderot, one of its main editors, described it. Its purpose was summed up by Kant's definition of Enlightenment: 'man realising his potential through the use of his mind' (quoted in Gay, 1973a, p.21).

The concept of the *Encyclopédie* was originally based on an English work, Ephraim Chambers's *Cyclopaedia or Universal Dictionary of Arts and Sciences* (1728). Although initially intended to be a translation of this popular and successful work, it soon became an original work in its own right, after Denis Diderot and Jean d'Alembert (a scientifically inclined *philosophe*) took over the editorship for its publisher, Le Breton. Virtually all of the major *philosophes* contributed to it, and its influence was very widespread in eighteenth-century Europe.

There are two striking characteristics of the *Encyclopédie* from our point of view. Firstly, in creating a plan for the enterprise — a way of linking all the articles together in a coherent manner — the decision was taken to place man at the centre; As Diderot said (in an entry in the *Encyclopédie* under the heading 'Encyclopédie'), what he and his associates wanted for the *Encyclopédie* was a plan or design that would be 'instructive and grand' — something which would order knowledge and information as 'a grand and noble avenue, stretching into the distance, and along which one would find other avenues, arranged in an orderly manner and leading off to isolated and remote objects by the easiest and quickest route' (*Encyclopédie*, Volume V, 1755).

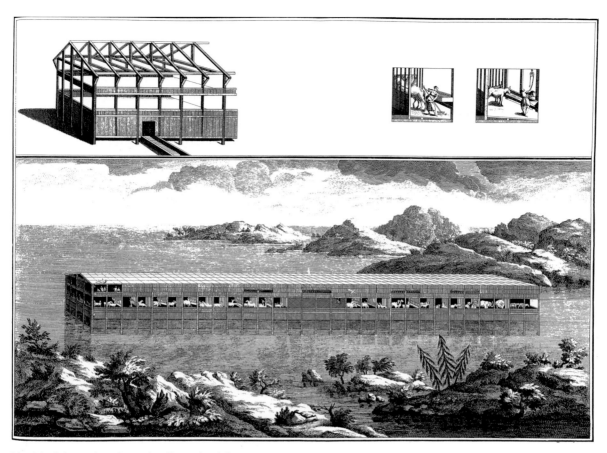

Noah's Ark: a plate from the *Encyclopédie*

Secondly, the *Encyclopédie* is truly 'universalistic' in its approach.
Diderot and his colleagues wanted it to be the sort of work from which,
should a disaster overtake civilization, all human knowledge could be
reconstructed. As a result, it is a vast publication: it took over twenty
years to be published, from 1751 to 1772, and amounts to seventeen
volumes of text and twelve volumes of plates.

The pre-eminence in the eighteenth century of French as the language
of culture and of ideas made the *Encyclopédie* a widely-known work —
some 50 per cent of the 25,000 copies in various editions which sold
before 1789 were purchased outside of France. It is not surprising
perhaps that from a modern standpoint this endeavour should seem to
support the idea of an 'Enlightenment project', the notion that a
planned and influential intellectual movement, designed to popularize
certain key notions to do with science, reason and progress, was at work
in the eighteenth century. But from the evidence available on those who
purchased copies of it, the *Encyclopédie* sold more because of its
critical and irreverent notoriety than for any specific programme or
project which it represented (Doyle, 1989, p.52). What is more, it is

clear that the term 'Encyclopedism' was quite widely used at the time as a synonym for the refusal to accept anything uncritically.

Indeed, a key feature of the whole Enlightenment period is the influence of a wide range of individual writers on educated and cultivated opinion. Thinkers such as Voltaire, Montesquieu, Diderot, Hume, Smith, Ferguson, Rousseau, and Condorcet — to mention only some of the most notable — produced a large collection of novels, plays, books, pamphlets and essays which became bestsellers amongst an audience which was avid for new and exciting ideas, and receptive to the notion that the application of reason to the affairs of men would encourage a general advance of civilization. This audience was not however dominated by the 'new' social groups, the emergent middle classes of manufacturers and merchants, but by members of more traditional élite groups — nobles, professionals (especially lawyers), academics and the clergy. The idea of disciplinary demarcation was foreign to such people, for whom the ideal of Renaissance Man was the archetype of cultivated knowledge — a person whose knowledge and understanding enabled him or her to pick up a book on physics, read a text of Tacitus, design a Palladian villa, paint a *Mona Lisa*, or compose a sonnet with equal facility. They had for the most part received a classical education (in French colleges of the mid-eighteenth century, for example, four hours a day were given over to the study of the classics), but also some introduction to the sciences. Men (and the much smaller number of women educated to the same level) would expect to understand and participate in the spread of knowledge about new ideas, whether in the field of moral philosophy or physical science. Yet women, though they played a major part in the development and diffusion of Enlightenment ideas, found themselves in a contradictory position in the application of such ideas to their social condition. We shall return to this in Section 2.5.

2.3   TRADITION AND MODERNITY

The *philosophes* took a very clear position in their writings on certain important transitions underway within European society. These involved the move from a traditional social order and a traditional set of beliefs about the world to new forms of social structure and ways of thinking about the world which were distinctively modern. The modernity of these modes of thought lay in the innovative way in which the *philosophes* sought to demolish and replace *established* forms of knowledge dependent on religious authority, such as the biblical account of the creation of the world, with those new forms of knowledge which depended upon experience, experiment and reason — quintessentially, science.

Until the eighteenth century, what passed in Europe for knowledge about the creation of the world, about man's place in that world, about nature and society, and about man's duties and destiny, was dominated by the Christian churches. Knowledge was continually referred to scriptural sources in the Bible, and was transmitted through the religious institutions of universities, colleges, religious orders, schools and churches. A typical visual representation of the traditional world-view shows heaven and earth as physically contiguous (see page 23). Even Bossuet's *Histoire Universelle* (Universal History) of 1681 began its account of human history over the previous 6,000 years with Adam and Eve's departure from the Garden of Eden, and did not mention the Chinese once. Yet, as Voltaire pointed out (in his *Lettres Philosophiques*), the Chinese could trace their civilization back through '36 recorded eclipses of the sun to a date earlier than that which we normally attribute to the Flood'.

The astronomic discoveries in the sixteenth and seventeenth centuries of Kepler and Copernicus about the nature of the universe, the observations of Galileo concerning the movements of the planets, the lessons of empirical science, and the increasingly common accounts of distant and exotic societies available through travellers' tales, combined to provide an effective scientific and empirical base from which to challenge traditional cosmologies (a cosmology is an intellectual picture or model of the universe) founded upon Christian belief, which placed the earth at the centre of the universe, and Christendom at the centre of the world. This was fertile ground for the *philosophes*, who opposed traditional religious authority and the false knowledge which it ordained.

The particular form in which Enlightenment anti-traditionalism appears, then, is as a debunking of outmoded, scripturally-based concepts of the universe, the earth and human society. Although we must be clear that many of the *philosophes* were in fact believers in a God, or at least a divine entity, this did not prevent much of their writing from heaping scorn upon religious teaching, and being virulently anti-clerical. The *philosophes* challenged the traditional role of the clergy as the keepers and transmitters of knowledge: because they wished to redefine what was socially important knowledge, to bring it outside of the sphere of religion, and to provide it with a new meaning and relevance. As a result, they typically presented traditional religious world-views as attempts to keep people in a condition of ignorance and superstition, and thus reserved much of the most pointed of their intellectual attacks for key elements in what they saw as the ideological window-dressing of the Church, such as miracles and revelations.

Religious ideas and knowledge also underpinned the absolute claim to power exercised by the French, Austrian and German kings, and the Russian Czar, and were also used, in a modified form, to support the claim on the British throne of the Hanoverians. Some of the *philosophes* were quite explicitly antithetical to 'despotism' (the Enlightenment's code-word for absolutism); others were more equivocal about the virtues of a strong monarch, and both Voltaire and Diderot were virtually apologists for the absolutist regimes of Frederick the Great of Prussia, and Catherine the Great of Russia.

An idealized view of Louis XV which represents his stature as an absolute monarch

The ideas developed and disseminated by the *philosophes* touched critically upon nearly all aspects of the traditional societies in which they operated, and sought to question virtually all (the condition of women being, perhaps, the main exception) of the forms which that society took. One of the main sources of their approach to the critique of traditional society is found in their enthusiasm for science, and the notions of progress and reason for which it seemed to provide a guarantee. We shall return to the connection between the Enlightenment and the emergence of modern science in Section 3.1.

2.4   SOCIAL ORDERS AND SOCIAL STRUCTURE

Despite their secular radicalism, the ideas of the typical *philosophes* were not as subversive of the traditional social structure in which they lived as might have been the case. There is perhaps a simple reason for this: self-interest. The English historian Edward Gibbon described himself as fortunate to have been placed by the lottery of life amongst a cultured and leisured élite, the 'polished and enlightened orders of society', which he contrasts with the condition of the masses:

> The most numerous portion of it [society] is employed in constant and useful labour. The select few, placed by fortune above necessity, can, however, fill up their time by the pursuits of interest or glory, by the improvements of their estate or of their understanding, by the duties, the pleasures, and even the follies of social life.
> (Gibbon, 1966, p.207)

Most of the *philosophes* came from the higher orders of society. Many were of noble birth, whilst some came from the gentry classes or from a professional milieu. Montesquieu, for example, was a great landowner in the Bordeaux region of France. Diderot and Rousseau came from the traditional middle class — Diderot's father was a master-cutler, Rousseau's a watchmaker.

Peter Gay describes the *philosophes* as a 'solid, respectable clan of revolutionaries' (Gay, 1973a, p.9). Most were born into a cultured élite, and in the main their works were circulated amongst other members of that élite. It was not until almost the eve of the French Revolution, in the 1780s, that a new social group emerged, concerned with popularizing Enlightenment ideas (Darnton, 1979).

This new group was composed largely of lower-middle-class hack journalists and other writers, who supplied the growing number of popular newspapers with a diet of scandal mixed up with simplified Enlightenment ideas. Their audiences were the disaffected and propertyless lower middle classes, for whom the traditional social structure had little to offer.

The traditional social structure of eighteenth-century Europe was essentially based upon the ownership of land and landed property. It was a society composed of orders, rather than economically defined classes, although class formations were beginning to appear. The great noble landowners formed the dominant ruling order (of which a Louis XV or a George III was simply a leading member), and although there was considerable variation within Europe over the extent of their political power — in France, for example, feudal rights over land still remained, whilst in Russia serfdom was the norm on the great estates — they dominated an economy in which at least 80 per cent of the population derived their employment and income from agriculture in one form or another.

Beneath the landed nobility there existed a stratum of 'traditional' professional orders which had changed little since the feudal period — lawyers, clerics, state officials, etc. — and also a stratum of small landowners or gentry-farmers. In France the latter group (the *hobereaux*, or gentry) was quite numerous, but often possessed only modest means. Frequently reasonably well-educated, they were the social group from which many of the lesser figures of the Enlightenment emerged, for an acceptable profession for this social group was that of 'writer'. There was an emergent and growing 'new' middle class involved in new forms of manufacture and trade, as well as the traditional merchant order of feudalism, which included the quite large numbers of urban craftsmen — from the wealthy goldsmiths, perfumiers or tailors who worked for the nobility, through to an assortment of printers, furniture makers, or carriage makers, down to the modest shoemaker or mason. Below the urban middle class was to be found a large class of domestic servants, and a small urban working class, supplemented on a daily or seasonal basis by day labourers from the countryside. Peasants or smallholders made up the great mass of the population — in mid-eighteenth century France they probably accounted for eighteen of the twenty million or so of the population.

In eighteenth-century France, these social orders were represented as three 'Estates' — Clergy, Nobility, and the 'Third Estate', which comprised everyone else, from wealthiest bourgeois to poorest peasant. Some *philosophes* were members of the Second Estate, which perhaps also indicates why they should be less explicitly subversive of the traditional social order than of the traditional religious order.

For the lower orders of European eighteenth-century society, the Enlightenment had apparently little to offer. Voltaire was fond of describing the peasantry in terms which put them hardly above the beasts of the field, in order to criticize the sort of social system which reduced men to such a level of ignorance and bestiality. However, he showed little interest in a levelling of social distinction. Few indeed of the *philosophes* were interested in the greater involvement of the great mass of the population in the government of society, for the most part favouring a system *à la* Great Britain, where political power was extended to the propertied classes and the landed gentry, but not beyond.

The Enlightenment certainly propagated concepts of equality, (limited) democracy and emancipation. But in the societies in which it flourished

A cartoon depicting the condition of the French peasantry prior to the Revolution of 1789: the taxes paid by the peasantry supported the clergy and the nobility

its ultimately revolutionary implications were not grasped by (or meant to be extended to) the mass of poor and uneducated people. None the less, ruling élites in particular saw the ideas of the Enlightenment as a threat to the established order. Because they discerned in it certain dangerous and revolutionary elements, both secular and religious authorities tried to control the spread of Enlightenment culture. However, the *philosophes* themselves refused to believe that they were rebels or revolutionaries: they thought that progress could come about within the existing social order by the spread of their ideas among men of influence. As Diderot once said, their aim was to 'change the general way of thinking', and was revolutionary only insofar as it sought 'the revolution which will take place in the minds of men' (quoted in Eliot and Stern, 1979, p.44).

2.5   WOMEN AND ENLIGHTENMENT: THE SALON

Although there were some wealthy and powerful women manifestly involved in the propagation of its principles — Catherine the Great of Russia was one of its staunchest supporters at one stage — the Enlightenment was essentially promoted and prosecuted, at least in its public face, by a male intellectual élite. Women figured as either silent partners in the intellectual enterprises of their more famous consorts (Voltaire spent much time performing scientific experiments with the aid of his mistress Madame du Châtelet, whilst much of what we know of the intellectual society of the times comes from Diderot's voluminous correspondence with his mistress, Sophie Volland), or as the (frequently brilliant) hostesses of the regular salons and soirées where the *philosophes* and other members of the cultivated élites would meet.

The institution of the salon had begun in seventeenth-century Paris, the invention of the Marquise de Rambouillet in 1623, who created 'a space in which talented and learned women could meet with men as intellectual equals, rather than as exceptional prodigies' (Anderson and Zinsser, 1990, vol.II, p.104). Yet the salon proved to be a rather double-edged sword in the expansion of women's rights. Although many of those set up in imitation of Mme de Rambouillet's were presided over by women who, like her, refused sexual liaisons so as to free themselves for a role beyond that of wife or courtesan, many salons were also the locus for affairs between talented or titled men and intellectual women, and the reputation of all *salonières* (chaste or otherwise) was affected: it was assumed that relations between men and women, however intellectual or artistic they might appear, could not remain platonic. In Reading A, we examine the social institution of the Enlightenment salon, and follow through some of its rather contradictory implications for the way in which women's rights were perceived.

An eighteenth-century
French salon

ACTIVITY 1   Now read **Reading A, 'Women in the salons'**, by Anderson and Zinsser
(which you will find at the end of this chapter). While reading the
article, I suggest you make notes on the following questions:

1   How would you account for the differences between the public and
the private faces of the Enlightenment in respect of women's roles?

2   To what extent did the institution of the salon confine women to the
domestic sphere?

3   ENLIGHTENMENT AS THE PURSUIT OF MODERNITY

A specifically 'modern' concern with man conceived of as a social being was forged by the key figures amongst the *philosophes* during the mid-eighteenth century, principally in France and Scotland, but with certain important contributions from thinkers in Italy and Germany.

Taking account of the diversity of views espoused by the *philosophes*, there are broadly four main areas which distinguish the thought of the *philosophes* from that of other intellectuals of their period, and from earlier intellectual approaches:

- **Anti-clericalism:** the *philosophes* had no time for the Church (especially the Catholic Church) and its works — a perspective summed up in Voltaire's phrase '*Écrasez l'infâme*' ('crush the infamous thing', the 'thing' being the authority of the Catholic Church). They were particularly opposed to religious persecution, and although some went further, denying the existence of a God altogether, most acknowledged that reason indicates the likely existence of a God, but not one who has provided a 'revelation' of Himself through scripture, the life of Christ, miracles, or the Church.
- **A belief in the pre-eminence of empirical, materialist knowledge**: the model in this respect being furnished by science.
- **An enthusiasm for technological and medical progress**: scientists, inventors, and doctors were seen as the curers of society's ills.
- **A desire for legal and constitutional reform**: in the case of the French *philosophes*, this was translated into a critique of French absolutism, and an admiration for the British constitution, with its established liberties.

This qualitatively new mode of thought about man and society, which had its roots in the Scientific Revolution of the seventeenth century and the subsequent diffusion from about 1700 onwards of scientific concepts and methods, led to the creation of a small group of 'moral sciences' as David Hume called them, which included what we would now call sociology. The word 'sociology', as a description of a science, does not appear until the nineteenth century: but that is of little importance in the sense that characteristically *sociological* concerns about the ways in which societies are organized and developed, and about human social relationships, are clearly identifiable from the middle of the eighteenth century in the writings of a number of *philosophes*.

It is these 'moral sciences' which, concerning themselves with the deeper understanding of the human condition as a prelude to the emancipation of man from the ties of superstition, ignorance, ideology and feudal social relationships, constituted the turning point for sociology and the other social sciences, and eventually formed the basis of their professionalized disciplines in the early nineteenth century.

As part of this concern with reformulating moral philosophy as 'moral science', the understanding of *human nature* was regarded as the key to an objective 'science of man'. Indeed it was also the key to a secure foundation for *all* science, natural as well as social. As David Hume put it: 'the Science of man is the only solid foundation for the other sciences' and 'Human Nature is the only science of man' (Hume, 1968, pp.xx and 273).

In their aim to destroy the Christian view of man's nature and place in the world, the *philosophes* gave a particular conception of human psychology a central and strategic scientific position. Their basic assumption was that human nature possesses an essential *uniformity*, though it does exhibit a wide empirical variation. Following in part the philosopher John Locke (1632–1704), the *philosophes* took over his 'empiricist' ideas that the mind of the human being at birth is, in important respects, comparable to an empty sheet of paper, and that all his or her knowledge and emotions are a product of experience. Locke may, in this regard, be looked upon as the founder of the philosophy of *empiricism,* which holds to this doctrine of knowledge proceeding only out of experience. The science of man that the *philosophes* of the Enlightenment developed was distinctly empiricist; it follows that the social sciences that they inaugurated reflected both this concern with understanding social phenomena on the basis of human experience, and a scientific approach to those phenomena.

3.1   ENLIGHTENMENT, SCIENCE AND PROGRESS

As we have seen, for the intellectuals of the Enlightenment, science was the epitome of enlightened reason. Both were vehicles which — together — would move human society onwards and upwards to a more enlightened and *progressive* state.

The founding concepts of social science were intimately bound up with the Enlightenment's concept of *progress*, the idea that through the application of reasoned and empirically based knowledge, social institutions could be created that would make men happier and free them from cruelty, injustice, and despotism. Science played an important role in this process for the men of the eighteenth century, because it seemed to offer the prospect of increasing man's control over those aspects of nature most harmful to human interests. Science could ensure a more efficient and productive agriculture, and thus the elimination of famine; it could lead to the invention of processes and machines which would convert raw materials into goods that would be of benefit to mankind; it could ensure the reduction of illness and infirmity, and the prospect of a population no longer kept in 'ignorance and superstition' by received wisdom about the Christian creation myth, and religious concepts of cause and effect. The discovery that smallpox could be prevented by simple inoculation was only one amongst a great range of scientific innovations which seemed to roll back the frontiers of a nature hitherto quite hostile to man.

The great impact of the achievements of science, and especially the work of Newton, led the *philosophes* to believe that scientific method might be applied to society, and that science could become the basis of future social values, which could be selected rationally in relation to predetermined goals. Indeed Newton himself held this view. In his *Opticks* (1663) he had written: '... if natural philosophy, in all its parts, by pursuing this method, shall at length be perfected, the bounds of moral philosophy will also be enlarged.'

Sir Isaac Newton: hero of the Enlightenment (1642–1727)

The wit, playwright, historian, novelist and philosopher Voltaire had a good deal to do with the emergence and diffusion of the fashion for science within Enlightened thought. Voltaire embraced certain ideas and principles which had impressed him during a visit to England in the 1720s: Locke's empiricism, with its notion of our psychological pliability to the impressions we receive; Bacon's ideas about the use of empirical methods; Newton's great achievements in scientific knowledge of the universe; and the religious pluralism and tolerance which he found in British society. He melded them in a persuasive mix of new ideas which he published in his *Lettres Philosophiques* of 1732. The book was immediately banned and publicly burned, naturally becoming as a result a huge publishing success. It was largely responsible for the rapid spread of knowledge about the new scientific method, making both Locke and Newton household names in cultivated

circles. The well-known story about Newton discovering gravity as a
result of an apple falling on his head, which Voltaire invented to help
non-scientists understand the concept, is typical of Voltaire's urge to
popularize and make more accessible the new 'natural philosophy'.

Voltaire (1694–1778)

Voltaire's success was due not merely to his genius as a writer: what his
work evoked in his audience was a great desire for new ideas, for an
understanding of how society could progress through an application of
the best knowledge available in the arts and sciences. This belief in the
new, in progress and change through the application of reason and
knowledge, represented a qualitative shift in the attitudes of the literate
élite (although we should be careful about assuming that literacy was
confined only to the cultured élite: by the time Louis XVI came to the
French throne in 1774, about a third of the French population could
read and write). We might characterize this shift as a new thirst for
modernity in all its possible forms. As Peter Gay points out in his
classic study of the Enlightenment:

In the century of the Enlightenment, educated Europeans awoke to a new sense of life. They experienced an expansive sense of power over nature and themselves: the pitiless cycles of epidemics, famines, risky life and early death, devastating war and uneasy peace — the treadmill of human existence — seemed to be yielding at last to the application of critical intelligence. Fear of change, up to that time nearly universal, was giving way to fear of stagnation; the word innovation, traditionally an effective term of abuse, became a word of praise. The very emergence of conservative ideas was a tribute to the general obsession with improvement: a stationary society does not need conservatives. There seemed to be little doubt that in the struggle of man against nature the balance of power was shifting in favour of man. (Gay, 1973b, p.3)

3.2   THE COMMUNICATION OF ENLIGHTENMENT

As I have argued in the previous section, the emergence of prototypical social sciences owes much to the fascination of the *philosophes* with natural sciences, and the applications of their methods to medicine, agriculture and industry. The *philosophes* saw science as an ally in their common desire to combat religious intolerance and political injustice, and their writings are full of discussions of the way in which science contests theological representations of the earth's history, of man's constitution, and of divine rights.

However, the Enlightenment was not simply a set of ideas. It helped to create a new secular intelligentsia, and to give the role of the intellectual a social and cultural base independent of traditional institutions such as the Church. It also represented (perhaps more significantly) a great cultural and social change in the way in which ideas were created and disseminated, and was a truly modern intellectual movement in the sense that its propagation depended upon the creation of secular and cross-cultural forms of communication. The Enlightenment forged the intellectual conditions in which the application of reason to practical affairs could flourish — principally through the invention of such modern institutions as the scientific academy, the learned journal, and the conference. It also helped establish a modern 'audience' for social, political, philosophical and scientific ideas, and thus created the circumstances in which a class of intellectuals could live from writing about them.

The case of France, centre of European cultural and intellectual life, demonstrates this 'explosion' of new forms of communication very well. During the eighteenth century, a welling tide of journals, concerned with literary matters, news, art, science, theology, philosophy, law and other matters of contemporary concern, appeared and were distributed throughout Europe. Between 1715 and 1785 the number of such regularly published journals grew from twenty-two to seventy-nine (Doyle, 1989, p.45). The boldest journals, those with the most radical or 'dangerous' ideas, were published beyond the frontiers of France. Some, such as Baron Grimm's *Correspondance Littéraire,* which had a Europe-wide circulation, were extremely costly and went only to such people as rulers and monarchs anxious to keep up with the heady life of the Parisian salons, and to keep abreast of new knowledge. Although publishing was (technically) strictly supervised by a system of censorship, there were many ways in which books and journals which were contrary to the government, to morals and to religion could be published without receiving the official 'privilege', and very few were banned. From the 1770s, book and journal publishing accelerated enormously, with newspapers starting to be available as well.

The audience for this massive explosion of printed material was potentially very large. However, access to this material was greatly restricted by two things: cost (a subscription to a journal could cost 20–50 *livres* per year, when the wages of the most skilled craftsman would not exceed 30 *livres* a week, with most earning half that sum or less); and restricted availability of the cultural education necessary to understand and take part in the debates about new ideas. Access to books and journals was facilitated for the impecunious by the rapid growth, after the mid-century, of subscription libraries and reading rooms, which had membership fees of about the cost of a single journal subscription. Some of these had conversation rooms set aside, but in the main discussion took place in a different and equally popular institution, the literary society. These also had libraries where journals could be read, but in addition they held regular public sessions where their members read their own works or debated questions of the day. They organized essay competitions, public lectures and other cultural events, and were popular with the educated classes in all French towns: 'One sees societies of this sort in almost all the towns of the kingdom … such an agreeable resource for the select class of citizen in all walks of life', noted a Dijon newspaper in 1787 (Doyle,1989, p.47). Even more select were the academies. Their members were elected, their membership carefully restricted, their constitution recognized by royal letters-patent. Apart from the three main Parisian academies founded in the seventeenth century, there were only seven provincial academies in 1700: this number had grown to thirty-five by the 1780s, although their combined membership throughout the entire period only amounted to some 6,000, of whom 37 per cent were nobles. The academies were culturally pre-eminent, international bodies in the sense that they included distinguished foreign associates and correspondents on their lists (Adam Smith was a correspondent of the Academy of Toulouse, for example). Success in their regular essay competitions could launch careers — Rousseau's triumph in the Dijon Academy's competition of 1750 being a notable example (Doyle, 1989, pp.47–8).

The consumers of this intellectual culture were mainly nobles, clerics and the professional bourgeoisie — members of the traditional social orders. They were mostly residents of towns, and particularly those towns *least* influenced by commerce or manufacturing. The new, 'modern' middle classes of merchants and manufacturers were seemingly not so interested in the world of ideas. 'I do not expect you will be able to sell any here' writes a bookseller of Bar-Le-Duc, an eastern French textile manufacturing town, to the publishers promoting a new edition of the *Encyclopédie* in 1780: 'Having offered them to everybody here, nobody so far has come looking for a copy. They are more avid for trade than for reading, and their education is quite neglected ... the merchants prefer to teach their children that 5 and 4 make 9 minus 2 equals 7, than in telling them to refine their minds' (quoted in Doyle, 1989, p.48).

In this context it is perhaps not surprising that for the *philosophes*, as for the consumers of their writings, the domain of enlightened thought was not subdivided by a barrier between the disciplines which studied natural and social worlds: the implication of this for an emergent sociology and the other social sciences is of fundamental importance. It is not until the late nineteenth century and early twentieth century that a gulf begins to emerge between natural and social sciences, exemplified particularly by the great *methodenstreit* or methodological argument which raged in Germany from the 1880s, and which turned upon the question of whether the sciences which study history, society and culture share the same scientific methods as those which study matter.

3.3   ENLIGHTENMENT AND SOCIAL SCIENCE

As the *philosophes* saw it, science was the epitome of reason because it made possible objective statements which were beyond philosophical, theological or ideological dispute. Indeed, the concern of the Enlightenment thinkers with science was not in any sense the espousal of mere principles alone, but in many cases proceeded from a very full immersion in scientific knowledge and practices. As we noted above, Voltaire, who visited England in 1726–9, produced a lucid and popular exposition of Newton's major scientific achievements. Voltaire idealized Newton as a sort of new hero; one more fitting to an age which was concerned with reason, progress, the future:

> If true greatness consists of having been endowed by heaven with powerful genius, and of using it to enlighten oneself and others, then a man like M. Newton (we scarcely find one like him in ten centuries) is truly the great man, and those politicians and conquerors (whom no century has been without) are generally nothing but celebrated villains.
> (quoted in Gay, 1973b, pp.128–9)

The deification of Newton was in fact a common theme of the Enlightenment. Jean-Jacques Rousseau was at one point called the 'Newton of the moral world' by Kant, and to be a 'Newton' was just about the most flattering thing anybody could say about a *philosophe* (Gay, 1973b, p.129). A number of central figures of the Enlightenment (David Hume, Jean d'Alembert, Étienne de Condillac, and Immanuel

Kant) made significant contributions to the philosophical understanding of science, and thus to the acceptance of scientific method as the basis for an understanding of human nature.

The achievements of science were of signal importance, for they pointed to the possibility of a rational and empirically-based method for creating a form of knowledge which was not conditioned by religious dogma or superstition. The *philosophes* were concerned with moral issues, but they wished to free moral philosophy from its reliance upon theology, put it upon a scientific and rational base and derive objective knowledge from it. Their critical rationalism and their support of science were in certain respects a confusion of two different intellectual strands, and the progressive espousal by the sciences of what are termed *positivist* methods, which make a very rigid distinction between fact and value, ultimately caused them some philosophical problems. They wished to use science and reason to counteract the founding of social institutions on what they saw as repressive values derived from Christianity or feudalism: but they did not foresee that the separation of fact and value implicit in scientific method would make it difficult to establish a scientific basis for the societal and cultural values which they espoused. If science is indeed value-neutral, then the knowledge it creates confers no special status on any social arrangement, however 'enlightened' it may appear.

None the less, the long love-affair of the *philosophes* with science was important in the emergence of social science. The prototypical social sciences required two basic conditions in order to develop coherent areas of study and methods of enquiry, which they derived from the example of the natural sciences: *naturalism* and the *control of prejudice*. Naturalism, the notion that cause and effect sequences in the natural world (rather than a spiritual or metaphysical world) fully explain social phenomena, was provided by the Enlightenment emphasis on scientific method. The control of prejudice is necessary in the social sciences as a means of preventing value-judgements from unduly influencing the results of empirical study. It is arguable whether it is possible to eliminate prejudice or value-judgements completely from the selection of a topic of research, but it is clear that in the evaluation or analysis of evidence and data the social scientist must prevent his or her prejudices from influencing the results. The *philosophes* — although they were on many occasions prey to prejudice in their work (and nowhere is this clearer than in their treatment of the rights and condition of women) — wanted to let facts, rather than values, test their theories. The presence of these two conditions in the intellectual climate of the Enlightenment fertilized the growth of the social sciences, but it also created a number of major philosophical difficulties which remained essentially unresolved.

The overarching emphasis of the *philosophes* on rationalism, empiricism and humanitarianism was largely responsible for their work in the new social sciences having two distinct characteristics:

1   the use of *scientific methods* in attempting to justify the reform of
     social institutions; and

2   *cultural relativism*: the realization, by many *philosophes,* that the
     European society in which they lived did not represent the best or
     most developed form of social organization.

The first of these is evidenced by the widespread belief amongst the
philosophes that scientific knowledge of human affairs could be directly
applied to the transformation of human institutions. Believing, as
Voltaire put it, that men were corrupted by 'bad models, bad education,
bad laws', the *philosophes* placed a great reliance on the functions of
knowledge itself as an agent of social change. Man's natural innocence
and his dependence on himself as an adult would provide the material,
with objective knowledge to reject corrupt influences. Diderot wrote a
play *Est-il Bon? Est-il Méchant?* (Is he Good? Is he Wicked?), which
aptly sums up the wholly *modern* way in which questions about human
morality were to be treated by the Enlightenment: as problems to be
solved by intellectual enquiry, rather than by the imposition of an
external authority.

The second major characteristic of the new social sciences was their
new mood of *cultural relativism*: the notion that there was no single
culture, and certainly not any Christian culture, which could provide a
standard of perfection by which to judge others. This mood was by no
means universal amongst the *philosophes*, but it was a strong feature of
the approach we associate with the French Enlightenment. Scottish
Enlightenment figures (especially Hume, Smith and Ferguson) were
attached to a stage-model of human development, in which modern
European society appeared to be the most advanced. The French
philosophes were frequent users of the literary ruse of providing a
critique of some aspect of European society with which they disagreed,
by means of an account written by what would have been considered in
their time as a 'barbarous' non-European — Montesquieu's *Lettres
Persanes*, a criticism of absolute monarchy as practised by Louis XIV
and XV, is a classic of the genre. Apparently written by a Persian
traveller, it inverts the classic western assumption that despotism is
only practised in the East.

The *philosophes* were extensive if somewhat uncritical users of the
reports of travellers, explorers, or even missionaries about foreign lands
and other cultures (a theme explored in much more detail by Stuart Hall
in Chapter 6). They employed these in the service of their important
contention that human nature was basically uniform, and varied only in
response to certain local conditions and particular circumstances,
ranging from the ecological to the political. As Montesquieu put it, the
Enlightenment's maxim of cultural relativism worked like this: 'one
should not sit in judgement upon the ways of other people, but rather
seek to understand them in the context of their circumstances, and then
use one's knowledge of them to improve understanding of oneself'
(Porter, 1990, p.63). Although they were often a little credulous in their
usage of some of the more dubious of these travellers' tales, the

philosophes' passionate interest in other cultures was crucially important to the development of a basic component of social science: cross-cultural comparison. For it is a central methodological tenet of the social sciences that theories and hypotheses should be formulated in a way which allows their employment in comparative studies. It is important to separate this cultural relativism from the belief in progress — the idea that the application of science and enlightened thought to the improvement of man's lot could make the European societies in which the *philosophes* lived the most advanced in the world. And we should be aware that intellectually the key figures of the Enlightenment stood in opposition to the domination of alien cultures and civilizations, and especially to the enslavement of their populations.

It is important to observe that the treatment of other cultures is one where the contradictions and inconsistencies of the Enlightenment are most evident. Several French *philosophes* used the example of other cultures to point up the 'barbarism' of the French state. Some, like Rousseau, used the example of 'savage society' to demonstrate how civilization makes men subvert their natural humanity and create inequalities. His idea of the 'noble savage', the notion that man is naturally good and is only made bad by society, fits well with the Enlightenment concept of the uniformity of human nature. By contrast, the Scottish Enlightenment developed several 'stadial models' of the historical stages though which human society was supposed to have evolved. These models typically set up the Scottish society of the eighteenth century as the pinnacle of human development, with the 'savage' or 'barbarous' societies discovered by colonial exploration in the Americas and elsewhere at the other end of the scale.

Although these two ways of using other cultures in the emergent social science of the Enlightenment clearly differ, they do have one important common characteristic: the need to compare European society with that of other cultures and to understand its characteristics and history in a wider context.

4 HUMAN NATURE AND HUMAN SOCIETY

It is arguable that the sociological ideas developed by the Enlightenment were preoccupied with the advancement of freedom and humanity.

In this section, the emergence of a specifically modern approach to the scientific study of man in society will be analysed, as it appears principally in the work of two Enlightenment writers, Montesquieu (Charles de Secondat), and Adam Ferguson.

We shall approach this through a consideration of Reading B, 'The science of society', by Peter Gay.

ACTIVITY 2   At this point, you should read **Reading B, 'The science of society'**, by
Peter Gay. The reading is part of a chapter from Gay's classic study *The
Enlightenment: An Interpretation*, originally published in the 1960s. In
this book Gay set out to present a reinterpretation of the Enlightenment
as a 'momentous event in the history of the Western mind', and his
approach is one which maintains that there is a holistic unity in
Enlightenment thought over and above the evident disunity of its many
protagonists. Gay discerns a 'program' in the Enlightenment, and his
view of the Enlightenment is essentially positive.

**Adam Ferguson
(1723–1816)**

As you read the extract from Gay's chapter, I suggest you make brief
notes on the following:

1   How did the *philosophes* put their ideas about society together: in
     particular, what sorts of sources did they use?

2   What was the form taken by their social science? For example, are
     their propositions formulated in a form which makes them testable
     by some form of social research? Or are they essentially literary
     ideas?

3   What would you say are the main differences and similarities Gay
     identifies between the ideas of Montesquieu and Ferguson?

The emphasis Gay puts upon the *critical* and *programmatic* nature of Enlightenment rationalism is of importance to an understanding of the emergence of the social sciences. Mere curiosity, scepticism and a belief that scientific principles could be applied to human affairs were not enough. The distinctive character of the emergent social sciences was given them by the commitment of their practitioners to *social change*, to a transformation of human affairs by means of extending man's understanding of himself.

5   REVOLUTION AND REFORMATION

In the emergence of distinctively modern societies, the social and political transformations which occurred in the American and French Revolutions of 1776 and 1789 appear to be intimately linked. They are widely represented as the thresholds between traditional and modern society, symbolizing the end of feudalism and absolutism, and the rise of the bourgeoisie as the dominant class in capitalist society, as well as major steps along the roads to both liberal democracy and totalitarianism. But what is the precise nature of the relationship between the Enlightenment and the French and American Revolutions? This topic has been hotly debated for the last 200 years, and we are not going to resolve it in this chapter. Our concerns are more with some of the implications of these Revolutions for the emergence of sociology and the other social sciences as institutionalized disciplines.

The American Revolution and the War of Independence which followed it (1776–83) appeared to prove that a new Republic could be created, that it could defeat a powerful monarchy and that it could encapsulate Enlightenment ideas. A number of the central figures of the new American Republic — notably Thomas Jefferson, Benjamin Franklin, John Adams, and Alexander Hamilton — were *philosophes* in the sense of being part of the wider circle of intellectuals in touch with the key figures of the Enlightenment. The Republic's constitution enshrined a number of central precepts of the Enlightenment: the uniformity of human nature (equality), tolerance, freedom of thought and expression, the separation of powers. It owed a lot to Montesquieu's ideas about the social basis of political order, to Hume's conception of the universality of human nature, and to Voltaire's concern with freedom of thought. Yet like most products of the Enlightenment it had its dark side: slavery paradoxically remained legal (Jefferson was himself a plantation owner and a slave-master).

The success of the American Revolution — helped to no small degree by aid from the French state, as part of its long struggle with Britain for European dominance — encouraged those in France who wished to see an end to the 'despotism' of absolute monarchy in Europe.

It was widely thought at the time that the French Revolution was in part at least a by-product of the dangerous ideas proposed by the *philosophes*. As Catherine the Great of Russia wrote in 1794 to the Baron Grimm:

> Do you remember that the late King of Prussia claimed to have been told by Helvétius that the aim of the *philosophes* was to overturn all thrones, and that the *Encyclopédie* was written with no other end in view than to destroy all kings and all religions? Do you also remember that you never wished to be included among the *philosophes*? Well, you were right ... The sole aim of the whole movement, as experience is proving, is to destroy.

Yet, as we have noted, the *philosophes* for the most part thought that progress could come about *within* the existing social order. As Diderot once said, their aim was revolutionary only insofar as it sought 'the revolution which will take place in the minds of men' (quoted in Eliot and Stern, 1979, p.44). Indeed, Voltaire believed in the necessity of absolute monarchs (like Louis XV, whose historiographer-royal he became) because only they would have the power to sweep away the institutions and outmoded laws which kept men in a state of ignorance and superstition.

In Britain, Edmund Burke (1729–97), a political theorist of the Whig party, put forward what was to be an influential conservative interpretation of the Enlightenment, which saw it as an intellectual or philosophic conspiracy, fomented by a 'literary cabal', and designed to destroy Christianity, and in the process bring down the French state. To support his case he used the example of the Bavarian *Illuminati*. There had been a notorious conspiracy by a group of Enlightenment-influenced intellectuals in Bavaria — the *Illuminati* — to use freemasonry to bring down the Church-dominated government of the German principality in 1787.

In his widely read *Reflections on the Revolution in France* (1790), Burke laid responsibility for the Revolution squarely at the door of the *philosophes*. He told the French that there was nothing fundamentally wrong with the *ancien régime*, and that they had no need to bring the monarchy down: 'You had the elements of a constitution very nearly as good as could be wished ... but you chose to act as if you had never been moulded into civil society and had everything to begin anew' (quoted in Doyle, 1989, p.166).

Burke's ideas were vigorously contested by Thomas Paine (1737–1809), amongst others, in his *Rights of Man*, a strong case for the republican argument, and one which stressed that the French were creating a new constitution on the basis of Enlightenment thinking — rational, equitable, based on natural law and scientific principles. The debate between Burke and Paine was linked quite closely to a wider political struggle over parliamentary reform in England, and continued until about 1800. Although Paine's ideas were highly influential in Britain, in

Europe Burke's argument that societies were very unwise to abandon heritage and established traditions struck a strong chord — particularly among the cultivated and ruling élites who perceived that the example of the French Revolution threatened their own vested interests.

In one sense, the *philosophes* were a key factor in the French Revolution. As Albert Sorel, writing a century later would say:

> The Revolutionary situation was a result of the faults of the Government, but the philosophes gave it leaders, cadres, a doctrine, direction, the temptation of illusions and the irresistible momentum of hope. They did not create the causes of the Revolution, but they made them manifest, actuated them, gave them emotive force, multiplied them and quickened their pace. The writings of the philosophes were not responsible for the disintegration of the ancien régime: it was because it was disintegrating of its own accord that their influence promoted the Revolution.
> (Sorel, 1969, pp.238–9; first published 1885)

As Sorel and many historians since have made very clear, the conditions for revolution existed at least as early as the reign of Louis XV: only a certain sense of optimism that his successor would put things right, founded in the residual legitimacy of the monarchy for most of the French, delayed the events which finally occurred in 1789. Despite the *philosophes'* own protestations to the contrary, the Enlightenment was a radical force in undermining the legitimacy of the *ancien régime*. The main factor in this was the great popularity of Enlightenment thinking among the educated élites. We have noted the virtual explosion in the number of books, newspapers, journals, literary societies, and subscription libraries between 1725 and 1789. This provoked a growth in the number of state censors, from 41 in 1720 to 148 by 1789. The expulsion of the Jesuit order in 1764 as a result of a long dispute between the order and the French *Parlements* (which seriously disrupted the French educational system: about a quarter of the French *collèges* were run by Jesuits) also gave a boost to the mounting tide of irreligion and to demands for greater religious tolerance, largely emanating from the *philosophes*. The Church itself tried to stem this tide by publishing refutations of philosophic impieties, and getting pious laymen in positions of authority to suppress dissent, but of course as a result it only succeeded in encouraging the wider debate of central issues of Enlightenment thought.

The French Revolution became, as the historian William Doyle has said, 'an opportunity for enlightened men to bring about a more rational, just and humane organisation of the affairs of mankind'. The National Assembly, which launched the Revolution in 1789, included 'the cream of the country's intelligentsia, who consciously saw themselves as the products and the instruments of the triumph of Enlightenment. All over

France men of similar background rallied to them, inspired by the same ideals' (Doyle, 1989, p.393). The revolutionary constitution which that Assembly produced in 1791 was directly based upon ideas first enunciated in *De l'Esprit des Lois* by Montesquieu, especially those relating to the separation of powers between executive, legislature and judiciary.

It would be misleading to see the French Revolution as no more than the putting into practice of the intellectual principles of the Enlightenment. As Mounier, the moderate royalist leader of 1789, argued much later, 'it was not the influence of those principles which created the Revolution, it was on the contrary the Revolution which created their influence' (quoted in Hampson, 1969, p.256).

As a socio-political event, the French Revolution stands at the threshold of the modern world, and that world is arguably inconceivable without it, for it transformed men's outlook on the nature and organization of society. If we then look at the chief architects of that Revolution, and ask from where their own outlook was derived, we come back to the main figures of the Enlightenment — to Voltaire, Montesquieu, Diderot, Rousseau, Condorcet, Bejamin Franklin.

It is in the areas of civil law, parliamentary control of taxation, the liberties of the press and of the individual, religious tolerance, and the wholesale sweeping away of feudal laws and obligations ('privilege') that the influence of the Enlightenment on the Revolution is clearest. The *philosophes* believed that 'men would live with greater happiness and dignity if their social institutions were determined by what was considered reasonable or scientific rather than regulated by prescription' (Hampson 1969, p.252). With this went the assumption that men had certain inalienable rights, such as unrestricted freedom of access to information, freedom of speech, freedom from arbitary arrest, and freedom of economic activity. Taken overall, they appear as the Revolution's drive to institutionalize a greater degree of social, political and economic equality within the state, to counter the natural inequality of man which underpinned the whole complex system of law, taxation and local government of the *ancien régime.* Yet, at least in its early stages, the ideal of equality was a limited one, and not as radical as it might appear. What the revolutionaries of 1789–91 wanted was an opening up of French society to those men — essentially the educated, cultivated 'gentlemen' who had been some of the main consumers of Enlightenment thought — then excluded from power and influence. In many ways they wanted a society like that of England, where a limited democracy was available.

The Revolution took a different turn after 1792, entering a clear second phase and becoming both more radically republican and Rousseauist in its form. The Republic was engaged in a war against numerous absolutist or monarchist states on its frontiers (Austria, Prussia, Holland, Spain, Britain) and internally against those who opposed the increasingly democratic and totalitarian directions which its institutions were taking. It had progressively less to do with the basic principles of the *philosophes*, and became closer in spirit to the ideas of Jean-Jacques Rousseau,with the Republic represented as a sort of Ideal City, and society seen as a means for reinforcing the morality of its members. The execution of Louis XVI in 1793, and the Terror unleashed against many of those who had been the main supporters of the Revolution of 1789, seemed to many outside of France to be proof that the Enlightenment had created a monster. Many European intellectuals — Kant among them — were repelled by the violence of the Revolution, and the increasingly belligerent nationalism of France.

The latter history of the Revolution, and its transformation into a new form of absolutism under Napoleon, thus helped to accelerate a move away from the ideals of the Enlightenment. Only those measures which helped national efficiency (e.g. internal free trade, technical education) remained. Basic liberties, such as freedom of the press and freedom from arbitrary arrest, were suspended. The Enlightenment as a force for progress and intellectual change was effectively at an end. Nevertheless, the intellectual principles which it had institutionalized amongst the cultivated élite survived, and formed the basis of a new set of reflections upon the ordering of a post-revolutionary society.

6   THE BIRTH OF SOCIOLOGY: SAINT-SIMON AND COMTE

Although the Revolution and its aftermath carried away with it some of the 'momentum of hope' engendered by the Enlightenment, the intellectual advances it brought in ways of thinking about man and society were not jettisoned in the process. Other intellectual fashions — especially, in the more conservative forms of Romanticism, a return to a belief in order and tradition — held sway, but the palpable advances of the natural sciences and their progressive institutionalization as professionalized disciplines continued to provide a model for the social sciences to follow. The social changes which the French Revolution had brought in its train — notably the emergence of an economically powerful middle class — also provided a new social force in the constitution of civil society, and with it the creation of new social theories which could make sense of the new directions in which an emergent 'modern' and 'industrial' society was heading.

Although a properly professionalized sociology was not to appear until the latter half of the nineteenth century, it is in the carry-over of ideas and concepts from the Enlightenment into the 'classical sociology' formulated in the first decades of the nineteenth century that we can discern its roots. In the writings and activities of Saint-Simon and Comte, a theory was elaborated about the emergent 'industrial society' forming itself in post-revolutionary Europe, and this constituted an agenda of interests for the new science of sociology which was still being debated by Émile Durkheim and Max Weber in the 1890s.

6.1 SAINT-SIMON

When Henri de Saint-Simon (1760–1825) set out to construct a new science of society from the wreckage of the Enlightenment, he saw himself as carrying the *philosophes'* ideas on to a new plane: 'The philosophy of the eighteenth century has been critical and revolutionary; that of the nineteenth century will be inventive and constructive' (quoted in Taylor, 1975, p.22).

Saint-Simon was a typical product of the Enlightenment. From a noble family, he received an education steeped in the classics, the new science of Newton, and the writings of the *philosophes*, typical of the second half of the eighteenth century. As he later wrote: 'Our education achieved its purpose: it made us revolutionaries' (quoted in Taylor, 1975, p.14).

Saint-Simon narrowly escaped becoming a victim of the Terror before a series of successful financial speculations made him (briefly) a rich man. He used the leisure this brought him to follow and even finance courses in the study of science and physiology, the latter because he held the view that a new science of society — a 'social physiology' — would be necessary if order and stability were to become possible again. Saint-Simon came to believe that modern society was threatened by the forces of anarchy and revolution, and that society would only progress beyond this stage if science and industry were put at the service of mankind through a major social reorganization. Scientists would become the new religious leaders because, as human thought had become more enlightened since the Middle Ages, the Catholic clergy could no longer demonstrate the spiritual power required to hold society together. Saint-Simon proposed a 'religion of Newton' organized on both national and international levels, with the world's most eminent scientists and artists at its head. Temporal power would belong with the property owners, representatives of the new industrial class.

Although these notions received relatively little attention, Saint-Simon's ideas about the need for a science of man and society became progressively more influential as war and social disorder engulfed Europe in the first two decades of the nineteenth century. His *Memoire sur la Science de l'Homme* (Memoir on the Science of Man) and *Travail sur la Gravitation Universelle* (Work on Universal Gravitation), both written in 1813, received wide recognition as an appeal to found a new social science which would counteract the forces of conflict and disorder. As a result of this and later work, Saint-Simon became a key figure in the 'liberal' political movements of post-Napoleonic Europe. In his journal *L'Industrie*, Saint-Simon used the term 'liberal' to describe economic and political values which were in favour of greater freedom for manufacture and trade, and a bigger say in how the country was run for those who owned factories and other businesses.

Henri de Saint-Simon (1760–1825)   Auguste Comte (1798–1857)

6.2 COMTE

Auguste Comte (1798–1857) was the first person to use the term
'sociology' to describe the scientific study of society. Comte's work has
been presented as a synthesis of the writings of key Enlightenment
figures such as Montesquieu, the physiocratic economist Turgot, and
Condorcet, and of his erstwhile patron and collaborator, Saint-Simon.
Although the *philosophes* clearly inspired Comte, his work in defining
the subject matter and methods of the new science — sociology — goes
far beyond them, and offers a clear link to the professionalized
discipline of the twentieth century (Thompson, 1976, p.6).

Comte wished to create a naturalistic science of society capable of both
explaining its past and predicting its future. He developed a theory
which has many affinities with those of the Enlightenment *philosophes*,
in that it proposed a series of stages (The Law of Human Progress or the
Law of Three Stages), through which society has progressed. Unlike the
stadial (staged) theories of Ferguson or Smith however, his notion of
development was based on the idea of a development of the human
mind, and societal stages thus mirrored these developments in terms of
social organization, types of social unit and forms of social order. Like
the *philosophes*, he saw society as developing progressively through the
emancipation of the human intellect. Where he differed from them most
substantially was in the notion that societies are in effect like giant
biological organisms. Their evolution and development thus follow
well-defined, law-like stages, much as the development of an animal
follows a clear pattern.

Comte believed that sociology was the study of such patterns of societal evolution, and that it would proceed through an analysis of both *static* and *dynamic* aspects of social organization. He distinguished these two not by empirical criteria, but methodologically. Static and dynamic, order and progress are always present in an interconnected way, and thus their differentiation in any empirical context is always a matter of methodological distinction, based on theoretical concepts. It is often very hard to make a purely empirical distinction between these elements in a given situation, where the point at which progress ends and order begins becomes a matter of interpretation. Comte's insight is that these distinctions are theoretical, rather than simple observations.

Like Saint-Simon, Comte used ideas about the function of religion as a sort of social cement which binds societies together. Language also performs this function, but without some form of religion (adapted to the stage of society in which it is found) governments would possess no legitimacy, and society would be torn apart by factional violence. Comte also used a further notion, derived essentially from the Scottish Enlightenment, to explain social order — the division of labour. Men are:

> bound together by the very distribution of their occupations; and it is this distribution which causes the extent and growing complexity of the social organism.

> The social organization tends more and more to rest on an exact estimate of individual diversities, by so distributing employments as to appoint each one to the destination he is most fit for, from his own nature ... from his education and his position, and, in short, from all his qualifications; so that all individual organizations, even the most vicious and imperfect ... may finally be made use of for the general good.
> (Comte, *Cours de Philosophie Positive*, 1830–2, vol.II; quoted in Thompson, 1976)

Many of Comte's ideas are remarkably close in spirit to the sociology developed by Émile Durkheim at the end of the nineteenth century: especially his emphasis on the clear definition of sociology's subject matter, and on the methodological principles underlying the new science — observation, experimentation, comparison. Durkheim was also concerned with the role of religion in generating social cohesion or solidarity, in the role of the division of labour within industrial societies, and in the forms of solidarity which modern societies required. Indeed, all of Durkheim's most characteristic ideas have close affinities with those of Comte and Saint-Simon, although it is also quite evident that Durkheim departed from their perspective in a number of respects. But the crucial point is that Émile Durkheim provided theories, methodologies and subject matter for the earliest institutionalization of sociology as a university-based discipline. With Comte and Saint-Simon, then, we are at one of the crucial bridges between the ideas of the Enlightenment and those of modern sociology. They provided the conduit along which certain central principles of the Enlightenment's world-view flowed into modern sociology.

7   CONCLUSION

The Enlightenment, which its proponents saw as spreading reason like light, played a critically important part in the emergence of the social sciences. It formed the first stage in the forging of a modern conception of society as an entity open to human agency, whose workings are in principle open to our scrutiny. It created the elements from which intellectuals could begin to construct an image of society which reflected human interests. The *philosophes* certainly believed that human agency, if properly informed by enlightened self-knowledge, was perfectly capable of controlling society — for what was the latter but the aggregated wills of individual men and women? We can be sceptical about the extent to which they really wanted to change society as a result of that self-knowledge, and there is little doubt that most of the major figures in the movement wished only for the end of absolutist rule, and for a political regime which extended if only in a limited way the liberties of the social orders from which they issued.

It is also clear that, like all knowledge, that of the Enlightenment spilled over from the narrow cup into which it was poured by the *philosophes,* and washed over those for whom it was not originally intended, being take up by a wide range of popularizers and political activists of many hues. When the great rupture between traditional and modern society first took shape in the French Revolution, the jettisoning of traditional values based on Christianity and absolutism must have seemed to many people a logical outcome of the radical programme of the Enlightenment — its hatred of religious orthodoxy and the clergy, its opposition to the political controls of the absolutist state, and its egalitarian ideology. Having prepared — even unwittingly — the ground for Revolution, it is not surprising that the Enlightenment's central ideas were tarred by the ruling élites of post-1815 Europe with the brush of sedition, subversion, and disorder. Indeed, it is a paradox of some magnitude that whilst the Enlightenment never developed a coherent theory or model of the society from which it issued, it produced enough elements of a *critique* of that society to help it along the way to an eventual demise.

How does the Enlightenment link to later stages in the emergence of a science of society? To begin with, we can assess its impact as an early and rather rickety sociological 'paradigm' — a cluster of interconnected ideas which were influential in the ways people thought about the social world and human relationships. If we think of Kant's motto *sapere aude* — dare to know — we can capture the essence of this new approach, this new paradigm. For the first time, man could 'dare to know' about the social arrangements under which he lived, rather than have them presented to him through the obscuring haze of a religious ideology. By knowing about these social arrangements, their operation would become clear, and thus open to change. Much in the same way as knowing about the cause of smallpox enabled man to devise a way of preventing it, it seemed to the *philosophes* self-evident that knowing about the cause of a social injustice, like religious persecution, would enable men to stop it occurring. Rather than a model of society, the Enlightenment had a model of how to think about social arrangements. Its practitioners were not loth to use the term 'society', but rarely even approached a definition of what could be meant by the word. The nearest the *philosophes* got to achieving a modern concept of society is thus the Scottish Enlightenment's ideas about human civilization going through a series of stages, which become the progressive unveiling of the uniformity of human nature. Ferguson's concept of 'civil society' thus appears as a setting in which the uniformity of human nature is finally allowed to operate as a set of arrangements for conducting the business of a nation in an enlightened fashion. It is in 'civil society' that the division of labour enables human nature to work most efficiently, and without unnecessary restraint.

We must not forget that the Enlightenment also encompassed medical, scientific, technological and other innovations, and that as a result it was widely thought of as part of a society-wide process of improving human life. It also made a big impact on education and therefore came to be part of the body of knowledge and ideas which were passed on in the process of schooling. In a general sense, once ways of thinking have been changed, they rarely go back to an earlier state. If I tell you something important which you did not already know, it will be hard for you to forget it. Those who thought and wrote about the society which emerged from the ashes of Revolutionary France, like Saint-Simon and Comte, could not escape their upbringing, which was steeped in the ideas and learning of the *philosophes*. They could not forget the Enlightenment, but they could react against it, and attempt to surpass it. The very thing that was deficient in Enlightenment thought — its inability to provide a coherent explanatory model of the society in which it existed — was precisely the thing that Saint-Simon and Comte tried to improve. They used the concept of society to describe the new combination of people, institutions, social groups and manufacturing processes which was emerging from the wreckage of the traditional European world. But their aim was not merely to describe and understand: like the *philosophes* their objective was to change society. Saint-Simon and Comte wished to see created the 'industrial society' dealt with in their writings.

By contrast, most *philosophes* stopped short of a properly worked out model of society, because they held an essentially 'individualist' conception of man, and because their social theory hardly needed the explicit conception of society as an entity. Once we 'know' that all men share a uniform human nature, it appears possible to construct an explanation of the behaviour of a multitude of people by simply aggregating individual characteristics (as a way of explaining social behaviour, this approach is known by the term 'methodological individualism'). Saint-Simon and Comte went beyond this to write quite explicitly about society as an entity which can be 'known' independently of individual men, as a force which can coerce and constrain individuals to behave in certain ways. Their ideas were influenced both by the traditionalism and romanticism of their time (a sort of reaction to the Enlightenment idea that man is a self-sufficient individual), and by the success of life-sciences such as biology and medicine, in which understanding the interconnections of organic processes played a crucial role. In Comte's work, man becomes subject to society once more, no longer self-sufficient but pushed and pulled by the twin forces of statics and dynamics. Comte presents society as a system which obeys certain laws — the laws which his positive sociology was established to study. His approach is often called 'organicism' because it uses the idea of society as a huge organism, as something more than the sum of its parts. If we take out one unit of that society — a particular person, for instance — we can know something about him or her, but not about how the whole society operates. But in the Enlightenment model, that person is a microcosm of society: by studying him or her we can build a picture about how society as a whole will operate — there are no 'laws of society' which are independent of the individual.

The history of sociology since the Enlightenment can be presented as the tension between the two approaches to society outlined above: one based in the *philosophes*' idea that society is no more than an aggregate of individuals, the other in Comte's idea that society is a super-individual entity, with a life of its own. Such a tension appears in the approaches of the central figures of nineteenth-century sociology, from J.S.Mill and Herbert Spencer to Émile Durkheim and Max Weber. Durkheim developed his own version of organicism, whilst Weber's approach recast the 'methodological individualism' of the Enlightenment in a modern form.

The Enlightenment, then, is one of the starting points for modern sociology. Its central themes formed the threshold of modern thinking about society and the realm of the social. Perhaps of equal importance is that it signalled the appearance of the secular intellectual within western society, a figure whose role is intimately bound up with the analysis and critique of society. It is from that role that emerged, amongst other intellectual positions, the modern conception of the professional sociologist, based in a specific institution. It may be that we have to thank Comte for the name 'sociology', but it is arguably to the Enlightenment that we should turn to see the emergence of the profession of sociologist.

REFERENCES

Anderson, B. and Zinsser, J. (1990) *A History of their Own: Women in Europe from Prehistory to the Present*, 2 vols, Harmondsworth, Penguin.

Black, J. (1990) *Eighteenth Century Europe 1700–1789*, London, Macmillan.

Brinton, C. (1930) 'The Revolutions', *Encyclopaedia of the Social Sciences*, vol.1, Macmillan, New York.

Darnton, R. (1979) *The Business of Enlightenment. A Publishing History of the Encyclopédie 1775–1800*, Cambridge, Mass., Harvard University Press.

Doyle, W. (1989) *The Oxford History of the French Revolution*, Oxford, Clarendon Press.

Eliot, S. and Stern, B. (eds) (1979) *The Age of Enlightenment: An Anthology of Eighteenth Century Texts*, London, Ward Lock Educational.

Gay, P. (1973a) *The Enlightenment: An Interpretation. Vol.1: The Rise of Modern Paganism*, London, Wildwood House.

Gay, P. (1973b) *The Enlightenment: An Interpretation. Vol.2: The Science of Freedom,* London, Wildwood House.

Gibbon, E. (1966) *Memoirs of my Life* (ed. by G. A. Bonnard), London, Nelson.

Hampson, N. (1969) *The Enlightenment*, Harmondsworth, Penguin.

Nisbet, R. (1967) *The Sociological Tradition*, London, Heinemann.

Porter, R. (1990) *The Enlightenment*, London, Macmillan.

Sorel, A. (1969) *Europe and The French Revolution: The Political Traditions of the Old Regime* (first published 1885), London, Collins.

Taylor, K. (1975) *Henri Saint-Simon 1760–1825: Selected Writings on Science, Industry and Social Organisation*, London, Croom Helm.

Thompson, K. (1976) *Auguste Comte: The Foundation of Sociology*, London, Nelson.

READING A   WOMEN IN THE SALONS

Bonnie Anderson and Judith Zinsser

One hundred and fifty years after Rambouillet's creation — in the second half of the eighteenth century — the salon achieved its greatest influence and prestige in Europe. In the leading capital cities, salons flourished, and their existence signaled an active intellectual and cultural life. Appearing in many nations, the salon reached its apogee in eighteenth-century France. There, where women's influence in the courts — as *maîtresse-en-titre,* as queen, as courtier — increased, women's influence also flourished outside the court, in the salons. In the relatively rigid hierarchical society of pre-revolutionary France, where a person had to prove four quarters of nobility to hold many important posts, the salon allowed both women and men a social mobility which existed nowhere else. The salon mixed elements of the nobility, bourgeoisie, and intelligensia and enabled some women to rise through both marriage and influence. ...

Intellectually, the salon provided shelter for views or projects unwelcome in the courts: when Voltaire was *persona non grata* with Louis XV because of his critical views of monarchy, he was deluged with invitations from Parisian salonières eager to be his hostess. The great Enlightenment project of the *Encyclopédie,* which sought to categorize, define, and criticize all existing knowledge, was suppressed by the French court, but completed in secret with Mme. Geoffrin's social and financial assistance. She welcomed the Encyclopedists to her salon, and their presence was sought by other salonières as well. The great French salonières both competed with and helped each other. Rivals for prestigious, usually male, guests, they often bequeathed their salons to younger female protegées. ...

Some salons were hosted by men. The focus in all the salons was attracting male guests. Men's superior prestige and power gave them precedence, and a salonière made her name by attracting male luminaries to her drawing room.

Despite this male predominance, both French and foreign commentators stressed and even exaggerated the power of 'female influence' in France. Traditional male fears about what might happen if women were 'out of place' and influenced government combined with the conspicuous role of women in the French court and salons to produce this view. In France, wrote the Scottish philosopher David Hume, 'the females enter into all transactions and all management of church and state: and no man can expect success, who takes not care to obtain their good graces.'

Rational conversation, sociability between women and men, delight in the pleasures of this world are the hallmarks of Enlightenment culture. The men who mingled with the Bluestockings and frequented the salons were the men who produced the Enlightenment. It is a tragedy for women that

Source: Anderson, B. S. and Zinsser, J. P. (1990) *A History of their Own: Women in Europe from Prehistory to the Present,* vol.II, Harmondsworth, Penguin Books; pp.106–9, 112–15, 118–20.

these men, who were aided, sponsored, and lionized by the salonières, produced — with very few exceptions — art and writing which either ignored women completely or upheld the most traditional views of womanhood. Just as there was no Renaissance or Scientific Revolution for women, in the sense that the goals and ideals of those movements were perceived as applicable only to men, so there was no Enlightenment for women. Enlightenment thinkers questioned all the traditional limits on men — and indeed challenged the validity of tradition itself. They championed the rights of commoners, the rights of citizens, the rights of slaves, Jews, Indians, and children, but not those of women. Instead, often at great cost to their own logic and rationality, they continued to reaffirm the most ancient inherited traditions about women: that they were inferior to men in the crucial faculties of reason and ethics and so should be subordinated to men. In philosophy and in art, men of the Enlightenment upheld the traditional ideal of woman: silent, obedient, subservient, modest, and chaste. The salonière — witty, independent, powerful, well-read, and sometimes libertine — was condemned and mocked. A few Enlightenment thinkers did question and even reject subordinating traditions about women. But those who argued for a larger role for women — like the Englishwoman Mary Wollstonecraft in her *Vindication of the Rights of Woman* (1791), the French Marquis de Condorcet in his *Admission of Women to Civic Rights* (1790), the German Theodor von Hippel in his *On the Civic Improvement of Women* (1792), the Spaniard Josefa Amar y Borbón in her *Discourse in Defense of Women's Talent and Their Capacity for Government and Other Positions Held by Men* (1786) — prompted outrage and then were forgotten. Instead, most philosophers and writers reiterated the most limiting traditions of European culture regarding women, often in works which condemned traditional behaviour for men. John Locke, the English philosopher, had a profound influence on Enlightenment thought when he argued that every man has an equal right 'to his natural freedom, without being subjected to the will or authority of any man.' But he thought women (and animals) exempt from 'natural freedom' and declared they should be subordinate: he upheld 'the Subjection that is due from a Wife to her Husband.' The Scottish philosopher David Hume delighted in his visits to the Paris salons of Deffand, Lespinasse, and Geoffrin, so much so that in his autobiography he declared he had once thought 'of settling there for life' because of 'the great number of sensible, knowing, and polite company with which that city abounds above all places in the universe.' Yet he simultaneously condemned France, which 'gravely exalts those, whom nature has subjected to them, and whose inferiority and infirmities are absolutely incurable. The women, though without virtue, are their masters and sovereigns.' Like Hume, other Enlightenment authors connected the rule of women — and especially of unvirtuous women — to the end of good government. Women who wielded the indirect power and influence of the salonières and the women of the courts were condemned.

The *Encyclopédie* could not have been written without the support of the salonières, yet there is no mention of the salons within its pages. Instead, articles about women concentrated on their physical weakness, their emotional sensitivity, and their role as mothers. While a few articles discussed equality, most accepted the traditional view that women were men's inferiors and often their opposites. By the eighteenth century, the idea that what is a virtue for one sex is a defect in the other had become a cliché: 'An effeminate behaviour in a man, a rough manner in a woman; these are ugly because unsuitable to each character', wrote Hume. Moreover, there was concern that each sex remain in its proper place. Joseph Addison and Richard Steel's influential journal, the *Spectator*, consistently condemned women who encroached on male territory by being too independent, too forward, or too 'impertinent'. 'I think it absolutely necessary to keep up the Partition between the two Sexes and to take Notice of the smallest Encroachments which the one makes upon the other,' wrote Addison in 1712, expressing a sentiment increasingly common in the eighteenth century.

… Voltaire lived for many years with Emilie du Châtelet (1706–1749), one of the most learned women of her age, who was famous for her scientific writings and her commentary on Leibnitz. Justifying her encroachment into the male domain of philosophy, Voltaire explained in his memoirs that 'Mme. du Châtelet did not seek to decorate philosophy with ornaments to which philosophy is a stranger; such affectation never was part of her character, which was masculine and just.' Despite his pleasure in his educated mistress, Voltaire wrote very little on women's education, function, or role in society — a glaring omission in a body of work which criticized so many other traditional institutions. He also seems to have been at best ambivalent about Châtelet's intellect. 'Emilie, in truth, is the divine mistress, endowed with beauty, wit, compassion and all of the other womanly virtues', he wrote a friend. 'Yet I frequently wish she were less learned and her mind less sharp.' In this, as in little else, Voltaire was in agreement with his arch-rival, the philosopher Jean-Jacques Rousseau. Rousseau, introduced to the Paris salons by Diderot in the 1740s, condemned the salonières in his influential novel *Émile* (1762):

> I would a thousand times rather have a homely girl, simply brought up, than a learned lady and a wit who would make a literary circle of my house and install herself as its president. A female wit is a scourge to her husband, her children, her friends, her servants, to everybody. From the lofty height of her genius, she scorns every womanly duty, and she is always trying to make a man of herself, like Mlle. de L'Enclos.

… As well as extolling the domestic virtues for women, the men of the Enlightenment, like so many generations of European men before them, insisted that chastity was woman's highest virtue and left the double standard of sexual behaviour intact. 'Modesty' and 'chastity' are duties which 'belong to the fair sex', argued David Hume. The double standard was essential to 'the interest of civil society … and to prove this', he concluded, 'we need only appeal to the practice and sentiments of all nations and ages.' Hume expressed the sentiments of his era. Regardless of whether or not they had sexual liaisons with the salonières, the men of the Enlightenment united in condemning the woman who had sex outside of marriage. Johnson thought she 'should not have any possibility of being restored to good character'; Rousseau equated her crime with treason:

> The faithless wife is worse [than the faithless husband]; she destroys the family and breaks the bonds of nature; when she gives her husband children who are not his own, she is false both to him and society; thus her crime is not infidelity, but treason. To my mind, it is the source of dissension and of crime of every kind.

In addition, they believed that women's supposed sexual power, so frightening and threatening to men, must be controlled for the good of society. Women who used their sexual power, as salonières or royal mistresses, could only meet with condemnation. ...

By the end of the eighteenth century, the salonière was repudiated in favor of more traditional women. This change occurred very rapidly during the era of the French Revolution and the Napoleonic Wars (1789–1815). The social and political power which the salonières had wielded in pre-revolutionary France became a leading criticism of the old monarchy, and people of differing classes and political philosophies united in condemning this 'female influence'. 'Women ruled [in the eighteenth century]', the French artist and Marie Antoinette's portraitist, Elizabeth Vigée-Lebrun remarked in her memoirs, 'The Revolution dethroned them.' Vigée-Lebrun exaggerated women's powers, but accurately perceived their decline in influence. The revolution unleashed a flood of criticism about women's 'unnatural' usurpation of the male domain of politics. Female political activity was outlawed in 1793, and male politicians, journalists, and philosophers condemned women's political influence whether it was republican or monarchist, revolutionary or counter-revolutionary.

READING B THE SCIENCE OF SOCIETY

Peter Gay

Whatever may have become of sociology in the nineteenth century, when the discipline got its name and took a distinctly conservative and nostalgic turn, in the Enlightenment, when it was invented, it was a science designed to advance freedom and humanity. 'The philosophy of the eighteenth century', wrote Saint-Simon, 'has been critical and revolutionary; that of the nineteenth century will be inventive and constructive.' Like other intellectual instruments devised or perfected in the eighteenth century, sociology suffered from bouts of self-confidence that its practitioners could not suppress. ... For all this lack of clarity and lack of modesty, the aims of eighteenth-century sociology were clear enough: to substitute reliable information and rational theory for guessing and metaphysics, and to use the newly won knowledge in behalf of man.

Source: Gay, P. (1973) *The Enlightenment: An Interpretation. Vol.2: The Science of Freedom,* London, Wildwood House; pp.323–8, 330–3, 336–42.

Montesquieu, the first and the greatest sociologist in the Enlightenment, embodies this scientific reformism perhaps more strikingly than anyone else. As he insisted in the Preface to his *De l'esprit des lois,* he was indeed a scientist: 'I have not drawn my principles from my prejudices, but from the nature of things'; and he reassured his readers that he was merely a reporter: 'I do not write to criticize whatever is established in any country.' At the same time, and in the same place, he made it plain that facts, for him, were in the service of values: 'I should think myself the happiest of mortals if I could help men to cure themselves of their prejudices'; indeed, 'it is not unimportant to have the people enlightened.' His intentions, at least, were clear and pure.

His execution was something else again. *De l'esprit des lois* is a flawed performance; even contemporaries who admired its originality and shared its pagan philosophy tempered their praise with reservations. It is the most unkempt masterpiece of the century: short chapters, some only one sentence in length, alternate with long disquisitions, and, especially in the later books, topics appear and reappear in bewildering sequence. The work has a certain coherence imposed on it by its author's passion for finding law behind the apparent rule of chance and general themes in the fragmented mosaic of particular facts, but the order is concealed behind digressions, abrupt shifts of theme, and rhetorical outbursts. Roughly the first third of *De l'esprit des lois* — doubtless the most important — deals with the nature and forms of government and the rights of subjects; the book then turns to an analysis of the impact of environment on politics and concludes with a potpourri which contains, among other things, discussions of political economy, French politics, and legal theory. No wonder Voltaire called the book 'a labyrinth without a clue, lacking all method' and thought that its strength lay in particular ideas, in its 'true, bold, and strong things'. Moreover, as Voltaire also complained, not without cause, Montesquieu was uncritical of the facts he had drawn from histories and travelers' reports, and his citations were often inaccurate: 'He almost always mistakes his imagination for his memory.' Finally, Montesquieu, no doubt unconsciously, smuggled ideology into his science: his definition of political freedom, his analysis of the British Constitution, and his advocacy of powerful aristocracies made him into a partisan in the great struggle that divided the French state in the eighteenth century rather than a neutral observer transcending his time and class. His claim that he had freed himself from his prejudices was not borne out by his performance.

Yet whatever his ambiguous role in French politics, whatever the limitations on his vision and the defects in his scholarship — and I make this assertion after due deliberation and with due consideration for the claims of potential rivals — Montesquieu was the most influential writer of the eighteenth century. Horace Walpole, who read *De l'esprit des lois* as soon as it became generally available, in January 1750, called it without hesitation 'the best book that ever was written — at least I never learned half so much from all I ever read'; when he heard that Montesquieu's reputation in France had suffered, he declared his contempt for French *'literati'* and reiterated his initial response: 'In what book in the world is there half so much wit, sentiment, delicacy, humanity?' The world agreed with Walpole. The men of the Scottish Enlightenment studied *De l'esprit des lois* with great care and great profit. ...

The real originality and lasting importance of *De l'esprit des lois,* however, lie in the particular relation it established between reason and decency. Montesquieu's argument is fairly simple, and its materials are old; what was complex, and new, was his manner of combining what others had known. His system is imperfectly perspicuous, for it depends on intellectual procedures — deduction and induction — that Montesquieu neither clarified nor reconciled. On the [one] hand, he professes to deduce his sociological laws from first principles; on the other, his laws group particular experiences into intelligible wholes — in Montesquieu's sociology the great contest between rationalism and empiricism was never settled. It was 'Descartes and Malebranche far more than Locke', Franz Neumann has written, 'who determined Montesquieu's scientific method' — but the importance of Locke was not negligible. The two principles on which he constructed his system — the uniformity of human nature and the diversity produced by environment and culture — have an independent validity. But they are also at times in tension.

Whatever these tensions, his argument was, as I have said, plain enough. There are, Montesquieu reasons, certain laws of nature that apply to all men, since they are derived from 'the constitution of our being.' But these laws find different expression in different situations; they are bent into individual shape by physical causes like climate, soil, size of the country, and by what Montesquieu calls 'moral' causes like customs and religion. The task of social science is to find both the universal laws and their appropriate application to each situation. The logic of Montesquieu's social science is the logic of cultural relativism: [as Neumann says,] 'There is, he believes, no universally applicable solution. There are only types of solutions.'

The configuration of laws appropriate to a certain nation is 'the spirit of the laws', and Montesquieu's book is an attempt to discover and define that spirit in all its multiformity. He begins, conventionally enough, with a classification of government by types of rulership — an enterprise as old as Plato and Aristotle, although his classification differs from theirs. He finds essentially three forms of government: republics, monarchies, and despotisms. This classification caused some dissent in his day; but it is only a prelude to what really matters: the 'principles' actuating each of these forms. The history of political sociology begins at this point. The principle of republics, Montesquieu argues, is 'virtue', and, as there are two kinds of republics, there are two kinds of virtue: democratic republics rest on public spirit; aristocratic republics on the moderation and self-restraint of the ruling families. Monarchies for their part are animated by what Montesquieu calls 'honor' — a keen awareness of status, accompanied by aspiration to preferment and titles. Despotism, finally, is actuated by fear. Montesquieu knows perfectly well that there is an admixture of each of these elements in all states; what matters is which predominates.

When one principle powerfully invades a state to which it is not suited, pernicious consequences are inescapable: the right principle will be corrupted, then collapse and revolution must follow.

This is a fertile scheme. It permits Montesquieu to penetrate beyond forms to substance; to discover, behind institutions, the forces that make them cohere, persist, or falter. It permits him, further, to find the institutions appropriate to each state: a monarchy needs schools, or a family organization, quite different from those needed in a republic. And finally it permits him to address himself to the dynamic of social change: 'The corruption of every government', Montesquieu writes, in one of those one-sentence chapters that so amused Voltaire, 'begins almost always with the corruption of its principles.' *De l'esprit des lois* takes a comprehensive view of political sociology: it finds room for the sociology of law and of education, and suggests a sociological view of history.

… Montesquieu's purpose, Raymond Aron has said, 'was to make history intelligible', and he realized that purpose, if incompletely, by seeking causes rather than ascribing everything to inscrutable fortune, and by grouping causes into small, manageable groups. The road to positivist sociology was thus open.

It is worth repeating that Montesquieu was never satisfied to formulate general laws and leave value judgments to others; he was too much the classicist, too much the humanist, too much the philosophe for that. He recognized that his commitment to facts and values sometimes involved him in paradoxes and contradictions. It is touching to see him struggling with himself: thus he speaks at length, and quite coolly, about slavery, and argues that in the West at least slavery is useless and uneconomical — then he adds a little pathetically, 'I do not know if this chapter was dictated to me by my mind or my heart'. The distinction between causal and normative inquiry was hard to maintain, even for him.

His analysis of despotism reveals both his ambivalence and his intentions. On the one hand, Montesquieu lists despotism among forms of government and assigns to it a principle as he has assigned principles to others. On the other hand, he sets off despotism from all other forms: monarchies, aristocracies, and democracies are legitimate forms, despotism is always bad. It is a 'monstrous' form of government; it 'takes glory in despising life'. Despotism may aim at tranquillity, but its tranquillity is only terror: 'It is not peace; it is the silence of towns the enemy is ready to occupy.' Despotism enlists religion in the regime of fear — 'fear added to fear' — depoliticizes its subjects, and treats men like animals by subjecting them to corruption and police brutality under capricious and unknown laws. As a sociologist, Montesquieu found it appropriate to analyze the phenomenon of despotism, to acknowledge its plausibility in vast empires and hot climates, but as a moralist he found nothing worthy in a regime whose principle was fear, whose policy was tyranny, and whose consequence was inhumanity. …

Like another French philosophe — Diderot — Montesquieu was more influential abroad than at home. I have indicated the range of his empire

— from America to Russia, from the Scotland of Ferguson to the Naples of Filangieri — but among all his dependencies Scotland must rank first. Hume, though critical of Montesquieu's 'abstract theory of morals' and sparing with hyperbole, thought him an 'author of genius, as well as learning.' Ferguson treated him as a modern classic: he lectured on Montesquieu, recommended him to his students, quoted him without criticism and paraphrased him without acknowledgment; indeed, acknowledgment would have been otiose: *De l'esprit des lois* was the common coin of learned discussion.

There was good reason for Scotland's receptivity to Montesquieu: his particular mixture of philosophy and science was wholly congenial to the Scottish Enlightenment, which had been developing its own tradition of secular sociological inquiry since the beginning of the eighteenth century. Francis Hutcheson, moral philosopher and student of society, had many disciples, a brilliant assembly of intellectuals — David Hume, John Millar, Adam Ferguson, Lord Kames, Lord Monboddo, William Robertson — followed, in the next generation, by Adam Smith and Dugald Stewart. All were to a degree moral philosophers, all turned under the pressure of their inquiries to the scientific study of society. The problems these Scots addressed became the classical problems of sociology: the origins of civilization, man's place in society, the development of language, the relations of classes, the rise and fall of population and their interplay with cultivation and prosperity, and the forms of government. ... However much their researches varied in effectiveness and direction, the intentions of the Scottish school were united in a single pursuit: to place moral philosophy on a sound, that is to say, a scientific, basis. By mid-century, the Scots could equate morals and science — Hume spoke of 'Moral philosophy, *or* the science of human nature'. Scientific metaphors were always in their minds: 'The great Montesquieu pointed out the road', wrote John Millar in acknowledging the debt he owed to Adam Smith, his teacher and friend. 'He was the Lord Bacon in this branch of philosophy. Dr. Smith is the Newton.' The comparison was trite when Millar made it in the 1780s, and its application doubtful, but it confirms the aspiration of the Scottish school toward a science of society. ...

In 1767, Hume's friend Adam Ferguson, a former chaplain, lapsed Christian, Professor of Moral Philosophy and Pneumatics at Edinburgh, published his first and, it was to turn out, his most important book, *An Essay on the History of Civil Society*. ... Like Hume, Ferguson was an enemy to fictions, and like Hume, he undertook the scientific study of society for moral reasons. Men shall know the truth — this, in sum, is Ferguson's motive and program — and the truth shall permit them to break the traditional cycles of civilization and decay. But the truth is elusive: Ferguson punctuates his *Essay* with warnings against rash conjectures, easy generalizations, and mere book learning. The warnings are repetitious and seem a little insistent, but they were not without point: only five years before, Adam Smith had told his students that 'the practical sciences of Politics and Morality or Ethics have of late been treated too much in a Speculative manner.' The very obscurity of man's origins, Ferguson argues, has seduced modern investigators into that supreme intellectual vice — system-making. 'The desire of laying the foundation of a favourite system, or a fond expectation, perhaps, that we may be able to penetrate the secrets of nature, to the very source of existence, have, on this subject, led to many fruitless inquiries, and given rise to many wild suppositions.' After all, Ferguson complains, other scientists do not follow such dubious methods: 'In every other instance … the natural historian thinks himself obliged to collect facts, not to offer conjectures'. But, it seems, when he studies himself, 'in matters the most important, and the most easily known', the student of society 'substitutes hypothesis instead of reality, and confounds the provinces of imagination and reason, of poetry and science'; he selects a few human characteristics, abstracts from current experience, and invents feeble fictions like the state of nature or the noble savage. 'The progress of mankind from a supposed state of animal sensibility, to the attainment of reason, to the use of language, and to the habit of society, has been accordingly painted with a force of imagination, and its steps have been marked with a boldness of invention, that would tempt us to admit, among the materials of history, the suggestions of fancy, and to receive, perhaps, as the model of our nature in its original state, some of the animals whose shape has the greatest resemblance to ours.' The sarcasm is heavy and its target obvious, but Ferguson does not permit his readers a moment's uncertainty: a footnote refers them to Rousseau's *Discours sur l'origine de l'inégalité parmi les hommes*. Rousseau's way, Ferguson insists, is not the way of science; the student of society must rest his case on 'just observation'. Human nature cannot be discovered by stripping away the contributions of culture to arrive at the naked, original being: 'Art itself is natural to man'. So, significantly but not surprisingly, Ferguson begins his *History* of *Civil Society* with an attempt to arrive at a realistic appraisal of human nature — not its origins but 'its reality' and 'its consequences'. …

The first victim of Ferguson's empiricism is the state of nature, the second is the legislator who supposedly transforms the horde into a society. 'Man is born in society', Ferguson writes, quoting Montesquieu, 'and there he remains'. There can be no doubt: 'Mankind have always wandered or settled, agreed or quarrelled, in troops and companies'. The study of man and the study of society are thus wholly interdependent. What they show at the outset — here Ferguson turns to Hume — is both the unity and the diversity of man's nature. 'The occupations of men, in every condition, bespeak their freedom of choice, their various opinions, and the multiplicity of wants by which they are urged; but they enjoy, or endure, with a sensibility, or a phlegm, which are nearly the same in every situation. They possess the shores of the Caspian, or the Atlantic, by a different tenure, but with equal ease'. The claim that man has changed fundamentally by moving from the state of nature to the civil state is a total misreading of his history. If we ask, 'Where [is] the state of nature to be found?' the answer must be, 'It is here; and it matters not whether we are understood to speak in the islands of Great Britain, at the Cape of Good Hope, or the Straits of Magellan'. And, just as travel in space offers the spectacle of uniformity, so does travel in time: 'The latest efforts of human invention are but a continuation of certain devices which were practised in the earliest ages of the world, and in the rudest state of mankind'.

This uniformity is the expression of certain 'universal qualities' in man, certain 'instinctive propensities', which are 'prior to the perception of pleasure or pain'. Most notable among these propensities is man's instinct for self-preservation, which expresses itself in automatic self-protection, in sexuality, and in his sociable traits. Man's reason is equally composite: God — a singularly shadowy figure in Ferguson's philosophy — has endowed man with reason to permit him to know and to judge. But neither the urge for self-preservation nor the capacity to reason makes man essentially into a calculating and selfish animal: hedonistic psychology is, in Ferguson's judgment, shallow at its best and in general contrary to experience. Man is a creature of habit as much as of reason, the prey to ambition as much as the victim of conformity, and, above all, he is an active being, happiest when he exercises his powers. 'Man is not made for repose', Ferguson writes, sounding much like Diderot. 'In him, every amiable and respectable quality is an active power, and every subject of commendation an effort. If his errors and his crimes are the movements of an active being, his virtues and his happiness consist likewise in the employment of his mind'. ...

While Ferguson insists on the uniformity of man's nature, he insists just as emphatically on the diversity of institutions and ideals, and it is here — in accounting for this diversity — that social science finds its proper employment. It is a difficult task, for 'the multiplicity of forms' that the social scientist must take into account 'is almost infinite'. After all, as Montesquieu had recognized, 'forms of government must be varied, in order to suit the extent, the way of subsistence, the character, and the manners of different nations'. Paradoxically enough, it is precisely the propensities of human nature — the principles, that is, of its unity — that lead to the diversity of human experience. For the urge to ally oneself with some implies the urge to divide oneself from others. 'They are sentiments of generosity and self-denial that animate the warrior in defence of his country; and they are dispositions most favourable to mankind, that become the principles of apparent hostility to men'. This is not a perverse pleasure in paradox: the dialectical character of human experience is for Ferguson an overwhelming fact. Civilization is natural; all civilizations are natural. But — and here we seem to hear the language of Freud's *Civilization and its Discontents* — all civilizations exact their price, all are a mixture of cooperation and conflict, of decay implicit in progress. To condemn all conflict indiscriminately is to read out of court half of human nature — 'He who has never struggled with his fellow-creatures, is a stranger to half the sentiments of mankind.' — and to misunderstand, and misunderstand disastrously, the positive function of conflict in culture. ...

Ferguson's science of man does not end here. It is not enough to analyze and then fold one's hands, watching tyrants or corrupt politicians misuse one's work. Precisely like the other social scientists of his time, Ferguson refuses to equate objectivity with neutrality. Whether we are 'actors or spectators', we perpetually 'feel the difference of human conduct', and are 'moved with admiration and pity, or transported with indignation and rage'. These emotions, 'joined to the powers of deliberation and reason,' constitute 'the basis of a moral nature'.

It is with this sense of being an engaged scholar that Ferguson delineates his virtuous man and describes the threats to flourishing civilizations. Fortunately, private happiness and public prosperity are consonant; benevolence gives pleasure not solely to the receiver but to the giver as well, and the vigorous exercise of one's public spirit is at once a source of personal gratification and of national well-being. Activity is praiseworthy, but it 'may be carried to excess', and then it deserves censure. Similarly, while conflict is valuable, not every conflict is creditable in origins or beneficial in consequences — 'the quarrels of individuals, indeed, are frequently the operations of unhappy and detestable passions; malice, hatred, and rage' — and it should be possible to devise a kind of moral equivalent for detestable quarrels by sublimating them into praiseworthy competition. This kind of discrimination that the student of society should apply to activity and conflict he must apply to other forms of social experience, all for the sake of moral judgment and sound public policy. ...

To Ferguson's mind, perhaps the most extraordinary instance of the paradox of progress is the division of labor. On the one hand, the division of labor is essential to social advance. Savages and barbarians are men of all trades, too worn out from their labors to improve their fortune, too scattered in their pursuits to acquire commendable skill in any single occupation. As the manufacturer, the merchant, the artist, the consumer discover, 'the more he can confine his attention to a particular part of any work, his productions are the more perfect, and grow under his hands in the greater quantities'. But just as the division of labor in public affairs brings efficiency in administration and alienation from politics, the division of labor in industrial or mercantile or artistic matters brings skill and prosperity — and alienation as well. Man (as Ferguson's admirer Karl Marx would put it) is alienated from his community, his labor, and himself; he is fragmented and mechanized: the community falls apart, divided between lowly mechanics and proud practitioners of the liberal arts, and the general increase in wealth is unevenly distributed, to the benefit of an elite and at the expense of the mass: 'In every commercial state, notwithstanding any pretension to equal rights, the exaltation of a few must depress the many'. Thus the division of labor produces conceit and selfishness in some, envy and servility in most; it is a blessing and a curse, creating vast possibilities and great dangers. The economic problem is, for Ferguson, a social and, even more, a political problem.

CHAPTER 2   THE DEVELOPMENT OF THE MODERN STATE

David Held

CONTENTS

1 INTRODUCTION

This chapter has three overall purposes: first, to introduce the diversity of state forms which have existed over time and which constitute the broad historical context for understanding the nature of the modern state; secondly, to explore the question: Why did the nation-state become the supreme form of the modern state?; thirdly, to examine competing conceptions of the modern state — its sovereignty, authority and legitimacy. These objectives are clearly wide-ranging; but by devoting attention to all three I hope to shed some light on the key formative processes of the modern state and the controversies that surround it.

The prime focus of this chapter will be the making of the modern state in Europe. There are a number of important reasons for this geographic restriction. In the first instance, the story of the formation of the modern state is in part the story of the formation of Europe, and vice versa. The development of a distinctive 'European' identity is closely tied to the creation of Europe by states. Moreover, the states system of Europe has had extraordinary influence in the world beyond Europe: European expansion and development has had a decisive role in shaping the political map of the modern world. Furthermore, debates about the nature of the modern state in large part derive from European intellectual traditions, notably the Enlightenment, although to recognize this is by no means to suggest that everything of importance about the state was understood and expressed in Europe alone.

1.1 SOME PRELIMINARY DEFINITIONS

It is intriguing to note that for the greater part of human history states have not existed at all. States are *historical* phenomena, constructed under particular conditions, and far from fixed or 'natural' entities. In hunting-and-gathering communities, in small agrarian cultures, and in the regions wandered by semi-nomadic or nomadic peoples there has been no recognizably separate state or political organization. Today, there are still many communities which anthropologists refer to as 'stateless' — communities such as the Jale people of the New Guinea highlands, the pastoral Nuer of the South Sudan, the M'dendeuili and Arusha of East Africa. 'Stateless', however, should not be taken to mean the absence of any mechanisms of regulation or government through which decisions affecting the community can be made and disputes settled. A diverse array of such mechanisms have existed, from family and kinship structures to the rules and norms of custom or tradition, and to the established powers of a chief (a warrior or priest, or both), often assisted by a council or court.

Table 2.1 provides a useful starting point by juxtaposing stateless and state societies in order to bring the latter's broad characteristics into relief. Table 2.1 offers only rudimentary definitions. One reason for this is that states, like other social phenomena, have changed over time, partly in relation to the transformation of the conditions of the societies

Table 2.1   Features of stateless and state societies

Stateless societies	State societies
informal mechanisms of government	political apparatus or governmental institutions differentiated from other organizations in the community
no clear boundaries to a society	rule takes place over a specific population and territory
disputes and decisions settled by family or kin groups, or by larger tribal structures headed by a chief with the support of a council	legal system, backed by a capacity to use force
relationships and transactions significantly defined by custom	institutional divisions within government (the executive, civil service and army, for example) are formally coordinated

in which they arose. There have been many different state forms which have set down elements of rule in a succession of different ways. Rule or rulership has no single 'essence' or fixed quality. Examples which will be drawn upon to highlight this are empires, feudal political relations and absolutist monarchies.

This chapter distinguishes the characteristics of stateless and state societies from those of the modern state. Several key features of the latter will be elucidated in Section 2.5, but for the present it is sufficient to stress that the concept of the modern state refers to that type of state which emerged in the European states system from the sixteenth century onwards. The concept connotes an impersonal and privileged legal or constitutional order with the capability of administering and controlling a given territory; that is, a distinct form of public power, separate from both ruler and ruled, and forming the supreme political authority within certain defined boundaries (Skinner, 1978, p.353; cf. Neumann, 1964). The 'other side' of the modern state is 'civil society'. Civil society — like nearly all concepts in social and political analysis — has a long and complex history; but by 'civil society' I will here mean those areas of social life — the domestic world, the economic sphere, cultural activities and political interaction — which are organized by private or voluntary arrangements between individuals and groups outside the *direct* control of the state (cf. Bobbio, 1989; Pelczynski, 1985; Keane, 1988). The modern state and civil society were formed, as will be seen, through distinct but interrelated processes.

1.2   THE STRUCTURE OF THE CHAPTER

This chapter has three main parts which correspond to the aims stated at the outset. The objective of the first part (Section 2) is to provide a brief chronological sketch of the development of the state in Europe, and an account of its chief variants. It is not my intention here to suggest that the variants followed one another according to an evolutionary pattern through which states passed from the 'primitive' to the 'civilized', from the 'simple' to the 'complex', or from 'lower' to 'higher' stages — far from it! My aim is to establish a political map or set of bearings which can become a basis for asking in the next section

(Section 3): What explains the movement and change among state forms, and how can one understand the rise of the nation-state? If Section 2 expounds a *typology* of states, Section 3 seeks to explicate the *underlying processes* or *causal patterns* which might illuminate why particular types of state have taken the form they have, and why one of these types — the modern nation-state — became the dominant form over time.

In the third major part of the chapter (Section 4), the meaning and significance of the development of the modern state is explored via an introduction to the work of some of its leading political interpreters. It will be readily seen that the history of the interpretation of the modern state contains sharp conflicts of view. It will be my aim to explicate these conflicts, rather than to try and resolve the differences among them. However, I hope also to establish a framework which will aid an assessment of the relevance of the various interpretations to an understanding of the modern state, as it was and is.

The particular emphasis of this chapter is on the active role played by the state in the making and shaping of modernity. Throughout the nineteenth and twentieth centuries most of the leading perspectives on social change emphasized that the origins of social transformation were to be found in processes *internal* to society and, above all, in *socio-economic* factors. In many of these perspectives, the interrelations *among* states and societies were barely explored. By focusing on the war-making capacity of states, and on the role of the state in domestic *and* international affairs, this chapter sets itself against this neglect. In so doing, it aligns itself with a notable strand of recent scholarship on the history of states (much of it referred to in the pages which follow), which emphasizes the independent and autonomous part played by *political* and *military* factors in the formation of Europe and the modern world. While this story could be told from a number of different starting points, the initial focus will be a sketch of the history and geography of European states, beginning with Rome. This sketch provides a useful background to the diversity of states and their alteration over time.

2 A BRIEF HISTORY AND GEOGRAPHY OF EUROPEAN STATES

Sixteen hundred years or so ago 'Europe' was dominated by the Roman Empire, albeit an empire divided and disintegrating. Theodosius I (AD 379–95) was the last 'sole ruler' of the Roman Empire, which, after his death, split into the Western and Eastern Roman Empires. The Western Empire suffered from repeated attacks and grew weak in comparison with the East. In 410, the city of Rome was sacked by the Visigoths, a wandering Germanic people from the North-east. The fall of Rome was completed in 476, when the last Roman emperor of the West was deposed. The Eastern Empire, economically securer than its Western counterpart owing to spice and other exports, continued as the Byzantine Empire through the Middle Ages until it was successfully challenged and displaced by the Islamic Ottoman Empire in 1453.

In the centuries which succeeded the disintegration of the Roman Empire, 'Europe' did not experience the rise of another imperial society, although it was chronically engaged in war and harassed from outside. A contrast has often been drawn between an essentially civilized Europe and a despotic or barbarous East. There are many reasons for distrusting this contrast (see Bernal, 1987; Springborg, 1991). Some of these reasons will be explored in Chapter 6 of this volume, but two should be emphasized here. First, as recent historical and archaeological research has shown, some of the key political innovations, conceptual and institutional, of the putatively western political tradition can be traced to the East; for example, the 'city-state' or *polis* society can be found in Mesopotamia long before it emerged in the West. Second, 'Europe' was the creation of many complex processes at the intersection of 'internal' and 'external' forces and relations. A thousand years ago Europe as such did not exist. The roughly thirty million people who lived across the European landmass did not conceive of themselves as an interconnected people, bound by a common history, culture and fate (Tilly, 1990, p.38).

The larger power divisions on a map of 'millennial Europe' (c. AD 1000) to some extent mask the area's fragmented and decentred nature. Those who prevailed over territories — emperors, kings, princes, dukes, bishops and others — did so above all as military victors and conquerors, exacting tribute and rent to support their endeavours; they were far from being heads of state governing clearly demarcated territories according to formal law and procedure. As the historian Charles Tilly put it, 'nothing like a centralized national state existed anywhere in Europe' (1990, p.40).

Yet one can talk about the beginnings of a recognizable states system at the millenium. In the Italian peninsula, the Papacy, the Holy Roman Empire and the Byzantine Empire claimed most of the territory, even though these claims intermingled and were contested routinely by many localized powers and independent and semi-autonomous city-states. But the political map of Europe was to be shaped and reshaped many times. For example, the European map of the late fifteenth century included some five hundred more or less independent political units, often with ill-defined boundaries. By 1900 the number had dwindled to about twenty-five (Tilly, 1975, p.15). It took a long time for national states to dominate the political map, but the era they ushered in was to change fundamentally the nature and form of political life itself.

ACTIVITY 1   Examine Figures 2.1–2.4 and ask yourself the following questions:

1   Which political boundaries, if any, have persisted over time?

2   Can one recognize modern Europe in the political map of 1478?

3   How would the political map of 1980 have to be redrawn today?

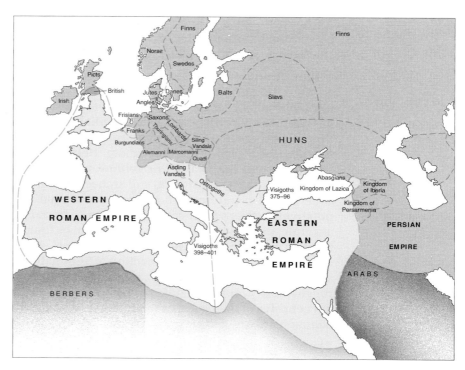

Figure 2.1   Europe in AD 406

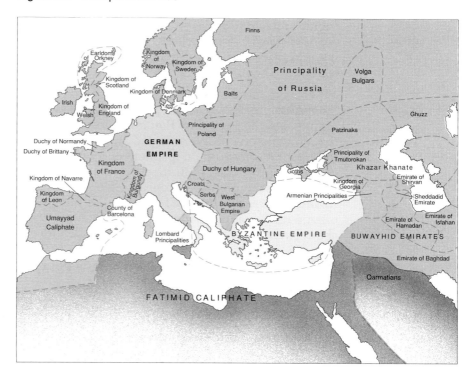

Figure 2.2   Europe in AD 998

Figure 2.3   Europe in AD 1478

Figure 2.4   Europe in AD 1980

Since the fall of Rome, it is not just the number of states which has altered dramatically, but the forms and types of states as well. There are five main clusters of state systems which can be distinguished:

1   traditional tribute-taking empires;
2   systems of divided authority, characterized by feudal relations, city-states and urban alliances, with the Church (Papacy) playing a leading role;
3   the polity of estates;
4   absolutist states;
5   modern nation-states, with constitutional, liberal democratic or single party polities locked progressively into a system of nation-states.

Figure 2.5 provides an approximate guide to the periods in which each type of state system could be found. For the remainder of this section, I shall examine each type in turn before pursuing the question: What accounts for the eventual dominance of the nation-state?

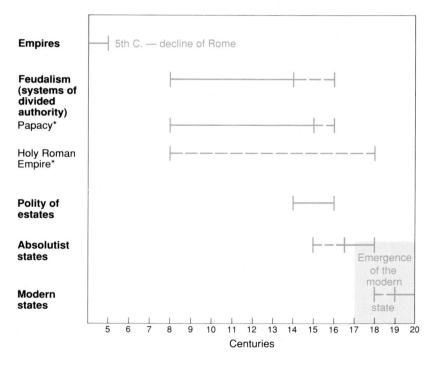

Broken lines indicate that a political system's influence was not continuous, but rather broken from time to time.

* The Papacy and the Holy Roman Empire, while at certain stages essential elements of the feudal system of authority, have been separated out for later reference.

Figure 2.5   State forms and historical periods

2.1   EMPIRES

Empires or imperial systems have dominated the history of states over the centuries, particularly in their size and grandeur. Some, notably Rome (and China in the East), retained identifiable institutional forms over long periods. Empires required an accumulation and concentration of coercive means — above all, of war-making ability — to sustain themselves. When this ability waned, empires disintegrated. All 'traditional' empires developed as a result of expansion from initially more restricted power bases and confined states. Moreover, the deployment of military strength was uppermost in the creation and maintenance of frontiers or territorial boundaries, though the latter were often in flux and shifted according to patterns of rebellion and invasion. Territorial boundaries were by no means yet 'fixed borders' (Giddens, 1985, pp.80–1).

While empires frequently were crossed by long-distance trading routes, and indeed often engaged directly in long-distance trade themselves, their economic requirements were largely met through the exaction of *tribute,* some of which was used to buy off threatened assaults if military power fell short. The tribute system supported the emperor, his administrative apparatus and the military. But however powerful empires might have been relative to contending power centres, they could sustain only limited administrative authority. Empires stretched over a plethora of communities and societies which were culturally diverse and heterogeneous. Empires were *ruled* but they were not *governed;* that is to say, emperors dominated a limited social and geographical space, but lacked the administrative means — the institutions, organizations, information, personnel and so on — to provide regularized administration over the territories they claimed as their own. The polities of empires busied themselves with conflicts and intrigue within dominant groups and classes and within local urban centres; beyond that the resort to military force was the key mechanism for binding and integrating peoples and territories. Although force was frequently effective, its significance should not be exaggerated. For the size, mobility and deployment of armies depended on the availability of water and local harvests to plunder. The military depended on the countryside and could move no more quickly than its men could march in a day, subject to the availability of foodstuffs.

2.2   SYSTEMS OF DIVIDED AUTHORITY IN MEDIAEVAL EUROPE

Feudalism — a political system of overlapping and divided authority — assumed many forms between the eighth and the fourteenth centuries. But it is probably fair to say that it was distinguished in general by a network of interlocking ties and obligations, with systems of rule fragmented into many small, autonomous parts (Poggi, 1978, p.27). Political power became more local and personal in focus, generating a 'social world of overlapping claims and powers' (Anderson, 1974, p.149). Some of these claims and powers conflicted; and no ruler or state was sovereign in the sense of being supreme over a given territory and population (Bull, 1977, p.254). Within this system of power, tensions were rife and war was frequent.

The early roots of feudalism can be traced to left-overs of the Roman Empire and to the militaristic culture and the institutions of Germanic tribal peoples (Poggi, 1990, pp.35–7). A concern with loyalty in war and effective leadership among these peoples led to a special relationship between a ruler or lord or king (generally acclaimed or 'appointed' by his followers on the basis of his military and strategic skills) and the tribe's leading warriors, called *vassi* ('vassals'; 'servants'). The warriors declared bonds of loyalty and homage to their lord in return for privileges and protection. In the late seventh century, Frankish rulers connected the idea of a vassalic bond not just to military endeavour, but to the governing of territories more generally: rulers endowed vassals with rights of land, later called *feudum* ('fief'), in the hope of securing continued loyalty, military service and flows of income. The result, however, was rarely a simple hierarchy of lord, vassal and peasants; rather, the hierarchy was often characterized by a great chain of relations and obligations as major vassals 'sub-contracted' parts of their lands to others. At the bottom of the hierarchy was, of course, the vast majority of the population: 'the object of rule ... but never the subject of a political relationship' (Poggi, 1978, p.23).

While feudal kings were *primus inter pares* ('first among equals'), they were locked (with certain exceptions, notably in England and northern France) into wide-ranging systems of privileges and duties which often imposed on them a requirement to consult and negotiate with the most powerful lords or barons, when taxes or armies were to be raised. Lords were expected to maintain an autonomous military capability to support their kings; but it was a capability that provided them with an independent power base which they could be tempted to use to further their own interests. With some political forces seeking to centralize power and others seeking local autonomy, the feudal states system contained significant disintegrative tendencies.

Within mediaeval Europe the economy was dominated by agriculture, and any surplus generated was subject to competing claims. A successful claim constituted a basis to create and sustain political power. But the web of kingdoms, principalities, duchies and other power centres which depended on these arrangements was complicated further by the emergence of alternative powers in the towns and cities. Cities and urban federations depended on trade and manufacture and relatively high accumulations of capital. They developed different social and political structures and frequently enjoyed independent systems of rule specified by *charters*. Among the best known were the Italian cities of Florence, Venice and Sienna, but across Europe hundreds of urban centres developed. Nowhere, however, did they (and the web of feudal relations in the countryside) alone determine the pattern of rule or political identity. For in the Middle Ages 'Europe' more accurately meant 'Christendom'. And the Papacy and the Holy Roman Empire gave Christendom what overarching unity it had.

The Holy Roman Empire existed in some form from the eighth until the early nineteenth century. For while the Roman imperial title had lapsed in the fifth century, it was revived in 800 by Pope Leo III and conferred on Charlemagne, King of the Franks. Later, the title Holy Roman Emperor was borne by successive dynasties of German kings, although its actual significance, like that of the Empire more generally, varied considerably over time. At its height, the Holy Roman Empire represented an attempt, under the patronage of the Catholic Church, to unite and centralize the fragmented power centres of western Christendom into a politically-unified Christian empire. The countries federated under the Empire spread from Germany to Spain, and from northern France to Italy. However, the actual secular power of the Empire was always limited by the complex power structures of feudal Europe on the one hand, and the Catholic Church on the other.

The chief rival power to the mediaeval feudal and city networks was the Catholic Church itself. Throughout the Middle Ages the Catholic Church sought to place spiritual above secular authority. While it would be quite misleading to suggest that the rise of Christianity effectively banished secular considerations from the lives of rulers and ruled, it unquestionably shifted the source of authority and wisdom from this-worldly to other-worldly representatives. The Christian world-view transformed the rationale of political action from an earthly to a theological framework; it insisted that the Good lay in submission to God's will.

In mediaeval Europe there was no theoretical alternative — no alternative 'political theory' — to the theocratic positions of Pope and Holy Roman Emperor. The integration of Christian Europe came to depend above all on these authorities. This order has been characterized as the order of 'international Christian society' (Bull, 1977, p.27). International Christian society was conceived as being Christian first and foremost; it looked to God for the authority to resolve disputes and conflicts; its primary political reference point was religious doctrine, and it was overlaid with assumptions about the universal nature of human community.

It was not until western Christendom was under challenge, especially from the conflicts generated by the rise of national states and by the Reformation, that the idea of the modern state was born, and the ground was created for the development of a new form of political identity — national identity.

2.3   THE POLITY OF ESTATES

Some date the crisis of feudalism as early as 1300. But whether or not one accepts this date, the decay of feudalism can be detected over a substantial period as competing claims to more extensive and penetrating political power were fought out. Within this process of transformation, new understandings about political arrangements emerged. Some writers argue that these 'new' concepts and ideas — for example, the claims of various social groups or 'estates' (the nobility, clergy, and leading townsmen or burghers) to political prerogatives, particularly to rights of representation — were merely extensions of existing feudal relations. However, others emphasize their novel and distinctive qualities.

Those that emphasize the innovative nature of the post-feudal system of rule draw attention to a number of larger territories in which successful rulers created new kinds of political relations with various elements of society. One observer has described the arrangements thus:

> In the first place, in the polity of estates the rulers present themselves primarily not as feudal superiors, but as the holders of higher, public prerogatives of non- and often pre-feudal origins, surrounded by the halo of a higher majesty; often imparted by means of sacred ceremonies (for example, the *sacre du roi* ['consecration of a king']).
>
> In the second place, the counterpart to the ruler is typically represented not by individuals, but by constituted bodies of various kinds: local assemblies of aristocrats, cities, ecclesiastical bodies, corporate associations. Taken singly, each of these bodies — the 'estates' — represents a different collective entity: a region's noblemen of a given rank, the residents of a town, the faithful of a parish or the practitioners of a trade. Taken together, these bodies claim to represent a wider, more abstract, territorial entity — country, *Land, terra, pays* — which, they assert, the ruler is entitled to rule only to the extent that he upholds its distinctive customs and serves its interests.
>
> In turn, however, these interests are largely identified with those of the estates; and even the customs of the country or the region in question have as their major components the different claims of the various estates. Thus, the ruler can rule legitimately only to the extent that periodically he convenes the estates of a given region or of the whole territory into a constituted, public gathering. (Poggi, 1990, pp.40–1)

In these circumstances, rulers had to deal with estates and estates had to deal with rulers. Out of this emerged a variety of estates-based assemblies, parliaments, diets and councils which sought to legitimate and enjoy autonomous faculties of rule. The 'polity of estates' was characterized by a 'power dualism': power was split between rulers and estates.

This 'power dualism' did not endure; it was challenged by the estates seeking greater power and by monarchs hoping to subvert the assemblies in order to centralize power in their own hands. As the grip of feudal traditions and customs was loosened, the nature and limits of political authority, law, rights and obedience emerged as a preoccupation of political thought.

2.4   ABSOLUTIST STATES

The historical changes that contributed to the transformation of mediaeval notions of politics were complicated. Struggles between monarchs and barons over the domain of rightful authority; peasant rebellions against the weight of excess taxation and social obligation; the spread of trade, commerce and market relations; the flourishing of Renaissance culture with its renewed interest in classical political ideas (including Athenian democracy and Roman law); changes in technology, particularly military technology; the consolidation of national monarchies (notably in England, France and Spain); religious strife and the challenge to the universal claims of Catholicism; the struggle between Church and State — all played a part. In the sections that follow, I shall return to discuss a number of these developments, but it is important first to clarify the notion of the 'absolutist' state.

From the fifteenth to the eighteenth century two different forms of regime can be distinguished in Europe: the 'absolute' monarchies of France, Prussia, Austria, Spain, Sweden and Russia, among other places, and the 'constitutional' monarchies and republics found principally in England and Holland (Mann, 1986, p.476). There are important conceptual and institutional differences between these regime types, although in terms of the history of state/society relations some of the differences have, as we shall see, been more apparent than real. I shall discuss constitutional states shortly, but will focus in the first instance on absolutism.

Absolutism signalled the emergence of a form of state based upon: the absorption of smaller and weaker political units into larger and stronger political structures; a strengthened ability to rule over a unified territorial area; a tightened system of law and order enforced throughout a territory; the application of a 'more unitary, continuous, calculable, and effective' rule by a single, sovereign head; and the development of a relatively small number of states engaged in an 'open-ended, competitive, and risk-laden power struggle' (Poggi, 1978, pp.60–1). Although the actual power of absolutist rulers has often been exaggerated, these changes marked a substantial increase in 'public authority' from above. Certainly, absolutist rulers claimed that they alone held the legitimate right of decision over state affairs. One of the most remarkable statements of this view has been attributed to Louis XV, king of France from 1715 to 1774:

> In my person alone resides the sovereign power, and it is from me alone that the courts hold their existence and their authority. That ... authority can only be exercised in my name ... . For it is to me exclusively that the legislative power belongs ... . The whole public order emanates from me since I am its supreme guardian. ... The rights and interests of the nation ... are necessarily united with my own and can only rest in my hands.
> (quoted in Schama, 1989, p.104)

The absolutist monarch claimed to be the ultimate source of human law, although it is important to note that his broad writ was understood to derive from the law of God. The king's legitimacy was based on 'divine right'. In this very particular sense, political authorities were regarded as being as much under the law as any other corporate institution (Benn and Peters, 1959, p.256).

In a striking and somewhat (maliciously) humorous account of the public standing of the French monarch, perhaps the supreme example of an absolutist figure, the sociologist Gianfranco Poggi has written:

> [The] King of France was thoroughly, without residue, a 'public' personage. His mother gave birth to him in public, and from that moment his existence, down to its most trivial moments, was acted out before the eyes of attendants who were holders of dignified public offices. He ate in public, went to bed in public, woke up and was clothed and groomed in public, urinated and defecated in public. He did not copulate in public; but near enough, considering the circumstances under which he was expected to deflower his august bride. He did not much bathe in public; but then, neither did he in private. When he died (in public) his body was promptly and messily chopped up in public, and its severed parts ceremoniously handed out to the more exalted among the personages who had been attending him throughout his mortal existence.
> (Poggi, 1978, pp.68–9)

The absolutist monarch was at the apex of a new system of rule which was progressively centralized and anchored on a claim to supreme and indivisible power: *sovereign authority*. All these qualities were manifest in the routines and rituals of courtly life.

However, linked to the court there developed a new administrative apparatus involving the beginnings of a permanent, professional bureaucracy and army (Mann, 1986, p.476). If the French monarchy of the seventeenth century represents the best example of an absolutist court, Prussia under the Hohenzollern dynasty provides the best example of the 'prototypes of ministries' (Poggi, 1990, p.48). These 'prototypes' increased the state's involvement in the promotion and regulation of a hitherto unparalleled diversity of activities. Six ensuing developments were of great significance in the history of the states system:

1   the growing coincidence of territorial boundaries with a uniform system of rule;

2   the creation of new mechanisms of law-making and -enforcement;

3   the centralization of administrative power;

4   the alteration and extension of fiscal management;

5   the formalization of relations among states through the development of diplomacy and diplomatic institutions; and

6   the introduction of a standing army (see Anderson, 1974, pp.15–42; Giddens, 1985, ch. 4).

Absolutism helped set in motion a process of state-making which began to reduce the social, economic and cultural variation *within* states and expand the variation *among* them (Tilly, 1975, p.19).

According to one interpretation of these changes, the expansion of state administrative power was made possible to a significant extent by the extension of the state's capacity for the surveillance of its subjects; that is, the collection and storing of information about members of society, and the related ability to supervise subject populations (Giddens, 1985, pp.14–15). However, as the state's sovereign authority expanded and its administrative centres became more powerful, there was not simply a concentration of power at the apex. For the increase in administrative power via surveillance increased the state's dependence on cooperative forms of social relations; it was no longer possible for the state to manage its affairs and sustain its offices and activities by force alone. As a result, greater reciprocity was created between the governors and the governed, and the more reciprocity was involved, the more opportunities were generated for subordinate groups to influence their rulers (Giddens, 1985, pp.198ff.). Absolutism, in short, created within itself a momentum toward the development of new forms and limits on state power — constitutionalism and (eventually) participation by powerful groups in the process of government itself.

Whatever the other merits of this particular interpretation, it usefully draws attention to the gulf that existed between the claims of the absolutist monarch, on the one hand, and a reality, on the other hand, which imposed on the monarch requirements of negotiation and cooperation if the state was to function effectively. This gulf has been explored further in the recent work of the sociologist Michael Mann, who distinguishes between a 'strong' regime's power to effect its will over civil society, which he calls 'despotism', and its power to coordinate civil society, which he refers to as 'infrastructural strength' (1986, p.477). Comparing a range of absolutist regimes, Mann argues that the absolute monarch was 'no ancient emperor — he was not the sole source of law; of coinages, weights and measures; of economic monopolies … . He could not impose compulsory cooperation. He owned only his own estates' (Mann, 1986, p.478). Absolutist regimes, Mann concludes, had limited despotic reach; they were weak in relation to powerful groups in society, for example, the nobility, merchants and urban bourgeoisie. But, like their constitutional counterparts, they were engaged increasingly in the coordination of the activities of these groups and in building up the state's infrastructural strength.

By the end of the seventeenth century Europe was no longer a mosaic of states. For the 'consolidated independent sovereignty of each individual state … was at the same time part of a process of overall inter-state integration' (Giddens, 1985, p.91). A concomitant of each and every state's claim to uncontestable authority was the recognition that such a claim gave other states an equal entitlement to autonomy and respect within their own borders. The development of state sovereignty was part of a process of mutual recognition whereby states granted each other rights of jurisdiction in their respective territories and communities.

In the international context, sovereignty has involved the assertion by the state of independence; that is, of its possession of sole rights to jurisdiction over a particular people and territory. This dimension of sovereignty has, in addition, been associated with the claim that, by virtue of the very argument which establishes the sovereignty of a particular state, that state must accept that it will be one among many states with, in principle, equal rights to self-determination. In the world of relations among states, the principle of the sovereign equality of all states was to become paramount in the formal conduct of states towards one another.

The conception of international law which emerged within the new 'international society of states' has been referred to by international lawyers, notably Richard Falk and Antonio Cassese, as the 'Westphalian model' (after the Peace of Westphalia of 1648, which brought to an end the Eighty Years War between Spain and the Dutch and the German phase of the Thirty Years War). The model covers the period of international law from 1648 to 1945 (although some would say it still holds today). It depicts the emergence of a world community consisting of sovereign states which settle their differences privately and often by force; which engage in diplomatic relations but otherwise minimal cooperation; which seek to place their own national interest above all others; and which accept the logic of the principle of effectiveness, that is, the principle that might eventually makes right in the international world — appropriation becomes legitimation. The model of Westphalia can be summarized by the following seven points (see Cassese, 1986, pp.396–9; Falk, 1969):

The model of Westphalia

1 The world consists of, and is divided by, sovereign states which recognize no superior authority.

2 The processes of law-making, the settlement of disputes and law-enforcement are largely in the hands of individual states subject to the logic of 'the competitive struggle for power'.

3 Differences among states are often settled by force: the principle of effective power holds sway. Virtually no legal fetters exist to curb the resort to force; international legal standards afford minimal protection.

4 Responsibility for cross-border wrongful acts are a private matter concerning only those affected; no collective interest in compliance with international law is recognized.

5 All states are regarded as equal before the law: legal rules do not take account of asymmetries of power.

6 International law is oriented to the establishment of minimal rules of co-existence; the creation of enduring relationships among states and peoples is an aim only to the extent that it allows military objectives to be met.

7 The minimization of impediments on state freedom is the 'collective' priority.

The new international order, ushered in by the era of the absolutist state (and its constitutional counterpart, a discussion of which follows), had a lasting and paradoxical quality rich in implications: an increasingly integrated states system simultaneously endorsed the right of each state to autonomous and independent action. The upshot of this development was, as one commentator has aptly noted, that states were 'not subject to international moral requirements because they represent separate and discrete political orders with no common authority among them' (Beitz, 1979, p.25). According to this model, the world consists of separate political powers pursuing their own interests, and backed ultimately by their organization of coercive power.

2.5   MODERN STATES

The proximate sources of the modern state were absolutism and the interstate system it initiated. In condensing and concentrating political power in its own hands, and in seeking to create a central system of rule, absolutism paved the way for a secular and national system of power. Moreover, in claiming sovereign authority exclusively for itself, it threw down a challenge to all those groups and classes which had had a stake in the old order (the polity of estates), and to all those with a stake in the new developing order based on capital and the market economy. It forced all these collectivities to rethink their relationship to the state, and to re-examine their political resources. In addition, the myriad battles and wars fought out in the interstate system altered fundamentally the boundaries of both absolutist states and the emerging modern states — the whole map of Europe changed as territorial boundaries progressively became fixed borders.

Although the transition from the absolutist to the modern state was marked by dramatic events and processes such as the English (1640–88) and French (1789) Revolutions, an exclusive focus on these hinders an understanding of the way in which the absolutist state itself was crucial in the development of modern political rule. It was the confluence of 'internal' transformations in European states with shifting geopolitical relations and forces which provided a, if not *the*, key impetus to the formation of the modern state. I shall return to elements of these 'macropatterns' in Section 3; in the meantime, what should be understood by the term 'modern state'?

All modern states are nation-states — *political apparatuses, distinct from both ruler and ruled, with supreme jurisdiction over a demarcated territorial area, backed by a claim to a monopoly of coercive power, and enjoying a minimum level of support or loyalty from their citizens* (cf. Skinner, 1978, pp.349–58; Giddens, 1985, pp.17–31, 116–21). Like all definitions in the social sciences, this one is controversial; and Section 4 of this chapter will, as previously noted, focus directly on the controversy about how the modern state should be understood. But for my purposes here, this particular definition is useful because it underscores a number of the crucial innovations of the modern states system; these are:

1　*Territoriality*. While all states have made claims to territories, it is only with the modern states system that exact borders have been fixed.

2　*Control of the means of violence*. The claim to hold a monopoly on force and the means of coercion (sustained by a standing army and the police) became possible only with the 'pacification' of peoples — the breaking down of rival centres of power and authority — in the nation-state. This element of the modern state was not fully present until the nineteenth century.

3　*Impersonal structure of power*. The idea of an impersonal and sovereign political order — i.e. a legally circumscribed structure of power with supreme jurisdiction over a territory — could not predominate while political rights, obligations and duties were conceived as closely tied to property rights, religion and the claims of traditionally privileged groups such as the nobility. This matter was still in contention in the eighteenth and nineteenth centuries.

4　*Legitimacy*. It was only when claims to 'divine right' or 'state right' were challenged and eroded that it became possible for human beings as 'individuals' and as 'peoples' to be active citizens of a new order — not merely dutiful subjects of a monarch or emperor. The loyalty of citizens became something that had to be *won* by modern states: invariably this involved a claim by the state to be legitimate because it reflected and/or represented the needs and interests of its citizens.

There is a further clarification which should be made at this juncture. The concept of the nation-state, or national state, as some prefer, ought not to be taken to imply that a state's people necessarily 'share a strong linguistic, religious, and symbolic identity' (Tilly, 1990, pp.2–3). Although some nation-states approximate to this state of affairs, many do not (for example, in the United Kingdom there are significant differences in national tradition). It is therefore important to separate out the concepts of 'nation-state' and 'nationalism'. Anthony Giddens has made the point succinctly: '... what makes the 'nation' integral to the nation-state ... is not the existence of sentiments of nationalism but the unification of an administrative apparatus over precisely defined territorial boundaries (in a complex of other nation-states)' (Giddens, 1987, p.172). The concept of 'nationalism' — denoting the existence of symbols and beliefs which create patterns of ethnic, or religious, or linguistic commonality and political ambition — should be reserved for highlighting particular types of configuration of peoples and states.

It has been argued that the difference between absolute and modern states is not as great as conventionally thought, for two reasons (see Mann, 1986, pp.450–99). First, absolutist states, as already noted, had less power over civil society than is frequently claimed. Second, modern states are rarely 'bounded' by their constitutions and borders and, hence, have often behaved like arrogant 'absolutist' states, especially in their dealings with peoples and cultures overseas. Both points carry weight and need to be borne in mind in what follows. However, neither point negates fully the conceptual and institutional innovations introduced by the modern state. In order to highlight these, it is useful to draw attention to a number of forms of the modern state itself. These are the *constitutional state*, the *liberal state*, the *liberal-democratic state*, and the *single-party polity*.

Forms of the modern state

1 *Constitutionalism* or the *constitutional state* refers to implicit and/or explicit limits on political or state decision-making, limits which can be either procedural or substantive; that is, specifying how decisions and changes can be made (proceduralism), or blocking certain kinds of changes altogether (substantivism) (see Elster, 1988). Constitutionalism defines the proper forms and limits of state action, and its elaboration over time as a set of doctrines and practices helped inaugurate one of the central tenets of European liberalism: that the state exists to safeguard the rights and liberties of citizens who are ultimately the best judges of their own interests; and, accordingly, that the state must be restricted in scope and constrained in practice in order to ensure the maximum possible freedom of every citizen.

2 The *liberal state* became defined in large part by the attempt to create a private sphere independent of the state, and by a concern to re-shape the state itself, i.e. by freeing civil society — personal, family and business life — from unnecessary political interference, and simultaneously delimiting the state's authority (Held, 1987, chs 2–3). The building blocks of the liberal state became constitutionalism, private property, the competitive market economy and the distinctively patriarchal family (see Chapter 4 of this volume). But while liberalism celebrated the rights of individuals to 'life, liberty and property' (John Locke), it should be noted from the outset that it was generally the male property-owning individual who was the focus of so much attention; and the new freedoms were first and foremost for the men of the new middle classes or the bourgeoisie. The western world was liberal first, and only later, after extensive conflicts, liberal democratic; that is, only later was a universal franchise won which in principle allowed all mature adults the chance to express their judgement about the performance of those who govern them (Macpherson, 1966, p.6).

3 The third variant of the modern state is *liberal* or *representative democracy* itself, a system of rule embracing elected 'officers' who undertake to 'represent' the interests or views of citizens within the framework of the 'rule of law'. Representative democracy means that decisions affecting a community are not taken by its members as a whole, but by a sub-group of representatives whom 'the people' have elected for this purpose. In the arena of national politics, representative democracy takes the form of elections to congresses, parliaments or similar national bodies, and is now associated with the system of government in countries as far afield as the United States, Britain, Germany, Japan, Australia and New Zealand.

4 Finally, there is the form of the modern state known as the *one-party* or *single-party polity*. Until recently, the Soviet Union, many East European societies and some Third World countries have been governed

by this system. The principle underlying one-party polities is that a single party can be the legitimate expression of the overall will of the community. Voters have the opportunity to affirm the party's choice of candidate, or occasionally to choose from among different party candidates (although some may doubt whether this constitutes an opportunity for the exercise of choice at all).

Little further will be said about the single-party polity in this chapter. (For further discussion of this state form, see Book 2 (Allen *et al.*, 1992), Chapter 1, and Book 4 (Hall *et al.*, 1992), Chapter 1.) This chapter will instead attend to those elements of the first three state forms listed above which require elaboration and examination. But before turning to this task, it is important to respond to the question: What accounts for the emergence of the modern nation-state? In other words, why did national states come to predominate in the political world?

3   WHY DID NATION-STATES BECOME SUPREME?

In order to address the above question, this section will examine a number of key factors, or causal patterns, in the development of the states system and of the modern state in particular. The prime focus will be on war and militarism and on the relationship between states and capitalism, although other significant factors will be touched on. Once again, it will be useful to examine deeply structured processes of change taking place over long periods. It should be noted that the stress is on *processes, factors* and *causal patterns*; that is to say, this section is guided by the assumption that there is no mono-causal explanation — no single phenomenon or set of phenomena — which fully explains the rise of the modern state. States, like other collectivities and institutions, depend for their existence on broad experiences and diverse conditions. It is in a combination of factors that the beginnings of an explanation for the rise of the modern state can be found.

3.1   WAR AND MILITARISM

It has already been suggested that the nature and form of the states system crystallized at the intersection of 'international' and 'national' conditions and processes (the terms in inverted commas are so expressed because they did not take on their contemporary meaning until the era of fixed borders, i.e. the era of the nation-state). In fact, it is at this intersection that the 'shape' of the state was largely determined — its size, external configuration, organizational structure, ethnic composition, material infrastructure and so on (Hintze, 1975, chs 4–6, 11). At the heart of the processes involved was the ability of states to secure and strengthen their power bases and, thereby, to order their affairs, internally and externally. What was at issue, in short, was the capacity of states to organize the means of coercion (armies, navies and other forms of military might) and to deploy them when necessary. How important this element of state power has been to the history of states can be gleaned by examining the case of England/Britain.

From an analysis of state finances (how the state raised and spent what money it had) over several centuries, Michael Mann has shown that 'the functions of the state appear overwhelmingly military and overwhelmingly geopolitical rather than economic and domestic' (Mann, 1986, p.511; see also Mitchell and Deane, 1962; Mitchell and Jones, 1971). Mann calculates that from about the twelfth to the nineteenth century, between 70 and 90 per cent of the English state's financial resources were continuously devoted to the acquisition and use of the instruments of military force, especially in international wars. For most of this period the state grew slowly and fitfully (although when it did grow it was due to warfare and related developments), and its size, measured in relation to the resources of the economy and its impact on the daily life of most people, was small. But in the seventeenth and eighteenth centuries the state's real finances grew rapidly, largely in response to the escalating costs of the means of 'coercive power'; in this case, the growing professional, standing armies and navies. Expenditures on non-military civil functions remained minor.

Reliable annual sets of accounts are available for central government expenditure in Britain for the period after 1688. These are presented in Figure 2.6 and Table 2.3, both taken from Mann (1986).

ACTIVITY 2   Turn to Figure 2.6 and Table 2.3 (overleaf) now. Consider how military and total expenditure fluctuated together.

Mann's comments on Figure 2.6 and Table 2.3 are telling:

> Note first the upward trend in the financial size of the British state: Between 1700 and 1815 real expenditures rise fifteenfold (and the increase at current prices is thirty-fivefold!). This is easily the fastest rate of increase we have seen for any century ... . But the upward trend is not steady. The total rockets suddenly six times. It will come as no surprise that all but one of these are at the beginning of a war, and all six are due primarily to a large rise in military expenditures. Furthermore debt repayment, used exclusively to finance military needs, rises toward the end of each war and is maintained in the first years of peace. The pattern is beautifully regular ... .
>
> These figures confirm every hypothesis made for previous centuries on the basis of sketchier data. State finances were dominated by foreign wars. As warfare developed more professional and permanent forces, so the state grew both in overall size and (probably) in terms of its size in relation to its 'civil society'.
> (Mann, 1986, pp.485–6)

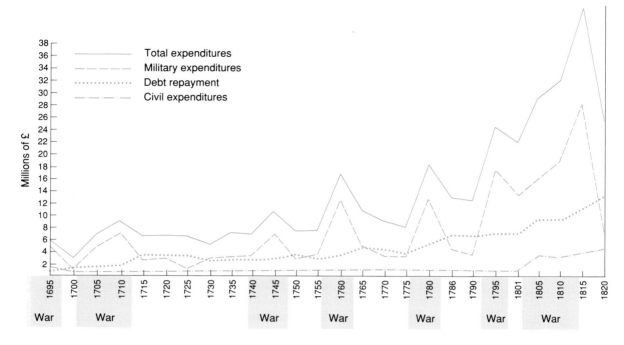

Figure 2.6   British state expenditure, 1695–1820 (at constant prices: 1690–9 = 100)
Source: Mann, 1986, p.484

The significance of these remarks is highlighted further if it is recalled that they bear on the activities and functions of a constitutional state. In fact, over the whole period in question, broadly the eighteenth and early nineteenth centuries, whether a state was 'constitutional' or 'absolutist' made little difference to the proportion of its expenditure on the military. This can be seen by comparing Table 2.3 with Table 2.2, which shows Austrian state expenditure for part of the same period.

Table 2.2   Austrian state expenditure, 1795–1817 (in percent)

Year	Military	Debt repayment	Civil	Total expenditure at current prices (in millions of guldern)
1795	71	12	17	133.3
1800	67	22	11	143.9
1805	63	25	12	102.7
1810	69	20	11	76.1
1815	75	4	21	121.2
1817	53	8	38	98.8

Source: Mann, 1986, p.487

Sketchier evidence appears to confirm a similar pattern of income and costs for France, Prussia and Russia, although each had its peculiarities.

The above material is not an argument for 'military determinism'; that is, for a view which asserts that changes in war and the military are the

Table 2.3   State expenditure for Great Britain, 1695–1820 (in millions of pounds at current and constant prices: 1690–9 = 100)*

Year	Price index	Military expenditure		Debt repayment		Civil expenditure		Total expenditure	
		Current	Constant	Current	Constant	Current	Constant	Current	Constant
1695	102	4.9	4.8	0.6	0.6	0.8	0.8	6.2	6.1
1700	114	1.3	1.1	1.3	1.1	0.7	0.6	3.2	2.8
1705	87	4.1	4.7	1.0	1.2	0.7	0.8	5.9	6.8
1710	106	7.2	6.8	1.8	1.7	0.9	0.8	9.8	9.2
1715	97	2.2	2.3	3.3	3.4	0.7	0.8	6.2	6.4
1720	94	2.3	2.4	2.8	3.0	1.0	1.0	6.0	6.4
1725	89	1.5	1.7	2.8	3.1	1.3	1.5	5.5	6.2
1730	99	2.4	2.4	2.3	2.3	0.9	0.9	5.6	5.6
1735	82	2.7	3.3	2.2	2.7	0.9	1.1	5.9	7.1
1740	90	3.2	3.6	2.1	2.3	0.8	0.9	6.2	6.8
1745	84	5.8	6.9	2.3	2.7	0.8	1.0	8.9	10.6
1750	93	3.0	3.2	3.2	3.5	1.0	1.1	7.2	7.7
1755	92	3.4	3.7	2.7	2.9	1.0	1.1	7.1	7.7
1760	105	13.5	12.8	3.4	3.2	1.2	1.1	18.0	17.1
1765	109	6.1	5.6	4.8	4.4	1.1	1.0	12.0	11.0
1770[a]	114	3.9	3.4	4.8	4.2	1.2	1.1	10.5	9.2
1775	130	3.9	3.0	4.7	3.6	1.2	0.9	10.4	8.0
1780	119	14.9	12.5	6.0	5.0	1.3	1.1	22.6	19.0
1786[b]	131	5.5	4.2	9.5	7.2	1.5	1.2	17.0	13.0
1790	134	5.2	3.9	9.4	7.0	1.7	1.3	16.8	12.5
1795	153	26.3	17.2	10.5	6.8	1.8	1.2	39.0	25.5
1801[c]	230	31.7	13.8	16.8	7.3	2.1	0.9	51.0	22.2
1805	211	34.1	16.2	20.7	9.8	7.8	3.7	62.8	30.0
1810	245	48.3	19.7	24.2	9.9	8.8	3.6	81.5	33.3
1815	257	72.4	28.2	30.0	11.7	10.4	4.0	112.9	44.0
1820	225	16.7	7.4	31.1	13.8	9.8	4.4	57.5	25.6

* NB: *Constant* prices are prices controlled for inflation; i.e. they compensate for the existence of inflation. *Current* prices are the real prices paid at the time of purchase; i.e. they include inflation.
[a] Between 1770 and 1801 the detailed items fall short of the total given by about £500,000. No reason for this is given in the source.
[b] 1785 figures follow an idiosyncratic budgeting system.
[c] 1800 figures are incomplete.
Source: Mann, 1986, p.485.

exclusive source of change in the state and the states system. However, it does indicate that the development and maintenance of a coercive capability was central to the development of the state: if states wished to survive they had to fund this capability and ensure its effectiveness. Precisely what this involved can be analysed further by means of Figure 2.7. (Note that the discussion which follows concentrates initially on the central and left-hand columns of Figure 2.7.)

The process of state-making, and the formation of the modern states system, was to a large degree the result, as Poggi has observed, 'of the

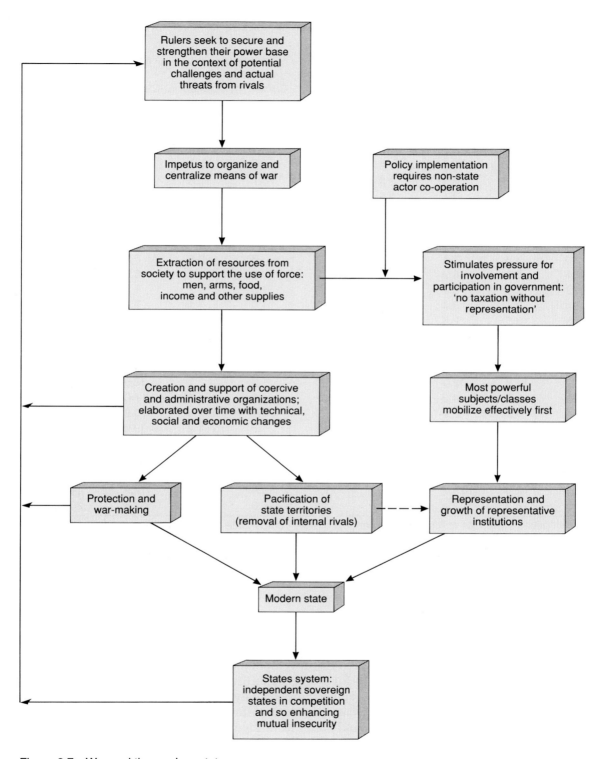

Figure 2.7   War and the modern state

strenuous efforts made by rulers, each by means of his/her apparatus of rule, to widen and secure their power base and to increase their own effectiveness and discretion in managing and mobilizing societal resources' (1990, p.101). State-makers were locked into an open-ended and ruthless competition in which, as Tilly put it, 'most contenders lost' (1975, p.15). The successful cases of state-making such as England, France and Spain were the 'survivors'.

The competition among states was driven not just by the ambitions of rulers and internal or domestic considerations, but also by the very *structure* of the international system: individual states, pursuing their own security, had to be prepared for war, a process which itself generated insecurity in other states which sought to respond in kind. In short, states armed and became militaristic partly to ensure their own safety and, in so doing, they ensured the insecurity of others who armed in turn — thus making all states less secure. (This vicious circle of mutual insecurity is often referred to as the 'security dilemma' of the state.)

The ability to wage war was dependent on a successful process of *extraction*; that is, on a state's capacity to extract resources — whether these be men, weapons, foodstuffs, taxes or income substitutes — in support of its endeavours. Few subjects, however, were willing to sacrifice their resources or lives without a struggle for some kind of return or recognition, and conflicts and rebellions against economic and political demands were rife. In response, state rulers built state structures — administrative, bureaucratic and coercive — in order to aid the coordination and control of their subject populations. In short, direct connections can be traced between a growth in the requirement for the means of waging war, an expansion in processes of extraction, and a concomitant formation of state executive and administrative offices to organize and control these changes. The development of some of the key organizations of the modern state emerged at the intersection of warfare and the attempt to pay for it. War and its financial burdens promoted 'territorial consolidation, centralization, differentiation of the instruments of government and monopolization of the means of coercion ...' (Tilly, 1975, p.42).

It has already been noted (in Section 2) that different state forms prevailed in Europe in different eras and regions. The organizational form of the state varied too. In his most recent work, Tilly has sought to examine this variation with reference to the ways state development was mediated by, or filtered through, the social structure of particular societies — that is, the particular constellation of social classes and groups which existed within the terrain of the state and which were either cooperative with or resistant to state-makers (Tilly, 1990, pp.15, 27–8, 57, 117ff.). The shape of each such constellation was significantly affected by the different kinds of resource base which could be drawn upon by the various groups and classes comprising it, and the options they had for involvement (or otherwise) in state politics. As Tilly explains:

> The organization of major social classes, and their relations to the
> state, varied significantly from Europe's coercion-intensive regions
> (areas of few cities and agricultural predominance, where direct
> coercion played a major part in production), to its capital-intensive
> regions (areas of many cities and commercial predominance,
> where markets, exchange, and market-oriented production
> prevailed). The demands major classes made on the state, and their
> influence over the state, varied correspondingly.
> (Tilly, 1990, p.15)

For example, in 'capital-intensive' regions, like those found in the
Dutch Republic in the seventeenth century, city-based merchants and
capitalists favoured, and sometimes achieved, state structures which
extended representation to include their interests. By contrast, in
'coercion-intensive' areas such as the Russian Empire, landlords gained
greater control of the state and were able to hinder or block the
development of representative councils or assemblies.

Over time it was the increasing scale of war, and particularly its growing
reliance on technological change, industrialization and specialization
which, in combination with the growth of commercial, legal and
diplomatic interaction among states, gave the modern centralized nation-
state its distinctive edge over other state forms. States that could mobilize
and sustain standing armies and/or navies gained a war-making
advantage. To quote Tilly again: '... states having access to a combination
of large rural populations, capitalists, and relatively commercialized
economies won out. They set the terms of war, and their form of state
became the predominant one in Europe. Eventually European states
converged on that form: the national state' (Tilly, 1990, p.15).

The above discussion has concentrated on the relationship between
warfare, state-building and the modern state. However, the relationship
between warfare, state-building and democratic representation — i.e.
the relationship set out on the right-hand side of Figure 2.7 — needs
further specification. Yet, here too the role and changing form of war
was important. It has been argued by a number of scholars that the more
military superiority depended on the ability of a state to mobilize large
numbers of soldiers, particularly large numbers of lightly-armed foot
soldiers, the greater have been the prospects for representative or
popular government (Dahl, 1989, p.245; Andreski, 1968). The subject–
soldier has often become, and struggled to become, a citizen–soldier
(Janowitz, 1978, pp.178–9; cf. Dahl, 1989, p.247). As the political
scientist Robert Dahl put it:

> ... to see oneself as a member of a nation, a privilege for which one
> was expected to make sacrifices, could also justify one in making a
> more expansive claim, including a right to a fair share in governing
> ... or at any rate [as] entitled to the franchise. Countries with mass
> armies now found that they had ushered in the Age of Democratic
> Revolutions. It was under these historical conditions in which

> military organisation and technology were more favourable to
> democratisation than they had been for many centuries that ... the
> institutions of polyarchy ['representative government'] took root in
> one country after another.
> (Dahl, 1989, p.247)

The more costly and demanding war became, the more rulers had to
bargain for and win the support of their subjects. And the more people
were drawn into preparations for war and war-making, the more they
became aware of their membership in a political community and of the
rights and obligations such membership might confer. While the nature
of this emergent identity was often initially vague, it grew more definite
and precise over time. The conditions for the development of
citizenship varied across countries and regions (see Therborn, 1977;
Mann, 1987; Turner, 1986). But the expansion of citizenship, or
membership of an overall political community, was undoubtedly bound
up with the military and administrative requirements of the modern
state and the 'politicization' of social relations and day-to-day activities
which followed in its wake (cf. Giddens, 1985, ch. 8). In fact, it has been
argued that the democratization of the modern nation-state was largely
'a martial accomplishment' (Therborn, 1977). Whether or not this
statement is fully justified, it usefully highlights the impetus received
by institutions of representation and democracy from the conditions of
mass mobilization and the political demands created by the modern
state, although it is also important to stress that while some democracies
were stimulated by processes of mass mobilization (Britain, Canada),
others became democracies by defeat (Austria, Germany, Italy and
Japan; see Therborn, 1977). It would be misleading to suggest that war
created any one single pattern of causation in the building of
democratic institutions.

There is not scope here to focus on nationalism as such, but it is useful to
add that nationalism was a critical force in the development of the
democratic nation-state. The conditions involved in the creation of the
modern state were also often the conditions which generated
nationalism. Nationalism has been closely linked to the administrative
unification of the state. For the process by which national identities were
formed was often the result of both a struggle for membership in the new
political communities, and a struggle by elites and governments to create
a new identity to legitimize the actions of the state. In other words, the
construction of national identity has been part of an attempt to bind
people together within the framework of a delimited territory in order to
gain or enhance state power. The requirements of political action have
led to the deployment of national identity as a means of ensuring the
coordination of policy, mobilization and legitimacy (Breuilly, 1982,
pp.365ff.). However, the conditions of 'state-making' and nationalism or
'nation-building' never fully overlapped — and nationalism itself,
especially in the late nineteenth and twentieth centuries, became a force
frequently deployed to challenge existing nation-state boundaries (e.g.
Northern Ireland; see Poggi, 1990, pp.26–7).

It is a paradoxical result of the waging of war that it stimulated the formation of representative and democratic institutions. But to note this is not to claim that democracy is fully explained by the pursuit of war. The historical conditions surrounding the rise of democracy have been complex and varied (Dahl, 1989; Held, 1991). It is one thing to suggest that there is a direct connection in certain countries between, for example, the extension of the universal franchise and the emergence of modern infantry armies, but it is quite another to argue that democracy is thereby fully explained. Furthermore, if war gave democracy an impetus within particular nation-states, the rights and principles of democracy were often explicitly denied to those who were conquered, colonized and exploited by powerful nation-states. While the expansion of Europe became the basis of the political unification of the world into a system of nation-states, the main purpose of this expansion was to further European commerce and trade; the rights of colonial subjects were a secondary matter, if a matter of concern at all.

3.2   STATES AND CAPITALISM

In the interpretation that has been offered so far about the development of the modern state, little has been said about the *economic motives* or *economic interests* of political and social actors, and about the economic conditions and limits of state action, other than to examine the issue of extraction of men, arms, income etc. (see Section 3.1). The main emphasis has been on the non-economic features of the modern state; that is, on the independent and autonomous capacities of its organizations and agencies. Does the introduction of an account of economic relations, and of the impact of the development of capitalism especially, alter the view set out so far of states as competing geopolitical institutions, above all else? Did the modern state system shape and constrain the modern capitalist economy as the latter developed after AD 1500? Or was the formation of the capitalist economy on a progressively more international basis a, if not the, prime determinant of the scope or limits of state power? As state boundaries became more fixed, did the formal state rulers 'rule the roost', or was the 'roost' impinged upon more and more by the rising economic classes? In short, what was the effect upon the nation-state of the development of the modern economic system; and who exactly rules the nation-state? As with previous sections, it is useful to take several steps back in time before seeking to discriminate among, and weigh up, the multifarious factors which were at play.

At about AD 1000 the nearest approximation to a worldwide order of politics and trade was the Moslem world. Its dominance, however, was slowly challenged: faced with Mongol invasions in the thirteenth and fourteenth centuries, on the one hand, and later outflanked by European naval expeditions, on the other, the vitality of the Islamic world declined (Modelski, 1972). Europe was to 'explode outward upon the world' (Mann, 1986, p.500). The growth of interconnections between states and societies — that is, of *globalization* — became progressively shaped by the expansion of Europe. Globalization meant western globalization. Key features of the modern states system — the centralization of political power, the expansion of administrative rule, the emergence of massed standing armies, the deployment of force — which existed in Europe in embryo in the sixteenth century were to become prevalent features of the entire global system. The chief vehicle for this was, to begin with, the European states' capacity for overseas operations by means of naval and military force capable of long-range navigation.

Among the early leaders in exploration were the Spanish and Portuguese (see Chapter 6, Section 2.3). If the Iberian monarchies led the first two centuries of 'European globalization', their position was eroded in the seventeenth century by the Dutch and then by the English. English influence was markedly in the ascendant in the eighteenth century and quite dominant in the nineteenth. British naval and military power conjoined with London as the centre of world trade and finance. However, it is doubtful whether any one single power was dominant until the nineteenth century. At least two powerful states were always contending for hegemony in Europe, and the expansion of world commerce drew in non-state actors as well (Tilly, 1990, p.189).

The expansion of Europe across the globe enhanced the demand, as one observer has noted, 'for organizations that would be capable of operating on such a scale. All the basic organization types of modern society — the modern state, modern corporate enterprise, modern science — were shaped by it and benefited greatly from it' (Modelski, 1972, p.37). In particular, globalization itself became a major source of expansion of state activity and efficiency. Governments organized and reaped some of the fruits of the 'discovery' and exploitation of non-European lands as it became essential to equip, plan and finance exploration and manage newly acquired posts and territories. In turn, state bureaucracies and executive powers were better resourced and this enhanced their autonomy in the face of local assemblies and parliaments. Once again, those states which were able to call upon an administrative infrastructure, substantial manpower and a wide tax base, alongside arms and shipbuilding industries, gained an advantage. In the seventeenth and eighteenth centuries this advantage was enjoyed by absolutist and constitutional governments; in the nineteenth century by the emergent leading nation-states.

If the consolidation of the modern European state was aided by globalization, this process involved great social costs: the progressive collapse of non-European civilizations, among them the Moslem, Indian and Chinese; the disorganizing effects of western rule on a large number of small societies; and the interlinked degradation of the non-European and European worlds caused by the slave trade. The benefits and costs were not, however, just the result of the expansion of the European states system: the picture was more complicated.

The diffusion of European power occurred mainly through the medium of sea-going military and commercial endeavours; and in the process

Europe became connected to a global system of trade and production relationships. At the centre of the latter were newly expanding capitalistic economic mechanisms which had their origins in the sixteenth century, or in what is sometimes called the 'long sixteenth century' running from about 1450 to 1640 (Braudel, 1973). One of the foremost analysts of this period is the sociologist Immanuel Wallerstein. As Wallerstein points out, 'capitalism was from the beginning an affair of the world economy and not of nation-states … . Capital has never allowed its aspirations to be determined by national boundaries' (1979, p.19). The emergence of capitalism ushered in a quite fundamental change in the world order: for the first time genuinely global interconnections were achieved among states and societies. Capitalism has been able to penetrate the distant corners of the world.

Wallerstein makes a fundamental distinction between two types of *world-system* which have existed historically: world-empires and world-economies. Whereas world-empires were political units characterized by imperial bureaucracies, with substantial armies to exact tax and tribute from territorially dispersed populations, their capacity for success depended upon political and military achievements. World empires were not as flexible and, ultimately, as adaptable as the emerging world-economy of the sixteenth and seventeenth centuries, and they were finally displaced by the European world-economy as it expanded globally. They were displaced, Wallerstein argues, because the new world economic system was based on a process of endless accumulation of wealth. This world-economy was an economic unit which transcended the boundaries of any given political structure. If it constrained anything it was states, not the process of economic expansion.

According to this view, the modern world-system is divided into three components: the core (initially located in north-west and central Europe); the semi-periphery (the Mediterranean zone after its decline from earlier prominence); and the periphery (colonized and captured territories), although where each of these three components is located has varied over time. Each zone of the world-economy is characterized, Wallerstein maintains, by a particular type of economic activity, state structure, class formation and mechanism of labour control. The world capitalist economy created a new world-wide division of labour. And while in the late twentieth century colonialism in its original form has practically disappeared, the world capitalist economy creates and reproduces massive imbalances of economic and political power among different component areas.

The development of the world capitalist economy initially took the form of the expansion of market relations, driven by a growing need for raw materials and other factors of production. Capitalism stimulated this drive and was stimulated by it. It is useful to make a distinction (which Wallerstein fails to do) between the expansion of capitalist market relations based on the desire to buy, sell and accumulate mobile resources or capital, and the formation of industrial capitalism involving highly distinctive class relations — based on those who own and control the means of production and those who have only their labouring capacity to sell. 'Capitalists', under the latter conditions, own factories and technology, while wage-labourers, or 'wage-workers', are without ownership in the means of production (see Chapter 4 for a further discussion of these issues). It is only with the development of capitalism in Europe after 1500, and in particular with the formation of the capitalist organization of production from the middle of the eighteenth century, that the activities of capitalists and the capitalist system began to converge (Tilly, 1990, pp.17, 189; Giddens, 1985, pp.122–47).

The development of capitalism itself can be explained as partly the result of long drawn-out changes in 'European' agriculture from as early as the twelfth century: changes resulting in part from the drainage and utilization of wet soils, which increased agricultural yields and created a sustainable surplus for trade. Linked to this was the establishment of long-distance trade routes in which the northern shores of the Mediterranean were initially prominent (Mann, 1986, p.504). Economic networks created 'north-south corridors' across the European landmass, with those networks in the North-west becoming progressively more dynamic over time. It was a combination of agricultural and navigational opportunities which helped stimulate the European economic dynamic, and the continuous competition for resources, territory and trade. Accordingly, the objectives of war gradually became more economic: military endeavour and conquest became more closely connected to the pursuit of economic advantage (Mann, 1986, p.511). The success of military conquest and the successful pursuit of economic gain were more directly associated.

The state slowly became more embroiled with the interests of civil society in part *for its own sake*. If state rulers and personnel wished to pursue and implement policy of their own choosing then they would require the financial wherewithall to do so; and the more successful the economic activity in their territories, the more — through customs, taxes, investments and other revenue-generating activity — they could sustain their own strategies and interests. By the seventeenth and eighteenth centuries absolutist and constitutional states were drawn steadily into a coordinating role with respect to the activities of civil society. The trigger for this growing responsibility almost always emanated from military commitments. But beneath this lay a general and growing requirement to regulate the developing capitalist economy and the spread of competing claims to property rights, if the economic basis of the state itself was to be properly protected (Mann, 1986, p.512). The other side of this process was, of course, the growing enmeshment of civil society with the state; for the latter's capacity in principle to stabilize and enforce law, contracts and currencies — to provide a coordinating framework for the new emerging capitalist economy — made it a growing object of attention for the powerful groups and classes of civil society who hoped to shape state action to suit their own interests.

What was the relationship between 'states' and 'classes' in the era of formation of the modern state? Any full answer to this question is likely to be controversial, and would have to be qualified in important details from one country to another. However, having said this, a pattern, first depicted by the sociologist Max Weber, can be uncovered between political rulers and the rising capitalist classes. Weber spoke of an 'alliance' between modern capitalism and the emergent modern state (Weber, 1923). Analysing the nature of this alliance further, Poggi has usefully drawn a distinction between two autonomous forces whose interests converged for a distinctive period (Poggi, 1990, pp.95–7). The forces consisted, on the one hand, of political rulers seeking to centralize political power and fiscal arrangements by disrupting and eradicating vestiges of power held by the nobility, the Church and various estate bodies, and, on the other hand, of the rising bourgeois classes seeking to remove impediments to the expansion of market relations based upon the trading arrangements established by powerful social networks, both country (aristocratic and landed power bases) and urban (the estate and guild systems). How the 'alliance' changed and crystallized over time into different constellations of class and state power is beyond the scope of this chapter. Nevertheless, it can be noted that the alliance appears to have endured up to the industrial revolution and aided both the expansion of commerce and the industrialization of the economy (Poggi, 1990, p.96).

If there was an alliance between the interests of powerful political and economic groupings during the formative phase of the modern state it was not without conflicts. For the new capitalist classes sought to struggle not only against the remnants of feudal privilege, but also to ensure the progressive separation of the economy from the state so that the economy was free from any risk of arbitrary political interference. It is at this juncture that the emerging economic classes often became the reforming classes of the eighteenth and nineteenth centuries, seeking to conjoin the struggle for an independent economic sphere with the struggle for representative government. The chief connecting mechanism was the attempt to establish civil and political rights (Marshall, 1973; Giddens, 1981; and see Book 2 (Allen et al., 1992), Chapter 4). For what was at issue in the establishment of these rights was the attempt to uphold 'freedom of choice' in areas as diverse as personal, family, business and political affairs. The pursuit of civil and political rights over time reconstituted the nature of both the state and the economy — driving the former toward a liberal democratic polity and the latter toward the capitalist market system. But the meaning of membership in the modern state, that is, of citizenship, remained contested — by political rulers, anxious to preserve their traditional privileges, by powerful social groups and classes, hoping to inscribe their interests into the polity, and by all those who remained excluded from political participation until well into the twentieth century: the working classes, women and many minority groups (see Book 2 (Allen et al., 1992), Chapters 1 and 4 for an account of the complex development of these conflicts). Moreover, as the coordinating role of the state expanded, and it became more involved in determining the conditions of civil society, the state became more intensely contested. The risk of unwanted political interference in economic affairs, and the requirement for a regulatory framework for trade and business, gave the emerging classes of capitalist society a double incentive for involvement in setting the direction of state action.

The process and outcome of the new social struggles, it should be stressed, cannot simply be understood in their own terms; for their form and dynamic were shaped and re-shaped by the states system itself. Mann has put the point sharply:

> ... by the time of the Industrial Revolution, capitalism was already contained within a civilization of competing geopolitical states ... [while] economic interaction was largely confined within national boundaries, supported by imperial dominions. Each leading state approximated a self-contained economic network. International economic relations were authoritatively mediated by states. Class regulation and organization thus developed in each of a series of geographical areas shaped by existing geopolitical units. (Mann, 1986, p.513)

Class conflicts were, in other words, framed in large measure by the nature and interrelations of states (cf. Tilly, 1981, pp.44–52, 109–44).

3.3   SUMMARY: THE STORY SO FAR

The formation of the modern state has to be related to at least two overarching phenomena: the structures of political and social groups and classes, and the relations among states — 'their position relative to each other, and their overall position in the world', as Hintze put it (1975, p.183). Struggles among social collectivities at home and conflicts among states abroad have had a dramatic impact on the nature, organization and dynamics of individual states. The modern state has a dual anchorage 'in class-divided socio-economic structures and an international system of states' (Skocpol, 1979, p.32). If this is the context in which the rise of the modern state must be understood, it remains to draw together the grounds for why it was that the modern state came to be a national or nation-state. Briefly put, this chapter has argued that nation-states became supreme because they won at war, were economically successful and, subsequently, achieved a significant degree of legitimacy in the eyes of their populations and other states.

They won at war because as warfare became more extended in scale and cost, it was larger national states which were best able to organize and fund military power; and as these states expanded overseas this ability increased (Tilly, 1990, pp.65–6, 190). They were economically successful because the rapid growth of their economies from the late sixteenth century, and particularly after the mid-eighteenth century, sustained the process of capital accumulation: as the economic basis of the centralized state expanded, it significantly reduced the war-making ability of smaller states (often with fragmented power structures) and traditional empires (which depended above all on coercive power for their success). And they gained in legitimacy because as they extended their military, organizational and coordinating activities, they came to depend more and more on the active cooperation, collaboration and support of their peoples, especially well-organized civil groups. In the wake of the erosion of the authority of the Church, the legitimacy of claims to political power came to depend on the view that such claims were justified and appropriate if popular or democratic. Calls for democratic government or democratic legitimacy became irresistible in the face of the expansion of state administrative power and the growth of new political identities — nationalism, citizenship and 'public' life.

However, the rise of Europe, of the European nation-state and of the modern states system is not fully explained by these factors and processes. There was, as there always is in politics, a fair degree of 'luck', 'uncertainty' or 'contingency'. The Mongol invasions (1206–60) could have penetrated further west with significant implications for the formation of Christian Europe; the Reformation could have drawn Europe into an endless vicious circle of religious war which might have undermined future European expansion; Napoleon Bonaparte might have conquered Russia and created a more durable empire; capitalism could have taken a firm hold in the East. The point of these and dozens of other 'what-ifs' is to remind one that history doesn't unfold according to one pattern, one logic, or one evolutionary scheme. History, if the above account is useful, is rather the result of the interplay of a number of causal patterns or processes which combine to produce particular trends and developmental trajectories. Moreover, these are never set in stone; they are always affected by and open to alteration by changing circumstances, and by the outcome of key historical events. In the case of the history of states these events have been wars, first and foremost, and the development of military power to back up negotiations on pressing issues.

4 SOVEREIGNTY AND THE MODERN NATION-STATE: COMPETING CONCEPTIONS

The focus of the ensuing section is a number of accounts of the modern state and the interrelated notion of sovereignty. The ideas of some of the key contributors to modern political thought are presented, and some of their major texts are introduced. While the previous sections of this chapter have offered, in broad terms, a *descriptive-explanatory* account of the development of the modern state, what follows is more directly concerned with the *normative problems* of political theory. However, before turning to the latter, it is useful to ask: What kind of distinction is being made here between types of political inquiry?

A contrast is often drawn between normative political theory or political philosophy, on the one hand, and descriptive-explanatory or analytical theories of the social sciences, on the other. The former refers to theories about the proper form of political institutions and includes accounts of such notions as sovereignty, authority and liberty. The latter refers to attempts to characterize actual phenomena and events and is marked by a strong empirical element. The distinction, thus, is between theories which focus on what is desirable — what should or ought to be the case — and those that focus on what has been or is the case. But it should be borne in mind that, while this distinction is helpful as an initial point of orientation, it is hard to use it as a precise classificatory device for theories of the modern state. For many political philosophers see what they think the state ought to be like in the state as it is. Social scientists, on the other hand, cannot escape the problem that facts do not simply 'speak for themselves'; they are, and they have to be, interpreted; and the framework we bring to the process of interpretation determines what we 'see' — what we notice and register as important.

The distinction between 'empirical analysis' and 'normative theory' is further complicated if one reflects on the interaction between 'ideas' and 'reality'. The process of analysing aspects of the political world contributes to an understanding of how people can, might or should act in the world; it can be reflexively applied to the transformation of the conditions of existence. Political enquiry, in fact, has often had a practical impact in the modern era, just as political, social and economic developments have had an influence on the nature and objects of enquiry. The debate in political theory about the modern state became a constitutive component of the concepts and theories which were utilized and applied in the formation and construction of the modern state itself (see Skinner, 1978). In what follows some of the leading contributions to this interchange are set out. It is an interchange which has had, and is likely to continue to have, significant political implications.

4.1 WHAT IS THE PROPER NATURE OF POLITICAL AUTHORITY?

The idea of the modern state is intimately linked to the idea of sovereignty: for its origin and history are closely connected to the origin and development of the concept of sovereignty itself. While the idea of sovereignty can be traced to the Roman Empire, it was not until the end of the sixteenth century, when the nature and limits of political authority emerged as a preoccupation of European political thought, that sovereignty became a major theme in political analysis. The theocratic concepts of authority which dominated mediaeval Europe were challenged both by the rise of centralized states, absolutist and constitutional, and by the Protestant Reformation.

The Reformation did more than just challenge Papal jurisdiction and authority across Europe; it raised questions about political obligation and obedience in a stark manner. The issue of whether allegiance was owed to the Catholic Church, a Protestant ruler, or particular religious sects did not easily resolve itself. Very gradually it became apparent, moreover, that the powers of the state would have to be separated from the duty of rulers to uphold any particular faith (Skinner, 1978, p.352). This conclusion alone offered a way forward through the dilemmas of rule created by competing religions, all seeking to secure for themselves the kind of privileges enjoyed by the mediaeval church.

In this context sovereignty became a new way of thinking about an old problem: the nature of power and rule. When established forms of authority could no longer be taken for granted it was the idea of sovereignty which provided a fresh link between political power and rulership. In the struggle between church, state and society, sovereignty offered an alternative way of conceiving the legitimacy of claims to power. In the debate about sovereignty which ensued, there was little initial agreement about its meaning; differing accounts were offered of the proper locus of 'supreme power' in society, the source of authority for that power, limitations upon that power (if any), and the ends to which that power might or should be directed. As the theory of sovereignty developed, however, it became a theory about the possibility of, and the conditions for, the rightful exercise of political power. It became the theory of legitimate power or authority. In examining the theory, we examine some of the most fundamental conceptions of the modern state; for the theory of sovereignty largely set down the terms of reference of political discussion.

While tension between the principles of rulership and self-government, between power and society, led to discrepant conceptions of the nature of sovereign power and of the criteria of legitimate government, two poles became clearly established in the emergent debate: state sovereignty and popular sovereignty. Where advocates of the former tended to grant the state ultimate authority to define public right, advocates of the latter tended to see the state as a mere 'commission' for the enactment of the people's will and, therefore, as open to direct determination by 'the public' (cf. Berlin, 1969, pp.164ff.). Traditionally, these positions are thought to have been articulated best by, respectively, Hobbes's classic statement about state sovereignty (*Leviathan*, 1651) and Rousseau's powerful account of the doctrine of popular sovereignty (*The Social Contract*, 1762).

4.2 HOBBES

In his great work *Leviathan,* Thomas Hobbes (1588–1679) provided one of the most elegant rationales for the primacy of the state, for the necessary unity of the state as the representative of the body politic, and for the necessity of the state as the creator and maintainer of positive law. Hobbes wrote against the background of social disorder and political instability — the English Civil War — and sought to establish the necessity of an all-powerful sovereign capable of securing the conditions of 'peaceful and commodious living'. His position was that individuals ought willingly to surrender their rights to a powerful single authority — thereafter authorized to act on their behalf — because, if all individuals were to do this simultaneously, the condition would be created for effective political rule. A unique relation of authority would be created — the relation of sovereign to subject — and a unique political power would be established: sovereign power or sovereignty — the authorized, hence rightful, use of power by the person (or assembly) established as sovereign.

The sovereign has to have sufficient power to ensure that the laws governing political and economic life are upheld. Since, in Hobbes's view, 'men's ambitions, avarice, anger and other passions' are strong, and the 'bonds of words are too weak to bridle them ... without some fear of coercive power', he concluded that, 'covenants, without the sword, are but words, and of no strength to secure a man at all' (Hobbes, 1968, p.223). Beyond the sovereign state's sphere of influence there will always be the chaos of constant warfare; but within the territory controlled by the state, with 'fear of some coercive power', social order can be sustained.

It is important to stress that, in Hobbes's opinion, sovereignty must be self-perpetuating, undivided and ultimately absolute (Hobbes, 1968, pp.227–8). The justification for this is 'the safety of the people'. By 'safety' is meant not merely minimum physical preservation. The sovereign must ensure the protection of all things held in property: 'Those that are dearest to a man are his own life, and limbs; and in the next degree, (in most men) those that concern conjugal affection; and after them riches and means of living' (Hobbes, 1968, pp.376, 382–3). Although Hobbes acknowledges certain limits to the legitimate range of the sovereign's actions, the state is regarded by him as pre-eminent in all spheres (see Hobbes, 1968, ch. 21). For the state is authorized to represent all individuals and, accordingly, absorbs all popular or public right. State sovereignty embraces, in principle, all elements of the body politic.

ACTIVITY 3   You should now read **Reading A, 'Leviathan'**, by Thomas Hobbes, which you will find at the end of this chapter. As you read, note the reasons why Hobbes thinks:

1   people require a 'common power' or state — what he calls a 'mortal God' — in order to live securely and prosperously;

2   people must live in fear of some 'coercive power'.

Additionally, consider:

3   on what basis Hobbes thinks a 'common power' can be established; and

4   what, in his view, is the nature of the relationship that ought to be created between ruler and ruled — sovereign and subject?

With Hobbes, the justification of state power received its fullest
expression and became a central theme in European political thought.
But his position was controversial and challenged on at least two
grounds (see Hinsley, 1986, pp.144ff.). The first objection raised the
fundamental question of where sovereign authority properly lay — with
the ruler, the monarch, the state or (as was increasingly to be argued)
with the people? The second objection was concerned with the proper
form and limits, the legitimate scope, of state action.

4.3   ROUSSEAU

Jean-Jacques Rousseau (1712–78) did not reject the concept of
sovereignty, but insisted on retaining for the people the sovereignty
which Hobbes had transferred to the state and its rulers. In Rousseau's
view, sovereignty originates in the people and ought to stay there
(Rousseau, 1968, p.141). For Rousseau, the very essence of sovereignty
is the creation, authorization and enactment of law according to the
standards and requirements of the common good. And the nature of the
common good can only be known through public discourse and public
agreement. Only citizens themselves can articulate 'the supreme
direction of the general will' — which is the sum of their publicly
generated judgements of the common good (Rousseau, 1968, pp.60–1).
Moreover, Rousseau argued, citizens can only be obligated to a system
of laws and regulations they have prescribed for themselves with the
general good in mind (Rousseau, 1968, p.65; cf. p.82).

Taking arguments about sovereignty in a new direction, Rousseau held
that, ideally, individuals should be involved directly in the creation of
the laws by which their lives are regulated. The sovereign authority is
the people making the rules by which they live. All citizens should
meet together to decide what is best for the community and enact the
appropriate laws. The ruled should be the rulers: the affairs of the state
should be integrated into the affairs of ordinary citizens (see Rousseau,
1968, pp.82, 114; and for a general account, ibid., pp.101–16). Rousseau
was critical of the classical Athenian conception of direct democracy
because it failed to incorporate a division between legislative and
executive functions and, consequently, became prone to instability,
internecine strife and indecision in crisis (Rousseau, 1968, pp.112–14,
136ff.). But while he wished to defend the importance of dividing and
limiting 'governmental power', the executive or government in his
scheme was legitimate only to the extent to which it fulfilled 'the
instructions of the general will'. In so arguing, Rousseau undermined
the distinction between the state and the community, the government
and 'the people', but in the opposite direction to that proposed by
Hobbes. Government was reduced to a 'commission'; public right, in
principle, absorbed the state.

ACTIVITY 4   You should now read **Reading B, 'The social contract'**, by Jean-Jacques Rousseau.

As you read, try to note the reasons Rousseau gives for holding that:

1   a 'social contract' must be established;

2   sovereignty originates in the people — and ought to stay there.

Reflect also on why Rousseau thinks:

3   citizens can legitimately be 'forced to be free'.

Finally, consider:

4   Rousseau's conception of the limits, if any, of popular 'sovereign power'.

Hobbes and Rousseau may be portrayed as representing opposing sides in the debate about the locus of sovereignty. However, both cast their arguments in such a way as to face a common objection: that they projected models of political power with potentially tyrannical implications. For if Hobbes placed the state in an all-powerful position with respect to community, Rousseau placed the community (or a majority thereof) in a position to wholly dominate individual citizens: the community is all-powerful and, therefore, the sovereignty of the people could easily destroy the liberty of individuals (Berlin, 1969, p.163). The problem is that just as Hobbes failed to articulate either the principles or institutions necessary to delimit state action, Rousseau assumed that minorities ought to consent to the decisions of majorities, and posited no limits to the reach of the decisions of a democratic majority, and therefore to political intervention. Such conceptions of sovereignty, which fail to demarcate the limits or legitimate scope of political action, need to be treated with caution.

An alternative to the contending theses of the sovereignty of the state and the sovereignty of the people is implicit in Locke's conception of an independent political community, and is essential to the traditions of political analysis which neither locate sovereignty in, nor reduce it to, either state or society. This tradition — above all, of constitutional thinking — sought to provide ways of mediating, balancing and checking the relationship between state and society such that some protection existed for both public and private right. The motivation for such a position lay precisely in doubts about unaccountable state power and in the necessity to provide limits to the legitimate scope of political action. Views such as these were given lasting expression in the constitutional arguments of John Locke (1632–1704).

4.4 LOCKE

Locke held that the institution of 'government' can and should be conceived as an instrument for the defence of the 'life, liberty and estate' of its citizens; that is, government's *raison d'être* is the protection of individuals' rights as laid down by God's will and as enshrined in law (see Dunn, 1969, part 3). He believed that the integrity and ultimate ends of society require a constitutional state in which 'public power' is legally circumscribed and divided. He argued on behalf of a constitutional monarchy holding executive power and a parliamentary assembly holding the rights of legislation, although he did not think this was the only form government might take. However, in Locke's view, the formation of the state does not signal the final transfer of all subjects' rights to the state (Locke, 1963, pp.402–3, para. II.135; pp.412–13, para. II.149). The rights of law-making and law-enforcement (legislative and executive rights) are transferred, but the whole process is conditional upon the state adhering to its essential purpose: the preservation of 'life, liberty and estate'.

It is important to emphasize that, in Locke's account, political authority is bestowed by individuals on government for the purpose of pursuing the ends of the governed; and should these ends fail to be represented adequately, the final judges are the people — the citizens of the state — who can dispense both with their deputies and, if need be, with the existing form of government itself. According to Locke, in the face of a series of tyrannical political acts, popular rebellion to form a new government might not only be unavoidable but justified. One commentator has summarized Locke's position thus:

> Rulers ... hold their authority under law; and entitlement to the obedience of their subjects derives from the impartial administration of this law. Where they act against or outside this law to the harm of their subjects, they become tyrants. Wherever law ends, tyranny begins [Locke, 1963, p.448, para. II.202]. For a ruler in authority to use force against the interests of his subjects and outside the law is to destroy his own authority. He puts himself into a state of war with his injured subjects, and each of these has the same right to resist him as they would have to resist any other unjust aggressor [Locke, 1963, p.448, para. II.202; p.467, para. II.232].
> (Dunn, 1984, p.54)

With these arguments Locke fashioned a doctrine which had an enduring impact on Western political thought. For it affirmed that supreme power was the inalienable right of the people; that governmental supremacy was a *delegated* supremacy held on trust; that government enjoyed full political authority so long as this trust was sustained; and that a government's legitimacy or right to rule could be withdrawn if the people judged this necessary and appropriate; that is, if the rights of individuals and 'ends of society' were systematically flouted.

ACTIVITY 5   Locke concludes his *Two Treatises of Government* with the following
passage. Note especially the conditions under which 'supreme power'
can legitimately revert to the people:

> To conclude, The *Power that every individual gave the Society*,
> when he entered into it, can never revert to the Individuals again,
> as long as the Society lasts, but will always remain in the
> Community; because without this, there can be no Community, no
> Common-wealth ... : So also when the Society hath placed the
> Legislative in any Assembly of Men, to continue in them and their
> Successors, with Direction and Authority for providing such
> Successors, *the Legislative can never revert to the People* whilst
> that Government lasts: Because having provided a Legislative with
> Power to continue for ever, they have given up their Political
> Power to the Legislative, and cannot resume it. But if they have set
> Limits to the Duration of their Legislative, and made this Supreme
> Power in any Person, or Assembly, only temporary: Or else when
> by the Miscarriages of those in Authority, it is forfeited; upon the
> Forfeiture of their Rulers, or at the Determination of the Time set,
> *it reverts to the Society*, and the People have a Right to act as
> Supreme, and continue the Legislative in themselves, or erect a
> new Form, or under the old form place it in new hands, as they
> think good.
> (Locke, 1963, p.477, para. II.243)

However, with these arguments Locke also ran into distinct difficulties.
He did not explore systematically how possible tensions might be
resolved between the sovereignty of the people — the idea of the people
as an active sovereign body with the capacity to make or break
governments — and the government as the trustee of the people with
the right to make and enforce the law. At the root of this lies a failure to
draw an effective contrast between the power of the people and the
powers of the state (Skinner, 1989, p.115). As Locke put it, 'the
community perpetually retains a supreme power' over its prince or
legislative (quoted in ibid.). Accordingly, what constitutes the precise
autonomy or independence of state powers remains unspecified. While
Locke's attempt to transcend the dualism between ruler and people,
state and community, became highly influential, as did his attempt to
enshrine this new political understanding in the notion of constitutional
government — a legal and institutional mechanism to protect both the
'sovereign people' and 'the sovereign state' — his solution was far from
complete.

Modern liberal and liberal-democratic theory has constantly sought to
justify the sovereign power of the state while at the same time justifying
limits upon that power. The history of this attempt is the history of
arguments to balance might and right, power and law, duties and rights.

On the one hand, states must have a monopoly of coercive power in order to provide a secure basis upon which trade, commerce and family life can prosper. On the other hand, by granting the state a regulatory and coercive capability, political theorists were aware that they had accepted a force which could, and frequently did, deprive citizens of political and social freedoms.

It was the liberal democrats who provided the key institutional innovation to try to overcome this dilemma — representative democracy. The liberal concern with reason, law and freedom of choice could only be upheld properly by recognizing the political equality of all mature individuals. Such equality would ensure not only a secure social environment in which people would be free to pursue their private activities and interests, but also that the state's personnel would do what was best in the general and public interest; for example, pursue the greatest satisfaction of the greatest number. Thus, the democratic state, linked to other key institutional mechanisms, above all the free market, resolved, the liberal democrats argued, the problems of ensuring both authority and liberty.

4.5   MILL

A classical statement of the new position can be found in the philosophy of John Stuart Mill (1806–73). In his hands the theory of liberal democracy received a most important elaboration: the governors must be held accountable to the governed through political mechanisms (regular voting, competition between potential representatives, the struggle among free opinion) which alone can give citizens the satisfactory means for choosing, authorizing and controlling political decisions. And with these means, he further contended, a balance could finally be obtained between might and right, authority and liberty. But who exactly was to count as a 'citizen' or an 'individual', and what their exact role was to be, remained unfortunately either unclear or unsettled: the idea that *all* citizens should have equal weight in the political system remained outside Mill's actual doctrine.

The idea of the modern democratic state remains complex and contested. The liberal democratic tradition itself comprises a most heterogeneous body of thought. However, the whole liberal democratic tradition stands apart from an alternative perspective — the Marxist tradition. It is worth briefly dwelling on this, since it remains the key counterpoint to liberal democracy.

ACTIVITY 6   Before reading further you should note down some of the key features of liberal democracy in order that the contrast with Marxism is brought more sharply into view.

4.6   MARX AND ENGELS

The struggle of liberalism against tyranny and the struggle by liberal democrats for political equality represented, according to Karl Marx (1818–83) and Frederick Engels (1820–95), a major step forward in the history of human emancipation. But for them, and the Marxist tradition more broadly, the great universal ideals of 'liberty, equality and justice' could not be realized simply by the 'free' struggle for votes in the political system and by the 'free' struggle for profit in the market place. The advocates of the democratic state and the market economy present them as the only institutions under which liberty can be sustained and inequalities minimized. However, by virtue of its internal dynamics the capitalist economy inevitably produces, Marxists aver, systematic inequality and massive restrictions on real freedom. While each step towards formal political equality is an advance, its liberating potential is severely curtailed by inequalities of class, wealth and opportunity.

In class societies the state cannot become the vehicle for the pursuit of the common good or public interest. Far from playing the role of emancipator, protective knight, umpire or judge in the face or disorder, the agencies of the liberal representative state are meshed in the struggles of civil society. Marxists conceive of the state as an extension of civil society, reinforcing the social order for the enhancement of particular interests — in capitalist society, the long-term interests of the capitalist class. Marx and Engels' argument is that political emancipation is only a step towards human emancipation: that is, the complete democratization of society as well as the state. In their view, liberal democratic society fails when judged by its own principles; and to take these seriously is to become a communist. Marx himself envisaged the replacement of the 'machinery' of the liberal democratic state by a 'commune structure': the smallest communities would administer their own affairs, elect delegates to larger administrative units (districts, towns) and these would, in turn, elect candidates to still larger areas of administration (the national delegation). This arrangement is known as the 'pyramid' structure of direct democracy: all delegates are revocable, bound by the instructions of their constituency and organized into a 'pyramid' of directly elected committees.

ACTIVITY 7   Note Marx and Engels' emphasis on the interconnections between social power, class and state. Consider the stress they place on these interconnections. How convinced are you by their view that the state is an extension of civil society — that is, a political apparatus structured and shaped by class relations?

4.7   WEBER

One of the toughest (yet not wholly unsympathetic) critics of the
Marxist tradition was the sociologist Max Weber (1864–1920). Weber
believed that Marxists' political ambitions were premised on a deficient
understanding of the nature of the modern state and of the complexity
of political life. In Weber's account, the history of the state and the
history of political struggle could not in any way be reduced to class
relations: the origins and tasks of the modern state suggested it was far
more than a 'superstructure' on an economic 'base'. Moreover, even if
class relations were transformed, institutions of direct democracy could
not replace the state; for there would be a massive problem of
coordination and regulation which would inevitably be 'resolved' by
bureaucracy, and by bureaucracy alone, unless other institutions were
created to check its power. The problems posed by the liberal pursuit of
a balance between might and right, power and law, are, Weber thought,
inescapable elements of modernity.

Weber developed one of the most significant definitions of the modern
state, placing emphasis upon two distinctive elements of its history:
territoriality and violence. The modern state, unlike its predecessors
which were troubled by constantly warring factions, has the capability
of monopolizing the legitimate use of violence within a given territory;
it is a nation-state in embattled relations with other nation-states rather
than with armed segments of its own population. 'Of course', Weber
emphasized, 'force is certainly not the normal or only means of the state
— nobody says that — but force is a means specific to the state … . The
state is a relation of men dominating men, a relation supported by
means of legitimate (i.e. considered to be legitimate) violence' (Weber,
1972, p.178). The state maintains compliance or order within a given
territory; in individual capitalist societies this involves crucially the
defence of property and the enhancement of domestic economic
interests overseas, although by no means all the problems of order can
be reduced to these. The state's web of agencies and institutions finds
its ultimate sanction in the claim to the monopoly of coercion, and a
political order is only, in the last instance, vulnerable to crises when
this monopoly erodes.

However, there is also a third key element in Weber's definition of the
state: legitimacy. The state is based on a monopoly of physical coercion
which is legitimized (that is, sustained) by a belief in the justifiability
and/or legality of this monopoly. Today, Weber argued, people no longer
comply with the authority claimed by the powers-that-be merely on the
grounds, as was common once, of habit and tradition or the charisma
and personal appeal of individual leaders. Rather, there is general
obedience by 'virtue of "legality", by virtue of the belief in the validity
of legal statute and functional "competence" based on rationally created
rules' (Weber, 1972, p.79). The legitimacy of the modern state is
founded predominantly on 'legal authority', that is, commitment to a
'code of legal regulations'.

Foremost among the state's institutions are, Weber held, the administrative apparatuses — a vast network of organizations run by appointed officials. Weber feared that political life in West and East would be ever more ensnared by a rationalized, bureaucratic system of administration — a 'steel-hard cage', as he wrote. Against this he championed the countervailing power of private capital, the competitive party system and strong political leadership to secure national power and prestige — all of which could prevent the domination of politics by state officials. Two-hundred-and-fifty years after Hobbes wrote *Leviathan*, the conception of the state as a potentially omnipotent and all-embracing entity remained a deep concern.

ACTIVITY 8 Before reading further, you should note down the key differences between the Marxist and Weberian accounts of the modern state. Which position do you find the more plausible, and why? Consider your response in relation to the historical material presented in the earlier parts of the chapter, especially Section 3.

5 CONCLUSION

What should be made of these various conceptions of sovereignty, state power and democracy today? The difficulties of coming to a judgement about the modern state are acute, especially if one examines it in relation to the history both of the states system and of the interconnections of the world economy. (For a discussion of these points, see Book 4 (Hall *et al.*, 1992), especially Chapter 1.) By way of a conclusion, however, a number of points from the chapter as a whole can be usefully brought together, and left for you to reflect upon. These can be put briefly:

1   To understand the formation of the state it is necessary to grasp the intersection of national and international conditions and processes. The state faces inwards toward its subjects and citizens, and outwards toward the states system and international economy. It has an anchorage in both the organizations and relations of socio-economic groups and in the international order.

2   The modern state became the supreme form of the state because it most successfully marshalled the means of waging war, economic resources and claims to legitimacy. Modern states mobilized effectively for war, for the enhancement of economic activity (capitalist expansion) and for their own legitimation. It is at the intersection of these particular formative processes that the distinctive organization and form of the modern state emerged.

3   The democratization of the modern state, that is, the establishment of the universal franchise, can be related directly to the state's search for loyalty and resources when it has been most pressed (before, during and after wars), and to its claim to a distinct form of legitimacy. Unlike its predecessors, the modern state heralds its separateness from both ruler and ruled. At the centre of the self-image and representation of the modern state lies its claim to be an 'independent authority' or 'circumscribed impartial power' accountable to its citizens. To the extent that this claim has been redeemed, the modern state has been able to enjoy an advantage against rival political forces in the battle for legitimacy in the modern world. However, the nature and meaning of this claim have been contested from the outset of the modern state to the present day. The legitimacy of the modern state remains controversial.

4   The modern state has been neither simply a detached 'judge' of the affairs of civil society, nor merely an epiphenomenon. Rather, it is best understood as a system of organizations and relations which can make and shape social, political and economic change. The state apparatus has sufficient primacy over social classes and collectivities that discrete political outcomes — constitutional forms, coalitional arrangements, particular exercises of state coercion, and so on — cannot be inferred directly from the movements and activities of those in civil society. Political life, and state action in particular, are by no means wholly determined by socio-economic life.

5   The modern state, like its predecessors, is a system of power in its own right; it has to be understood as a set of organizations and collectivities concerned with the institutionalization of political power. While the independent and autonomous capacities of state organizations and agencies have been stressed, so have the latter as sites of contestation and conflict. The history of the modern state is also the history of the way in which social struggle has been 'inscribed' into, that is, embedded in, the organization, administration and policies of the state. As states came to depend on their citizens for support and resources, their structures and policies became subject, some would say ever more subject, to political negotiation and compromise.

6   The proper locus and form of the sovereignty of the modern state have been in dispute from Hobbes to Rousseau to Marx and Weber. Conceptions of sovereignty which neither locate sovereignty exclusively in, nor reduce sovereignty to, either state or society seem compelling; yet, these are far from secure. What is meant by the rightful exercise of political authority remains open to dispute. Further, the operation of states in the complex international system of economics and politics raises questions about the role of sovereignty — its possible nature and extent — in a world in which powerful non-state actors, like international companies, have significant influence, and in which the fate of peoples are interconnected. Sovereignty is moulded and re-moulded in the international world of states and societies.

7   The processes and conflicts which have centred on and crystallized around the modern state have been the result of complex interactions between political, economic, military and social factors, among other things. These factors cannot simply be ranked in a fixed order of importance in the explanation of the rise and development of the modern state. For it is in a combination of factors that a satisfactory explanation can be found for the major trends and developments of the modern political world. While this amounts to a rejection of arguments for economic determinism, or cultural determinism, or military determinism (and other positions which advocate focusing on one set of causal factors), it allows that one or more of these factors could have causal primacy under particular conditions and circumstances. The modern state escapes the categories of deterministic theories; but economic relations, political forces and military might have all been fundamental to elements of its form and dynamics.

REFERENCES

Allen, J., Braham, P. and Lewis, P. (eds) (1992) *Political and Economic Forms of Modernity,* Cambridge, Polity Press.

Anderson, P. (1974) *Passages from Antiquity to Feudalism*, London, New Left Books.

Andreski, S. (1968) *Military Organization and Society*, Berkeley, University of California Press.

Beitz, C. (1979) *Political Theory and International Relations*, Princeton, Princeton University Press.

Benn, S.I. and Peters, R.S. (1959) *Social Principles and the Democratic State*, London, Allen & Unwin.

Berlin, I. (1969) *Four Essays on Liberty*, Oxford, Oxford University Press.

Bernal, M. (1987) *Black Athena*, vol. 1, London, Free Association Books.

Bobbio, N. (1989) *Democracy and Dictatorship*, Cambridge, Polity Press.

Braudel, F. (1973) *Capitalism and Material Life*, London, Weidenfeld & Nicolson.

Breuilly, J. (1982) *Nationalism and the State*, Manchester, Manchester University Press.

Bull, H. (1977) *The Anarchical Society*, Cambridge, Macmillan.

Cassese, A. (1986) *International Law in a Divided World,* Oxford, Clarendon Press.

Dahl, R. (1989) *Democracy and its Critics*, New Haven, Yale University Press.

Dunn, J. (1969) *The Political Thought of John Locke,* Cambridge, Cambridge University Press.

Dunn, J. (1984) *Locke*, Oxford, Oxford University Press.

Elster, J. (1988) 'Introduction', in Elster, J. and Slagstad, R. (eds) *Constitutionalism and Democracy*, Cambridge, Cambridge University Press.

Engels, F. (1972) *The Origins of the Family, Private Property and the State*, New York, International Publishers.

Falk, R. (1969) 'The interplay of Westphalia and Charter conceptions of international law', in Black, C.A. and Falk, R. (eds) *The Future of the International Legal Order*, vol.1, Princeton, Princeton University Press.

Giddens, A. (1981) *A Contemporary Critique of Historical Materialism,* London, Macmillan.

Giddens, A. (1985) *The Nation-State and Violence*, Cambridge, Polity Press.

Giddens, A. (1987) *Social Theory and Modern Society*, Cambridge, Polity Press.

Hall, S., Held, D. and McGrew, A. (eds) (1992) *Modernity and its Futures,* Cambridge, Polity Press.

Held, D. (1987) *Models of Democracy*, Cambridge, Polity Press.

Held, D. (1991) 'Democracy, the nation-state and the global system', in Held, D. (ed.) *Political Theory Today*, Cambridge, Polity Press.

Hinsley, F. H. (1986) *Sovereignty*, 2nd edn, Cambridge, Cambridge University Press.

Hintze, O. (1975) *Historical Essays*, New York, Oxford University Press.

Hobbes, T. (1968) *Leviathan*, Harmondsworth, Penguin.

Janowitz, M. (1978) *The Last Half-Century*, Chicago, University of Chicago Press.

Keane, J. (1988) *Democracy and Civil Society*, London, Verso.

Locke, J. (1963) *Two Treatises of Government*, Cambridge, Cambridge University Press.

Macpherson, C.B. (1966) *The Real World of Democracy*, Oxford, Oxford University Press.

Mann, M. (1986) *The Sources of Social Power,* vol. 1, Cambridge, Cambridge University Press.

Mann, M. (1987) 'Ruling strategies and citizenship', *Sociology*, vol. 21(3).

Marshall, T.H. (1973) *Class, Citizenship and Social Development*, Westport, Greenwood Press.

Marx, K. and Engels, F. (1948) *The Communist Manifesto*, New York, International Publishers.

McEvedy, C. (1961) *The Penguin Atlas of Medieval History*, Harmondsworth, Penguin.

McEvedy, C. (1982) *The Penguin Atlas of Recent History: Europe since 1815*, Harmondsworth, Penguin.

Mill, J.S. (1951) *Considerations on Representative Government*, in Acton, H.B. (ed.) *Utilitarianism, Liberty and Representative Government*, London, Dent.

Mitchell, B.R. and Deane, P. (1962) *Abstract of British Historical Statistics*, Cambridge, Cambridge University Press.

Mitchell, B.R. and Jones, H.G. (1971) *Second Abstract of Historical Statistics*, Cambridge, Cambridge University Press.

Modelski, G. (1972) *Principles of World Politics*, New York, Free Press.

Neumann, F. (1964) *The Democratic and the Authoritarian State*, New York, Free Press.

Pelczynski, Z.A. (1985) *The State and Civil Society*, Cambridge, Cambridge University Press.

Poggi, G. (1978) *The Development of the Modern State*, London, Hutchinson.

Poggi, G. (1990) *The State: Its Nature, Development and Prospects*, Cambridge, Polity Press.

Rousseau, J.-J. (1968) *The Social Contract*, Harmondsworth, Penguin.

Schama, S. (1989) *Citizens*, New York, Knopf.

Skinner, Q. (1978) *The Foundations of Modern Political Thought* (2 vols), Cambridge, Cambridge University Press.

Skinner, Q. (1989) 'The state', in Ball, T. *et al.* (eds) *Political Innovation and Conceptual Change*, Cambridge, Cambridge University Press.

Skocpol, T. (1979) *States and Revolutions*, Cambridge, Cambridge University Press.

Springborg, P. (1991) *Western Republicanism and the Oriental Prince*, Cambridge, Polity Press.

Therborn, G. (1977) 'The rule of capital and the rise of democracy', *New Left Review*, vol. 103.

Tilly, C. (1975) 'Reflections on the history of European state-making', in Tilly, C. (ed.) *The Formation of National States in Western Europe*, Princeton, Princeton University Press.

Tilly, C. (1981) *As Sociology Meets Men*, New York, Academic Press.

Tilly, C. (1990) *Coercion, Capital and European States, AD 990–1990*, Oxford, Blackwell.

Turner, B.S. (1986) *Citizenship and Capitalism*, London, Allen & Unwin.

Wallerstein, I. (1979) *The Capitalist Economy*, Cambridge, Cambridge University Press.

Weber, M. (1923) *General Economic History*, London, Allen & Unwin.

Weber, M. (1972) 'Politics as a vocation', in Gerth, H. H. and Mills, C.W. (eds) *From Max Weber*, New York, Oxford University Press.

READING A LEVIATHAN

Thomas Hobbes

Nature hath made men so equal, in the faculties of the body, and mind; as that though there be found one man sometimes manifestly stronger in body, or of quicker mind than another; yet when all is reckoned together, the difference between man, and man, is not so considerable, as that one man can thereupon claim to himself any benefit, to which another may not pretend, as well as he. For as to the strength of body, the weakest has strength enough to kill the strongest, either by secret machination, or by confederacy with others, that are in the same danger with himself. ...

Hereby it is manifest, that during the time men live without a common power to keep them all in awe, they are in that condition which is called war; and such a war, as is of every man, against every man. For WAR, consisteth not in battle only, or the act of fighting; but in a tract of time, wherein the will to contend by battle is sufficiently known. ...

Whatsoever therefore is consequent to a time of war, where every man is enemy to every man; the same is consequent to the time, wherein men live without other security, than what their own strength, and their own invention shall furnish them withal. In such condition, there is no place for industry; because the fruit thereof is uncertain: and consequently no culture of the earth; no navigation, nor use of the commodities that may be imported by sea; no commodious building; no instruments of moving, and removing, such things as require much force; no knowledge of the face of the earth; no account of time; no arts; no letters; no society; and which is worst of all, continual fear, and danger of violent death; and the life of man, solitary, poor, nasty, brutish, and short. ...

It may peradventure be thought, there was never such a time, nor condition of war as this; and I believe it was never generally so, over all the world: but there are many places, where they live so now. For the savage people in many places of America, except the government of small families, the concord whereof dependeth on natural lust ['inclination'], have no government at all; and live at this day in that brutish manner, as I said before. Howsoever, it may be perceived what manner of life there would be, where there were no common power to fear, by the manner of life, which men that have formerly lived under a peaceful government, use to degenerate into, in a civil war. ...

The final cause, end, or design of men, who naturally love liberty, and dominion over others, in the introduction of that restraint upon themselves, in which we see them live in commonwealths, is the foresight of their own preservation, and of a more contented life thereby; that is to say, of getting themselves out from that miserable condition of war, which is necessarily consequent ... to the natural passions of men, when there is no visible power to keep them in awe, and tie them by fear of punishment to

Source: Hobbes, T. (1651) *Leviathan*; reproduced from Held, D. *et al.* (eds) (1983) *States and Societies*, Oxford, Martin Robertson, pp.68–71.

the performance of their covenants, and observation of those laws of nature … .

For the laws of nature, as *justice, equity, modesty, mercy,* and, in sum, *doing to others, as we would be done to,* of themselves, without the terror of some power, to cause them to be observed, are contrary to our natural passions, that carry us to partiality, pride, revenge, and the like. And covenants, without the sword, are but words, and of no strength to secure a man at all. Therefore notwithstanding the laws of nature, which every one hath then kept, when he has the will to keep them, when he can do it safely, if there be no power erected, or not great enough for our security; every man will, and may lawfully rely on his own strength and art, for caution against all other men. And in all places, where men have lived by small families, to rob and spoil one another, has been a trade, and so far from being reputed against the law of nature, that the greater spoils they gained, the greater was their honour; and men observed no other laws therein, but the laws of honour; that is, to abstain from cruelty, leaving to men their lives, and instruments of husbandry. And as small families did then; so now do cities and kingdoms which are but greater families, for their own security, enlarge their dominions, upon all pretences of danger, and fear of invasion, or assistance that may be given to invaders, and endeavour as much as they can, to subdue, or weaken their neighbours, by open force, and secret arts, for want of other caution, justly; and are remembered for it in after ages with honour.

Nor is it the joining together of a small number of men, that gives them this security; because in small numbers, small additions on the one side or the other, make the advantage of strength so great, as is sufficient to carry the victory; and therefore gives encouragement to an invasion. The multitude sufficient to confide in for our security, is not determined by any certain number, but by comparison with the enemy we fear; and is then sufficient, when the odds of the enemy is not of so visible and conspicuous moment, to determine the event of war, as to move him to attempt. …

The only way to erect such a common power, as may be able to defend them from the invasion of foreigners, and the injuries of one another, and thereby to secure them in such sort, as that by their own industry, and by the fruits of the earth, they may nourish themselves and live contentedly; is, to confer all their power and strength upon one man, or upon one assembly of men, that may reduce all their wills, by plurality of voices, unto one will: which is as much as to say, to appoint one man, or assembly of men, to bear their person; and every one to own, and acknowledge himself to be author of whatsoever he that so beareth their person, shall act, or cause to be acted, in those things which concern the common peace and safety; and therein to submit their wills, every one to his will, and their judgements, to his judgment. This is more than consent, or concord; it is a real unity of them all, in one and the same person, made by covenant of every man with every man, in such manner, as if every man should say to every man, *I authorize and give up my right of governing myself, to this man, or to this assembly of men, on this condition, that thou give up thy right to him, and authorize all his actions in like manner.* This done, the multitude so united in one person, is called a COMMONWEALTH, in Latin CIVITAS. This is the generation of the great LEVIATHAN, or rather, to speak more reverently, of that *mortal god,* to which we owe under the *immortal God*, our peace and defence. ... And in him consisteth the essence of the commonwealth; which, to define it, is *one person, of whose acts a great multitude, by mutual covenants one with another, have made themselves every one the author, to the end he may use the strength and means of them all, as he shall think expedient, for their peace and common defence.*

And he that carrieth this person is called SOVEREIGN, and said to have *sovereign power;* and every one besides, his SUBJECT.

The attaining to this sovereign power, is by two ways. One, by natural force; as when a man maketh his children, to submit themselves, and their children to his government, as being able to destroy them if they refuse; or by war subdueth his enemies to his will, giving them their lives on that condition. The other, is when men agree amongst themselves, to submit to some man, or assembly of men, voluntarily, on confidence to be protected by him against all others. This latter may be called a political commonwealth, or commonwealth by *institution*; and the former, a commonwealth by *acquisition.*

READING B   THE SOCIAL CONTRACT

Jean-Jacques Rousseau

Man was born free, and he is everywhere in chains. Those who think themselves the masters of others are indeed greater slaves than they. How did this transformation come about? I do not know. How can it be made legitimate? That question I believe I can answer. ... The social order is a sacred right which serves as a basis for all other rights. And as it is not a natural right, it must be one founded on covenants. The problem is to determine what those covenants are. ...

The social pact

I assume that men reach a point where the obstacles to their preservation in a state of nature prove greater than the strength that each man has to preserve himself in that state. Beyond this point, the primitive condition cannot endure, for then the human race will perish if it does not change its mode of existence. ...

'How to find a form of association which will defend the person and goods of each member with the collective force of all, and under which each individual, while uniting himself with the others, obeys no one but himself, and remains as free as before.' This is the fundamental problem to which the social contract holds the solution. ...

Source: Rousseau, J.-J. (1762) *The Social Contract;* reproduced from Held, D. *et al.* (eds) (1983) *States and Societies*, Oxford, Martin Robertson, pp.71–5.

[The] articles of association, rightly understood, are reducible to a single one, namely the total alienation by each associate of himself and all his rights to the whole community. Thus, in the first place, as every individual gives himself absolutely, the conditions are the same for all, and precisely because they are the same for all, it is in no one's interest to make the conditions onerous for others.

Secondly, since the alienation is unconditional, the union is as perfect as it could be, and no individual associate has any longer any rights to claim; for if rights were left to individuals, in the absence of any higher authority to judge between them and the public, each individual, being his own judge in some causes, would soon demand to be his own judge in all; and in this way the state of nature would be kept in being, and the association inevitably become either tyrannical or void.

Finally, since each man gives himself to all, he gives himself to no one; and since there is no associate over whom he does not gain the same rights as others gain over him, each man recovers the equivalent of everything he loses, and in the bargain he acquires more power to preserve what he has.

If, then, we eliminate from the social pact everything that is not essential to it, we find it comes down to this: 'Each one of us puts into the community his person and all his powers under the supreme direction of the general will; and as a body, we incorporate every member as an indivisible part of the whole.'

Immediately, in place of the individual person of each contracting party, this act of association creates an artificial and collective body composed of as many members as there are voters in the assembly, and by this same act that body acquires its unity, its common *ego*, its life and its will. The public person thus formed by the union of all other persons was once called the *city*, and is now known as the *republic* or the *body politic*. In its passive role it is called the *state*, when it plays an active role it is the *sovereign*; and when it is compared to others of its own kind, it is a *power*. Those who are associated in it take collectively the name of a *people*, and call themselves individually *citizens*, in so far as they share in the sovereign power, and *subjects*, in so far as they put themselves under the laws of the state. ...

The sovereign

Now, as the sovereign is formed entirely of the individuals who compose it, it has not, nor could it have, any interest contrary to theirs; and so the sovereign has no need to give guarantees to the subjects, because it is impossible for a body to wish to hurt all of its members, and, as we shall see, it cannot hurt any particular member. The sovereign by the mere fact that it is, is always all that it ought to be. ... Every individual as a man may have a private will contrary to, or different from, the general will that he has as a citizen. His private interest may speak with a very different voice from that of the public interest. ...

Hence, in order that the social pact shall not be an empty formula, it is tacitly implied in the commitment — which alone can give force to all others — that whoever refuses to obey the general will shall be constrained to do so by the whole body, which means nothing other than that he shall be forced to be free; for this is the condition which, by giving each citizen to the nation, secures him against all personal dependence, it is the condition which shapes both the design and the working of the political machine, and which alone bestows justice on civil contracts — without it, such contracts would be absurd, tyrannical and liable to the grossest abuse. ...

Whether the general will can err

The people is never corrupted, but it is often misled; and only then does it seem to will what is bad.

There is often a great difference between the will of all [what all individuals want] and the general will; the general will studies only the common interest while the will of all studies private interest, and is indeed no more than the sum of individual desires. But if we take away from these same wills, the pluses and minuses which cancel each other out, the sum of the difference is the general will. ...

But if groups, sectional associations are formed at the expense of the larger association, the will of each of these groups will become general in relation to its own members and private in relation to the state; we might then say that there are no longer as many votes as there are men but only as many votes as there are groups. The differences become less numerous and yield a result less general. ...

The limits of the sovereign power

How should it be that the general will is always rightful and that all men constantly wish the happiness of each but for the fact that there is no one who does not take that word 'each' to pertain to himself and in voting for all think of himself? This proves that the equality of rights and the notion of justice which it produces derive from the predilection which each man has for himself and hence from human nature as such. It also proves that the general will, to be truly what it is, must be general in its purpose as well as in its nature; that it should spring from all and apply to all; and that it loses its natural rectitude when it is directed towards any particular and circumscribed object — for in judging what is foreign to us, we have no sound principle of equity to guide us. ...

Whichever way we look at it, we always return to the same conclusion: namely that the social pact establishes equality among the citizens in that they all pledge themselves under the same conditions and must all enjoy the same rights. Hence by the nature of the compact, every act of sovereignty, that is, every authentic act of the general will, binds or favours all the citizens equally, so that the sovereign recognizes only the whole body of the nation and makes no distinction between any of the members who compose it. ...

When the people as a whole makes rules for the people as a whole, it is dealing only with itself; and if any relationship emerges, it is between the entire body seen from one perspective and the same entire body seen from another, without any division whatever. Here the matter concerning which a rule is made is as general as the will which makes it. And *this* is the kind of act which I call a law. ...

The public force thus needs its own agent to call it together and put it into action in accordance with the instructions of the general will, to serve also as a means of communication between the state and the sovereign, and in a sense to do for the public person what is done for the individual by the union of soul and body. This is the reason why the state needs a government, something often unhappily confused with the sovereign, but of which it is really only the minister.

What, then, is the government? An intermediary body established between the subjects and the sovereign for their mutual communication, a body charged with the execution of the laws and the maintenance of freedom, both civil and political. ...

Just as the particular will acts unceasingly against the general will, so does the government continually exert itself against the sovereign. And the more this exertion increases, the more the constitution becomes corrupt, and, as in this case there is no distinct corporate will to resist the will of the prince and so to balance it, sooner or later it is inevitable that the prince will oppress the sovereign and break the social treaty. This is the inherent and inescapable defect which, from the birth of the political body, tends relentlessly to destroy it, just as old age and death destroy the body of a man. ...

The principle of political life dwells in the sovereign authority. The legislative power is the heart of the state, the executive power is the brain, which sets all the parts in motion. The brain may become paralysed and the individual still live. A man can be an imbecile and survive, but as soon as his heart stops functioning, the creature is dead.

CHAPTER 3 THE EMERGENCE OF THE ECONOMY

Vivienne Brown

CONTENTS

1   INTRODUCTION: THE ECONOMIC FORMATION OF MODERNITY

The 'economy' as an object of interest is so much a part of our everyday lives and concerns that it is easily taken for granted. Newspaper headlines provide the latest economic forecasts and economic gurus on TV offer a stream of opinions about any and every aspect of economic performance. In this way, economic terms and economic analysis have entered into the daily media coverage of events, and most people have some working understanding of these debates even if the points of economic detail seem arcane.

Though we take this kind of economic debate for granted, it is a 'modern' debate indicative of a 'modern' society. Its comparative modernity may be seen in a number of different ways. First, such a debate takes for granted a certain kind of economy: a modern economy where there is a highly specialized and educated workforce organized to produce a differentiated range of goods for sale on a worldwide market. This presupposes a multinational corporate structure which is itself organized on a global scale, together with a vast network of interlinking financial, marketing, scientific and technological agencies.

Second, such a debate is articulated within a set of economic terms and economic models that derive from a certain way of thinking about the economy; that is, from modern economic theory. Experts in the field of modern economic theory are specialists in the sense that they have undergone a lengthy period of training and are now employed in a range of specialist institutions, such as: universities and polytechnics, governmental and commercial organizations, and international agencies, such as the European Commission and the International Monetary Fund. Although it is these professional economists who develop economic theory and conduct economic research, many of the key terms of the economic debates are understood by a wider and ever more discerning public.

Third, such an ongoing economic debate presupposes not only a literate and informed public audience, but also one which considers that it has the political right to be well-informed about the performance of the economy. This itself presupposes a political context of open democratic debate (whatever the actual restrictions may be in practice), where critical arguments may take place over the conduct of economic policy.

Living and working as we do in the midst of this 'modern economy', it is easy to take it for granted. In this chapter we are going to pause to consider the emergence of the modern economy and ways of thinking about it. In line with other chapters, we shall examine the emergence of the economy as part of the more general emergence and definition of modernity that we now associate with Enlightenment thinking in the eighteenth century. As Chapter 1 showed, the Enlightenment was a period of intense questioning about the nature of society and, inevitably, some of this questioning was also directed towards those parts of society that we would now designate as 'economic', although this term, a modern one, was not used then.

In presenting a series of 'histories' of different aspects of the formation of modern societies, this book is underlining the multifaceted character and complexity of modern societies. This is an important point and one to which this book will frequently return. But these different 'histories' of the emergence of modern society also contribute to another and more fundamental point: that our understanding of modern society is itself closely linked to the kind of 'history' that we tell about it. The notion that there are different 'histories' of modern society as opposed to a single 'history' unsettles any idea that there is only one correct view either of a society or of its history. It also displaces any notion that historical time is a one-dimensional course of events or a single historical process. This means that a historical account of the formation of modernity will uncover discontinuities in the development of modernity as well as a continuous thread of progress, and that understanding any period in history entails looking backwards and sideways, as well as forwards.

By exploring the emergence of the economic formation of modernity, this chapter examines some of these issues. Section 2 compares the contours of the economy in eighteenth-century Britain with those of the modern UK economy of the twentieth century, and discusses the extent to which the rudiments of a modern economy can be discerned in the eighteenth century. Two different historical approaches to this issue are presented, thus providing two different 'histories' — or 'discourses' — of economic change during the period, but the overall conclusion of the section is that recent historical research has underlined the gradual nature of the economic changes taking place in the eighteenth century.

Section 3 investigates what are generally taken to be the origins of modern economic analysis in the eighteenth century. One of the reasons for the fascination of this period for those wishing to acquire an understanding of the development of modern economics is that it is regarded as the century which produced the first systematic treatise on the economy. In 1776, Adam Smith published *An Inquiry into the Nature and Causes of the Wealth of Nations*. Adam Smith is often regarded as the 'father' of economics because he published the first major book on the subject at just that moment in Britain's history when signs of the modern economy seemed to be appearing. Armed with prescient insight and a commitment to objective economic analysis, Adam Smith is thought to have initiated the scientific study of economics and to have heralded the new era of the modern, industrial, profit-seeking economy. Changes in the economy in the eighteenth century are thus thought to be 'mirrored' by corresponding changes in economic thinking, and both processes are seen as providing a clear overture to the later economic developments of the Industrial Revolution and beyond. This interpretation, which many historians and economists have found deeply compelling, is discussed in Section 3.

Just as Section 2 problematizes the notion that the eighteenth century could be understood in terms of later economic developments, Section 4 questions this popular view of Adam Smith as the spokesman for the emerging capitalist market order. It presents recent research on Adam Smith which locates his writings within the broad cultural context of the eighteenth century rather than seeing him as the originator and prophet of later economic developments.

Hence, the chapter concludes that one of the interesting links between the eighteenth century and ours is not so much that the eighteenth century and its thinking signposted modernity but that, looking back into the past, modernity retrospectively reinterprets the past. According to this view, writing 'histories' is also partly a process of constructing a story about society's own origins, and this process involves both self-recognition and self-reconstruction. It is also a process in which the 'classic' books of the past take on a new meaning as they are reinterpreted as signposts of the future order. This concluding account of the economic formation of modernity is presented in Section 5.

2　A MODERN ECONOMY IN THE MAKING?

2.1　A NEW COMMERCIAL SOCIETY IN THE EIGHTEENTH CENTURY?

Looking back, the eighteenth century seems to be the moment when the pace of economic life began to quicken. To those living and writing at that time, it was the age of 'commerce', the apex or culmination of a long period of social development in a country's manners, laws and government, as well as in its productive powers and patterns of consumption. The idea of a commercial society included social as well as economic considerations, with an emphasis on the polite, even polished, character of the manners of the time made possible by what was thought to be a more refined way of life and enlarged cultural horizons.

Differences in wealth and life style, however, were enormous: a great peer might get £10,000 per annum, a prosperous knight £800 per annum, and a poor labourer £10 per annum. But the social ladder was finely graduated along its entire length and so a certain degree of social mobility could take place across adjacent rungs, more so than in other European countries where the class structure was more ossified and the rungs of the ladder were further apart. While Enlightenment thinking may have opened up the intellectual and cultural horizons of the age, life still remained wretched for many. As a correspondent to the *Northampton Mercury* wrote in 1739: 'I never see lace and embroidery upon the back of a beau but my thoughts descend to the poor fingers that have wrought it ... What would avail our large estates and great tracts of land without their labours?' (quoted in Porter, 1990, p.87).

Even so, the increasingly commercial basis of social relations did make possible new standards of consumption for many that would have been inconceivable a generation earlier, even though these standards were not achieved uniformly or for everyone. Population increased, and so did the urban areas. The population of the UK increased from about 9.4 million in 1701 to 10.5 million in 1751, and 16.0 million in 1801, with a marked increase in the proportion living in urban areas. London dominated, but Manchester, Liverpool, Birmingham, Bristol, Leeds, Glasgow, Edinburgh and Dublin were all growth points. Urban growth was accompanied by the development of characteristic Georgian flat-fronted terraced brick houses which introduced a more wholesome and spacious style of living for many. Canals and road improvements opened up the regions to the cultural influences of the metropolis and they also provided vital infrastructure for the burgeoning trade links between the rapidly growing cities. Road travelling times were slashed: the Edinburgh to London journey was reduced from 256 hours in 1700 to 60 hours in 1800, and the journey from Bath to London was reduced from 50 hours to 16 hours over the same period. As in the twentieth century, improved roads led to increased travel, congestion, and moralists decrying the obsession with speed. In 1767, the *London Magazine* reported that: 'There is scarce a cobbler in the counties of York and Lancaster, but must now be conveyed to his cousin german [i.e. his first cousin] in Wapping in two days time' (quoted in Langford, 1989, p.407).

Improved communications meant that people and goods could travel more easily; so too could fashions and trends in consumer taste. The eighteenth century has been identified by some historians as the period of the 'birth of a consumer society' (McKendrick *et al.,* 1982), when social emulation manifested itself in a fast-moving fashion-consciousness in dress and in households goods. Although some manufacturers were careful to cultivate the patronage of royalty and the aristocracy in order to promote the fashionable credentials of their wares, the consumer markets thus developed were essentially popular rather than socially exclusive. Reading A is an account by Roy Porter of English society at this time. It describes how the growth of shops and advertising in newspapers enabled the new fashions to be quickly transmitted from London to the provinces, thus contributing to the first national market in clothing and household goods.

ACTIVITY 1   You should now read **Reading A, 'The birth of consumerism'**, by Roy Porter (which you will find at the end of this chapter).

In this extract Porter points to the development of a national market and the importance of the growth in advertising. Porter mentions the increased availability of home furnishings — hangings, blankets and rugs, together with mirrors and dinner services as well as fashion clothes. The eighteenth century was the age when Josiah Wedgwood commercialized the potteries and made expensive dinner and tea services which were eagerly sought after by the rich and fashionable; it was the age when Chippendale, Hepplewhite and Sheraton established new designs for elegant furniture; and it was the age of Georgian silver cutlery, buckles, buttons, new fabrics, high wigs, new breeds of animals, and new species of plants. Porter also refers here to a general paraphernalia of 'knick-knacks' and 'curios' which were bought on whim and appealed to a newly developing sense of novelty. Note too the development of retailing, with its alluring presentation of goods, and the power of advertising in stimulating a demand for the new products of the day. London acquired a reputation as the most dazzling shopping opportunity in all Europe, with its paved and well-lit shopping streets where even the most obdurate would be unable to resist the enticement of gorgeous displays presented in glass-fronted shop windows. Reading this description of eighteenth-century advertising and retailing, it comes as no surprise to recognize why many twentieth-century shopping malls and 'boutiques' are neo-Georgian in style, with bow windows and reproduction decors. Even the commercialization of commemorative mugs and handkerchiefs adorned with the symbols of national events have sound historical precedents!

Porter's account provides a telling insight into some of the changes taking place in eighteenth-century society, changes which were apparent to observers at the time and which were widely commented upon. These changes were also noted by visitors to Britain, who compared it in favourable terms with other European countries. Ordinary folk seemed to be better dressed, better fed and better housed than the native peasantry in other countries or, at least, in the words of one American traveller, 'the poor do not look so poor here as in other countries' (quoted in Porter, 1990, p.86). Ordinary folk seemed cleaner too; in the 1720s a visitor remarked: 'English women and men are very clean; not a day passes by without their washing their hands, arms, faces, necks and throats in cold water, and that in winter as well as in summer' (*ibid.*, p.221). As a mid-century commentator from Nottingham observed, imported goods such as tea, coffee, chocolate and sugar were no longer regarded as expensive luxuries reserved for the few but had entered the national diet: ' ... not only Gentry and Wealthy Travellers drink it constantly, but almost every Seamer, Sizer and Winder will have her Tea in a morning ... and even a common Washer woman thinks she has not had a proper Breakfast without Tea and hot buttered White Bread!' (*ibid.*, p.218). Entertainment, music and theatre were also becoming commercialized and available to a growing ticket-buying audience, and this brought with it a large increase in the number of pleasure gardens, pubs, coffee houses, theatres and concerts. In the middle of the century, for example, in 1749, 12,000 people paid 2s. 6d. each to hear Handel's *Fireworks Music* at Vauxhall in London, and in the last decade of the century when Hayden visited London, the concert halls were packed with enthusiastic and musically literate audiences.

This description of eighteenth-century English social life is an optimistic one, in which a more refined and comfortable way of life is

1784, or the Fashions of the Day, by Thomas Rowlandson: In a fashion-conscious society, personal dress and adornment achieved a new significance; wigs and headgear completed the outfit ...

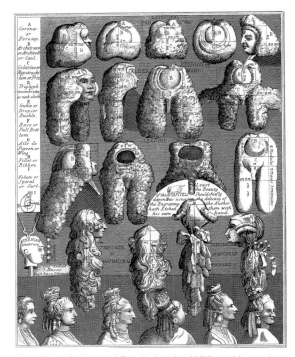

The Five Orders of Perriwigs, by William Hogarth

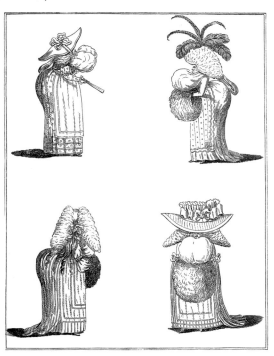

Such things are: that such things are we must allow but such things never were till now

seen to be spreading right down the social scale. Such accounts also have a directly modern ring to them; it seems easy to bridge the historical gap of 200 years or so by imagining those eighteenth-century folk on their shopping sprees, lounging in the newly-opened pleasure gardens, or doing some home improvements on the side. Porter's account is written in a very engaging style too; this isn't the formal history of kings and queens and high diplomatic manoeuvres, but the everyday history of ordinary folk — folk like us — going about their lives. Thus, the style that Porter uses to recount an engaging story about the new consumerism of the eighteenth century contributes to our sense that this early consumerism was not so unlike the consumerism of the 1980s and 1990s with which we are familiar.

Porter's account of eighteenth-century consumer society, and the informal style in which it is written, both contribute towards painting a distinctly 'modern' picture of the eighteenth century, and it is easy to conclude that the eighteenth century really did contain an embryonic version of the modern consumer economy of today which has developed directly from it. But this style of social history is itself new. This account of the eighteenth century reflects a relatively recent interest in the everyday facets of social history, and the wealth of detail that makes Porter's descriptions so fascinating is often culled from relatively new research. What this means is that his own project in writing this kind of social history, fascinating and scholarly though it is, is itself part of a relatively new trend in writing history. Porter's interest in the consumer activities of the eighteenth century is also partly the result of a recent trend in writing social history that attempts to counter what is seen as an excessive emphasis on the production aspects of the Industrial Revolution; in this approach, the 'consumer revolution' is seen as an essential precursor of the better publicized 'Industrial Revolution'.

But recent scholarly interest in the new consumer activities of the eighteenth century may also be seen partly as the result of the consumer orientations of the latter part of the twentieth century. Thus, interest in the consumer society of the late twentieth century has to some degree stimulated a lot of fine research on similar tendencies in eighteenth-century society. This contributes to our sense that the eighteenth century contained the seeds of modern society, but we must remember that it was modern society that itself produced the detailed research that made such a historical understanding possible. And furthermore, as you will discover in other books in this series, the consumer orientations and ideologies of late twentieth-century society are often taken as symptomatic of a *post-modern* social order, and sociological analyses of these are often denominated as 'post-modern' analyses. Thus, there is a sense in which Porter's account of eighteenth-century consumerism not only pulls that period into line with modernity, but even propels it beyond that and into line with current trends identified with post-modernity.

Porter's social history relies on anecdotal and literary evidence from a wide range of sources: from letters, journals, foreign visitors' accounts, newspapers, and private papers. Very often economic historians attempt to provide a quantitative estimate of the changes that were taking place. By collecting statistical evidence they try to answer questions such as: by how much were standards of living increasing over the period?; were trade and commerce expanding at a greater rate than agriculture during this period? The attraction of this kind of research is its generality and its precision; for example, if national output is increasing at 3 per cent per year and population at 1 per cent per year, then the society is able to support a rising population with an approximate 2 per cent annual increase in the standard of living. The great difficulty with this approach is that the statistics become increasingly unreliable as they are projected further back in time. The margin of error may then become so wide as to make the conclusion unreliable. If, in the above example, both statistics are subject to an error of 0.5 in either direction, then the result is that output increases by between 2.5 and 3.5 per cent while population increases by 0.5 to 1.5 per cent. In this case the average standard of living will be increasing by somewhere between 1 per cent and 3 per cent per annum approximately, a much less precise result. Here at least, in this example, the margin of error is known. A greater source of difficulty with historical statistics is that the degree of unreliability may also be subject only to informed guesswork.

In spite of these difficulties, research on the quantitative dimensions of the eighteenth century provides another way of understanding the changes taking place; it may not tell us what an individual family had for breakfast but it may indicate whether living standards were improving on average. This kind of historical research poses questions that are quantitative in nature and which require detailed statistical analysis in order to provide answers. Table 3.1 (from an article by the economic historian R. V. Jackson) shows the annual growth rates over two periods during the eighteenth century: from 1700–60 and from 1760–1800. The first row shows the annual percentage increase in real output, the second shows the annual percentage increase in population, and the third shows the annual percentage increase in output per head of population.

Table 3.1   Annual growth rates of output, population, and output per head in eighteenth-century Britain

	1700–60	1760–1800
	(per cent per annum)	
Output	0.58–0.60	1.04–1.20
Population	0.38	0.83
Output/head	0.20–0.22	0.21–0.37

Source: Jackson, 1990, pp.219, 225

The table suggests that output increased by between 0.58 and 0.60 per cent each year on average in the early period, and that this rate of growth increased to between 1.04 and 1.20 per cent each year on average in the later period. Taking account of population growth during the period, this means that real output per person grew at an average annual rate of between 0.20 and 0.22 per cent in the early period and between 0.21 and 0.37 per cent in the later period. Although highly tentative, these figures suggest that the rising output over the eighteenth century did enable a growing population to live at a rising standard of living, a standard which increased at a somewhat higher rate in the latter part of the century; but note how small these increases are. This suggests that the optimistic picture painted by Porter's account should perhaps be tempered a little by the realization that, although increased consumption was available for many members of a rising population, on average the rate of improvement was slow.

But to say that the rate of improvement was slow suggests a standard of comparison of some sort. What is the implicit standard of comparison that is being used in the previous paragraph? Compared with improvements in living standards in the seventeenth century, the figures in Table 3.1 may look substantial. For those living and writing during the eighteenth century, the point of comparison would have been either backwards to an earlier period, or sideways to other countries at the same period. And clearly, from Porter's account, many contemporary observers did find the changes remarkable. But if we are comparing the eighteenth with the twentieth century, then these figures do look small. Table 3.2 provides a modern point of comparison by presenting data for the UK, West Germany (as it then was), France, the USA, and Japan.

Table 3.2 Annual rates of growth of gross domestic product per head of total population, 1983–88

	1983–88 (per cent per annum)
UK	3.4
W. Germany	2.5
France	1.7
USA	3.4
Japan	3.8

Source: *Basic Statistics of the Community*, 1990, 27th edn, p.40, Eurostat, Luxembourg

The statistics in Table 3.2 were compiled on a different basis from those in Table 3.1 and so they are not directly comparable, but they are clearly of a different order of magnitude from those in Table 3.1. The range of figures is from 1.7 per cent for France to 3.8 per cent for Japan, with a UK figure of 3.4 per cent. The figure for the UK looks so good because the middle period of the 1980s was a period of rapid growth in the UK; if either the early or the late years of the decade had been included the figure would have been lower. None the less, this annual figure of 3.4 per cent for the mid-1980s is about fourteen times as great as the average figure for the eighteenth century in Table 3.1. Thus we can say that the annual increases in output during the eighteenth century were small by present-day standards, but they were significant and observable to many of those living in the eighteenth century.

The quantitative results shown in Table 3.1 may look firm and definite, giving us a clear bird's-eye view of the long term trajectory of economic change in the eighteenth century. For this reason they may appear more secure than the portrayal of contemporary life in Porter's account, especially in view of the realization that Porter's description is partly the result of modern research in social history and a recent interest in the consumer aspects of society. But Jackson's data in Table 3.1 are also representative of a relatively new style of economic history, known as 'cliometrics', where the statistical techniques and modelling methods of modern economic theory are applied to the past. So in Jackson's case, too, the insights provided into the course of economic development in the eighteenth century are the product of modern ways of analysing the economy. Thus, the statistics presented in Table 3.1 are the product of recent research, and reflect the belief of many economic historians that the rate of economic growth during the eighteenth century was lower than had previously been thought (see also Crafts, 1985). This new conventional wisdom suggests that there was a smaller increase in output over the course of the century, but that there was a smoother trend over the century as a whole; in particular, this implies that earlier views of the 1780s and 1790s, as marking a dramatic turning point in economic development and as heralding the onset of the 'Industrial Revolution', now seem to be an exaggeration. According to the new estimates, the Industrial Revolution took place in the nineteenth century rather than the late eighteenth century, and even then it was a more gradual and piecemeal affair than had previously been thought.

Furthermore, in the article from which these statistics were taken, Jackson goes on to present revised estimates that challenge even these more circumscribed views on the eighteenth-century pattern of economic change. Jackson argues in this article that inclusion of government activities seriously distorts the national output figures for purely statistical reasons; when government activities are excluded to provide an estimate of the growth of *private* sector output growth per head, the rate of growth of output per head falls *below* the level reported in Table 3.1. Jackson estimates that, on this revised basis, output growth per head was about 0.13 per cent per annum during the 1700–60 period and 0.19 per cent per annum from 1760–1800, but the article reiterates the important point that all these estimates must be regarded as highly approximate and that they are all subject to a very wide margin of error. As other economic historians readily agree, these economic statistics represent hypotheses for future research rather than final judgments about what actually happened.

2.2   DISCOURSES ON THE ECONOMY

Just as Porter's description of eighteenth-century consumerism is a 'modern' account of the eighteenth century, so are economic statistics such as those presented by Jackson. Both approaches to describing the eighteenth century are the product of modern intensive research by specialist professional historians using up-to-date resources and methods. And both accounts will surely need to be amended in the future as new historians construct new ways of formulating evidence and arguments from the archives. Thus, as more knowledge is produced about the eighteenth century, we can see how that knowledge is itself a product of modern society and would not have been available without the priorities, attitudes, perspectives, theories and research techniques that are themselves a product of modern society.

This underlines a more general point that knowledge about the eighteenth century does not exist in a pure or absolute form, just waiting for historians to come and record it. Knowledge about the period, about any period (including our own), has to be 'produced' and this process of reseach production necessarily takes place within the context of modern academic life. This means that the research produced will bear the marks of modern academic conventions concerning standards of scholarship, the questions which are deemed worthy of further investigation, and the institutional bases for funding research projects.

Further, as we have seen, each of these histories of the eighteenth-century offers its own insights into the social and economic processes of the time: the account of eighteenth-century consumerism offers us insights into early acquisitiveness and social emulation as structured by the commercialization of fashion; the account of national economic performance offers us insights into economic growth conceived as an aggregate or economy-wide process. Whichever approach we take, our insights are both opened up and closed off by the characteristics of that account itself.

Thus, we could say that our knowledge of the economy or of society is constituted by a series of 'discourses' on these topics, discourses which structure our thinking and predispose us towards specific asssumptions and specific forms of enquiry. Note too that this notion of 'discourse' is also comparatively recent, but it is one that is increasingly being adopted in a number of different areas in social analysis, and you will meet it again in later chapters of this book.

2.3 STRUCTURAL CHANGE IN THE EIGHTEENTH CENTURY

In trying to assess the extent to which an economy is becoming 'modernized', many economists and economic historians also look at changes in the structure of output; here they try to assess the relative importance of agriculture and industry as sources of employment and final output. It is generally thought that a 'pre-modern' economy is one where agriculture is more important than industry, whereas a 'modern' economy is one where industry is more important than agriculture. This is a very rough and ready rule of thumb as different economies develop according to their own particular characteristics, but it can prove a useful starting point.

If an increasing population was experiencing an increasing standard of living in the eighteenth century, where was this increased output coming from? In Reading B, a second extract by Roy Porter, you will find a brief summary of some of the sources of increased industrial output.

ACTIVITY 2   Now read **Reading B, 'Pre-modern manufacturing'**, by Roy Porter, and make brief notes on the main sources of increased output during the eighteenth century.

One of the remarkable features about the increased economic activity right up until the later part of the eighteenth century is that it was not based on major changes in technology nor on the reorganization of the workforce into factories, the features of change which characterized the Industrial Revolution of the nineteenth century. Change as Porter describes it here was on the whole small-scale and piecemeal; industry was labour-intensive and skill-intensive and was largely based on the work-unit of the household. This system economized on capital by operating on a low capital–output basis, and it was flexible in the face of unforeseeable changes in demand. With the opening up of both the domestic market and the international market, economies of scale were gradually incorporated and a host of minor improvements were made possible; in particular, the development of the canals and the turnpike system represented a considerable investment in transport which reduced transport costs and facilitated regional specialization. But industrial giants were the exception rather than the rule, and often these were linked (as is still the case) with large government defence contracts. This was to change somewhat later on, especially during the 1780s and beyond when the Lancashire cotton industry expanded as a result of the technical developments in spinning and weaving, and cotton became the single most important industry in Britain. Later on, in the nineteenth century, factory production and a factory workforce became more significant as features of industrial production but, even at this later stage, change was piecemeal and most workers were still craft workers rather than factory operatives tending the machinery of the new technology. Certainly during the eighteenth century, production remained labour-intensive and was based largely on the household and the small workshop. The main industries in the eighteenth century were the traditional ones of wool, leather and building, although by the end of the century cotton had caught up. The goods produced were mainly items intended for personal consumption; items such as textiles and clothing, leather goods and pottery, pots and pans, and the products of the Birmingham 'toy' trade such as buttons, buckles, jewellery, and a wide range of trinkets and novelties.

An iron works, Coalbrookdale, Shropshire, 1788.
Smoke from the stacks, but the scale is still near human-size.

An Iron Forge, by Joseph Wright of Derby, 1772: a family setting.
An artist's representation of a 'model' iron-founder with a water-driven tilt-hammer
to save effort in the swing of the hammer. Fashion makes its presence felt here too.

Again, Porter's account focuses in on the kaleidoscopic details of change. If we want to get an overall picture of structural shifts in the economy, say between agriculture and manufacturing, we need to take a quantitative approach. In an economy such as the one reported by Porter, we would not expect the annual increases in industrial output to be very large, nor perhaps would we expect those increases to be much greater than for agricultural output, and this is the picture that the statistics endorse. Table 3.3 shows the growth rates for different sectors for the same periods that were shown in Table 3.1.

Table 3.3   Annual growth rates for different sectors in eighteenth-century Britain (excluding government)

	1700–60	1760–1800
	(per cent per annum)	
Agriculture	0.47	0.43
Industry	0.71	1.81
Commerce	0.51	1.02
Services	0.38	0.83
Total private output	0.51	1.02
Output per head	0.13	0.19

Source: Jackson, 1990, p.232

Table 3.3 suggests that it was only in the later period that the performance of the different sectors began to diverge markedly. Although lagging behind industry and commerce, agriculture was growing at just under 0.5 per cent per year in the early period. This improved agricultural efficiency had its origins in the previous century; it resulted from improved husbandry and stock breeding, a more commercial approach to agricultural organization, and a keen interest in applying scientific techniques to agriculture. But in the later period agricultural growth was clearly overtaken by industrial and commercial growth, each of which exceeded one per cent per year; here the front runner is clearly industry with an annual growth rate of about 1.81 per cent.

The significance of these changes can also be seen in terms of the structure of output during the course of the eighteenth century. The statistics so far suggest an economy that was still marked by traditional features, with a small and unmodernized manufacturing sector, a large agricultural sector, and a large domestic service sector. It is difficult to be precise about the division of employment across these sectors, as much employment combined elements of more than one sector; for example, where the family was the unit of production, the domestic servant often performed the work of the agricultural labourer as well as of the tradesman's assistant. Table 3.4 shows estimates of the proportion of national output accounted for by the agricultural sector and the industrial/commercial sector for the years 1700, 1760 and 1800.

Table 3.4   Proportion of national output produced by the agricultural and industrial/commercial sectors in the eighteenth century (England and Wales)

	1700 %	1760 %	1800 %
Agriculture	40	34	35
Industry/commerce	33	37	40
All other sectors (including government, domestic services and rent)	27	29	25
Total	100	100	100

Source: Cole, 1981, p.64

Even keeping in mind the reservations about the reliability of these statistics, this table clearly shows how agriculture and industry/commerce switched over in importance during the course of the eighteenth century. In the early part of the century, agricultural output was pre-eminent; it accounted for about 40 per cent of national output, whereas industry and commerce together accounted for about a third. By the end of the century the position was reversed, with agriculture contributing about a third of the national product and industry/commerce contributing about 40 per cent. Thus, Table 3.4 illustrates the transformation that took place in the course of the eighteenth century. At the beginning of the period the economy was very largely an agricultural one, although this does not mean that it was stagnant. But by the end of the period the agricultural sector contributed a smaller share of total output than industry/commerce, and its rate of growth also fell way behind that of the industrial sector.

As the nineteeth century progressed these trends became even more marked. By the end of the nineteenth century the agricultural share fell below 10 per cent, and the combined share of industry and commerce amounted to something like two-thirds of national output. This is typical of the proportionate contribution of agriculture, industry and commerce that has often been thought to characterize the 'modern' economy; most of its employment and output derive from industry and commerce, which are increasingly organized on an international basis. This has been the pattern for economies such as the UK, the USA and many other advanced industrial capitalist societies, at least until the middle of the twentieth century, and it has provided a model for what is often denoted as a 'modern' economy. Since that time, however, the size of the industrial sector in many countries has shrunk and that of the service sector has grown considerably. Table 3.5 shows the relevant data for the UK, West Germany as it then was, France, the USA, and Japan for 1987, the most recent year available.

Table 3.5 shows that the movement towards a larger service sector and a smaller industrial sector can be discerned in all the countries shown. This change has led to discussions about the 'deindustrialization' of the

Table 3.5   Composition of output in the UK, W. Germany, France, the USA, and Japan, 1987

	UK %	W. Germany %	France %	USA %	Japan %
Agriculture	1.2	1.5	3.7	1.9	2.7
Industry	36.7	40.3	31.5	28.5	39.0
Services	62.1	58.2	64.8	69.6	58.3
Total	100.0	100.0	100.0	100.0	100.0

Source: *Basic Statistics of the Commumity*, 1990, p.41, 27th edn, Eurostat, Luxembourg

advanced capitalist countries where the manufacturing sectors fail to compete with the low-wage, newly industrializing countries of South East Asia. This change has focused attention on new ways of organizing the industrial sector, with a renewed emphasis on flexibility and technological innovation. It has also led to discussions of a 'post-industrial' society, thought to be structurally and culturally distinct from the 'modern' or 'industrial' society which characterized the UK for the century and a half or so from the beginning of the Industrial Revolution. It is sometimes argued that this process of 'de-industrialization' is a disease peculiar to the UK, but note that Table 3.5 shows that the UK comes midway in terms of the relative sizes of the industrial and service sectors; West Germany and Japan both have larger industrial sectors and smaller service sectors than the UK, while France and the USA have smaller industrial sectors and larger service sectors.

So far these tables of statistics have painted a broad picture of the changing relative importance of agriculture and industry/commerce. In Table 3.4, the figures for industry and commerce were combined into a single sector, but to many eighteenth-century observers it was 'commerce' itself that seemed to provide the great impetus to growth. The acute contemporary observer Arthur Young estimated that commerce amounted to about 13 per cent of the national product in 1770 (leaving about 24 per cent for manufacture, mining and building) (Deane and Cole, 1967, p.156), but even by his time commerce was almost as much an international affair as a domestic one. During the course of the eighteenth century, exports increased more than fourfold, far faster than domestic output. International commerce was accompanied by an active colonial policy and a considerable amount of protective legislation intended to promote domestic interests:

> Commerce in an international setting was an acutely competitive affair, in which the full power of the States competing was exerted to strengthen the national economy. The struggle for raw materials and tropical commodities, as well as for markets and the carrying trade which served them, was central to international relations ... Every war during this period was in essence a commercial war ... (Langford, 1989, p.3)

Britain had for many years encouraged trade with old allies such as Portugal and Holland, and discouraged trade with old enemies such as France and Spain. This resulted in a complicated system of import tariffs to discourage imports (especially of what were seen as 'luxury' items), export bounties to promote exports, and colonial monopolies to encourage a favourable balance of colonial trade with the mother country. It meant that the British gentry got drunk on port (from Portugal) rather than on claret (from France), that aspiring ladies wore protected home-produced silk rather than French silk, and that colonial products such as tea and sugar became mainstays of the national diet as we saw earlier.

Thus, the state was seen to have an active role in maintaining British interests abroad. In normal years the expenditure of the state amounted to about 5 per cent of total national expenditure, but in extraordinary years associated with wartime, this could increase to 10–14 per cent of national expenditure. In spite of the active role of the state in pursuing international interests, the preference of the times was generally for fewer state restrictions at home, although this did not stop cartels from forming when the producers thought it was in their own interest.

2.4 CONCLUSION

This section has provided a broad view of the developing economy in the eighteenth century and has compared some of its structural characteristics with those of modern economies of the twentieth century. But in building up this picture we found that the canvas itself seemed to change shape depending on how it was being painted by the modern historians; we could say that different 'discourses' on the eighteenth century seemed to project us into different eighteenth-century worlds. The discourse on nascent consumerism in the eighteenth century seemed to provide a direct forerunner of twentieth-century consumerism, and here we could see the seeds of modernity, or even post-modernity itself. Porter's account of industrial activity, however, seemed to betoken an economy that was largely pre-modern, with its cottage industries and the absence of large-scale factory production. The cliometric discourse presented another view; here the quirks and details of the period were smoothed over to provide simple statistics for the aggregate economy over long historical periods.

The eighteenth century also seemed to become a less unified economic entity as we looked at it more closely, rather like an impressionist painting when studied close at hand. Agriculture was predominant in the early part of the century but it was gradually superseded by industry and commerce as the century progressed. Though the entire century became increasingly active in an economic sense, it was not until the later period that industrial output seemed to achieve a momentum of its own, but even here the introduction of new technology was slow and uneven. Descriptions of dramatic turning points in the 1780s which characterized earlier research seem now to have exaggerated the position, and current historical research is more inclined to emphasize that the acceleration in growth was a gradual affair, both for the eighteenth and the nineteenth centuries. Production was still largely organized on a household basis and this was only partially displaced by the factory system as the new century replaced the old.

An emphasis on the slow and piecemeal nature of the economic changes taking place is, however, still consistent with a recognition of the structural changes that were taking place in the eighteenth century as agriculture slowly became eclipsed by industry and commerce, a process of change that seemed to be more or less complete by the late nineteenth century. This structure then provided something of a model for modern industrial society, in spite of the variation across individual economies, but this pattern of output itself proved to be a historically transient form for advanced economies such as the UK. The passage of the twentieth century in its turn has shown that the sectoral composition of output is not a final or predetermined issue; as the industrial sector declines in importance and the service sector becomes a new source of dynamism and technological innovation, a new debate has emerged about the structural features of what has come to be known as 'post-industrial' society.

3   THE BEGINNINGS OF MODERN ECONOMICS

3.1   ADAM SMITH

One of the most famous books of the eighteenth century is Adam Smith's *An Inquiry into the Nature and Causes of the Wealth of Nations.* This was not Adam Smith's first book although it is the book for which he is now largely remembered. In 1759, when still working as a professor of moral philosophy at the University of Glasgow, Smith published *The Theory of Moral Sentiments,* and it was this book that establised his reputation as a major thinker and philosopher. On the basis of the reputation thus secured, Smith resigned his university appointment in 1764 to travel to France and Switzerland as tutor to a young Scottish nobleman, the Duke of Buccleuch. The strength of Smith's reputation was such that he was warmly received by the French *philosophes* and enjoyed the friendship and intellectual activities of the Parisian salons of the time. After returning from his travels, Smith received a generous pension and this enabled him to spend some considerable time working on *The Wealth of Nations* which was eventually published in 1776, the year in which the North American colonies achieved their independence.

Adam Smith (1723–90)

Writing on the eve of the Industrial Revolution, the celebrated Scottish professor who had been welcomed into the élite philosophical circles of France has seemed to epitomize the new, enlightened ways of thinking about the economy. In his account of the social history of the eighteenth century, Porter refers to Adam Smith as 'that high priest of capitalism' (1990, p.87), and an authority on Adam Smith writes that: 'The *Wealth of Nations* was adopted as the ideology of early liberal capitalism and its popularity may have been due as much to the way in which it accorded with the economic and political prejudices of the emergent bourgeoisie as to its intrinsic merits as a scholarly work' (Campbell, 1971, p.15). Thus, many commentators have read Smith's *The Wealth of Nations* as a prescient anticipation of the capitalist economy; it has seemed to be a book that extolled the benefits of the unregulated, profit-seeking market economy at a time when commercial market relations were becoming increasingly significant.

According to this view of *The Wealth of Nations*, its centrepiece is the analysis of the 'invisible hand', the mechanism by which the economic activities of profit-seeking individuals result in the greatest economic good for society as a whole. As Smith wrote of the profit-seeking individual: ' ... by directing that industry in such a manner as its produce may be of the greatest value, he intends only his own gain, and he is in this, as in many other cases, led by an invisible hand to promote an end which was no part of his intention' (Smith, 1976b, p.456). Although each individual is intending his own gain, it is argued that the overall effect is the promotion of the interest of society as a whole. Here is thought to lie the central core of the message of *The Wealth of Nations*: that there exists a fundamental harmony of interests between the activities of profit-seeking individuals and the general good of society as a whole. The remainder of this section will examine three aspects of the writings of Adam Smith that have achieved prominence as integral parts of this vision of the invisible hand: the competitive market (Section 3.2); the division of labour (Section 3.3); and the pursuit of self-interest (Section 3.4). This section will also consider very briefly how economics developed after Adam Smith (Section 3.5)

3.2 THE OPERATION OF THE FREE MARKET ECONOMY

By emphasizing the importance of profit-seeking and self-interest, Smith is thought to have been arguing in favour of free trade and against state involvement in the economy. The market mechanism works by allocating goods and resources by the free interplay of demand and supply, and so goods are produced only if they are thought to be profitable. In this situation, it is both unnecessary and inefficient for the state to take an active economic role. Smith's analysis of competitive markets and the formation of 'market price' has seemed to later economists to represent a high point in analytical precision. This analysis provides the core of Smith's 'allocation analysis', showing how resources in a capitalist economy are allocated by the operation of the price mechanism.

These points are illustrated in the passage from *The Wealth of Nations* reproduced as Reading C.

ACTIVITY 3   You should now read **Reading C, 'The market'**, from *The Wealth of Nations* by Adam Smith.

In this passage Smith is showing how the competitive market price is responsive to the difference between demand and supply. If demand is greater than supply, then the market price will increase, and if demand is less than supply then market price falls. In the longer term, the outcome is that the market price will eventually settle down at the level of the natural price; that is, at the level of costs of production, even though short-term shortages and surpluses will push the market price either above it or below it.

The influence of this competitive market analysis has been immensely far-reaching. The notion of the invisible hand at work in the competitive market came to form a powerful basis for the nineteenth-century argument in favour of *laissez-faire,* the admonition that government should 'leave well alone'. According to this view, the capitalist competitive market harnesses the natural self-interest of every individual person in such a way that the well-being of the society as a whole is promoted. If individuals are left alone to pursue their own profit, so the argument goes, the resulting outcome will be the most beneficial one.

The economic implication of this argument in favour of *laissez-faire* capitalism coincided with the obvious political inference to be made. As the competitive market, untrammelled by burdensome restrictions, would promote both individual prosperity and national prosperity, the state would be absolved from any duty of directing the economic affairs of private individuals, and would provide only the basic infrastructure of legal order, protection of private property — the linchpin of the system — and external defence. It was accepted that there would need to be some state provision of those items that could not be secured satisfactorily through the market. These items are sometimes known as public goods — goods such as education, transport and health services. Vital though these goods are, they are not supplied in sufficient quantity to all who need them when they are left to the free market, and so most modern economies have designed alternative methods of provision involving the state or other community-based organizations. Furthermore, the political liberties associated with the individual citizen were now seen to be part and parcel of a wider set of liberties connected with the use of private property and participation in competitive markets. This view seemed in many ways also to be a direct descendant of the writings of John Locke, according to which certain liberties and rights in the use of private property were 'natural' rights that every person had and which could not without injustice be encroached upon by the state.

The consequences of this view of the 'economy' as a self-regulating mechanism operating independently of the state were crucial for the future development of economic theory. Earlier concepts of the economy as an aspect of the political power of the state implied that the directing hand of the statesman was essential to the economic well-being of the state, but Smith's concept of the invisible hand seemed to make the statesman almost redundant in an economic sense. In the earlier writings of mercantilism, the statesman had performed vital functions for the economy, controlling its direction and securing a favourable balance of trade. Similarly, earlier paternalist concepts of the moral obligation of the state in ensuring a plentiful supply of provisions to the populace also seemed to become outmoded in the face of this new reliance on market provision. The new view of the competitive market as economic regulator meant that economic activities could be conceptualized independently of the role of the government in a way that had not been possible before *The Wealth of Nations*. A new understanding of the economy was thus being developed, one that enabled the 'economy' to be regarded as a separate domain or area of social life that was largely distinct from the political power and moral duties of the state.

As the process of industrialization gathered momentum in the nineteenth century, and as social and economic change became more pronounced, the issue of the role of the state became more pressing. The new analysis of the economy deriving from this reading of *The Wealth of Nations* was one that placed the state largely outside the main sphere of economic operations, and this had enormous repercussions for the actual role of the state during that time of social upheaval. It is arguable that the state was always more actively involved in the nineteenth-century economy than the official opinion of the times either sought or recognized, but the prevailing views about the limited economic role of the government did have a far-reaching effect on British public opinion. It is for this reason that Campbell could argue, as we have seen, that the influence of *The Wealth of Nations* resulted not only from its intrinsic merits as a scholarly work but also from its popularity as the 'ideology of early liberal capitalism'. And these political effects are still providing powerful reverberations in the last decades of the twentieth century, when a number of governments in both Eastern and Western Europe have been involved in a series of disengagements from their national economies. In the UK, the Conservative governments from 1979 initiated a series of moves intended to reduce government involvement in and responsibility for the overall economic performance of the country.

3.3   THE DIVISION OF LABOUR

Another area in which *The Wealth of Nations* has seemed to have its finger firmly on the pulse of the future is that concerning the economic advantages deriving from the 'division of labour'. Smith argues that the division of labour had made possible an enormous increase in the productivity of labour in what he terms 'opulent' countries. There are two aspects to this division of labour. First, there is the division of labour between different trades. Second, there is the division of labour within the manufacture of a single good; here Smith provides the example of pin-making, where the operation has been divided into as many as eighteen separate activities. The second extract from *The Wealth of Nations* (Reading D) is a very famous one which provides an account of the division of labour.

ACTIVITY 4   Now read **Reading D, 'The division of labour'**, by Adam Smith, which has been taken from the opening chapters of *The Wealth of Nations*.

As you read, make brief notes on what Smith has to say on:

1   the particular factors causing the increased output resulting from the division of labour;

2   the range and quality of the goods available to ordinary working people;

3   the factors which determine the extent to which the division of labour may actually be carried out.

1   In this extract Smith argues that the greatest improvements in the productive powers of labour have been the result of the division of labour, and he spends some time describing how this occurs in a trifling manufacture such as pin-making. He refers to the eighteen or so distinct operations involved, and argues that the division of labour increases a man's output from between one and twenty pins a day to about 4,800 pins a day. Smith gives the particular factors that cause this increased output as: the increased dexterity arising from the repetition of simple tasks; the saving of time lost in passing from one task to another; and the invention of specialized machines which this close division of work is thought to encourage.

2   The effect of this division of labour for the range and quality of goods is startling, and brings to mind Roy Porter's description of the shopping possibilities that developed during the eighteenth century. A consequence of this worldwide division of labour is that even a 'common artificer or day-labourer in a civilised and thriving country' has access to a wide range of commodities that represent the labour inputs of many thousands of other workers. Thus, even an ordinary workman takes for granted the extensive worldwide division of labour involved in providing his basic articles of consumption. The result of this division of labour for the workman's overall standard of living, Smith argues, is that, though the difference between his lifestyle and that of the rich in his own country might seem great, it is probably less than the difference between his own material standards and those of an 'African king, the absolute master of the lives and liberties of ten thousand naked savages'. Smith's acceptance of the cultural determinants of this comparison with an 'African king' points to the wide interest of the time in the experiences of other societies, something which will be explored critically in Chapter 6; the point to notice here is that Smith argues that even the humble day-labourer is the unknowing beneficiary of a worldwide division of labour.

3   The extent to which this division of labour can actually be carried out in any society depends on the extent of the market. A porter, for example, cannot find sufficient employment in a village, and in lone houses and small villages every farmer must also be butcher, baker and brewer to his own family. In Chapter 3 of *The Wealth of Nations*, from which the last two paragraphs of Reading D are taken, Smith goes on to recognize the productive possibilities opening up in the move towards larger urban centres and the improved transport and communications that were illustrated in Section 2 above. Smith's argument also provides powerful ammunition for the opening up of markets on both a regional and international level as, the larger the market, the greater are the possibilities for an increased division of labour and further improvements in productivity.

The two extracts from *The Wealth of Nations* in Readings C and D thus suggest a view of Smith's writings as endorsing the new market-orientated commerce of his own day and also presaging the later events of the Industrial Revolution. The passages on the competitive market take it for granted that any person will use his own property to his own individual advantage; in this Smith was very much following the general approach of the eighteenth century, which placed considerable importance on the right to use one's own property. Indeed, for Smith one of the social benefits of a commercial society was that the monetized relations replacing the older relations of servitude and dependence were conducive to greater liberty for all, including the lower ranks of society; but note that this independence was based on a generalized self-interest.

3.4   SELF-INTEREST

In *The Wealth of Nations* Smith discusses self-interest in the context of the need to save and increase the stock of capital so that production can be expanded. Smith also discusses ambition and self-interest in the context of his account of moral philosophy in *The Theory of Moral Sentiments,* first published in 1759 but extensively revised shortly before his death in 1790. In *The Wealth of Nations,* self-interest is discussed more narrowly in terms of its economic effects. Reading E, the third and final extract from Adam Smith's writings, has been selected from *The Theory of Moral Sentiments* where Smith discusses ambition and the desire to 'better our condition'.

ACTIVITY 5   You should now read **Reading E, 'The origin of ambition'**, which has been selected from *The Theory of Moral Sentiments* to give you the opportunity to read something of Smith's moral evaluation of social and economic ambition. As you read this piece, make brief notes on the basic reason why people desire to better their condition.

In this extract Smith argues that ambition is based on a person's desire to be approved by others. It is not ease but vanity, Smith argues, that promotes people to wish to better their condition. Smith says: 'To be observed, to be attended to, to be taken notice of with sympathy, complacency, and approbation, are all the advantages which we can propose to derive from it. It is the vanity, not the ease, or the pleasure, which interests us.' Smith's argument is that it is not the pursuit of riches or luxuries for their own sake that attracts people, but the effect which the possession of these items will have on other people. For this reason it is the conspicuous consumption of the rich which marks them off and guarantees the attention and approbation of other people. From an economic point of view, Smith is here referring to what modern economists refer to as 'positional goods'; that is, status goods which by definition cannot be owned by a large number of people without losing something of their appeal. Thus, Smith's analysis of human ambition is not restricted to its economic dimension. He argues that people very often strive after material goods not for the sake of those goods themselves but because of the social esteem and respect that they think such wealth will bring them. In this sense, such goods are not so much an end in themselves, but a means to an end, that of social approbation.

Adam Smith's writings on the economy formed just a part of his larger intellectual interests, which included moral philosophy, jurisprudence, history, science, rhetoric and the study of fine writing. In spite of the comprehensiveness of Smith's interests, however, the separation between his writings on moral philosophy (in *The Theory of Moral Sentiments*) and his writings on the economy (in *The Wealth of Nations*) has set the pattern for much economic writing since which has aspired to join the scientific rather than the moral or social approach to economic analysis. This separation has reinforced the view that *The Wealth of Nations* can be read independently of Smith's other works and that it exemplifies the new Enlightenment approach to a rational and scientific study of society. It has also provided a famous precedent for the later professionalization of economics as a discipline purportedly characterized by a scientific rather than a moral approach to economic issues.

3.5   AFTER ADAM SMITH

Adam Smith's analysis was developed by other writers in the course of the nineteenth century, although most of these later writers took a narrower approach to the economy which excluded a historical or moral dimension.

One such writer was the economist David Ricardo (1772–1823). He took a more abstract approach to economic issues, and was particularly concerned to refine what he took to be the glimmer of a labour theory of value in *The Wealth of Nations*. In developing his own labour theory of value in his book *On the Principles of Political Economy and Taxation* (1817), Ricardo put at centre stage the issue of the distribution of income between the three main classes of society (landlords, capitalists and labourers) in his analysis of the relationship between rent, profits and wages.

Karl Marx (1818–83) challenged Smith in a number of different ways and argued that *The Wealth of Nations* was essentially an ideological defence of emerging capitalism. *Das Kapital* was published in 1867 and translated into English in 1887 under the title *Capital*; in this book Marx argued that capitalism was characterized not by an underlying harmony of interests but by an irreconcilable conflict of interest between capital and labour. Marx's analysis therefore challenged the doctrine of the invisible hand, and instead emphasized the exploitation of the working class and the revolutionary need to overthrow the capitalist system.

In the twentieth century, one of the greatest challenges to the doctrine of the invisible hand came from John Maynard Keynes (1883-1946), whose most famous book *The General Theory of Employment, Interest and*

Money was published in 1936 during a period of high unemployment. The issue that Keynes addressed was not exploitation but unemployment; he argued that, contrary to the doctrine of the invisible hand, it may not always be the case that the pursuit of individual interest is consonant with the general interest. In particular, Keynes argued that the failure of 'aggregate demand' is the fundamental cause of prolonged unemployment in the modern economy, and that governments should take upon themselves the responsibility for increasing aggregate demand and reducing unemployment. Keynes' analysis was intended as an answer to the socialist challenge; by making capitalism function more efficiently and more equitably, it was thought that its revolutionary overthrow would become unnecessary.

Keynes' doctrines became influential both at the level of government economic policy and at the level of popular debate, but by the late 1970s the twin problems of 'stagflation' — stagnation and inflation — were associated with a new anti-Keynesianism. By the late 1970s and early 1980s, a new free-market and anti-statist approach had become dominant in many countries including the UK, and this approach explicitly looked back to the tradition of *The Wealth of Nations* for political and analytical support. Adam Smith was then popularly cited not only as the 'father' of economics but as the original architect of a free-market, capitalist order in which the economic role of the state would be minimal.

3.6   CONCLUSION

Section 3 of this chapter has shown how Adam Smith's *The Wealth of Nations* has been understood as the beginning of a new kind of scientific analysis of the capitalist market economy. In particular, the section has outlined the theory of the invisible hand as an account of the capitalist market mechanism, the division of labour as an explanation of the sources of increased productiveness, and the pervasiveness and strength of the motive to 'better one's condition' as a spur to individual profit-seeking behaviour. In laying down this framework for the objective study of the capitalist economy, Smith's influence was also enhanced by the fact that he correctly anticipated the actual development of the UK economy. Writing before the period when the largely agricultural economy of the UK turned into the workshop of the world, Smith was able to point to just those developments that were going to prove decisive for the industrial growth of the capitalist economy during the nineteenth and twentieth centuries. The power and appeal of *The Wealth of Nations* at both the economic and the ideological level are thus thought to be a direct result of the timely nature of its analysis.

4   A MODERN ECONOMICS?

Seeing the analysis of *The Wealth of Nations* as a direct response to changes in the economy gives a robustness to the account of its enormous influence; as a tract for the times it spoke directly to the economic interests of its own day, and in the same vein it is thought to speak directly to us today. This approach to the founding or 'classic' texts of an academic discipline is a common one, but it is a view that is not well borne out by recent research. In this section I shall draw on recent research which has attempted to understand Adam Smith's writings as part of the broader context of the eighteenth-century Enlightenment, where questions of commerce and wealth were indissolubly linked with questions of history, jurisprudence, law, government and morality (Winch, 1978; Haakonssen, 1981; Hont and Ignatieff, 1983; Teichgraeber, 1986; Brown, 1991).

4.1   ANTICIPATING THE MODERN ECONOMY?

This newer approach to Adam Smith's writings points up a number of weaknesses in the traditional interpretation presented in Section 3. First, the traditional interpretation results in a process of 'historical foreshortening' that overlooks the differences between the modern period and the earlier period when *The Wealth of Nations* was written. Seeing *The Wealth of Nations* as an embryonic description of 'early liberal capitalism' tends to exaggerate the extent to which the eighteenth century of Smith's own day had already embarked on an irreversible process of modern economic transformation. This reduces the historical distance between *The Wealth of Nations* and our own period, thus contributing to our sense that such a book, although written over 200 years ago, may yet speak directly to us now. But as we saw in Section 2 of this chapter, the process of economic change in the eighteenth century was slow and uneven. The economy of the eighteenth century was a pre-industrial economy, and it is anachronistic to think that Adam Smith could have had in mind a later modern industrial economy.

If we reconsider the passage on the division of labour in Reading D and read it in the context of the small-scale, unmodernized state of British industry at that time, a different impression is given. In this extract, we have already seen that Smith was capturing something of the new developments of his own day, but, at the same time, we should note what he does *not* say. Smith's discussion is framed in terms of a trifling manufacture involving very little in the way of capital investment, where the production process is very labour-intensive. Smith describes how 'One man draws out the wire, another straights it, a third cuts it, a fourth points it … ' etc. In the middle of the eighteenth century, pin production was organized as a cottage industry, with a hundred or more pin 'manufactories' employing a handful or so of workers each, although much of this work was located in workhouses; the little pin manufactory that Smith himself had apparently witnessed employed only ten men. It

Wedgwood cameos in Boulton cut steel frames

Matthew Boulton's Soho Manufactory, near Birmingham, c.1781: a 'model' eighteenth-century manufactory

Boulton's manufactory was something of a showpiece for its forward-looking approach. In 1770, about 700 workers were employed, producing a range of metal goods, including 'toy' goods such as the Wedgwood cameos set in steel frames shown above. James Watt's famous 'lap' engine, which used steam power for driving the laps or polishing buffs, was not introduced until 1788, twelve years after the publication of *The Wealth of Nations*.

was not until the nineteenth century that machine production of pins was introduced and it was this, rather than the division of labour as such, that vastly increased labour productivity in pin production (Pratten, 1980). Thus, what is *not* included in Smith's account is the impact of machine production on the division of labour and how this affects the size of factories and the structure of industry. We should therefore be cautious about assuming that the example of the pin manufactory provides an astute anticipation of the enormous productive potential that lurked in the shadows of the Industrial Revolution of the future. In the case of the division of labour, as elsewhere, Smith's examples are typically of small-scale, low-technology industries requiring little in the way of capital equipment, industries that were more characteristic of the small-scale manufactories and cottage industries of his own time than the factories that came in the following century.

A second major problem with the traditional view of Adam Smith is that it is based on an implicit selection of those passages that seem to speak directly to an audience of modern economists and a relative neglect of those passages that fail to do so. Thus, those passages that refer to the debates that were current in the eighteenth century gradually become invisible as they become meaningless to later readers who are unfamiliar with those earlier debates. This means that many passages containing economic arguments, historical comparisons, political analyses, juristic comment, or moral assessments that relate to an eighteenth-century context, are simply ignored as irrelevant. In this way, the main thrust of the argument of the book is reconstructed retrospectively in terms of the interests and preconceptions of a later age.

In interpreting *The Wealth of Nations* as a signpost for the emerging liberal capitalist order, this implicit selection of passages is based on their congruence with modern notions of the superior productiveness and underlying harmony of the free-market order as represented by the invisible hand. But *The Wealth of Nations* also contains passages criticizing the effects of the division of labour and the unfettered pursuit of individual self-interest. The passage on the division of labour which is reproduced as Reading D is a very famous one; less famous is the following passage from a later chapter on the harmful effects of the division of labour:

> The man whose whole life is spent in performing a few simple operations, of which the effects too are, perhaps, always the same, or very nearly the same, has no occasion to exert his understanding, or to exercise his invention in finding out expedients for removing difficulties which never occur. He naturally loses, therefore, the habit of such exertion, and generally becomes as stupid and ignorant as it is possible for a human creature to become. The torpor of his mind renders him, not only incapable of relishing or bearing a part in any rational conversation, but of conceiving any generous, noble, or tender sentiment, and consequently of forming any just judgment concerning many even of the ordinary duties of private life. Of the great and extensive interests of his country, he is altogether incapable of judging; and unless very particular pains have been taken to render him otherwise, he is equally incapable of defending his country in war.
> (Smith, 1976b, p.782)

A life spent repeating a few simple operations is thought to lead to stupidity and ignorance; the torpor of the mind thereby induced, Smith argues, renders a person incapable of entering into rational conversation and unable to make moral or political judgments. A man's natural courage is corrupted, making him incapable of defending his country. Smith's condemnation here is unequivocal and contrasts strongly with an idealized picture presented later in *The Wealth of Nations* of a person's intellectual and moral capabilities in the early stages of society before the advent of commercial society. This shows that Smith's attitude towards commercial society was not one of undiluted approval. He recognized and appreciated the improved productive power arising from the division of labour, especially as this led to an improvement in the living conditions of the poor, but he clearly disapproved of what he saw as the intellectual, moral and martial impoverishment of the 'inferior ranks' of society in the commercial stage of society.

Furthermore, as this chapter proceeds, Smith compares the degraded 'inferior ranks' of his own society with both the 'barbarous' nations which preceded commercial society and with the ancient republics of

Greece and Rome. These comparisons show that Smith admired the classical notion of an active and virtuous citizenry, which included the capacity to bear arms in defence of the republic. Smith argued that, in the commercial stage of society, the inevitable division of labour had proceeded to such a point that a professional army had become a more practical proposition than arming the citizenry. Nevertheless, the classical model remained something of an ideal for Smith, and it was one against which the actual experience of commercial society compared unfavourably in a number of respects. In these passages, Smith is responding to a specifically eighteenth-century context formed partly by a new interest in comparing the development of society through a number of different historical stages, and also by an older discourse on the nature of 'civic virtue' which tended to take the ancient republics of Greece and Rome as models for a particular kind of active and participatory citizenship for a favoured male élite. Smith's own framework for assessing the effects of the division of labour therefore derived from a set of concerns that were specific to the eighteenth century.

Smith's solution to the degrading effects of the division of labour was the public provision of elementary school education for the poor, which would compensate to some extent for the debilitating effects of the division of labour, as well as equipping young minds more effectively for later adult work. Smith's argument here is that this provision should be made irrespective of any direct economic advantage that may accrue to the state, although in his view there would be a considerable advantage. In particular, Smith points to the political and public order implications of having a decent and respectable populace which is able to make political judgments calmly, free of either political or religious faction.

This example shows how ready Smith was to recommend state involvement where arguments of social benefit or political expediency seemed to call for it, and is a far cry from the traditional picture of him as the opponent of all state activities. In spite of references in his writings to the harmony of interests in society, there are also many references to the conflict of interests between different groups and classes in society, and there are also many practical instances throughout *The Wealth of Nations* of cases where the state should intervene in one way or another, in addition to what Smith saw as the three basic state functions of defence, justice, and maintenance of public institutions and works.

A third problem with the traditional interpretation of Adam Smith is that it is blind to the textual nuances evident in Smith's writings, even in those passages that seem to speak more directly to a later time. This leads it to overlook the range of other influences at work in Smith's texts that make the meaning of even these familiar passages much more problematic than the traditional interpretation accepts. As an example of this, consider again Readings C and E from Adam Smith's writings, which you studied in Sections 3.2 and 3.4.

Taking the first extract on the operation of the competitive market in Reading C, re-read this passage and make a note of any words or expressions that you would not expect to see in a modern piece of economic analysis.

This is not an easy activity. Having already read the extract as a piece of modern economic analysis, it is not easy to re-read it looking for elements that stand apart from modern economics.

As I re-read this passage I noted two expressions that I would not expect to see in a modern piece of economic writing. The first expression is that of 'natural price', an expression that would not even occur to a modern economist. The traditional interpretation of *The Wealth of Nations* regards this as a reference to 'long run costs'; the passage is thus taken to mean that in a competitive market the market price will eventually settle down at the level of long run costs, a result that is fully consonant with modern economic analysis. But the expression derives from a long tradition of 'natural law' treatises where the natural price is discussed along with the market price. Indeed, Smith first used this expression in the course of his lectures on jurisprudence, law and government, which were delivered at the University of Glasgow during the period 1752–64; these lectures were not published during Smith's lifetime but students' notes have since been published, providing modern scholars with the content of these lectures (Smith, 1978). The natural law treatises are in turn linked to the broader tradition of Stoic philosophy, a philosophy which greatly influenced Adam Smith. Within the Stoic philosophy, a person is enjoined to live 'according to nature' and so the attribute 'natural' was permeated with normative and philosophical overtones. The natural law tradition is also linked to mediaeval discussions of the 'just price', and for this reason some commentators have argued that the expression 'natural price' carries with it some of the moral resonances of the earlier just price discussions.

The second expression that I would not expect to see in a modern piece of economic writing is that of the 'wanton luxury' of those demanding a good, which pushes its market price above the natural price. Modern economic analysis accepts that high-income consumers have a relatively large influence on market outcomes, but the expression 'wanton luxury' carries with it a set of value judgments that modern economists would normally avoid. The expression can however be located within the context of eighteenth-century mercantilist and moral debates about the effect of 'luxury' (i.e. consumerism) on morals, manners and the employment of labour. A famous contribution to this debate was Bernard Mandeville's *The Fable of the Bees* (1714), which argued that private vices (i.e. 'luxury' or consumerism) lead to public benefits (i.e. increased demand for goods and hence increased employment).

ACTIVITY 7 Now look again at the third of the Smith extracts, Reading E, from *The Theory of Moral Sentiments*. Re-read this long paragraph, and consider what you think is Smith's attitude towards the ambition to 'better our condition'. Do you think that the tone of the piece changes as it progresses?

Stylistically this passage is more complex than much of *The Wealth of Nations*. Consider the place where Smith asks from whence arises the emulation which runs through all the different ranks of men. Read the answer which follows directly ('To be observed, to be attended to ... ' etc.), and consider whether you think that Smith is endorsing this answer in the sense of justifying or defending ambition.

It seems to me that the tone changes markedly in the course of this long paragraph. The paragraph starts by appearing to identify with the man of ambition; the voice in which the text is couched is that of the first person plural, which seems to include us all in the scope of the human naturalness of ambition. But in the course of the paragraph there is a shift to a more detached voice which refers to the man of ambition in the third person and, with critical reserve, notes that ambition inevitably involves anxiety, mortification and the loss of ease and security.

In a later passage Smith refers to 'wealth and greatness' as 'mere trinkets of frivolous utility, no more adapted for procuring ease of body or tranquility of mind than the tweezer-cases of the lover of toys' (1976a, p.181). He also argues that power and riches are 'enormous and operose machines contrived to produce a few trifling conveniencies to the body' (ibid., pp.182–3). Here we see Smith the moral philosopher inveighing against the consumerism of his own time and the futility of worldly ambition by deploying the language and argument of Stoic philosophy. In *The Theory of Moral Sentiments* there are many references to the Stoics, whose philosophy influenced Smith more deeply than any other, although he did not accept it in its entirety. According to the Stoic philosophy, a person's happiness and virtue are not dependent on material well-being; a person may be happy and virtuous in a cottage as well as a palace, more so most likely, and Smith generally went along with this view.

Thus, recent research on Adam Smith has argued that the traditional interpretation of his writings is inadequate, and this section has suggested some of the ways in which the traditional interpretation leads to historical foreshortening, retrospective selectivity, and textual blindnesses. Different writers within the research approach outlined in this section stress different aspects of this, but what they all share is an awareness of the historical complexity of Adam Smith's writings. Drawing on the notion of 'discourse' from Section 2, we could say that the new approach attempts to understand Adam Smith's writings as a distinct form of discourse according to its own terms of reference and its own framework of assumptions. This means that it has to be situated with respect to other discourses of the eighteenth century in order to identify its own internal points of reference which determine its meaning. As we saw in this section, this implies that Adam Smith's discourse can be understood only with respect to other writings of the eighteenth century and earlier, writings such as the natural law discourse, the mercantilist discourse, and the stoic discourse. It also implies that the detailed linguistic and stylistic features of Adam Smith's writings are also significant.

If Adam Smith was not the 'prophet of capitalism', how are we to understand *The Wealth of Nations*? The following section will present a brief account of an alternative reading.

4.2   THE SYSTEM OF NATURAL LIBERTY

One of the objects of enquiry during the Enlightenment was the idea of social progress and the way that a society's laws, government and mode of subsistence were uniquely linked. Underlying this interest was a concern with the apparently unstable or cyclical nature of much historical development. We have seen how Smith was fascinated with the ancient Greek and Roman republics, but these republics eventually fell into decline or absolutism and were overtaken by other forms of government. Within the mercantilist discourse too, concern was expressed about the long-term course of international trade; it was feared that a rich country would eventually find itself unable to compete internationally unless the statesman intervened. This raised a serious question about the long-term trajectory of the commercial system in which Smith himself lived. What was the place of international trade in the progress of 'opulence' — Smith's own term for economic growth — and what were the respective roles for agriculture and manufactures?

Smith's answer to this problem was to propose a scheme of the 'natural' progress of opulence; that is, a scheme whereby the natural order of economic progression for any country, reflecting people's natural preferences, was also the best possible order of development. In this way, a system of 'natural liberty', where economic agents would choose freely how to use their economic property, would best promote a country's opulence. In this scheme of development, Smith argued that agriculture was the sector that would inevitably be developed first. He based his claim on the idea of a natural division of labour between the country and the towns, in which the development of the towns would necessarily be subsequent to the development of agriculture which produced the food and raw materials required by the towns. The sector which would naturally be developed next was that of domestic manufactures, which was responsible for working up the raw materials into the goods required by the domestic population. According to this scheme, foreign trade would be developed last in the sequence and only when the needs of domestic agriculture and manufactures required it. Foreign trade was thus seen as following the development of domestic output rather than leading it:

> According to the natural course of things, therefore, the greater
> part of the capital of every growing society is, first, directed to
> agriculture, afterwards to manufactures, and last of all to foreign
> commerce. This order of things is so very natural, that in every
> society that had any territory, it has always, I believe, been in some
> degree observed.
> (Smith, 1976b, p.380)

When Smith then analysed the actual development of Europe he found
that this 'natural' order had been inverted by the mercantilist policies of
Europe which had developed the towns before the country, and
promoted foreign commerce before domestic production was ready for
it. This inversion of the natural sequence of development, Smith argued,
resulted in an 'unnatural and retrograde order' where agriculture had
been relatively neglected in the mercantilist race for exploiting new
foreign markets. Smith of course poured scorn on the mercantilist
concern with the balance of trade and the beggar-my-neighbour
attitudes that this had fostered. Smith argued that it was always in a
country's best economic interest to buy from the cheapest supplier and
devote its own resources to producing what it could produce most
efficiently at lowest cost. Exceptions there may be for reasons of
national security, but on straight economic grounds Smith argued that
trade protection and colonial monopolies could not pay their way.

Smith therefore charged the mercantilist system with leading
governments into misconceived policies, but note that his arguments
were based on the superiority of agriculture over manufactures, and
manufactures over foreign trade. In the absence of government
restrictions and in the absence of the monopoly with the North American
colonies, Smith argued that more resources would be devoted first to
agriculture and then to domestic manufactures and that this rerouting of
resources would be beneficial in promoting opulence. By arguing for free
trade Smith was not promoting trade and commerce, but was opposing
what he saw as their artificial and harmful overdevelopment.

This interpretation makes it easier to understand how Smith could
speak so harshly about manufacturers and traders, masters and
employers. Throughout *The Wealth of Nations* there are adverse
comments on the 'mean and rapacious spirit' of manufacturers and
traders, comments that fall into place when it is realized that *The
Wealth of Nations* was not written as a eulogy to trade and
manufactures but as an analysis of their undue pervasiveness and
influence. Smith spoke bitterly of the activities of manufacturers and
traders, and he advised that any proposal for a new law or regulation on
trade 'ought always to be listened to with great precaution' because it
comes from 'an order of men, whose interest is never exactly the same
with that of the publick, who have generally an interest to deceive and
even to oppress the publick, and who accordingly have, upon many
occasions, both deceived and oppressed it' (Smith, 1976b, p.267). These
passages show that Smith was not putting forward a simple-minded

theory of the invisible hand, according to which the pursuit of individual interest always resulted in a benefit to the public interest. Smith tended to be somewhat sceptical of the motivations and the claims made by any particular order of men, whether they were manufacturers, the clergy, professors or statesmen, and his general stance on many issues of policy was one of sceptical analyst rather than ardent reformer.

As Smith argued that the 'natural' order of development from agriculture through manufactures to commerce would be pursued in the absence of government intervention, he was able to provide a scheme of economic development, based on his system of natural liberty, that was not dependent on state direction. As we have seen, however, this does not imply that Smith saw no role for the government, nor does it imply that he wanted a sudden dismantling of the existing regulations on trade. Smith's preference was always for gradual change that would take public opinion into acount, even where he felt that opinion to be misguided.

Britain's dependence on foreign trade continued unabated into the nineteenth century and beyond. At the end of the twentieth century one of the weak features of the UK economy is its ability to provide enough exports to pay for imports, a trend which appears to be worsening. But economists do not now hold to the view that there is a natural or normal course of development from agriculture to manufactures to commerce that every economy has to follow. Furthermore, economists do not now agree with Smith that agriculture, taken by itself, is the most beneficial form of economic activity. Here Smith was influenced by a group of French writers who have come to be known as the physiocrats, and who formed a group around the physician François Quesnay. These writers were active in the 1760s when Adam Smith was visiting France as tutor to the young Duke of Buccleuch. The physiocrats had argued that only the agricultural sector was productive in producing a net product out of which taxes to the government could be paid. Smith disagreed with the physiocratic argument that all sectors other than agriculture were unproductive, but in formulating his criticisms of their theory he adopted the physiocrats' approach of identifying different sectors according to their contribution to society's annual revenue. Whereas the physiocrats argued that only agriculture contributes to annual revenue, Smith argued that all sectors contribute, but that agriculture contributes the most, followed by manufactures, followed by commerce and trade.

Thus, the theoretical basis of Smith's conception of the natural progress of opulence was derived in part from the physiocrats; this was because Smith partly adopted their own perspective in categorizing and ranking different sectors of the economy, even as he was developing his own criticisms of their theories. Here, then, we see another example of how *The Wealth of Nations* derives from and can be understood only in terms of its relationship with other discourses of the eighteenth century. The physiocrats' approach is one that rapidly fell into disfavour; by the early nineteenth century their theories were being heavily criticized and little of their work found its way into mainstream economics, although Marx developed the notion of productive and unproductive labour which Smith derived from the physiocrats. These sections of *The Wealth of Nations* have become largely neglected areas of his book. Smith's analysis of the inversion of the natural progress of opulence as the basis for his extended criticisms of the mercantile system has thus slipped from sight in many of the interpretations of *The Wealth of Nations*. Conversely, because Smith's analysis of the competitive market (reviewed above in section 3.2) is a form of analysis that modern commentators can make sense of in terms of their own understanding of demand and supply, it has been reinterpreted as the most prominent feature of his system of natural liberty.

Thus, what we see happening is that those parts of *The Wealth of Nations* that seem to relate most readily to modern forms of economic analysis are the parts that are emphasized in modern interpretations of Smith's work, and those parts that refer to other forgotten or neglected approaches slip gradually from view. In this way, over a period of time, the picture of *The Wealth of Nations* that has emerged is one that is made consonant with modern interests and perspectives.

5 CONCLUSION: SIGNPOSTING THE FUTURE?

One reason why the Enlightenment period is so challenging is that it seems to present social science with an account of its own origins. By searching for its origins, modern social science attempts to understand the course of its own development and hence arrive at a deeper understanding of its present state of knowledge. But this chapter has argued that we have no direct entry route into the eighteenth century, into either the course of its economic development or its writings about economic development. Any intellectual process of exploring the eighteenth century and its literary products must take place within a discursive framework of one sort or another that provides us with a way of reading and understanding those eighteenth-century materials.

In the case of the economic changes taking place in the eighteenth century, we reviewed two different approaches, each of which may be seen as a different kind of historical discourse. The discourse on nascent consumerism provided us with one way of understanding changing attitudes to the acquisition and display of material goods; it provides an interpretation of diverse materials such as newspaper advertisements, fashion reports, and retailing developments, and the output of satirists such as Hogarth, within the same unifying discursive framework. The statistical analysis of the economic historians or cliometricians represents another kind of historical discourse; employing modern economic theories and statistical methods, modern estimation techniques are used to construct a unified account of the momentum of economic development from the scattered data of the eighteenth century.

Similarly, in the case of Adam Smith's writings, or Adam Smith's discourse if you like, alternative interpretative strategies were reviewed. Section 3 outlined a traditional reading of Adam Smith's discourse which located it firmly within the context of what were perceived to be immanent changes in economic activity. According to this interpretation, *The Wealth of Nations* was a signpost for the newly emerging liberal capitalist order which became pre-eminent in the nineteenth century. According to this approach, Adam Smith is also regarded as the 'father' of modern economics; by this is meant that his work laid the analytical foundations on which modern economics has been built. A sign of his own times and a sign of the future, Adam Smith's writings were seen as the fountainhead and guiding spirit for an entirely new economic order.

But Section 4 of this chapter argued that Smith's own writings do not unambiguously lend support to such an interpretation. Smith's own system of natural liberty was based not only on the traditional analysis of the competitive market, but more signficantly on the natural progress of opulence from agriculture to manufactures to commerce. The guiding hand of the statesman was replaced by the invisible hand, but this still allowed scope for state involvement in the economy in a number of ways. Smith was so far from being an uncritical supporter of an economic system motivated entirely by self-interest that he frequently made harsh judgments on the activities of employers, manufacturers and dealers; and he was so far from recommending an expansion of commerce and manufactures that he argued instead that these sectors had been overdeveloped in relation to agriculture, a more beneficial activity.

It was argued further that *The Wealth of Nations* has been interpreted in terms of modern discourses on the economy and that in this process large sections of the book have been overlooked. The effect of this approach has been to reconstruct *The Wealth of Nations* in the image of the concerns of a later time, and thence to find in it the origins of a later course of development. The alternative account of Adam Smith's discourse that was presented in Section 4 was one that involved using a different interpretative matrix; here Adam Smith's discourse was interpreted in terms of other discourses of the Enlightenment which were held to account for the particular positioning and textual resonances of the arguments of *The Wealth of Nations*. For example, Smith's own moral evaluation of commercial society was interpreted in terms of his attachment to Stoicism and his interest in jurisprudence, and was not located on a spectrum of left–right political positions which mark the ideological parameters of a later age. But note that this approach to reading *The Wealth of Nations* also embodies a view of history: one that sees it as a less deterministic process, in which *The Wealth of Nations* was not the necessary embodiment of an age that was yet to come, but the complex product of a range of political, economic and moral discourses that were influential at the time.

Our attempt to understand the course of economic change in the eighteenth century, together with its most famous economics treatise, has resulted in the conclusion that both have been subject to a range of interpretations that may well tell us a good deal about the present as well as the past. In this process, views about the development of the economy become intermingled with views about the classic books on the economy. Thus, the interpretation of Adam Smith presented in Section 3 tends to be associated with a view of the eighteenth century as the clear beginning of industrial capitalism, and also with an interpretation of the modern economy as the inevitable result of those early eighteenth-century beginnings.

The view of Adam Smith presented in Section 4, however, emphasizes that his works can only be understood historically in terms of the other discourses of the Enlightenment period. At the same time, however, it recognizes that the power and the historical significance of a book is not necessarily related to this historically-situated reading, but depends precisely on the ways in which the book's arguments have been taken over by later generations and made their own. For it is one of the characteristics of a classic book — one that has been raised to canonical status — that instead of simply pointing the way of the future, it often becomes part of the process of struggle and debate out of which that future emerges. In the course of this untidy and loose-ended process of social change, the book's meaning and significance may well change along with the perceptions and political requirements of the age. In retrospect, it seems to have had the power to predict that change, but this power of prediction may well be the result of the book's canonization rather than its cause.

REFERENCES

Brown, V. (1991) 'Signifying voices: reading the "Adam Smith problem" ', *Economics and Philosophy*, vol. 7, no. 2.

Campbell, T.D. (1971) *Adam Smith's Science of Morals*, London, Allen and Unwin.

Cole, W.A. (1981) 'Factors in demand 1700–80', in Floud, R. and McCloskey, D. (eds) *The Economic History of Britain Since 1700,* Cambridge, Cambridge University Press.

Crafts, N.F.R. (1985) *British Economic Growth During the Industrial Revolution,* Oxford, Clarendon Press.

Deane, P. and Cole, W.A. (1967) *British Economic Growth 1688–1959,* 2nd edn, Cambridge, Cambridge University Press.

Haakonssen, K. (1981) *The Science of a Legislator: The Natural Jurisprudence of David Hume and Adam Smith*, Cambridge, Cambridge University Press.

Hont, I. and Ignatieff, M. (eds) (1983) *Wealth and Virtue: The Shaping of Political Economy in the Scottish Enlightenment*, Cambridge, Cambridge University Press.

Jackson, R.V. (1990) 'Government expenditure and British economic growth in the eighteenth century: some problems of measurement', *Economic History Review,* 2nd series, vol. XLIII, pp.217–35.

Langford, P. (1989) *A Polite and Commercial People: England 1727–1783*, Oxford, Clarendon Press.

McKendrick, N., Brewer, J. and Plumb, J.H. (1982) *The Birth of a Consumer Society: The Commercialization of Eighteenth-Century England,* London, Europa.

Porter, R. (1990) *English Society in the Eighteenth Century*, 2nd edn, Harmondsworth, Penguin.

Pratten, C. F. (1980) 'The manufacture of pins', *Journal of Economic Literature*, vol. XVIII, pp.93–6.

Smith, A. (1976a) *The Theory of Moral Sentiments*, edited by D.D. Raphael and A.L. Macfie; vol.I of The Glasgow Edition of the Works and Correspondence of Adam Smith, Oxford, Oxford University Press; reprinted by Liberty Press, 1982.

Smith, A. (1976b) *An Inquiry into the Nature and Causes of the Wealth of Nations*, edited by R.H. Campbell and A.S. Skinner; vol.II of The Glasgow Edition of the Works and Correspondence of Adam Smith, Oxford, Oxford University Press; reprinted by Liberty Press, 1981.

Smith, A. (1978) *Lectures on Jurisprudence*, edited by R.L. Meek, D.D. Raphael and P.G. Stein; vol.V of The Glasgow Edition of the Works and Correspondence of Adam Smith, Oxford, Oxford University Press; reprinted by Liberty Press, 1982.

Teichgraeber, R.F., III (1986) *Free Trade and Moral Philosophy: Rethinking the Sources of Adam Smith's 'Wealth of Nations'*, Durham, NC, Duke University Press.

Winch, D. (1978) *Adam Smith's Politics: An Essay in Historiographic Revision*, Cambridge, Cambridge University Press.

READING A   THE BIRTH OF CONSUMERISM

Roy Porter

A thousand other developments expedited trade. For instance, foreigners complimented the English on their retailing. 'The magnificence of the shops,' wrote Von Archenholz, 'is the most striking thing in London.' Defoe underlined the key distributive role of shops (bright, glass-fronted and bow-windowed) in serving householders with goods from the length and breadth of the country — hangings from Kidderminster, a looking-glass from London, blankets from Witney, rugs from Westmorland. He rhapsodized over their sheer number: 'I have endeavoured to make some calculation of the number of shop-keepers in this kingdom, but I find it is not to be done — we may as well count the stars' (yet the old Puritan in him begrudged the outlay lavished on their tinsel display). Advertising swelled enormously, especially in newspapers. Between 1747 and 1750 Bottely's *Bath Journal* carried 2,740 advertisements, between 1780 and 1783, well over twice as many. Provincial newspapers especially alerted readers to metropolitan tastes. Thus a North Walsham staymaker told lady readers of the *Norwich Mercury* in 1788 'that he is just returned from Town with the newest Fashions of French and Italian Stays, Corsetts and Riding Stays ... their Orders will be executed in an Height of Taste not inferior to the first shops in London' (who could resist?). A Newcastle-on-Tyne lady was demanding a Wedgwood dinner service with an 'Arabesque Border' before her local shopkeeper had even heard of it; she insisted on that precise pattern, having discovered it was 'much used in London at present', and refused to be fobbed off with substitutes. In 1777 Abigail Gawthern noted in her diary that she 'used a parasol for the first time ... the first in Nottingham'. Advertising's role in puffing demand was clear to all. 'Promise, large promise, is the soul of advertisement,' wrote Dr Johnson, who believed 'the trade of advertising is now so near perfection that it is not easy to propose any improvement'. Advertising's allure whipped up demand for knick-knacks, curios and all manner of disposable items, bought upon whim, and increased turnover in fashion. Handkerchiefs were hawked with Marlborough's five great victories painted on them; other designs celebrated Dr Sacheverell or the Peace of Utrecht. The radical John Wilkes's squinting face was plastered over mugs, jugs, teapots, plaques and plates.

Source: Porter, R. (1990) *English Society in the Eighteenth Century,* 2nd edn, Harmondsworth, Penguin, p.190.

READING B   PRE-MODERN MANUFACTURING

Roy Porter

Until late in the century, output operated almost exclusively through small-scale crafts, cottage and workshop industry. Expansion did not hinge on revolutionary innovations in technology, but on the steady sucking of accumulated wealth into circulation, better use of labour reserves, and new techniques facilitating exchange of goods and services. The heroes of this steady, inexorable march of commercial capitalism are largely anonymous: rank-and-file distributors, hauliers, shippers, transporters, and thousands of humble waggoners, packmen, tinkers, carters and hucksters. Up to 1760, no decisive breakthroughs had occurred in mechanization, in work organization, in the scale of the workplace, in sources of industrial power. The agricultural sector remained paramount, the fluctuating price of corn still largely dictating the tempo of commercial and industrial activity. Thus when agricultural profits were low in the 1730s, turnpiking tailed off. In mid-century, two thirds of British iron was still being used for agricultural purposes.

Even profit-conscious expanding trades continued to organize their labour force in traditional ways, often within guild or company rules. Such regulation after all ensured stability and rarely proved a brake upon expansion. Manufacturing typically remained in workshops, based on the work-unit of the household. Putting out was perfect for expansion in textiles. Master-clothiers supplied workers — carders, rovers, spinners, weavers — with materials, usually a week's supply, which they worked up on their own premises, using their own or rented wheels and looms. This system was a cost-effective use of capital. The capitalist needed to freeze little fixed capital in plant, and had flexibility in hiring and firing labour. Sub-contracting remained ubiquitous as a mode of employment and industrial organization, for instance in the 'butty' system used in shallow Midlands coal-mining. It shared investment risks, profits and the problems of managing the workforce. (Publishing books by subscription could be seen as a parallel case, obviating the need for the author and printer to lock up too much capital in the project.) Where metal extraction was regulated by ancient court jurisdictions, as in Cornish tin-mining and Peak District lead-mining, each sinking was under-taken by a gang supplying its own capital and equipment, and getting its return, not in wages, but in shares of ore sales. In all such trades, 'middle management' had hardly emerged as a regular profession. Most intermediaries in businesses were not salaried foremen or 'executives' but were part of the family, bosses in their own right. Employment was direct, responsibility personal, rewards proportionate to success.

Industry remained largely labour-intensive and skill-intensive. Weaving, smithying, hat-making, the furniture and cutlery trades, metal-working and thousands more besides expanded by recruiting more hands. When

Source: Porter, R. (1990) *English Society in the Eighteenth Century,* 2nd edn, Harmondsworth, Penguin, pp.193–6.

demand was high it was easy to take up the slack (and especially from mid-century, population pressure made the labour market a buyers' market). Women and children in particular could easily be drafted into the labour force.

There were, of course, a handful of mammoth factories in the first half of the century. Thomas Lombe's silk-throwing mill in Derby employed 500, his twenty-three-foot water-wheel driving 26,000 spindles. But this was highly exceptional — and not very successful (nor indeed original: Lombe merely copied Italian factories). There were also a few colossal entrepreneurs. Around 1700, Ambrose Crowley, the iron-master who got rich on navy contracts, commanded a workforce of nearly 1,000 and pioneered the techniques of shop-floor organization, discipline and welfare taken up in later generations by industrialists such a Josiah Wedgwood (Cowley had no alternative: he directed his Tyneside works by letter from London). In his 'Law Book of the Crowley Ironworks', all instructions begin 'I DO ORDER'. Crowley knew it paid to take pains over workers. He housed his employees on company property — but enforced a 9 p.m. curfew — and provided a doctor and poor relief, but the recipients had to wear a badge inscribed 'Crowley's Poor'. Yet such a man was utterly exceptional — a 'giant in an age of pygmies' as his biographer has called him. Only a vast purchaser such as the wartime navy could create such concentrated demand: civilian consumer requirements did not support titan captains of industry so early. Even with later industrialization, the expansion of great iron firms such as the Carron Works, Walkers, and Wilkinsons depended largely on military contracts. Indeed, only naval dockyards themselves had a comparable scale and division of functions. 'The building-yards, docks, timber-yard, deal-yard, mast-yard, gun-yard, rope-walks; and all the other yards and places, set apart for the works belonging to the navy, are like a well-ordered city,' was Defoe's comment on Chatham in the 1720s, 'and tho' you see the whole place as it were in the utmost hurry, yet you see no confusion, every man knows his own business.'

Furthermore, in the first two thirds of the century, it was highly exceptional for technological innovations to revolutionize a trade. The development of the coke-smelting of iron by the Darbys of Coalbrookdale was, of course, to prove vital in facilitating mass iron-casting. But despite rising charcoal prices, this innovation made slow headway (the Darbys kept it secret). New textile machinery such as Kay's flying shuttle also came in slowly. Newcomen's steam engine was used almost solely for pumping mines, and industrial power still came from animals, hands and feet, wind and water. Improvements occurred through the piecemeal modification of existing technologies within traditional employment stuctures. England consolidated her skills-base.

READING C   THE MARKET

Adam Smith

The market price of every particular commodity is regulated by the proportion between the quantity which is actually brought to market, and the demand of those who are willing to pay the natural price of the commodity, or the whole value of the rent, labour, and profit, which must be paid in order to bring it thither. Such people may be called the effectual demanders, and their demand the effectual demand; since it may be sufficient to effectuate the bringing of the commodity to market. It is different from the absolute demand. A very poor man may be said in some sense to have a demand for a coach and six; he might like to have it; but his demand is not an effectual demand, as the commodity can never be brought to market in order to satisfy it.

When the quantity of any commodity which is brought to market falls short of the effectual demand, all those who are willing to pay the whole value of the rent, wages, and profit, which must be paid in order to bring it thither, cannot be supplied with the quantity which they want. Rather than want it altogether, some of them will be willing to give more. A competition will immediately begin among them, and the market price will rise more or less above the natural price, according as either the greatness of the deficiency, or the wealth and wanton luxury of the competitors, happen to animate more or less the eagerness of the competition. Among competitors of equal wealth and luxury the same deficiency will generally occasion a more or less eager competition, according as the acquisition of the commodity happens to be of more or less importance to them. Hence the exorbitant price of the necessaries of life during the blockade of a town or in a famine.

When the quantity brought to market exceeds the effectual demand, it cannot be all sold to those who are willing to pay the whole value of the rent, wages and profit, which must be paid in order to bring it thither. Some part must be sold to those who are willing to pay less, and the low price which they give for it must reduce the price of the whole. The market price will sink more or less below the natural price, according as the greatness of the excess increases more or less the competition of the sellers, or according as it happens to be more or less important to them to get immediately rid of the commodity. The same excess in the importation of perishable, will occasion a much greater competition than in that of durable commodities; in the importation of oranges, for example, than in that of old iron.

When the quantity brought to market is just sufficient to supply the effectual demand and no more, the market price naturally comes to be either exactly, or as nearly as can be judged of, the same with the natural price.

Source: Smith, A. (1976) *An Inquiry into the Nature and Causes of the Wealth of Nations,* 1776 (first published 1776), edited by R.H. Campbell and A.S. Skinner, vol. II of The Glasgow Edition of the Works and Correspondence of Adam Smith, Oxford, Oxford University Press; reprinted by Liberty Press, 1981; pp.73–4.

The whole quantity upon hand can be disposed of for this price, and cannot be disposed of for more. The competition of the different dealers obliges them all to accept of this price, but does not oblige them to accept of less.

READING D   THE DIVISION OF LABOUR

Adam Smith

The greatest improvement in the productive powers of labour, and the greater part of the skill, dexterity and judgment with which it is any where directed, or applied, seem to have been the effects of the division of labour. ...

To take an example, therefore, from a very trifling manufacture; but one in which the division of labour has been very often taken notice of, the trade of the pin-maker; a workman not educated to this business (which the division of labour has rendered a distinct trade), nor acquainted with the use of the machinery employed in it (to the invention of which the same division of labour has probably given occasion), could scarce, perhaps, with his utmost industry, make one pin in a day, and certainly could not make twenty. But in the way in which this business is now carried on, not only the whole work is a peculiar trade, but it is divided into a number of branches, of which the greater part are likewise peculiar trades. One man draws out the wire, another straights it, a third cuts it, a fourth points it, a fifth grinds it at the top for receiving the head; to make the head requires two or three distinct operations; to put it on, is a peculiar business, to whiten the pins is another; it is even a trade by itself to put them into the paper; and the important business of making a pin is, in this manner, divided into about eighteen distinct operations, which, in some manufactories, are all performed by distinct hands, though in others the same man will sometimes perform two or three of them. I have seen a small manufactory of this kind where ten men only were employed, and where some of them consequently performed two or three distinct operations. But though they were very poor, and therefore but indifferently accommodated with the necessary machinery, they could, when they exerted themselves, make among them about twelve pounds of pins in a day. There are in a pound upwards of four thousand pins of a middling size. Those ten persons, therefore, could make among them upwards of forty-eight thousand pins in a day. Each person, therefore, making a tenth part of forty-eight thousand pins, might be considered as making four thousand eight hundred pins in a day. But if they had all wrought separately and independently, and without any of them having been educated to this peculiar business, they certainly could not each of them have made twenty, perhaps not one

Source: Smith, A. (1976) *An Inquiry into the Nature and Causes of the Wealth of Nations,* 1776 (first published 1776), edited by R.H. Campbell and A.S. Skinner, vol. II of The Glasgow Edition of the Works and Correspondence of Adam Smith, Oxford, Oxford University Press; reprinted by Liberty Press, 1981; pp.13–17; 22–4; 31.

pin in a day; that is, certainly, not the two hundred and fortieth, perhaps not the four thousand eight hundredth part of what they are at present capable of performing, in consequence of a proper division and combination of their different operations.

In every other art and manufacture, the effects of the division of labour are similar to what they are in this very trifling one; though, in many of them, the labour can neither be so much subdivided, nor reduced to so great a simplicity of operation. The division of labour, however, so far as it can be introduced, occasions, in every art, a proportionable increase of the productive powers of labour. The separation of different trades and employments from one another, seems to have taken place, in consequence of this advantage. This separation too is generally carried furthest in those countries which enjoy the highest degree of industry and improvement; what is the work of one man, in a rude state of society, being generally that of several in an improved one. In every improved society, the farmer is generally nothing but a farmer; the manufacturer, nothing but a manufacturer. The labour too which is necessary to produce any one complete manufacture, is almost always divided among a great number of hands. How many different trades are employed in each branch of the linen and woollen manufactures, from the growers of the flax and the wool, to the bleachers and smoothers of the linen, or to the dyers and dressers of the cloth! ...

This great increase of the quantity of work, which, in consequence of the division of labour, the same number of people are capable of performing, is owing to three different circumstances; first, to the increase of dexterity in every particular workman; secondly, to the saving of the time which is commonly lost in passing from one species of work to another; and lastly, to the invention of a great number of machines which facilitate and abridge labour, and enable one man to do the work of many ...

It is the great multiplication of the productions of all the different arts, in consequence of the division of labour, which occasions, in a well-governed society, that universal opulence which extends itself to the lowest ranks of the people. Every workman has a great quantity of his own work to dispose of beyond what he himself has occasion for; and every other workman being exactly in the same situation, he is enabled to exchange a great quantity of his own goods for a great quantity, or, what comes to the same thing, for the price of a great quantity of theirs. He supplies them abundantly with what they have occasion for, and they accommodate him as amply with what he has occasion for, and a general plenty diffuses itself through all the different ranks of the society.

Observe the accommodation of the most common artificer or day-labourer in a civilized and thriving country, and you will perceive that the number of people of whose industry a part, though but a small part, has been employed in procuring him this accommodation, exceeds all computation. The woollen coat, for example, which covers the day-labourer, as coarse and rough as it may appear, is the produce of the joint labour of a great multitude of workmen. The shepherd, the sorter of the wool, the wool-comber or carder, the dyer, the scribbler, the spinner, the weaver, the fuller, the dresser, with many others, must all join their different arts in order to complete even this homely production. How many merchants and carriers, besides, must have been employed in transporting the materials from some of those workmen to others who often live in a very distant part of the country! How much commerce and navigation in particular, how many ship-builders, sailors, sail-makers, rope-makers, must have been employed in order to bring together the different drugs made use of by the dyer, which often come from the remotest corners of the world! What a variety of labour too is necessary in order to produce the tools of the meanest of those workmen! ... if we examine, I say, all these things, and consider what a variety of labour is employed about each of them, we shall be sensible that without the assistance and co-operation of many thousands, the very meanest person in a civilized country could not be provided, even according to, what we very falsely imagine, the easy and simple manner in which he is commonly accommodated. Compared, indeed, with the more extravagant luxury of the great, his accommodation must no doubt appear extremely simple and easy; and yet it may be true, perhaps, that the accommodation of an European prince does not always so much exceed that of an industrious and frugal peasant, as the accommodation of the latter exceeds that of many an African king, the absolute master of the lives and liberties of ten thousand naked savages ...

As it is the power of exchanging that gives occasion to the division of labour, so the extent of this division must always be limited by the extent of that power, or, in other words, by the extent of the market. When the market is very small, no person can have any encouragement to dedicate himself entirely to one employment, for want of the power to exchange all that surplus part of the produce of his own labour, which is over and above his own consumption, for such parts of the produce of other men's labour as he has occasion for.

There are some sorts of industry, even of the lowest kind, which can be carried on no where but in a great town. A porter, for example, can find employment and subsistence in no other place. A village is by much too narrow a sphere for him; even an ordinary market town is scarce large enough to afford him constant occupation. In the lone houses and very small villages which are scattered about in so desert a country as the Highlands of Scotland, every farmer must be butcher, baker and brewer for his own family. In such situations we can scarce expect to find even a smith, a carpenter, or a mason, within less than twenty miles of another of the same trade. ...

READING E   THE ORIGIN OF AMBITION

Adam Smith

It is because mankind are disposed to sympathize more entirely with our joy than with our sorrow, that we make parade of our riches, and conceal our poverty. Nothing is so mortifying as to be obliged to expose our distress to the view of the public, and to feel, that though our situation is open to the eyes of all mankind, no mortal conceives for us the half of what we suffer. Nay, it is chiefly from this regard to the sentiments of mankind, that we pursue riches and avoid poverty. For to what purpose is all the toil and bustle of this world? what is the end of avarice and ambition, of the pursuit of wealth, of power and preheminence? Is it to supply the necessities of nature? The wages of the meanest labourer can supply them. We see that they afford him food and clothing, the comfort of a house, and of a family. If we examined his oeconomy with rigour, we should find that he spends a great part of them upon conveniencies, which may be regarded as superfluities, and that, upon extraordinary occasions, he can give something even to vanity and distinction. What then is the cause of our aversion to his situation, and why should those who have been educated in the higher ranks of life, regard it as worse than death, to be reduced to live, even without labour, upon the same simple fare with him, to dwell under the same lowly roof, and to be clothed in the same humble attire? Do they imagine that their stomach is better, or their sleep sounder in a palace than in a cottage? The contrary has been so often observed, and, indeed, is so very obvious, though it had never been observed, that there is nobody ignorant of it. From whence, then, arises that emulation which runs through all the different ranks of men, and what are the advantages which we propose by that great purpose of human life which we call bettering our condition? To be observed, to be attended to, to be taken notice of with sympathy, complacency, and approbation, are all the advantages which we can propose to derive from it. It is the vanity, not the ease, or the pleasure, which interests us. But vanity is always founded upon the belief of our being the object of attention and approbation. The rich man glories in his riches, because he feels that they naturally draw upon him the attention of the world, and that mankind are disposed to go along with him in all those agreeable emotions with which the advantages of his situation so readily inspire him. At the thought of this, his heart seems to swell and dilate itself within him, and he is fonder of his wealth, upon this account, than for all the other advantages it procures him. The poor man, on the contrary, is ashamed of his poverty. He feels that it either places him out of the sight of mankind, or, that if they take any notice of him, they have, however, scarce any fellow-feeling with the misery and distress which he suffers. He is mortified upon both accounts; for though to be overlooked, and to be disapproved of, are things entirely different, yet as

Source: Smith, A. (1976) *The Theory of Moral Sentiments* (first published 1759), edited by D.D. Raphael and A.L. Macfie, vol.I of The Glasgow Edition of the Works and Correspondence of Adam Smith, Oxford, Oxford University Press; reprinted by Liberty Press, 1981; pp.50–1.

obscurity covers us from the daylight of honour and approbation, to feel that we are taken no notice of, necessarily damps the most agreeable hope, and disappoints the most ardent desire, of human nature. The poor man goes out and comes in unheeded, and when in the midst of a crowd is in the same obscurity as if shut up in his own hovel. Those humble cares and painful attentions which occupy those in his situation, afford no amusement to the dissipated and the gay. They turn away their eyes from him, or if the extremity of his distress forces them to look at him, it is only to spurn so disagreeable an object from among them. The fortunate and the proud wonder at the insolence of human wretchedness, that it should dare to present itself before them, and with the loathsome aspect of its misery presume to disturb the serenity of their happiness. The man of rank and distinction, on the contrary, is observed by all the world. Every body is eager to look at him, and to conceive, at least by sympathy, that joy and exultation with which his circumstances naturally inspire him. His actions are the objects of the public care. Scarce a word, scarce a gesture, can fall from him that is altogether neglected. In a great assembly he is the person upon whom all direct their eyes; it is upon him that their passions seem all to wait with expectation, in order to receive that movement and direction which he shall impress upon them; and if his behaviour is not altogether absurd, he has, every moment, an opportunity of interesting mankind, and of rendering himself the object of the observation and fellow-feeling of every body about him. It is this, which, notwithstanding the restraint it imposes, nothwithstanding the loss of liberty with which it is attended, renders greatness the object of envy, and compensates, in the opinion of mankind, all that toil, all that anxiety, all those mortifications which must be undergone in the pursuit of it; and what is of yet more consequence, all that leisure, all that ease, all that careless security, which are forfeited for ever by the acquisition.

CHAPTER 4 CHANGING SOCIAL STRUCTURES: CLASS AND GENDER

Harriet Bradley

CONTENTS

1   INTRODUCTION

Most social scientists agree that contemporary Britain is a society marked by divisions and cleavages. There are divisions between rich and poor, divisions of social class, divisions between regions and between the different nationalities that go to make up the British Isles; divisions between people of different religions and between those of different ethnic origins, or races, to use the more popular term. Although we perhaps do not think of them in quite the same way, there are also divisions between the sexes, in terms of the typical patterns of their life histories and the different positions they occupy in the family and at work. All these divisions are aspects of what sociologists call *social structure*. This concept more generally refers to regular patterns which can be discerned in the way societies are organized; the types of divisions I have listed above are regular patterns of inequality which are deeply built into our society and tend to persist over time. Nevertheless they have not remained unchanged. The structure of social divisions in pre-industrial society was very different from what it is today. This chapter, then, is concerned with how class and gender divisions evolved with the formation of a modern social structure.

People have sometimes claimed that these divisions are disappearing over time. In the 1950s and 1960s, for instance, some social scientists believed that the working classes were being absorbed into the middle-classes, a process they described as 'embourgeoisement'. But both statistical evidence and general consensus in the 1980s suggest a deepening of some of these divisions. The gap between the top 20 per cent of households and the bottom 20 per cent has been steadily increasing over the past two decades, and a survey commissioned by the EEC in 1990 found that 80 per cent of people in the United Kingdom agreed with the statement, 'The rich get richer and the poor get poorer'.

This chapter is concerned with two types of social division and the inequalities they generate: those of gender and class. It tries to help you understand why these forms of inequality are so persistent by exploring their history. The chapter considers the changes in social structure brought about by industrialization and investigates the way contemporary patterns of class and gender inequality emerged. Emile Durkheim, one of the first academic sociologists, argued in his book *The Rules of Sociological Method* that to gain a complete understanding of any social phenomenon we have to understand why it came into existence in the first place (its causes and origins) and the reason it goes on existing (its effects or functions). This chapter is especially concerned with the former.

The chapter will also discuss some of the theories and ideas of the classical sociologists, Marx, Durkheim and Weber. We shall be considering their work partly because of the historical interest of their influential accounts of social change and social structure, but also because, as you will see in later chapters, many of their concepts and assumptions — the tools which they developed in their search for an understanding of how societies work — are still used by social scientists today to analyse contemporary societies.

2 PRE-INDUSTRIAL SOCIETY

2.1 'THE WORLD WE HAVE LOST'

The economic and social structure of pre-industrial Britain (i.e. roughly before 1780) was markedly different from the world we have come to regard as 'natural' today, as Peter Laslett shows in his imaginative and influential study *The World We Have Lost*.

Laslett (1965) paints a picture of an essentially rural world. Although there was some manufacture of goods, the central focus of the economy was agricultural production. At the end of the seventeenth century, about three quarters of the population earned most of their livelihood from some type of agricultural work, with the majority living in villages and small towns. Gregory King's estimates of the occupations of the English population carried out in the 1690s show that a fairly small minority of families worked as merchants, shopkeepers and artisans (see Table 4.1). Possession of land was the crucial factor in determining people's social status, with the great aristocratic estate owners at the top of the hierarchy. Manufacture was largely carried out in the towns and was organized through the craft guilds; they controlled entry to a trade through the apprenticeship system and laid down thorough regulations for the practice of each trade, providing at least a hope for a young entrant of working up through the ranks of journeymen and -women to become a master or mistress of a craft in his or her own right.

But for Laslett the most significant feature of the pre-industrial economy was that it was organized on a household basis (which is why Gregory King organized his census in terms of families). We could say that in the sixteenth and seventeenth centuries Britain was made up of small family businesses. Each member of the household was expected to make some contribution to the joint resources. It was absolutely normal practice for women, married or single, to work, and children started work at an early age, sometimes well before their teens. Household members might work cooperatively on the family farm or smallholding, or at a single trade like shoemaking: men cutting out the leather and lasting, women sewing up the pieces of the shoe, children threading laces and polishing. In other cases, especially in poorer families, household members were sent out to earn; young girls, in particular, went to work as servants in richer households.

Table 4.1   Gregory King's census of the English population in the 1690s

Number of families	Ranks, degrees, titles and qualifications	Number of persons per family	Total number of persons
160	Temporal lords	40	6,400
26	Spiritual lords	20	520
800	Baronets	16	12,800
600	Knights	13	7,800
3,000	Esquires	10	30,000
12,000	Gentlemen	8	96,000
5,000	Persons in greater offices and places	8	40,000
5,000	Persons in lesser offices and places	6	30,000
2,000	Eminent merchants and traders by sea	8	16,000
8,000	Lesser merchants and traders by sea	6	48,000
10,000	Persons in the law	7	70,000
2,000	Eminent clergymen	6	12,000
8,000	Lesser clergymen	5	40,000
40,000	Freeholders of the better sort	7	280,000
120,000	Freeholders of the lesser sort	5.5	660,000
150,000	Farmers	5	750,000
15,000	Persons in liberal arts and sciences	5	75,000
50,000	Shopkeepers and tradesmen	4.5	225,000
60,000	Artisans and handicraftsmen	4	240,000
5,000	Naval officers	4	20,000
4,000	Military officers	4	16,000
50,000	Common seamen	3	150,000
364,000	Labouring people and out-servants	3.5	1,274,000
400,000	Cottagers and paupers	3.25	1,300,000
35,000	Common soldiers	2	70,000
–	Vagrants; as gipsies, thieves, beggars, etc.	–	30,000
1,349,586	Grand totals		5,499,520

Source: Laslett, 1965, p.36

I have used the term *household* rather than *family* to indicate that these family enterprises often contained individuals who were not part of the core nuclear unit (parents and dependent children) which we in the twentieth century have come to think of as the 'normal' family. Laslett's work certainly shows that, on the whole, apart from the great aristocratic clans, English pre-industrial families were fairly small and often of the nuclear type: looking at Table 4.1, you can see that as a general rule the poorer the family the smaller it was likely to be. But many households also contained members of the wider kinship group (grandparents, aunts and uncles, nephews and nieces), and others contained non-kin members (servants, apprentices, lodgers) who were integrated into the household and joined in its communal work activities.

It was common practice in the sixteenth and seventeenth centuries to send children in their teens away from their parental homes for training: boys were commonly apprenticed and girls became household or farm servants. It is estimated that some 40 to 50 per cent of young people spent some time living in another household. So widespread was this practice that shocked continental observers accused the English of hating their children; an Italian diplomat attached to the court of Henry VII wrote:

> The want of affection in the English is strongly manifested towards their children; for having kept them at home till they arrive at the age of 7 or 9 years at the utmost, they put them out, both males and females, to hard service in the houses of other people, binding them generally for another 7 to 9 years ... . They like to enjoy all their comforts themselves and they are better served by strangers than they would be by their own children ... . If they had their own children at home they would be obliged to give them the same food they made use of for themselves.
> (quoted in Macfarlane, 1978, p.174)

2.2   PATRIARCHY AND MALE POWER IN PRE-INDUSTRIAL FAMILIES

As the above description suggests, families (or households) were the basic social units of these societies. A key feature of the pre-industrial family or household, noted by Laslett, was that it was *patriarchal.* Patriarchy is an important concept in contemporary sociology, but there is much disagreement over its meaning. The word literally means 'rule of the father' and Laslett uses it in much this sense to denote a system of family authority which is often linked to a system of inheritance in which property is transferred through the male line. The sociologist Max Weber used the term to describe what he saw as one fundamental model of social power: for Weber, patriarchy or 'patriarchalism' was a system of power common in traditional societies, 'where, within a group which is usually organized on both an economic and a kinship base, as a household, authority is exercised by a particular individual who is designated by a definite rule of inheritance' (Weber, 1964, p.346). Weber saw patriarchy as closely related to the feudal system which linked a lord and his male vassals in a power relationship, so in this sense patriarchy is not just about the relations between the sexes: the patriarch uses his power over both men and women. As head of the household, he has total control over the economic activities and behaviour of the other members. Laslett's work suggests that this was true for families in pre-industrial England, which displayed clear hierarchies usually linked to age and sex. The only exception would be where a widow took over management of the household, and this would usually be only until she remarried.

The concept of patriarchy has frequently been used, however, in a much more general way to denote the whole system of male dominance in society. Feminist sociologists often use the term in this way and suggest that patriarchy is not only manifested in family authority relationships but in the whole set of social arrangements which serve to ensure that men remain in control and that women are subordinate. This approach is exemplified in the following quotation from Kate Millett's *Sexual Politics*: 'Our society, like all other societies is a patriarchy. The military, industry, technology, universities, science, political office, finances — in short every avenue of power within the society, including the coercive force of the police, is entirely in male hands.' (Millett, 1971, p.25.) To describe pre-industrial societies as patriarchal in this sense would mean looking beyond the family — for example, at the exclusion of women from important roles in public life, particularly from political and military activity, and their allocation to inferior jobs in the occupational structure.

One trouble with Millett's definition is that it is very general and lacks the precision of Weber's approach. Critics have argued that if we use the term in this loose way it inevitably leads us to conclude that all societies are patriarchal and allow us no way of distinguishing between them. Yet it is clear that relations between men and women were very different in Tudor Britain from what they are in Britain in the 1980s, just as they are at the present time different in Britain, in India and in Saudi Arabia. Recent feminist analysts have, therefore, tried to make the concept more precise in two ways, while retaining Millett's implication that it relates specifically to gender relations. First, they have tried to develop accounts of how structures of patriarchy have varied in different times and places. We shall be thinking more about this later in this chapter. Secondly, they have tried to specify the base of patriarchy — that is, to identify the particular set of social relationships in which it is founded. Unless this is achieved, they argue, the concept will remain descriptive, rather than explanatory. Just as class relationships, as we shall see, are generated by changing forms of economic relations, so, if we are to arrive at a causal explanation of patriarchy, we must find the social arrangements from which it originates.

Feminists have not, however, been able to agree on what the basis of patriarchy is. Some, such as Shulamith Firestone, see it as springing from the family, and as being rooted in the control that men have exercised over women's reproductive powers. Others, such as Heidi Hartmann, argue that it is based on men's control of women's labour power; that is, the ability men have to force women to contribute free domestic labour in the home, and the use of male authority to exploit women as cheap labour outside the home. (These theoretical disagreements are explored more fully in Book 3 (Bocock and Thompson, 1992), Chapter 1.) For the moment, our concern is with patterns of power between men and women in a particular historical situation and we will return to that issue now.

On the face of it, historical evidence would suggest that pre-industrial Britain was patriarchal in both senses examined above. However, considerable debate exists among historians about power in the family. One important contribution to this debate was an early feminist classic, Alice Clark's *Working Life of Women in the Seventeenth Century*, first published in 1919. Clark argues strongly that marriage in pre-industrial England was more egalitarian than after industrialization. Basing her theory on the undisputed fact that married women were economically active, she sees marriage as a partnership where the importance of women's economic contribution gave them comparable status to that of men and a good degree of independence. She believes that both productive and domestic work were shared among the sexes so that there was no automatic identification of a married woman with the role of housewife.

Wool-spinning in a cottage

For Clark, industrialization brought a drastic decline in women's status and economic power, forcing them into dependence on men. The separation of the workplace from the family home which came with the factory system meant that women no longer learned craft and productive skills from their fathers and husbands. Aristocratic women and the wives of merchants and craftsmen gave up working altogether and either led a life of leisure or took on purely domestic housewifely tasks; labourers' wives continued to be forced to work because of family poverty, but they had, like their husbands, to 'go out to work' in factories or workshops where they were paid wages of below-subsistence level, forcing them into greater dependence on their husbands. For Clark, then, the pre-industrial economy was marked by greater gender equality.

ACTIVITY 1 You should now read **Reading A, 'Capitalism and women's labour'**, by Alice Clark, which you will find at the end of this chapter.

Not everybody agrees with Clark's account. One critic is Edward Shorter, who has argued that in pre-industrial society there was a clear sexual division of labour in which women were confined to a limited range of tasks, many of which were considered subsidiary to men's work. Consequently, women had a lower economic and social status than that of men and were subordinate to them in the family. These female tasks typically centred on the home, while men's work took them out into the public sphere. Shorter claims that women were responsible for what he calls 'the three big Cs' — cooking, cleaning and childcare — and that men took no part in these domestic tasks. Shorter believes, then, that pre-industrial families were patriarchal with a clearly established sexual division of labour. He states that only after industrialization did patriarchy begin to weaken; only when women were able to go out to work as wage labourers were they liberated from a purely domestic life and provided with some measure of independence from fathers and husbands. In his words: 'It was in the traditional moral economy that women suffered the most serious lack of status, and it was under capitalism that working women advanced to within at least shouting distance of equality with men.' (Shorter, 1976, p.513.)

Other historical research also suggests that Clark's picture of pre-industrial gender relations is too rosy. There is considerable evidence of a well-established division of labour within both agricultural and manufacturing work. Men took the tasks that were conventionally viewed as most important (such as ploughing or minding horses and cattle), while women were assigned tasks seen as less responsible and skilled (such as weeding the fields or caring for poultry and pigs). Women did do some skilled work, such as dairying, brewing, sewing and nursing, but it tended to be in areas which had been labelled 'women's work' and which often had domestic associations. Although it is possible to find examples, as Clark has done, of women practising virtually every guild craft or trade, including traditionally male skills such as masonry, carpentry, shoemaking and metalwork, such women were in a minority and usually gained access to the guild through family connections, being wives or daughters of craftsmen. More normally, they were found clustered in jobs traditionally designated as female, like spinning and shopkeeping. Yet there was also a certain flexibility in the assignment of tasks to women and men, which is reflected in the examples of female craftworkers and similar cases of women doing heavy farmwork such as ploughing or shepherding. Moreover, there were marked regional variations; in Scotland and the Northeast, for example, women were more likely to be involved in the 'heavier' forms of farmwork, like stock-keeping or shepherding. This makes it hard to decide finally whether Clark or Shorter is the more correct.

I think that one reason for the ambiguity of the evidence may be the variability of family arrangements. As you will know from personal experience, families are more different from one another than are, say, factories, offices or schools. No doubt there were henpecked husbands and bossy wives in pre-industrial families, just as there are today, even if pre-industrial society gave legal and formal sanction to male domination both in the family and at work. On the other hand, married women had fewer legal rights than men and it was socially and legally acceptable for a man to use violence to force his wife and children to obey him. In theory, if not in practice, a married woman was expected to subordinate herself entirely to her husband's wish and to practise complete obedience towards him.

Reading B, a passage from *For Her Own Good* by Barbara Ehrenreich and Deidre English, discusses this issue and suggests a compromise position. Ehrenreich and English believe that pre-industrial England was patriarchal but that it was also *gynocentric*, by which they mean that women's traditional skills, both productive and domestic, were seen as vital to the survival of families and thus of society as a whole. Women were the pivot of family life. The authors argue that when industrialization occurred, towards the end of the eighteenth century, it broke down male control within the family as women gained independence through wage labour, but at the same time the family became less important as an economic institution, so that women's value declined. Furthermore, their traditional skills, such as baking, brewing and preparing herbal medicine, were lost as the economy became commercialized. Women were less dominated by husbands, but became subject to the authority of male employers; and the new industrial society was reshaped in a way that ensured the dominance of male ideas and interests in the public world of work and politics. All these changes created a problem which the Victorians named 'the woman question': what would be the appropriate social role for women in the new industrialized society?

ACTIVITY 2   You should now read **Reading B, 'The woman question'**, by Barbara Ehrenreich and Deidre English.

As you do so, pay particular attention to the question of male dominance in the public sphere.

Finally, in trying to judge which of these accounts is most accurate, we have to bear in mind that historical 'facts' do not speak for themselves. We should note that both Clark and Shorter were committed to particular views of history which may have influenced the kind of evidence they looked for and selected to illustrate their arguments. Clark, who was born into a business family (Clarks' Shoes), idealized the small family business and favoured a return to an economy based upon it. Shorter, by contrast, is associated with 'modernization' theory, which sees industrial development as part of the advance of progress, inevitably leading to a better and freer society. These perspectives and commitment to the values which are associated with them inevitably tend to colour people's interpretations of history. One of the tasks which face us as social scientists is the need to move perpetually between concepts and the evidence used to support them, in order to perceive the biases associated with particular standpoints and thereby to refine our concepts and work towards a more adequate reading of the 'facts'. This is no easy task, as you will quickly discover when you try it for yourself!

ACTIVITY 3   Before reading further you should spend some time on the following:

1   Summarize the main points of difference between the positions of Clark, Shorter, and Ehrenreich and English.

2   In what senses could pre-industrial England be described as patriarchal? (Consider the definitions of patriarchy I have discussed in this section and the extent to which each of them could be applicable to pre-industrial England.)

3   Consider some of the ways in which women's lives seem to have changed since the pre-industrial period. Are Ehrenreich and English correct in their belief that patriarchy has declined?

2.3   CLASSES AND POWER IN PRE-INDUSTRIAL SOCIETY

One difficulty in assessing the position of women in pre-industrial society is that it varied according to their place in the social hierarchy. The strong, independent women whom Clark so admired were typically the wives of wealthier farmers and tradesmen; the position of labouring women was less enviable. This points to the way in which gender relations and class relations link together so that it is difficult to understand one without considering the other.

Class is a notoriously difficult concept to define, both in its sociological and common-sense usages, and there is considerable disagreement between different sociologists of different theoretical perspectives over the basis of class. However, there is general agreement that classes are produced by the economic arrangements within society. Here is my own definition, which pulls together some of the common themes from the different perspectives: a class is a group whose members share a common economic position, often involving a common lifestyle, and which is differentiated from other groups in terms of power and status, and the chances its members have of succeeding or bettering themselves in material terms. Obviously, as the pre-industrial economy was so different from ours, it generated different economic groups. Indeed, the very word class was not commonly used before the nineteenth century. People tended to talk of ranks or orders, or simply of the rich and the poor. Nevertheless, society was sharply divided on an economic basis in terms of wealth, property and how people made their living.

At the top of the hierarchy, as we noted before, were the landowning classes, ranging from the monarch and nobility to the gentry and local squires who dominated one particular small village. This group, defined by possession of land as the basis of its wealth, was a small elite. One historian, Robert Malcolmson, estimates that 75 to 80 per cent of the English population at the end of the seventeenth century were labourers (Malcolmson, 1981). Most of these were dependent on the elite for their livelihood, renting land from them, or hiring themselves out to them as labourers. There were many gradations within this group, ranging from small farmers to poor cottagers to paupers, but what they had in common was lack of any real wealth, dependence on the rich for work or sale of their produce, and the possibility of falling into poverty because of their limited resources. Craftsmen and tradesmen can be seen as a kind of middle class between the two agricultural groupings of landowners and labourers, and different from them in that their livelihood did not depend on land. Karl Marx saw these urban groups as the forerunners of the new industrial society. The guild organizations, granted rights by the monarch with legal backing, gave the artisans some degree of independence and security, and higher status than that of the common agricultural labourers.

These three major class groupings had been in existence right through from the mediaeval period until the end of the seventeenth century; but the eighteenth century brought important changes in the social structure. Even before the advent of the Industrial Revolution the economy was changing with the development of what has been called 'proto-industry'. This was the beginning of large-scale industry run on a capitalist basis — that is, organized and controlled as a profit-making speculation by non-labouring entrepreneurs who provided the initial investment. In what was also known as the 'putting-out system', many families continued to work in their own homes, but with raw materials and tools provided by the entrepreneurs, who also specified what work should be done and marketed the finished goods. This new class of entrepreneurs emerged from many backgrounds: some were originally merchants or master-craftsmen, some were farmers branching out into manufacture, some rose from the ranks of the labouring poor. But their rise to power heralded the collapse of the independent household work-unit. At the same time, changes in methods of agriculture meant that many peasants or farm-labouring families lost possession of their smallholdings or tenancies, or found them no longer viable as a means of livelihood. The enclosure of common land, on which villagers had been able to graze livestock and which provided them with such necessities as fuel and building materials, also made it harder for the poor to make a living from the land. Both in manufacture and agriculture more and more people had to work as 'day' or wage labourers.

The eighteenth century, then, saw the emergence of the two social groups which were held by Karl Marx to be the two great classes of industrial society: the entrepreneurial capitalists and the landless wage-earners or *proletariat*. While a large landowning class remained, by the beginning of the nineteenth century the possession of capital (the money, property and equipment needed to carry out a profit-making business) was becoming as important a source of social and economic power as the possession of land, and the capitalists were getting ready to challenge the political power of the landowners.

2.4   CLASSICAL THEORIES OF PRE-INDUSTRIAL SOCIETIES

One of the major concerns within sociology has always been the construction of categories — what sociologists call *social typologies* — to describe different types of society. The classical sociologists, Marx, Weber and Durkheim, were all concerned to distinguish and analyse different stages in social development and to identify the causes of the transition from one stage to another. They did not develop typologies as ends in themselves; rather, by comparing and contrasting different types of society, they hoped to understand why these societies had come into existence, how they worked and what were the most important features of each type, particularly the societies in which they themselves lived. This relates to what I said at the beginning of the chapter about the need to look at the history of our society and its formation if we want to understand the present.

Karl Marx

Marx (1818–83) developed a very powerful method of constructing such a typology. He categorized societies in terms of their *mode of production* — that is, the relationships between groups of people who combine to produce goods and services. The term 'mode of production' does not refer just to techniques and methods of economic production (like steam power, or the factory system), but also to the division of labour in society and the distribution of power, wealth and property. Another key aspect in his thinking is the idea of *surplus*, that is the stock of spare goods and wealth left over after the basic subsistence needs of the labourers who produce the wealth have been met. Those who control the surplus become the dominant group in society. Each mode of production has its own characteristic pattern of class relations and in each mode of production surplus is extracted and expropriated in a distinctive way. This is what Marx meant by the term 'exploitation'. In the capitalist mode of production, the surplus takes the form of the value left over from the production of goods after wages and other costs of production have been subtracted.

The type of society I have been describing Marx called *feudal* because it was founded on property and landholding arrangements developed in the Middle Ages. Feudal societies were based on agricultural production, and in them power depended on the possession of land. The two major classes were the landlords and the peasants (or, in the Middle Ages, serfs). Agricultural work was carried out by the peasants in exchange for grants of land and through this arrangement the landlords were able to extract, often by brute force, the agricultural surplus from the peasants. This form of surplus extraction, based on the legal and political power of the lords and often involving the squeezing of ever greater 'dues' out of the peasants, was fiercely resented. It resulted in hostility and bitterness towards the lords, in line with Marx's belief that conflict was inevitable in all societies divided by class. Indeed, for Marx, it was conflict between the various classes, arising from the structural weaknesses or 'contradictions' in any mode of production, which was the 'motor of history', eventually bringing about change from one mode of production to another. Conflicts between peasants and masters, such as the Peasants' Revolt led by Jack Straw and Wat Tyler in England in 1381, were signs of the instability of such a system. In addition, men fleeing from the tyranny of the landlords tended to settle in the towns and turn to manufacture for their livelihood. This provided another threat to feudalism, especially as the expansion of manufacture depended on the free availability of labour while the feudal relationship tied people to particular masters and their land. The demand for free labour was one factor in a growing competition between the landlords and the emergent class of manufacturing entrepreneurs. According to Marx, a combination of peasant unrest and the emergence of capitalist manufacture in the towns eventually led feudal societies to collapse and industrial societies to emerge.

Max Weber

Weber (1864–1920) shared some of Marx's ideas about the economic relationships of feudal societies and the industrial societies which succeeded them, but his interests were broader than those of Marx. He was particularly interested in human motivation and the role of ideas in bringing about change. He drew a contrast between *traditional* and *rational* motivations which were, he argued, characteristic of agrarian and industrial societies respectively. Traditional motives are based on respect for custom and acceptance of long-standing forms of behaviour, often backed by religious or superstitious beliefs. People do things 'because they've always been done that way'. Weber argued that peasants holding traditional values, if offered an increase in daily earnings, would simply work fewer days rather than improve their living standards or start saving up the extra cash! All they wanted was to continue their normal standard of living. Reading C, an excerpt from Weber's classic study *The Protestant Ethic and the Spirit of Capitalism,* elaborates this idea.

ACTIVITY 4   You should now read **Reading C, 'Traditionalism and capitalism'**, by Max Weber.

Traditional motivation was, therefore, resistant to change and also to the habits of thrift, hard work, accumulation and reinvestment of earnings, which Weber saw as the 'spirit of capitalism', the typical form of behaviour in industrial society. This capitalist spirit embodied the idea of rational motivation and behaviour. Rational behaviour implied finding the best means to a given end, the ends in this case being bettering oneself and the accumulation of profit. Protestantism had an important role to play here as it encouraged these forms of behaviour rather than either the pursuit of a gentlemanly life of leisure and conspicuous consumption or, alternatively, an unworldly devotion to spiritual things, which Weber believed characteristic of traditional religions like Catholicism or Buddhism. Later on, as societies were secularized and belief in Protestant dogma died away, people would have become habituated to rational forms of behaviour and to the objectives of rational capitalism, and would follow the spirit of capitalism as an end in itself. This cultural shift is discussed at greater length in the next chapter.

Emile Durkheim

Durkheim (1858–1917) provided yet another way of distinguishing between types of society. He was much less interested than were Marx and Weber in economic aspects of social structure. His major concern was with social or moral solidarity — what it is that holds society together and stops it breaking down into chaos and anarchy. Durkheim distinguished between societies characterized by what he called *mechanical* and *organic solidarity.* Mechanical solidarity is exemplified by societies with a very low division of labour, like tribal societies, where most people follow the same occupation. In these societies people are held together by common experience and shared beliefs. There is little room for individual dissent and indeed in such societies each individual matters little; each is like a cog in a machine which if lost or broken can easily be replaced by an identical piece. Organic solidarity, on the other hand, occurs in societies with a highly developed division of labour; such societies are held together by interdependence and people's awareness that they cannot survive without the specialized and skilled contributions of others. Without power workers, or nurses, or street cleaners, or bankers, society will grind to a halt, just as a body cannot function, or cannot function successfully, if it loses a vital organ or limb which cannot be replaced (Durkheim was writing before the days of heart transplants!) In societies characterized by organic solidarity, the individual is much more valued and given the scope to develop personal inclinations and talents. Pre-industrial Britain, in Durkheim's terms, still displayed a fair degree of mechanical solidarity and social conformism. Industrialism represented the triumph of organic solidarity and individualism.

As perhaps you will have perceived, these three thinkers, despite their very different focuses of interest, were all trying to explain the distinctiveness of traditional societies and the transition to a new capitalist social order, and they all saw the decline of feudal or traditional societies and the emergence of capitalist industrial ones as a progressive development. Although Marx and Weber were very aware of the negative features of capitalist society, they nevertheless believed it to be economically more productive and efficient, and all three believed it offered greater scope for individual creativity. Yet for those caught up in the switch to the new type of society the immediate result was often misery and confusion, as we shall see in the following section.

ACTIVITY 5   Before reading further, consider the following questions:

1   What were the different ways in which Marx, Weber and Durkheim distinguished between agrarian and industrial societies?

2   What seem to you to be the major points of difference between the three theorists?

---

3   CLASS, GENDER AND INDUSTRIALIZATION

3.1   INDUSTRIALIZATION AND SOCIAL CHANGE

As we have seen, early capitalist development was agrarian in form. It was the rise of manufacturing industry which completed the transition from traditional societies to the type of modern capitalist societies we know today. Industrialization in Britain was a long, slow and uneven process. Economic historians date the beginning of what has rather misleadingly become known as the 'Industrial Revolution' at about 1780, but the process of changing to a mechanized, factory-based industrial economy was not completed until 1850, or even later in the case of particular industries. Its impact and the disruption to existing ways of life were therefore experienced variably across the population. Yet the changes involved were so momentous that their shadow fell across the lives even of those who were not directly affected.

Table 4.2   Urbanization in England: populations of towns (in thousands)

Town	1801	1821	1841	1861	1881	1901	1921	1931
Bath	33	47	53	53	52	50	69	69
Birmingham*	71	102	202	351	546	760	919	1,003
Blackpool	–	1	2	4	14	47	100	102
Bolton	18	32	51	70	105	168	179	177
Bradford	13	26	67	106	183	280	286	298
Bristol	61	85	124	154	207	329	377	397
Cardiff	2	4	10	33	83	164	200	224
Exeter	17	23	31	34	38	47	60	66
Glasgow*	77	147	287	443	673	904	1,034	1,088
Halifax	12	17	28	37	74	105	99	98
Kings Lynn	10	12	16	16	19	20	20	21
Liverpool*	82	138	299	472	627	685	803	856
Manchester*	75	135	252	399	502	645	730	766
Middlesbrough	–	–	6	19	55	91	131	138
Northampton	7	11	21	33	52	87	91	92
Norwich	36	50	62	75	88	112	121	126
Oxford	12	16	24	28	35	49	57	81
Sheffield	46	65	111	185	285	381	491	512
Southampton	8	13	28	47	60	105	161	176
York	17	22	29	40	50	78	84	94
Greater London	1,117	1,600	2,239	3,227	4,770	6,586	7,488	8,216

* Including environs
Source: Mathias, 1969, p.451.

One of the immediate results of industrialization was the growth of the towns, as is shown in Table 4.2. In 1750 there were only two cities in Britain with a population of over 50,000 inhabitants — London and Edinburgh; by 1801 there were 8 such cities and by 1851, 29 (Hobsbawm, 1968). People, especially dispossessed agricultural workers, flooded into these towns for work, in much the same way as people in the developing societies are attracted today to their cities. The influx of new inhabitants to urban areas was combined with dramatic population growth over the country as a whole: between 1750 and 1850 the population of England and Wales virtually trebled, rising from about 6.5 to about 18 million. The population rose at the rate of 10% each decade (Mathias, 1969). These factors led to gross overcrowding in the towns and the hasty erection of cheap housing. The works of Dickens and other nineteenth-century novelists give some impression of the terrible conditions that resulted, with thousands of people living in conditions of filth, disease and penury. For the first time masses of people in Britain experienced urban rather than rural poverty, arguably much worse, because of the isolation from village communities with the traditional forms of support for the poor, sick and disadvantaged which had grown up within them. The provisions of the new Poor Law of 1834, notably the infamous workhouse system, were an ineffective and unacceptable substitute. In the first half of the nineteenth century the threat of the workhouse hung continually over the lives of thousands of working people.

The classic slum (Gustav Doré, 1870)

At the same time, conditions of work were changing, although this occurred slowly and not for everyone. It is worth remembering that in 1850 there were still three times as many agricultural workers as textile workers, and it was not until the twentieth century that agriculture ceased to be the major employer of labour. Similarly, far more women worked in domestic service than in factories. In 1851 there were over a million women servants. (Table 4.3 overleaf gives you some indication of the direction and pace of change.) But the new ways of work which evolved in the new factories set the pattern for working conditions for the whole of the labouring population. Even more important than the application of steam and the use of machinery was the subdivision of labour — a key feature of industrial organization based on capitalist investment. As you saw in Chapter 3 on the emergence of the economy, Adam Smith in *The Wealth of Nations* described the tremendous effects of the subdivision of manufacture in terms of increased efficiency and productivity, using the example of the manufacture of a pin. He calculated that one worker carrying out all the operations to make a pin could make perhaps 20 pins in a day. Once the job had been divided up into something like 18 separate minute operations, each performed by a different worker, the output of each worker was equivalent to 4,800 pins a day.

In their search for ever greater profits many capitalists applied these principles in reorganizing their production methods. The traditional

Table 4.3 Numbers of men and women in *selected* areas of employment in Great Britain, 1841–1921 (in thousands)[*]

	Men				Women		
	1841	1861	1881	1901	1861	1881	1901
Professional occupations and their subordinate services	113	179	254	348	126	203	326
Domestic offices and personal services	255	195	238	341	1407	1756	2003
Commercial occupations	94	130	352	597	2	11	76
Transport and communications	196	579	870	1,409	11	15	27
Agriculture, horticulture and forestry	1,434	1,779	1,517	1,339	163	116	86
Mining and quarrying and associated industries	218	457	604	931	6	8	6
Metal manufacture	396	747	977	1,485	45	49	84
Building and construction	376	593	875	1,216	1	2	3
Textiles	525	612	554	557	676	745	795
Clothing	358	413	379	423	596	667	792
Food, drink and tobacco	268	386	494	701	71	98	216
Total occupied in workforce	5,093	7,266	8,852	11,548	3,254	3,887	4,751

[*] The figures are based on census data. Figures for women from the 1841 census have been omitted as the data have been shown to be unreliable.
Source: Mitchell and Deane, 1962, p.60

craft-based way of manufacture, whereby apprentices learned all the techniques and processes by which raw materials became a finished product, was vanishing for ever. Craftsmen who took pride in skills which had been handed down through generations were faced with the redundancy of their knowledge, as many of these new subdivided jobs could be performed by young men and women with little or no training. Even Adam Smith, with his admiration for the efficiency of the new methods, acknowledged the stupefying effect such work could have on the labourer:

> The man whose life is spent in performing a few simple operations ... has no occasion to exert his understanding, or to exercise his invention in finding out expedients for difficulties which never occur. He naturally loses, therefore, the habit of such exertion and generally becomes as stupid and ignorant as it is possible for a human creature to become.
> (Smith, 1937, p.734)

Thus the worker not only lost skills and control over the task he or she was carrying out, but his or her ingenuity was destroyed, all of which served to render working people more and more powerless in the face of their employers. Although the artisans struggled for decades to maintain apprenticeship rules, to retain the old techniques and customs of their trades, and to keep out unskilled entrants, their efforts were in many cases ultimately doomed; though it should be said that at the same time the new system did create some new forms of skilled work, especially in the machine-engineering industry.

3.2   PROLETARIAT AND BOURGEOISIE: THE NEW CLASSES OF INDUSTRIAL SOCIETY

Marx has provided us with the most influential account of how all these changes affected the class structure. For him, industrialization consolidated the existence of the two new classes which had been developing from, or to use his own words, 'maturing in the womb' of, the old feudal society. For Marx, the most important feature of the industrial society he was analysing was that it was capitalist; that is, it was based on the private ownership of the means of production (machines, factories, raw materials) by non-labouring entrepreneurs. In his massive study *Das Kapital,* Marx stated that capitalism exists when the owner of capital meets the seller of labour in the free market. This definition gives us the three central elements of the new society: the capitalists, the wage labourers and the market.

Marx called the two new classes the *bourgeoisie* and the *proletariat*, although we might now prefer to use the terms 'capitalists' and 'working classes'. Like many nineteenth-century commentators, Marx also used the more abstract terms *capital* and *labour*. (This reminds us that in discussing classes we are not just talking about identifiable groups of individuals, but about a structured relationship between collectivities which embody different functions within a specific method of production.) The bourgeoisie now became the major holders of wealth and the social surplus, and thus the economically dominant class. In the first part of the nineteenth century they also attempted to consolidate their social and political power. On the local level they established their leadership in many towns, especially in the North and the Midlands, often through acts of public philanthropy such as establishing schools and leisure facilities. On the national level they challenged the old power group, the aristocracy, through various processes of Parliamentary reform. Especially important was the overthrow of the Corn Laws which kept agricultural prices artificially high, thereby protecting the landlords from the free market and helping to ensure their wealth and power. In political terms the bourgeoisie did not so much throw out the landed classes, as come to share the governing of the country with them.

Facing the bourgeoisie was the new urban working class, dispossessed of the means of producing their own livelihood and forced to sell their only possession, their labour, in order to survive. For Marx these two groups were locked in a relationship that was both dependent and antagonistic. The labourers needed the capitalists to provide them with work, and the capitalists needed the labourers to make profits; but the relationship was also one of inherent conflict because of the exploitative nature of these economic arrangements.

Like many other nineteenth-century commentators, Marx believed that the wages paid to the working people did not represent the full value of the goods they produced. During part of their working time, labourers produced goods of a value equivalent to the costs of their own subsistence needs (which would in turn be equivalent to a minimum wage). In the rest of the time they worked, the goods they produced represented extra value. Some of this value, 'surplus value' to use Marx's term, was taken by the capitalists in the form of profit. It could be argued that the capitalists deserved to take the surplus because of the risks they took in their investment and their initiative in deciding what goods were needed by the market. This is an important argument, and is used by many people today. However, Marx took the opposing view: that it was the labourers whose work had actually produced the goods by their skill and effort and that they consequently had a right to the surplus or, to use the nineteenth-century phrase, 'the full fruits of their labour'. However, the mechanism of the wage, apparently offering a fair reward for a fair day's work, concealed from the workers the fact that the surplus was indeed being taken from them. This was what Marx meant by *exploitation* and it was the distinctive form by which surplus was extracted in the capitalist mode of production. Moreover, it was in the interests of the capitalists to try to increase profits by raising the amount of surplus value they took from the workers, either through cutting wages or by forcing the workers to make more goods for the same wages (that is, raising productivity). This in turn would increase the tendency to subdivision which I described earlier, so that, along with exploitation, working-class people would experience ever greater levels of powerlessness and meaninglessness at work, as they carried out their repetitive and mindless labour.

Marx believed that when the working people came to understand how they were being exploited, they would see the system as unjust and seek to change it. The shared experience and awareness of exploitation would be the basis for unified class action, whereby the proletariat would eventually rise up to overthrow the whole economic order of capitalism, replacing it with a juster type of society in which the producers, not the capitalists, would control the surplus. For Marx, then, the working class was a class of revolutionary socialist potential. Reading D offers excerpts from *The Communist Manifesto* which Marx co-wrote with Frederick Engels; these excerpts give a fuller account of the emergence of the two key classes of capitalist society and their subsequent relationship.

ACTIVITY 6   You should now read **Reading D, 'Bourgeois and proletarians'**, by Karl Marx and Frederick Engels.

Marx recognized that other classes existed in society (for example, landlords and peasants left over from feudalism, or the growing intermediate class of administrators and professionals), but they seemed to him relatively insignificant in terms of the great struggle for power described above. It was left to Weber, writing at a much later date, to grasp the social importance of these intermediate classes, which sociologists now usually refer to as *the new middle classes*. These are the various groups of white-collar workers, from clerks to teachers to managers. Weber noted how the growth of bureaucracy had led to vast increases in their numbers. Like the industrial workers, these classes were relatively powerless since they, too, did not own the means of production within the bureaucracies but had to sell their labour; nevertheless, they received higher social rewards and therefore were placed in a situation of competition and rivalry with the proletariat. Weber, like many later sociologists, believed that the growth of the new middle classes added so greatly to the complexity of the class structure that the development of the revolutionary class struggle described by Marx would be blocked.

Weber's conceptualization of classes differed from Marx's in other important ways. While he accepted that there was a major division in society between the propertied and propertyless classes, he also emphasized very strongly that there were divisions *within* these groups. Not only was there the cleavage between the middle and working classes which we have described above, there were also splits within the working classes themselves. All these divisions were generated by the market, which gives different rewards to groups with different assets to sell. Skilled manual workers, for example, will be more highly rewarded than unskilled labourers because of their training and expertise, while the middle-class groupings have various levels of qualification, education and training to offer. The small propertied group, too, is split on the basis of different types of property held; one such division which still remains central to our economy today is that between finance capital (the city, bankers) and manufacturing capital. While Marx's theory of exploitation and class conflict led him continually to emphasize the potential for unity within the two major classes, Weber's stress on the divisive role of the market resulted in his view of a plurality of classes, or potential classes, all existing in a climate of competition and rivalry with one another; conflict was thus as great within the broader class groupings as between them.

This effect, which later sociologists have called *fragmentation* of classes, was increased, in Weber's view, because economic relations of class were further complicated by overlapping with two other sources of social division, which Weber called *status* and *party*. Status inequality refers to the differing amounts of prestige or social standing held by various groups (status groups tend to be held together by common lifestyles and patterns of consumption). Weber argued that status divisions within the working class (the old Victorian distinction between 'rough' and 'respectable' is one example) worked against the development of a unified class identity as envisaged by Marx. Finally, Weber believed that parties and other political organizations would often cut across class and status divisions in their membership as they sought to mobilize power to further the interests of their members. The sale of council houses to tenants by the Conservative party is a good example of how a party traditionally identified with bourgeois and middle-class interests can also cater to working-class needs, thereby encouraging political divisions within that class. In these ways, among others, Weber produced a model of the class structure which allowed for infinitely more complexity than Marx's polar model.

Weber did not, however, disagree with every aspect of Marx's thinking. Like Marx, he saw the capitalist entrepreneurs, the sellers of wage labour and the market as three of the core elements of industrial society. But as we have seen, Weber was particularly interested in motivation. He wanted to explain why people had initiated these new forms of production and new ways of developing wealth. This made him more interested in the capitalist class than in the labourers. He argued, as we saw earlier, that capitalist motivation had a particular link with Protestantism; what he called the 'Protestant ethic' encouraged the kind of behaviour necessary for capitalist success: hard work, systematic planning, saving and thrift, reinvestment of profits. In particular, certain Protestant sects, such as Calvinism, espouse the doctrine of predestination, which holds that men and women are doomed from birth to damnation or salvation. The only way Calvinists could deal with this depressing predicament was by demonstrating faith in the idea of being among the saved rather than the damned. This was achieved in part by steadily working away at their occupation or 'calling'. Weber had a gloomy view of the implications of this for people's lives. As religious motivations died away over the century, the capitalists would continue their pursuit of profit as an end in itself, not as a mark of faith and grace. Mankind would become trapped in the 'iron cage' of capitalist, bureaucratic society, which Weber believed posed a considerable threat to human freedom, stifling creativity and ingenuity. The importance, for Weber, of religion and culture in the transition to early capitalism forms one of the central themes of the next chapter.

Weber's thesis of the 'Protestant ethic' gains credibility from the fact that capitalism developed first in Protestant countries such as England. It is also true that many of the first capitalists were members, not of the Church of England, which had become the religion of the landed classes and gave support to the gentlemanly lifestyle, but of the various non-conformists sects like the Baptists, Congregationalists and Unitarians, which gave much more emphasis to the values of puritanism, thrift and hard work. Historians have argued about the evidence for the 'Weber thesis', but these debates about Weber's historical accuracy are less important to us as social scientists than the emphasis he puts on the role of ideas as a major influence in promoting or retarding social change.

Nevertheless, when I study the history of the early nineteenth century I find myself thinking of Marx's ideas rather than Weber's. The period between 1780 and 1850 was a time of constant upheaval, as working people struggled against the new industrial system and the hardship and poverty industrialism brought in its wake. There were food riots, hundreds of strikes and demonstrations in the industrial areas, rick-burning and riots in the countryside over agricultural wage levels; the Luddite movement smashed machinery as a result of its perceived threat to the wages of skilled workers, and the great Chartist movement of the 1840s sought political reforms, including universal male suffrage, in order to gain a Parliamentary voice for working people and then use it to address their economic grievances.

The 'Peterloo massacre', Manchester, 16 August 1819

Thousands of ordinary men and women set up clubs, joined trade unions, marched, went on strike, demonstrated and signed petitions. In one city alone, Nottingham, there were no fewer than thirty-nine riots between 1780 and 1850, as people sought redress for a range of social, economic and political grievances. Many of these riots caused substantial damage to the property of the wealthy mill- and landowners, including (in 1832) the looting and burning down of Nottingham Castle. However, these movements of resistance tended to be localized and small-scale, reflecting the fact that the development of capitalist industrialism was an extremely uneven process, which took different forms and occurred with varying speed around the country. Responses were far more militant in some areas than others, as, indeed, the degree of suffering experienced by the people varied from region to region, although the two were not necessarily linked. At times, however, as in the case of Chartism, these fragmented activities of the working class threatened to become a national movement.

A wonderful account of these conflicts has been provided by E. P. Thompson in his massive study, *The Making of the English Working Class*. Thompson is sympathetic to the ideas of Marx, but believes too many Marxist sociologists use the idea of class wrongly by ignoring the dimension of people's experiences and subjective responses. He declares that class is not a 'thing' that can be studied outside of the lived experience of the men and women who constitute it. Marx himself made a distinction between 'class in itself' (the economic conditions under which people live whether or not they realize it) and 'class for itself' (class as a politically aware and actively organized body). Thompson believes that these two aspects cannot be separated and that classes are therefore constantly changing as the people within them change their responses and behaviour. Reading E presents a short excerpt from Thompson's book in which he sets out his ideas on class and the necessity to understand it by viewing it historically — looking at patterns of behaviour over a period of time.

ACTIVITY 7   You should now read **Reading E, 'The making of a class'**, by E.P. Thompson.

In his book, Thompson argues that up to 1850 the working people of England, because of shared economic suffering, developed an awareness of common interests and grievances and attempted through the activities I have described above to redress them. Although this working-class movement might not have been quite the revolutionary force that Marx looked for, Thompson demonstrates in his book that these working people were highly critical of the industrial system and perceived it as unjust. They put forward, in numerous documents and pamphlets, plans for alternative ways of organizing society. Many of them favoured ideas of cooperative production, in which there would be no need for distinct classes of labour and capital and in which everybody would work collectively for the good of the community rather than for the profit of a few individuals. If we had been alive in 1840, Marx's ideas might have seemed much more pertinent than they do today.

ACTIVITY 8   Before reading further, you should spend some time answering the following questions:

1   Explain exactly what Marx meant by 'exploitation'.

2   Put forward the arguments for and against the idea that working people were being cheated of the possession of the surplus of their labour.

3   What are the main differences in the ways in which Marx and Weber thought about the new middle classes?

3.3   A NEW ROLE FOR WOMEN

The impact of industrialization on gender relations was less dramatic than on class relations, but just as far-reaching. Alice Clark, whose work we discussed in Section 2.2, may have had too optimistic a view of pre-industrial gender relations, but I believe she was correct about the immediate effects of industrialism on women's economic lives. We need, however, to distinguish carefully between women of the different classes. Working-class women shared in the deprivation and struggles of their menfolk. Women from the higher social groupings were obviously better-off materially, but in some ways their economic position relative to men deteriorated more sharply.

The breakup of the family unit was a slow and uneven process but its effects hit women from the higher classes more quickly. Such women lost their involvement in productive work and became quite dependent on fathers and husbands. Wives of the gentry and the entrepreneurs increasingly led a life of privileged idleness, which has been described as 'the gilded cage'. Only women in poorer families of, say, tradesmen or professionals, who did not succeed in finding a husband would be expected to earn, and these faced an unhappy future because of the very limited range of jobs considered respectable enough for 'genteel' women. Governessing was one such job, but it was ill-paid and commanded little social respect. Many such women ended up as paupers or dependent on charity. It is not surprising that the search for a husband often became the sole purpose of a young woman's life; without one the prospect was bleak.

These developments made what the Victorians called 'the woman question' an important issue of the day. If married women could not be earners what social function could they fulfil? The Victorians developed a whole new set of ideas about women which has been labelled the *ideology of domesticity*. You will find one account of this in Reading F, an excerpt from Catherine Hall's essay, 'The history of the housewife'.

ACTIVITY 9   You should now read **Reading F, 'The domestic ideal'**, by Catherine Hall.

At the core of this ideology was the now-familiar proposition that women's place is in the home. The Victorians acknowledged the seamier aspects of capitalism in representing the world of work as ruthless, polluted and dangerous. Women were seen as essentially pure, but easily led astray; if they went out to work they were considered to risk moral corruption and sexual seduction. Instead, they should devote themselves to domestic duties, restoring husbands after their return from work, raising children and setting a moral example to them, and making the home a comfortable place, either through their own housework or by managing a household of servants.

The ideal family (c.1850)

I want to emphasize again that this was largely a new view of women's role. In pre-industrial society it was seen as desirable and normal for women to be earners and contributers to the household income. But in Victorian England the only approved roles outside the home for women from wealthy families were unpaid charitable work, visiting the sick, and improving the lives and morals of their working-class sisters.

These ideas were based on the principle that women and men were naturally different — not just biologically, but in terms of inherent personality; they were believed therefore to be fitted by nature for different social roles. This was the doctrine of separate spheres. One classic and relatively sophisticated statement of this is found in John Ruskin's essay 'Of Queens' Gardens':

> Their separate characters are briefly these. The man's power is active, progressive, defensive. He is eminently the doer, the creator, the discoverer, the defender. His intellect is for speculation and invention; his energy for adventure, for war and for conquest ... But the woman's power is for rule, not for battle, and her intellect is not for invention or creation, but for a sweet ordering, arrangement and decision ... Her great function is Praise; she enters into no contest, but infallibly adjudges the crown of contest. By her office, and place, she is protected from all danger and temptation. The man, in his rough work in the open world, must encounter all peril and trial ... often he must be wounded or subdued ... and always hardened. But he guards the woman from all this ...
> (Ruskin, 1965, p.59)

The ideology of domesticity filtered down slowly to the working classes. In the 1830s some trade unions began to campaign against the employment of women in factories. Although this was chiefly because of fear of women's competition, they also made use of the domestic ideal. In 1842 the Mines Act prohibited women from working underground, and successive Factory Acts put limitations on women's working hours along with those of children. Although this legislation was the creation of middle-class reformers it was widely supported by working men. The Acts may have protected women from some of the worse aspects of unchecked exploitation, but they also served to suggest that women were in some way different from men as workers, an attitude that would grow in the course of the century. During the first half of the nineteenth century, however, the poverty and insecurity of working-class life ensured that most wives continued as earners where jobs were available to them.

Women without jobs often fell into destitution. The majority of paupers and occupants of workhouses were women. Many thousands more were forced into prostitution, which was extensive in Victorian England, especially in the cities. But most women managed to find work on farms, in domestic service (which remained the chief source of employment for women well into the twentieth century), in factories and in workshops and laundries. A growing problem in finding employment resulted from the separation of home and workplace, which made it hard to combine a job with the care of young children, especially before state education developed in the latter part of the century. Working-class women adopted the same range of solutions as they do today. Some continued to find work that could be done at home (such as sewing or washing); some took up casual or part-time tasks; others used relatives or childminders to care for their babies. Teenage daughters, whose earning potential was lower than that of their mothers, were often required to do housework and childminding. This growing burden of domestic responsibility was an additional restraint on women's opportunities compared to those of men.

Opportunities were also restricted by the sexual division of labour. Many of the new industrial jobs were seen by employers as ideal 'women's work', being repetitive and unskilled, and they preferred to employ women and children as their labour was cheaper and they were considered more docile and less likely to join trade unions. But this did not bring an end to the sexual division of labour, although there was some shifting in the labelling of jobs as men's or women's work. For example, in the pre-industrial economy spinning was a major female occupation while weaving was a traditional male skill. Mechanization took the skill from weaving which was then assigned to women, while men captured the more important and more highly-skilled machine-spinning tasks. These changes frequently provoked industrial conflict, as male workers struggled to retain their old jobs and skills, and the outcome was often a compromise with men being promised the best and most highly-paid of the reorganized tasks. The final result was that the sexual stereotyping of jobs as men's or women's work was strengthened rather than weakened. Campaigns were mounted against women, such as field workers or 'colliery lasses', working in jobs considered unsuitable because they were dirty, involved heavy labour or working beside men. Male control of the best, most highly-paid jobs was an important source of continued male dominance in industrial society.

In this period the family, too, continued to be patriarchal. This was especially the case in the families of the bourgeoisie and the upper classes, where women's total financial dependence on men deprived them of any base from which to resist male control. Among the working classes, women's continued labour-market participation gave them a stronger position with regard to their husbands. Moreover, working-class families were particularly vulnerable to breakup, because of the stresses of poverty, the need to move around the country to find work and the high mortality rates. Many widows and deserted wives found themselves in charge of the family, though husbands, when present, still held greater authority, and wives and children were often subjected to brutality and violence as men reaffirmed their right to be obeyed.

The legal position of married women remained weak. They had no rights to any property or earnings of their own, even those that they had possessed before marriage. They had no rights to divorce and men were empowered to keep children if a couple separated, although in practice most men left that responsibility to their wives. A woman's status was totally determined by that of her husband. If he became a pauper she had to accompany him to the workhouse.

In Section 2.2 we looked at the contention of Shorter, among others, that industrialization brought an end to patriarchy, or at least weakened its grip. But others, such as Sylvia Walby, have argued by contrast that Victorian society was a high point for patriarchy in Britain, as women were pressured to withdraw from economic activity and become more dependent on men. Similarly, Heidi Hartmann has argued that patriarchy did not disappear with industrial capitalism, but merely changed its form, becoming perhaps less centrally maintained by private relationships within the household, but instead being incorporated into the new capitalist relations of production. In her paper 'Patriarchy, capitalism and job segregation by sex', Hartmann argues that capitalism built upon existing patriarchal traditions at work and in the home by utilizing women as a source of cheap labour and by exploiting their weaker and subordinate social position. Sex segregation of jobs became a major vehicle for the continuing social dominance of men; the low pay given for women's work forced women into dependence on men and this encouraged the identification of women as domestic workers.

The Factory Acts can be seen to exemplify the way in which patriarchy and capitalism interacted. Patriarchal impulses from middle-class reformers who wished to push women into the home lay behind the legislation which many employers opposed since they preferred to use cheaper female labour. The motives of the working men who supported the Acts seem to have been a mix of economic consideration (fear of women's competition and the undercutting of wages) and acceptance of the domestic ideal for women which helped them to maintain their authority in the home. However, as Table 4.4 suggests, the end result of the Acts was not to exclude women altogether from industry, but to push them more firmly into jobs which were subsidiary to those of men. Men retained the best jobs and their economic superiority, while employers continued with their divisive tactics and exploitation of women's cheap labour. According to Hartmann, this demonstrates how patriarchy and capitalism work together to subordinate women.

Table 4.4 Total working population in England and Wales, 1861–1911

| Year | Combined total number | Men | | Women | |
		Total number	% of total working population	Total number	% of total working population
1861	9,818,994	6,469,674	65.9	3,349,320	34.1
1871	10,730,286	7,329,123	68.3	3,401,163	31.7
1881	11,187,564	7,783,646	69.6	3,403,918	30.4
1891	12,899,484	8,883,254	68.9	4,016,230	31.1
1901	14,328,727	10,156,976	70.9	4,171,751	29.1
1911	16,284,399	11,453,665	70.3	4,830,734	29.7

Source: Holcombe, 1973, p.213

Patriarchy did not come to an end with industrialization. I would accept the proposition that Victorian society saw patriarchy strengthened, as women's participation in the world outside the home diminished and sexual stereotyping became more pervasive. The doctrine of separate spheres meant that men were able to keep women out of the social institutions of the public sphere, to order them in line with male interests and ideas shaped by men, and to run them on male lines, as Ehrenreich and English argued.

ACTIVITY 10   Before reading further, you should consider the following questions:

1   What are the main points of the 'ideology of domesticity'?

2   In what ways does it appear that patriarchy survived into the industrial era?

(Remember the various definitions of patriarchy we discussed earlier.)

4   INDUSTRIAL SOCIETY AND THE GROWTH OF FEMINISM

4.1   THE MATURING OF INDUSTRIAL SOCIETY

In this, the final section of this chapter, I shall look briefly at changes which occurred between the mid-Victorian period and the end of the Second World War.

The period between 1850 and 1900 was a crucial one for stabilizing patterns of class and gender relations, which then persisted fairly unchanged until the epoch of post-war reconstruction. In these years industrial society became much more stable as it began to achieve its mature form. Relations between the classes became far more harmonious. Strikes, demonstrations and other manifestations of conflict still occurred, but the trend was for disputes to be settled by negotiation rather than confrontation.

Although the working classes continued to fight for their right to a decent standard of living, they no longer held so strongly to their visions of an alternative way of organizing society. The mass of the working class came to accept that industrial capitalism was inevitable, aspiring merely to improve their position within it.

Many factors contributed to this change. It has been argued that divisions were becoming more apparent within the working class. One example is the emergence of a *labour aristocracy*, an elite group of skilled workers, who, in return for high wages, were persuaded to abandon radical action. Such a division, if we follow Weber's thinking, would be only one of many. Perhaps the major division was that between the sexes; the exclusionary policies of trade unions which we discussed in the last section prevented working men and women from developing a common sense of identity. Another argument is that the bourgeoisie was able to use its control of social institutions, such as the education system, the churches, and later the mass media, to ensure that its own ideology became the dominant social viewpoint. Moreover, the working classes were now developing their own distinctive lifestyle, what sociologists call 'traditional working-class culture': football clubs and pools, racing and betting shops, 'the local' and working-men's clubs, music halls and dance halls. Sociologists suggest that this culture fostered defensive and fatalistic attitudes, leading to a resigned acceptance of the status quo. These and other factors contributed to a 'remaking of the working class', as the more politicized class described by Thompson was reshaped.

Major advances for working people were achieved in the early twentieth century with the gaining of the vote and the right to full political representation, along with the formation of a political party designed specifically to further the interests of labour. However, perhaps because of the disruptions caused by the two world wars and the international recession of the 1920s and 1930s, the working classes were unable to make use of their political muscle to improve their socio-economic position until after 1945. Nonetheless, this incorporation of the working classes into the political structure is seen by Anthony Giddens as a mark of the maturation of industrial capitalism and another factor contributing to more harmonious class relations (Giddens 1973).

Meanwhile, the middle classes were expanding, partly as a result of significant changes in the industrial economy. Private companies, owned by a single entrepreneur, were supplanted by public ownership; mergers and takeovers resulted in the formation of large companies with a wide range of production and financial interests. This promoted the growth of bureaucracy, which Weber considered to be a core feature of capitalist development, and produced new types of jobs. Such complex organizations needed armies of clerks, technicians, marketing specialists and managers in order to function effectively. The professions also expanded, partly as a response to the many problems thrown up by industrialization.

As we saw earlier, Weber believed that the expansion of middle-class occupations had radically transformed the class structure, with competition between the two different sorts of propertyless worker (middle-class and working-class) becoming just as important as the original split between propertied and propertyless. While Marx in some of his later works had discussed the role of the new middle classes, conceiving them as a buffer between capital and labour, he under-estimated the social and political implications of such a development. Durkheim's ideas suggest another approach to the implications of middle-class expansion: the increased complexity of the division of labour, he believed, would increase people's sense of the interdependence of the various social groups. Durkheim himself was not greatly interested in the concept of class, but his work has provided an alternative way of thinking about society to the class-based theories of Marx and Weber. The perspective known as 'functionalism', which draws on many of Durkheim's ideas, emphasizes the idea of integration and complementarity between classes. Functionalism suggests that people accept inequalities as a necessary consequence of the complex division of labour characteristic of industrial societies and that social solidarity is thus maintained.

4.2 SEXUAL SEGREGATION AND THE GROWTH OF FEMINISM

The expansion of the service sector had important effects for gender relations too. It provided new 'respectable' jobs for both working- and middle-class women, especially in retailing and clerical work. Teaching was another expanding area which provided many jobs for women, along with the modernized nursing service established by Florence Nightingale. However, these increased opportunities left the structure of segregation intact. Indeed, contemporary ideas about which jobs are suitable for each sex have their origins in the period between 1850 and 1900, during which the sexual division of labour stabilized into something similar to its contemporary form. Women were concentrated in light, repetitive factory work, in the caring professions and in lower-grade service jobs, just as they are today.

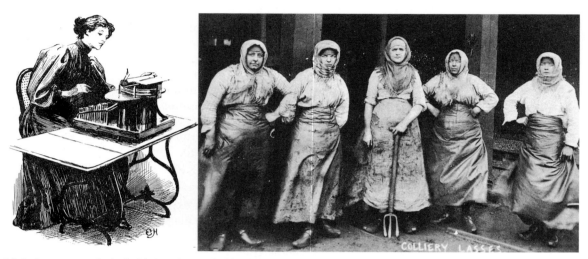

Victorian women in 'suitable' and 'unsuitable' forms of employment: a typist and 'colliery lasses'.

By the end of the nineteenth century the ideology of domesticity had become firmly established as the dominant way of thinking about women. It was now spreading to the working classes; the trade union movement endorsed the ideal of the family wage and the non-working wife (even if not many members achieved that ideal). Victorian ideas of sexual propriety also contributed to the segregation of the sexes (female and male office workers sometimes had to use separate doors to avoid bumping into one another!). The daily experience of men and of women was sharply differentiated.

But in opposition to this arose the movement for sexual equality, initiated by upper-class and middle-class women, like Florence Nightingale and Josephine Butler, who found the restrictions placed on them intolerable. The Victorian feminist movement started in the late 1850s and rapidly gained momentum and support. Its campaigns for educational, economic and social rights for women all had some effect. Higher education was slowly opened up to women (against voluble opposition from male students and professors); professions such as medicine admitted their first female entrants; women sat on school boards and local government bodies. Frances Power Cobbe's exposé of marital violence among the working classes, which she called 'wife torture', led to working-class women getting the right to legal separation in 1878, and divorce reform slowly followed. The Married Women's Property Acts of 1870 and 1882 allowed women control of their own earnings and the property they brought into marriage. Feminists also tried to improve the lot of working-class women, encouraging them to form their own trade unions. By 1900 the fight for female suffrage had become the key issue of the feminist movement and once it was achieved the movement lost its impetus, although women could then use parliamentary procedures to campaign on issues like the family allowance. At its height, however, the Victorian feminist movement posed an important challenge to the ideology of domesticity, although it can be argued that most of the benefits were felt by middle-class women and had little impact on working-class women's lives.

Victorian feminism represented the first major onslaught against the structures of patriarchal control, as feminists campaigned for greater equity within the family and started to push into the public sphere. However, they failed to break down the structure of gender-based job segregation which remained a key feature of the capitalist industrial system. (See also Book 3 (Bocock and Thompson, 1992), Chapter 1, which examines Sylvia Walby's argument that the twentieth century has seen a shift away from private patriarchy (based on the power of individual men within the family) but that gender hierarchies persist in the public domain.)

5 CONCLUSION

By 1900 the class and gender relations of the maturing industrial capitalist economy had consolidated themselves on a basis which would not alter much until the 1950s. Britain was still a society rigidly divided on class lines, with little contact between the classes. The material position of working people did not improve substantially. Their standard of living remained modest and the threat of destitution and the Poor Law continued. Foreign holidays, cars and refrigerators were as yet undreamed-of luxuries for the mass of working people.

Gender hierarchies, too, remained in place. Despite the fact that the legal framework of patriarchy was being dismantled, men continued in reality to dominate in the home and at work, and male control of the public sphere was furthered by the rigidifying of the sexual division of labour. Women's contributions to the economy in the First World War posed only a short-term challenge to established ideas about gender roles, with the pre-war division of labour rapidly being restored afterwards. Before the Second World War, the ideology of domesticity was as strong as ever, with marriage bars being introduced by many organizations. Women and men continued to inhabit separate spheres.

This chapter has traced inequalities of class and gender in Britain through from 1800 to 1945. I hope I have demonstrated to you how particular patterns of class inequality were generated by the emergence of an industrial system of production organized on a capitalist base. Gender inequalities were not produced by capitalism, as pre-industrial societies were already patriarchal. But my argument has been that male dominance at work was deepened by industrial capitalism, which produced a more rigid sexual division of labour, and that patriarchy in the family was also initially strengthened by the separation of home and work, although it began to break down at the end of the century.

The historical developments I have described are specific to Britain. In considering other societies, we would have to take into account variations caused by differing historical and cultural antecedents, differing political contexts and degrees of state intervention in social development, as well as the fact that capitalist economic development takes place at different paces, with a different balance of sectors and a different technological trajectory, in each society. Moreover, all these differences can also operate *within* each society, leading to marked local and regional variations. Nonetheless, we can still trace out broadly similar trends in other industrial societies. They share a common history of working-class deprivation with a struggle to improve living standards, and a common patriarchal legacy, fostering gender stereotyping and segregation. These similarities arise from their shared economic system and from the way that industrial capitalism was historically founded on a pre-industrial patriarchal base.

Since 1945, the British social formation has undergone some dramatic changes (which are examined in Book 3 (Bocock and Thompson, 1992), Chapter 1). But many of the conditions which generated the inequalities I have described still exist. Industrial production is still carried out on the basis of capitalist ownership, the profit imperative, the subdivision of the work process and the powerlessness of the labourers. Gender segregation in employment is still marked, and the domestic ideal still casts its shadow on women's lives. Although patriarchy has been greatly eroded and the class structure has been further fragmented, class and gender hierarchies remain in force; and, as individuals, our own life chances will in part be determined by the way in which those hierarchies interact. I hope this discussion of how those hierarchies originated and have shifted as societies have developed will help you towards an understanding of contemporary social formations.

REFERENCES

Bocock, R. and Thompson, K. (eds) (1992) *Social and Cultural Forms of Modernity*, Cambridge, Polity Press.

Clark, A. (1982) *Working Life of Women in the Seventeenth Century*, London, Routledge.

Ehrenreich, B. and English, D. (1979) *For Her Own Good*, London, Pluto.

Durkheim, E. (1933) *The Division of Labour in Society*, New York, Free Press.

Durkheim, E. (1964) *The Rules of Sociological Method,* New York, Free Press.

Firestone, S. (1979) *The Dialectic of Sex,* London, Women's Press.

Giddens, A. (1973) *The Class Structure of the Advanced Societies,* London, Hutchinson.

Hall, C. (1980) 'The history of the housewife', in Malos, E. (ed) *The Politics of Housework,* London, Allison and Busby.

Hartmann, H. (1976) 'Patriarchy, capitalism and job segregation by sex', *Signs,* vol. 1.3, pp.137–68.

Hartmann, H. (1981) 'The unhappy marriage of Marxism and feminism', in Sargent, L. (ed) *Women in Revolution*, London, Pluto.

Hobsbawm, E. (1968) *Industry and Empire,* Harmondsworth, Penguin.

Holcombe, L. (1973) *Victorian Ladies at Work*, Newton Abbot, David and Charles.

Laslett, P. (1965) *The World We Have Lost*, London, Methuen.

Macfarlane, A. (1978) *The Origins of English Individualism,* Oxford, Blackwell.

Malcolmson, R. (1981) *Life and Labour in England, 1700–80,* London, Hutchinson.

Marx, K. (1976) *Capital*, vol. 1, Harmondsworth, Penguin.

Marx, K. and Engels, F. (1934) *The Communist Manifesto,* in *Selected Works* (vol. 1), London, Lawrence and Wishart.

Mathias, P. (1969) *The First Industrial Nation,* London, Methuen.

Mitchell, B. and Deane, P. (1962) *Abstract of British Historical Statistics,* Cambridge, Cambridge University Press.

Millett, K. (1971), *Sexual Politics*, London, Sphere.

Ruskin, J. (1965) *Sesame and Lilies,* London, Dent.

Shorter, E. (1976) 'Women's work: what difference did capitalism make?', *Theory and Society*, vol. 3.4, pp.513–9.

Smith, A. (1937) *The Wealth of Nations,* New York, Random House.

Thompson, E.P. (1968) *The Making of the English Working Class,* Harmondsworth, Penguin.

Walby, S. (1988) 'The historical periodisation of patriarchy'; paper presented at the 1988 Annual Conference of the British Sociological Association.

Weber, M. (1938) *The Protestant Ethic and the Spirit of Capitalism,* London, Unwin.

Weber, M. (1964) *The Theory of Social and Economic Organization,* London, Macmillan.

READING A CAPITALISM AND WOMEN'S LABOUR

Alice Clark

In modern life the majority of Englishwomen devote the greater part of their lives to domestic occupations, while men are freed from domestic occupations of any sort, being generally engaged in industrial or professional pursuits and spending their leisure over public services or personal pleasure and amusement.

Under modern conditions the ordinary domestic occupations of Englishwomen consist in tending babies and young children, either as mothers or servants, in preparing household meals, and in keeping the house clean, while laundry work, preserving fruit, and the making of children's clothes are still often included in the domestic category. In the seventeenth century it embraced a much wider range of production; for brewing, dairy-work, the care of poultry and pigs, the production of vegetables and fruit, spinning flax and wool, nursing and doctoring, all formed part of domestic industry. Therefore the part which women played in industrial and professional life was in addition to a much greater productive activity in the domestic sphere than is required of them under modern conditions.

On the other hand it may be urged that, if women were upon the whole more actively engaged in industrial work during the seventeenth century than they were in the first decade of the twentieth century, men were much more occupied with domestic affairs then than they are now. Men in all classes gave time and care to the education of their children, and the young unmarried men who generally occupied positions as apprentices and servants were partly employed over domestic work. Therefore, though now it is taken for granted that domestic work will be done by women, a considerable proportion of it in former days fell to the share of men.

These circumstances have led to a different use of terms in this essay from that which has generally been adopted; a difference rendered necessary from the fact that other writers on industrial evolution have considered it only from the man's point of view, whereas this investigation is concerned primarily with its effect upon the position of women.

To facilitate the enquiry, organisation for production is divided into three types:

(a) Domestic Industry.

(b) Family Industry.

(c) Capitalistic Industry, or Industrialism.

No hard-and-fast line exists in practice between these three systems, which merge imperceptibly into one another. In the seventeenth century all three existed side by side, often obtaining at the same time in the same

Source: Clark, A. (1982) *Working Life of Women in the Seventeenth Century*, London, Routledge, pp.5–13.

industries, but the underlying principles are quite distinct and may be defined as follows:

(a) *Domestic Industry* is the form of production in which the goods produced are for the exclusive use of the family and are not therefore subject to an exchange or money value.

(b) *Family Industry* is the form in which the family becomes the unit for the production of goods to be sold or exchanged.

The family consisted of father, mother, children, household servants and apprentices; the apprentices and servants being children and young people of both sexes who earned their keep and in the latter case a nominal wage, but who did not expect to remain permanently as wage-earners, hoping on the contrary in due course to marry and set up in business on their own account. The profits of family industry belonged to the family and not to individual members of it. During his lifetime they were vested in the father who was regarded as the head of the family; he was expected to provide from them marriage portions for his children as they reached maturity, and on his death the mother succeeded to his position as head of the family, his right of bestowal by will being strictly limited by custom and public opinion.

Two features are the main characteristics of family industry in its perfect form: first, the unity of capital and labour, for the family, whether that of a farmer or tradesman, owned stock and tools and themselves contributed the labour; second, the situation of the workshop within the precincts of the home.

These two conditions were rarely completely fulfilled in the seventeenth century, for the richer farmers and tradesmen often employed permanent wage-earners in addition to the members of their family, and in other cases craftsmen no longer owned their stock, but made goods to the order of the capitalist who supplied them with the necessary material. Nevertheless, the character of family industry was retained as long as father, mother, and children worked together, and the money earned was regarded as belonging to the family, not to the individual members of it.

From the point of view of the economic position of women a system can be classed as family industry while the father works at home, but when he leaves home to work on the capitalist's premises the last vestige of family industry disappears and industrialism takes its place.

(c) *Capitalistic Industry,* or *Industrialism,* is the system by which production is controlled by the owners of capital, and the labourers or producers, men, women and children receive individual wages.

Domestic and family industry existed side by side during the middle ages; for example, brewing, baking, spinning, cheese and butter making were conducted both as domestic arts and for industrial purposes. Both were gradually supplanted by capitalistic industry, the germ of which was apparently introduced about the thirteenth century, and gradually developed strength for a more rapid advance in the seventeenth century. ...

The spread of capitalism affected the productive capacity of women:

1   In the capitalist class where the energy and hardiness of Elizabethan ladies gave way before the idleness and pleasure which characterised the Restoration period.

2   In agriculture, where the wives of richer yeomen were withdrawing from farm work and where there already existed a considerable number of labourers dependent entirely on wages, whose wives having no gardens or pastures were unable to supply the families' food according to old custom. The wages of such women were too irregular and too low to maintain them and their children in a state of efficiency, and through semi-starvation their productive powers and their capacity for motherhood were greatly reduced.

3   In the textile trades where the demand for thread and yarn which could only be produced by women and children was expanding. The convenience of spinning as an employment for odd minutes and the mechanical character of its movements which made no great tax on eye or brain, rendered it the most adaptable of all domestic arts to the necessities of the mother. Spinning became the chief resource for the married women who were losing their hold on other industries, but its return in money value was too low to render them independent of other means of support. There is little evidence to suggest that women shared in the capitalistic enterprises of the clothiers during this period, and they had lost their earlier position as monopolists of the silk trade.

4   In other crafts and trades where a tendency can be traced for women to withdraw from business as this developed on capitalistic lines. The history of the guilds shows a progressive weakening of their positions in these associations, though the corporations of the seventeenth century still regarded the wife as her husband's partner. In these corporations the effect of capitalism on the industrial position of the wage-earner's wife becomes visible.

Under family industry the wife of every master craftsman became free of his guild and could share his work. But as the crafts became capitalised many journeymen never qualified as masters, remaining in the outer courts of the companies all their lives, and actually forming separate organisations to protect their interests against their masters and to secure a privileged position for themselves by restricting the number of apprentices. As the journeymen worked on their masters' premises it naturally followed that their wives were not associated with them in their work, and that apprenticeship became the only entrance to their trade.

Though no written rules existed confining apprenticeship to the male sex, girls were seldom if ever admitted as apprentices in the guild trades, and therefore women were excluded from the ranks of journeymen. As the journeyman's wife could not work at her husband's trade, she must, if need be, find employment for herself as an individual. In some cases the journeyman's organisations were powerful enough to keep wages on a level which sufficed for the maintenance of their families; then the wife became completely dependent on her husband, sinking to the position of his unpaid domestic servant. ...

In estimating the influence of economic changes on the position of women it must be remembered that capitalism has not merely replaced family industry but has been equally destructive of domestic industry.

One unexpected effect has been the reversal of the parts which married and unmarried women play in productive enterprise. In the earlier stages of economic evolution, that which we now call domestic work, *viz.,* cooking, cleaning, mending, tending of children, etc., was performed by unmarried girls under the direction of the housewife, who was thus enabled to take an important position in the family industry. Under modern conditions this domestic work falls upon the mothers who remain at home while the unmarried girls go out to take their place in industrial or professional life. The young girls in modern life have secured a position of economic independence, while the mothers remain in a state of dependence and subordination — an order of things which would have greatly astonished our ancestors.

In the seventeenth century the idea is seldom encountered that a man supports his wife; husband and wife were then mutually dependent and together supported their children. ...

READING B   THE WOMAN QUESTION

Barbara Ehrenreich and Deirdre English

The Woman Question arose in the course of a historic transformation whose scale later generations have still barely grasped. It was the 'industrial revolution', and even 'revolution' is too pallid a word. From the Scottish highlands to the Appalachian hills, from the Rhineland to the Mississippi Valley, whole villages were emptied to feed the factory system with human labor. People were wrested from the land suddenly, by force; or more subtly, by the pressure of hunger and debt — uprooted from the ancient security of family, clan, parish. A settled, agrarian life which had persisted more or less for centuries was destroyed in one tenth the time it had taken for the Roman Empire to fall, and the old ways of thinking, the old myths and old rules, began to lift like the morning fog.

Marx and Engels — usually thought of as the instigators of disorder rather than the chroniclers of it — were the first to grasp the cataclysmic nature of these changes. An old world was dying and a new one was being born:

> All fixed, fast-frozen relations, with their train of ancient and venerable prejudices and opinions, are swept away, all new-formed ones become antiquated before they can ossify. All that is solid melts into air, all that is holy is profaned, and man is at last compelled to face

Source: Ehrenreich, B. and English, D. (1979) *For Her Own Good*, London, Pluto, pp.5–14.

with sober senses his real conditions of life and his relations with his kind.
(Marx and Engels, 1935, p.26)

Incredible, once unthinkable, possibilities opened up as all the 'fixed, fast-frozen relations' — between man and woman, between parents and children, between the rich and the poor — were thrown into question. Over one-hundred-and-fifty years later, the dust has still not settled.

On the far side of the industrial revolution is what we will call, for our purposes, the Old Order. ...

Three patterns of social life in the Old Order stand out and give it consistency: the Old Order is *unitary*. There is of course always a minority of people whose lives — acted out on a plane above dull necessity and the routines of labor — are complex and surprising. But life, for the great majority of people, has a unity and simplicity which will never cease to fascinate the 'industrial man' who comes later. This life is not marked off into different 'spheres' or 'realms' of experience: 'work' and 'home', 'public' and 'private', 'sacred' and 'secular'. Production (of food, clothing, tools) takes place in the same rooms or outdoor spaces where children grow up, babies are born, couples come together. The family relation is not secluded in the realm of emotion; it is a working relation. Biological life — sexual desire, childbirth, sickness, the progressive infirmity of age — impinges directly on the group activities of production and play. Ritual and superstition affirm the unity of body and earth, biology and labor: menstruating women must not bake bread; conception is most favored at the time of the spring planting; sexual transgressions will bring blight and ruin to the crops, and so on.

The human relations of family and village, knit by common labor as well as sex and affection, are paramount. There is not yet an external 'economy' connecting the fortunes of the peasant with the decisions of a merchant in a remote city. If people go hungry, it is not because the price of their crops fell, but because the rain did not. There are marketplaces, but there is not yet a *market* to dictate the opportunities and activities of ordinary people.

The Old Order is *patriarchal*: authority over the family is vested in the elder males, or male. He, the father, makes the decisions which control the family's work, purchases, marriages. Under the rule of the father, women have no complex choices to make, no questions as to their nature or destiny: the rule is simply obedience. An early nineteenth-century American minister counselled brides:

> Bear always in mind your true situation and have the words of the apostle perpetually engraven on your heart. Your duty is submission — 'Submission and obedience are the lessons of your life and peace and happiness will be your reward.' Your husband is, by the laws of God and of man, your superior; do not ever give him cause to remind you of it.
> (quoted in Ogburn and Nimkoff, 1955, p.167)

The patriarchal order of the household is magnified in the governance of village, church, nation. At home was the father, in church was the priest or minister, at the top were the 'town fathers', the local nobility, or, as they put it in Puritan society, 'the nursing fathers of the Commonwealth', and above all was 'God the Father'.

Thus the patriarchy of the Old Order was reinforced at every level of social organization and belief. For women, it was total, inescapable. Rebellious women might be beaten privately (with official approval) or punished publicly by the village 'fathers', and any woman who tried to survive on her own would be at the mercy of random male violence … .

And yet, to a degree that is almost unimaginable from our vantage point within industrial society, the Old Order is *gynocentric*: the skills and work of women are indispensable to survival. Woman is always subordinate, but she is far from being a helpless dependent. Women of the industrial world would later look back enviously on the full, productive lives of their foremothers. Consider the work of a woman in colonial America:

> It was the wife's duty, with the assistance of daughters and women servants, to plant the vegetable garden, breed the poultry, and care for the dairy cattle. She transformed milk into cream, butter and cheese, and butchered livestock as well as cooked the meals. Along with her daily chores the husbandwoman slated, pickled, preserved, and manufactured enough beer and cider to see the family through the winter.

> Still, the woman's work was hardly done. To clothe the colonial population, women not only plied the needle, but operated wool carders and spinning wheels — participated in the manufacture of thread, yarn and cloth as well as apparel. Her handwrought candles lit the house; medicines of her manufacture restored the family to health; her home-made soap cleansed her home and family. …
> (Ryan, 1975, p.31)

It was not only women's productive skills which gave her importance in the Old Order. She knew the herbs that healed, the songs to soothe a feverish child, the precautions to be taken during pregnancy. If she was exceptionally skilled, she became a midwife, herbal healer or 'wise woman', whose fame might spread from house to house and village to village. And all women were expected to have learned, from their mothers and grandmothers, the skills of raising children, healing common illnesses, nursing the sick.

So there could be no Woman Question in the Old Order. Woman's work was cut out for her; the lines of authority that she was to follow were clear. She could hardly think of herself as a 'misfit' in a world which depended so heavily on her skills and her work. Nor could she imagine making painful decisions about the direction of her life, for, within the patriarchal order, all decisions of consequence would be made *for* her by father or husband, if they were not already determined by tradition. The

Woman Question awaits the arrival of the industrial epoch which, in the space of a few generations, will overthrow all the 'fixed, fast-frozen relations' of the Old Order. The unity of biological and economic, private and public, life will be shattered; the old patriarchs will be shaken from their thrones; and — at the same time — the ancient powers of women will be expropriated. ...

With the triumph of the Market, the settled patterns of life which defined the Old Order were shattered irrevocably. The old unity of work and home, production and family life, was necessarily and decisively ruptured. Henceforth the household would no longer be a more or less self-contained unit, binding its members together in common work. When production entered the factory, the household was left with only the most personal biological activities — eating, sex, sleeping, the care of small children, and (until the rise of institutional medicine) birth and dying and the care of the sick and aged. Life would now be experienced as divided into two distinct spheres: a 'public' sphere of endeavour governed ultimately by the Market; and a 'private' sphere of intimate relationships and individual biological existence. ...

In the face of the Market, all that is 'human' about people must crowd into the sphere of private life, and attach itself, as best it can, to the personal and biological activities which remain there. Only in the home, or private life generally, can one expect to find the love, spontaneity, nurturance or playfulness which are denied in the marketplace. Sentiment may exaggerate the emotional nobility of the home, and gloss over its biological realities. But private life does, almost necessarily, invert the values of the Market: here what is produced, like the daily meals, is made for no other purpose than to meet immediate human needs; people are indeed valued 'for themselves' rather than for their marketable qualities; services and affection are given freely, or at least given. For men, who must cross between the two spheres daily, private life now takes on a sentimental appeal in proportion to the coldness and impersonality of the 'outside' world. They look to the home to fulfil both the bodily needs denied at the workplace, and the human solidarity forbidden in the Market.

At the same time, the forces which divide life into 'public' and 'private' spheres throw into question the place and the function of women. The iron rule of patriarchy has been shaken, opening up undreamed-of possibilities. But at the same time the womanly skills which the economy of the Old Order had depended on have been torn away — removing what had been the source of woman's dignity in even the most oppressive circumstances. Consider these changes, with their contradictory implications for women's status:

It was the end of the gynocentric order. The traditional productive skills of women — textile manufacture, garment manufacture, food processing — passed into the factory system. Women of the working class might follow their old labor into the new industrial world, but they would no longer command the productive process. They would forget the old skills. In time, as we shall see, even the quintessentially feminine activity of healing would be transformed into a commodity and swept into the Market. The homemade herbal tonic is replaced by the chemical products of multi-national drug firms; midwives are replaced by surgeons.

But, at the same time, it was the end of the rule of the father. Patriarchal privilege, of course, allows men to claim the new public world of industry and commerce as their own. But the ancient network of patriarchal social relations had been irreversibly undermined by the new economy. As the production of necessary goods goes out of the home, the organic bonds holding together the family hierarchy are loosened. The father no longer commands the productive processes of the home; he is now a wage-earner, as might be his son, daughter, or even wife. He may demand submission, may tyrannize his wife and children, may invoke the still-potent sanctions of patriarchal religion, but no matter how he blusters, now it is the corporation which brings in 'the fruits of the earth' and dictates the productive labor of the family. ...

The lives of women — always much more confined by nature and social expectation than those of men — were thrown into confusion. In the Old Order, women had won their survival through participation in the shared labor of the household. Outside of the household there was simply no way to earn a livelihood and no life for a woman. Women could be, at different ages or in different classes, wives, mothers, daughters, servants, or 'spinster' aunts, but these are only gradations of the domestic hierachy. Women were born, grew up, and aged within the dense human enclosure of the family.

But with the collapse of the Old Order, there appeared a glimmer, however remote to most women, of something like a choice. It was now possible for a woman to enter the Market herself and exchange her labor for the means of survival (although at a lower rate than a man would). ...

Entering the Market as a working woman might mean low wages and miserable working conditions, loneliness and insecurity, but it also meant the possibility — unimaginable in the Old Order — of independence from the grip of the family. ...

These were the ambiguous options which began to open up to women in the late eighteenth and early nineteenth centuries. In most cases, of course, the 'choice' was immediately foreclosed by circumstances: some women were forced to seek paid work no matter how much their working disrupted the family, others were inescapably tied to family responsibilities no matter how much they needed or wanted to work outside. But the collapse of the Old Order had broken the pattern which had tied every woman to a single and unquestionable fate. The impact of the change was double-edged. It cannot simply be judged either as a step forward or a step backward for women (even assuming that that judgment could be made in such a way as to cover all women — the black domestic, the manufacturer's wife, the factory girl, etc.). The changes were, by their nature, contradictory. Industrial capitalism freed women from the endless round of household productive labor, and in one and the same gesture tore away the skills which had been the source of women's unique dignity. It loosened the bonds of patriarchy, and at once imposed the chains of wage labor. It 'freed' some women for a self-supporting spinsterhood, and conscripted others into sexual peonage. And so on.

It was these changes — the backward steps as well as the forward ones — which provided the material ground for the emergence of the Woman Question. For women generally, from the hard-working women of the poorer classes to the cushioned daughters of the upper classes, the Woman Question was a matter of immediate personal experience: the consciousness of possibilities counterpoised against prohibitions, opportunities against ancient obligations, instincts against external necessities. The Woman Question was nothing less than the question of how women would survive, and what would become of them, in the modern world. ...

References

Marx, K. and Engels, F. (1935) 'The Communist Manifesto', in *A Handbook on Marxism*, New York, International Publishers.

Ogburn, W.F. and Nimkoff, M.F. (1955) *Technology and the Changing Family*, Boston, Houghton Mifflin.

Ryan, M.P. (1975) *Womanhood in America: From Colonial Times to the Present*, New York, New Viewpoints.

READING C TRADITIONALISM AND CAPITALISM
Max Weber

The most important opponent with which the spirit of capitalism, in the sense of a definite standard of life claiming ethical sanction, has had to struggle, was that type of attitude and reaction to new situations which we may designate as traditionalism. In this case ... every attempt at a final definition must be held in abeyance. On the other hand, we must try to make the provisional meaning clear by citing a few cases. We will begin from below, with the labourers.

One of the technical means which the modern employer uses in order to secure the greatest possible amount of work from his men is the device of piece-rates. In agriculture, for instance, the gathering of the harvest is a case where the greatest possible intensity of labour is called for, since, the weather being uncertain, the difference between high profit and heavy loss may depend on the speed with which the harvesting can be done. Hence a system of piece-rates is almost universal in this case. And since the interest of the employer in a speeding-up of harvesting increases with the increase of the results and the intensity of the work, the attempt has again and again been made, by increasing the piece-rates of the workmen, thereby giving them an opportunity to earn what is for them a very high wage, to interest them in increasing their own efficiency. But a peculiar difficulty has been met with surprising frequency: raising the piece-rates

Source: Weber, M. (1938) *The Protestant Ethic and the Spirit of Capitalism*, London, Unwin, pp.58–60.

has often had the result that not more but less has been accomplished in the same time, because the worker reacted to the increase not by increasing but by decreasing the amount of his work. A man, for instance, who at the rate of 1 Mark per acre mowed 2.5 acres per day and earned 2.5 Marks, when the rate was raised to 1.25 Marks per acre mowed, not 3 acres, as he might easily have done, thus earning 3.75 Marks, but only 2 acres, so that he could still earn the 2.5 Marks to which he was accustomed. The opportunity of earning more was less attractive than that of working less. He did not ask: how much can I earn in a day if I do as much work as possible? but: how much must I work in order to earn the wage, 2.5 Marks, which I earned before and which takes care of my traditional needs? This is an example of what is here meant by traditionalism. A man does not 'by nature' wish to earn more and more money, but simply to live as he is accustomed to live and to earn as much as is necessary for that purpose. Wherever modern capitalism has begun its work of increasing the productivity of human labour by increasing its intensity, it has encountered the immensely stubborn resistance of this leading trait of pre-capitalistic labour. And today it encounters it the more, the more backward (from a capitalistic point of view) the labouring forces are with which it has to deal. ...

READING D BOURGEOIS AND PROLETARIANS

Karl Marx and Frederick Engels

The history of all hitherto existing society is the history of class struggles.

Freeman and slave, patrician and plebian, lord and serf, guild-master and journeyman, in a word, oppressor and oppressed, stood in constant opposition to one another, carried on an uninterrupted, now hidden, now open fight, a fight that each time ended, either in a revolutionary reconstitution of society at large, or in the common ruin of the contending classes.

In the earlier epochs of history, we find almost everywhere a complicated arrangement of society into various orders, a manifold gradation of social rank. In ancient Rome we have patricians, knights, plebians, slaves; in the Middle Ages, feudal lords, vassals, guild-masters, journeymen, apprentices, serfs; in almost all of these classes, again, subordinate gradations.

The modern bourgeois society that has sprouted from the ruins of feudal society has not done away with class antagonisms. It has but established new classes, new conditions of oppression, new forms of struggle in place of the old ones.

Our epoch, the epoch of the bourgeoisie, possesses, however, this distinctive feature: it has simplified the class antagonisms. Society as a whole is more and more splitting up into two great hostile camps, into two great classes directly facing each other — bourgeoisie and proletariat.

Source: Marx, K. and Engels, F. (1934) *The Communist Manifesto*, in *Selected Works*, London, Lawrence and Wishart, pp.10–20.

From the serfs of the Middle Ages sprang the chartered burghers of the earliest towns. From these burgesses the first elements of the bourgeoisie were developed. ...

The feudal system of industry, in which industrial production was monopolised by closed guilds, now no longer sufficed for the growing wants of the new markets. The manufacturing system took its place. The guild-masters were pushed aside by the manufacturing middle class; division of labour between the different corporate guilds vanished in the face of division of labour in each single workshop.

Meantime the markets kept ever growing, the demand ever rising. Even manufacture no longer sufficed. Thereupon, steam and machinery revolutionised industrial production. The place of manufacture was taken by the giant, modern industry, the place of the industrial middle class, by industrial millionaires, the leaders of whole industrial armies, the modern bourgeois.

Modern industry has established the world market, for which the discovery of America paved the way. This market has given an immense development to commerce, to navigation, to communication by land. This development has, in its turn, reacted on the extension of industry; and in proportion as industry, commerce, navigation, railways extended, in the same proportion the bourgeoisie developed, increased its capital, and pushed into the background every class handed down from the Middle Ages.

We see, therefore, how the modern bourgeoisie is itself the product of a long course of development, of a series of revolutions in the modes of production and of exchange. ...

The bourgeoisie cannot exist without constantly revolutionising the instruments of production, and thereby the relations of production, and with them the whole relations of society. ... Constant revolutionising of production, uninterrupted disturbance of all social conditions, everlasting uncertainty and agitation distinguish the bourgeois epoch from all earlier ones. All fixed, fast-frozen relations, with their train of ancient and venerable prejudices and opinions, are swept away, all new-formed ones become antiquated before they can ossify. All that is solid melts into air, all that is holy is profaned, and man is at last compelled to face with sober senses his real conditions of life and his relations with his kind. ...

The bourgeoisie, during its rule of scarce one hundred years, has created more massive and more colossal productive forces than have all preceding generations together. Subjection of nature's forces to man, machinery, application of chemistry to industry and agriculture, steam-navigation, railways, electric telegraphs, clearing of whole continents for cultivation, canalisation of rivers, whole populations conjured out of the ground — what earlier century had even a presentiment that such productive forces slumbered in the lap of social labour?

We see then; the means of production and of exchange, on whose foundation the bourgeoisie built itself up, were generated in feudal society. At a certain stage in the development of these means of production and of exchange, the conditions under which feudal society produced and exchanged, the feudal organisation of agriculture and manufacturing industry, in one word, the feudal relations of property became no longer compatible with the already developed productive forces; they became so many fetters. They had to be burst asunder; they were burst asunder.

Into their place stepped free competition, accompanied by a social and political constitution adapted to it, and by the economical and political sway of the bourgeois class. ...

But not only has the bourgeoisie forged the weapons that bring death to itself; it has also called into existence the men who are to wield those weapons — the modern working class — the proletarians.

In proportion as the bourgeoisie, i.e. capital, is developed, in the same proportion is the proletariat, the modern working class, developed — a class of labourers, who live only so long as they find work, and who find work only so long as their labour increases capital. These labourers, who must sell themselves piecemeal, are a commodity, like every other article of commerce, and are consequently exposed to all the vicissitudes of competition, to all the fluctuations of the market.

Owing to the extensive use of machinery and to division of labour, the work of the proletarians has lost all individual character, and, consequently, all charm for the workman. He becomes an appendage of the machine, and it is only the most simple, most monotonous, and most easily acquired knack that is required of him. Hence, the cost of production of a workman is restricted, almost entirely, to the means of subsistence that he requires for his maintenance, and for the propagation of his race. ...

Modern industry has converted the little workshop of the patriarchal master into the great factory of the industrial capitalist. Masses of labourers, crowded into the factory, are organised like soldiers. As privates of the industrial army they are placed under the command of a perfect hierarchy of officers and sergeants. Not only are they slaves of the bourgeois class, and of the bourgeois state; they are daily and hourly enslaved by the machine, by the overlooker, and, above all by the individual bourgeois manufacturer himself. The more openly this despotism proclaims gain to be its end and aim, the more petty, the more hateful and the more embittering it is. ...

The proletariat goes through various stages of development. With its birth begins its struggle with the bourgeoisie. At first the contest is carried on by individual labourers, then by the work people of a factory, then by the operatives of one trade, in one locality, against the individual bourgeois who directly exploits them. They direct their attacks not against the bourgeois conditions of production, but against the instruments of production themselves; they destroy imported wares that compete with their labour, they smash to pieces machinery, they set factories ablaze, they seek to restore by force the vanished status of the workman of the Middle Ages.

At this stage the labourers still form an incoherent mass scattered over the whole country, and broken up by their mutual competition. ...

But with the development of industry the proletariat not only increases in number; it becomes concentrated in greater masses, its strength grows, and it feels that strength more. The various interests and conditions of life within the ranks of the proletariat are more and more equalised, in proportion as machinery obliterates all distinctions of labour, and nearly everywhere reduces wages to the same low level. The growing competition among the bourgeois, and the resulting commercial crises, make the wages of the workers ever more fluctuating. The unceasing improvement of machinery, ever more rapidly developing, makes their livelihood more and more precarious; the collisions between individual workmen and individual bourgeois take more and more the character of collisions between two classes. Thereupon the workers begin to form combinations (trades' unions) against the bourgeois; they club together in order to keep up the rate of wages; they found permanent associations in order to make provision beforehand for these occasional revolts. Here and there the contest breaks out into riots.

Now and then the workers are victorious, but only for a time. The real fruit of their battles lies, not in the immediate result, but in the ever expanding union of the workers. This union is helped on by the improved means of communication that are created by modern industry, and that place the workers of different localities in contact with one another. ...

This organisation of the proletarians into a class, and consequently into a political party, is continually being upset again by the competition between the workers themselves. But it ever rises up again, stronger, firmer, mightier. ...

Of all the classes that stand face to face with the bourgeoisie today, the proletariat alone is a really revolutionary class. The other classes decay and finally disappear in the face of modern industry; the proletariat is its special and essential product. ...

The essential condition for the existence and for the sway of the bourgeois class, is the formation and augmentation of capital; the condition for capital is wage-labour. Wage-labour rests exclusively on competition between the labourers. The advance of industry, whose involuntary promoter is the bourgeoisie, replaces the isolation of the labourers, due to competition, by their revolutionary combination, due to association. The development of modern industry, therefore, cuts from under its feet the very foundation on which the bourgeoisie produces and appropriates products. What the bourgeoisie therefore produces, above all, are its own grave-diggers. Its fall and the victory of the proletariat are equally inevitable.

READING E   THE MAKING OF A CLASS

E.P.Thompson

The working class did not rise like the sun at an appointed time. It was present at its own making. ...

By class I understand a historical phenomenon, unifying a number of disparate and seemingly unconnected events, both in the raw material of experience and in consciousness. I emphasize that it is a *historical* phenomenon. I do not see class as a 'structure', nor even as a 'category', but as something which in fact happens (and can be shown to have happened) in human relationships.

More than this, the notion of class entails the notion of historical relationship. Like any other relationship, it is a fluency which evades analysis if we attempt to stop it dead at any given moment and anatomize its structure. The finest-meshed sociological net cannot give us a pure specimen of class, any more than it can give us one of deference or of love. The relationship must always be embodied in real people and in a real context. Moreover, we cannot have two distinct classes, each with an independent being, and then bring them *into* relationship with each other. We cannot have love without lovers, nor deference without squires and labourers. And class happens when some men, as a result of common experiences (inherited or shared), feel and articulate the identity of their interests as between themselves, and as against other men whose interests are different from (and usually opposed to) theirs. The class experience is largely determined by the productive relations into which men are born — or enter involuntarily. Class-consciousness is the way in which these experiences are handled in cultural terms: embodied in traditions, value-systems, ideas, and institutional forms. If the experience appears as determined, class-consciousness does not. We can see a *logic* in the responses of similar occupational groups undergoing similar experiences, but we cannot predicate any *law*. Consciousness of class arises in the same way in different times and places, but never in just the same way.

There is today an ever-present temptation to suppose that class is a thing. This was not Marx's meaning, in his own historical writing, yet the error vitiates much latter-day 'Marxist' writing. 'It', the working class, is assumed to have a real existence, which can be defined almost mathematically — so many men who stand in a certain relation to the means of production. Once this is assumed it becomes possible to deduce the class-consciousness which 'it' ought to have (but seldom does have) if 'it' was properly aware of its own position and real interests. ...

If we remember that class is a relationship, and not a thing, we cannot think in this way. ...

If we stop history at a given point, then there are no classes but simply a multitude of individuals with a multitude of experiences. But if we watch

Source: Thompson, E.P. (1968) *The Making of the English Working Class*, Harmondsworth, Penguin, pp.9–11.

these men over an adequate period of social change, we observe patterns in their relationships, their ideas, and their institutions. Class is defined by men as they live their own history, and, in the end, this is its only definition.

READING F   THE DOMESTIC IDEAL
Catherine Hall

The ... definition of housework that I want to look at is the one which was current in early Victorian society. The dominant ideal definition was one which was established by the Victorian middle class and which was highly unsuited to working-class experience. One of the major functions of the Victorian family was to provide a privatised haven for the man who was subject day in and day out to the pressures of competition in the new industrial world. This feminine role was, one might say, a new aspect of the material reproduction of labour power — to provide men at home with the emotional support to face the world of work outside. As Engels says, the family is not only the sum of its economic functions; it is not just a serving-house for capitalism, standing in a one to one relationship with the mode of production — it is also itself a system of relations and emotional needs which shape responses in the world and are created and defined with peculiar strength within the intimate sphere of the family (Engels, 1940). So just as ... in the seventeenth century women became much less directly concerned with the creation of surplus value and much more concerned with the production of the proper conditions for capitalist production — so, with the coming of industrial capitalism, the more total separation of work from home and the public from the private, the proper role of women was increasingly seen to be *at home*. The family was at the centre of Victorian middle-class social life and the fulcrum for the complex set of social values which comprised middle-class respectability. We now know something of the degree of double standards and the mechanism of psychological projection which sustained this ethic. As Marx was the first to point out, the respectable middle-class lady and the prostitute were two sides of the same coin — one might almost say bedfellows! The rich harvest of Victorian pornography would not exist without the Victorian gentleman's ability to travel constantly between virginal ladies upstairs and easy prey below stairs. So it became essential for the preservation of family life that women should be at one and the same time exalted and despised. Thomas Arnold talked of that peculiar sense of solemnity with which the very idea of domestic life was invested: the conception of the home was a source of virtues and emotions which could not be found elsewhere. As Ruskin puts it in *Sesame and Lilies*, 'This is the true nature of home — it is the place of peace — the shelter not only from all injury, but from all terror, doubt and division. In so far as it is not this, it is not home; so far as the anxieties of the outer life penetrate into it, and the inconsistently minded, unknown, unloved, or hostile society of the outer

Source: Hall, C. (1980) 'The history of the housewife', in Malos, E. (ed.) *The Politics of Housework*, London, Allison and Busby, pp.61–3.

world is allowed by either husband or wife to cross the threshold, it ceases to be home.' (Quoted in Houghton, 1957, p.343.) William Thompson in his *Appeal on Behalf of One Half of the Human Race* (1825) was somewhat sceptical of the male-oriented view of the home. 'Home', he writes, 'was the eternal prison house of the wife; her husband painted it as the abode of calm bliss, but took care to find outside its doors a species of bliss not quite so calm, but of a much more varied and stimulating description.' (Thompson, 1970, p.79.) The Victorians needed to sentimentalise the home in order to give themselves some relief from the anxieties of the public world. Tennyson ironically epitomises the new tradition in *The Princess:*

> Man for the field and woman for the hearth;
> Man for the sword, and for the needle she;
> Man with the head and woman with the heart;
> Man to command, and woman to obey;
> All else confusion.
> (V.437–41)

As endless manuals reminded the Victorian wife and mother, their job was to be 'a companion who will raise the tone of a man's mind from low anxieties and vulgar cares' and preserve an exalted love free from the taint of sexuality or passion. Love should be an uplifting experience and belonged at home — sex was a different matter. Middle-class women who saw themselves as tending the household and maintaining its moral tone provided sex on demand for their husbands along with preserves, clean linen and roast meat. The notion of autonomous sexual pleasure for themselves was unthought of: sex was a necessary obligation owed to men and not one which women were permitted to talk or think about as owed to themselves. Mrs Ellis in her manual *Daughters of England* gives us a rich Victorian middle-class definition of love: "What, then, I would ask again, is love in its highest, holiest character?' It is woman's all — her health, her power, her very being. Man, let him love as he may, has ever an existence distinct from that of his affections. He has his worldly interests, his public character, his ambition, his competition with other men — but woman centres all in that one feeling, and 'in that *she* lives, or else *she* has no life'. In woman's love is mingled the trusting dependence of a child, for she ever looks up to man as her protector, and her guide; the frankness, the social feeling, and the tenderness of a sister — for is not man her friend? The solicitude, the anxiety, the careful watching of the mother — for would she not suffer to preserve him from harm? Such is love in a noble mind. ...' (Ellis, 1843, pp.99–100.)

As the rapidly expanding bourgeoisie extended its range of power and influence, as it established itself not only economically but also politically, so it took on — as the seventeenth-century bourgeoisie had done — the ideas of the ruling class about the proper activities of women: namely, economic idleness. As a result of the increase in wealth and consumer developments which came with the industrial revolution women's activities were restricted in various directions. The employment of servants and the mass production of articles formerly made in the home gradually made such idleness physically possible for the privileged. The industrialisation in textiles made redundant one of women's most traditional skills — that is, spinning — and the invention of the sewing-machine, for example, altered conditions even further in the direction of the leisured lady. Increasing wealth brought new standards of luxury and new ideas of refinement which prevented women in the trading and business classes from taking any further share in their husbands' concerns. In the eighteenth century many of women's entrepreneurial activities had been based on experience rather than training — but as the division of labour developed and education and skill became more important there was no provision for the training and education of women. The process which had begun in the seventeenth century with the emergence of capitalism was carried several stages further and affected much greater numbers of women in the nineteenth century. Margaretta Greg in her diary in 1853 wrote: 'A lady, to be such, must be a mere lady and nothing else. She must not work for profit … .' (Quoted in Pinchbeck, 1930, p.315.)

References

Ellis, Mrs S. (1842) *The Daughters of England: Their Position in Society, Character and Responsibilities*, London, Fisher.

Ellis, Mrs S. (1843) *The Wives of England: Their Relative Duties, Domestic Influence, and Social Obligations*, London, Fisher.

Engels, F. (1940) *The Origins of the Family, Private Property and the State*, London, Lawrence & Wishart.

Houghton, W.E. (1957) *The Victorian Frame of Mind, 1830–1870*, New Haven, Yale University Press.

Pinchbeck, I. (1930) *Women Workers and the Industrial Revolution, 1750–1850*, London, Routledge.

Thompson, W. (1970) *Appeal on Behalf of One Half of the Human Race, Women, Against the Pretentions of the Other Half, Men, to Retain them in Civil and Domestic Slavery*, Mallow, C.P. Hyland.

CHAPTER 5 THE CULTURAL FORMATIONS OF MODERN SOCIETY

Robert Bocock

CONTENTS

1   INTRODUCTION

> Culture is one of the two or three most complicated words in the
> English language ... This is so partly because of its intricate
> historical development, in several European languages, but mainly
> because it has now come to be used for important concepts in
> several distinct intellectual disciplines and in several distinct and
> incompatible systems of thought.
> (Williams, 1983, p.87)

In earlier units we looked at crucial moments, processes and ideas in
the historical development of the political, economic and social spheres
of modern societies. This chapter examines another part of the story —
namely, the formation of modern culture. As the quotation above
indicates, 'culture' is a complex term and carries particular meanings in
different disciplines. We shall start, therefore, in the next section, by
considering what the term 'culture' means and examining its use as a
sociological concept.

As we shall see, in the most important sociological use of the term,
culture is understood as referring to the whole texture of a society and
the way language, symbols, meanings, beliefs and values organize social
practices. The sociological analysis of culture in this sense has led to
the development of a distinctive 'tool-kit' of concepts and forms of
classification. A number of these derive from what is called a
structuralist approach and may at first seem rather abstract and
theoretical. These concepts will be introduced and explained in Section
3, which will also examine how they have been used to analyse cultural
formations and cultural phenomena in the work of Émile Durkheim and
Claude Lévi-Strauss.

The structuralist perspective has been criticized as of limited value in
addressing questions of cultural change, and therefore as being rather
different from more traditional sociological analyses of culture which
are very much concerned with questions of how cultures change.
Section 4 will consider the transition in western society from a feudal to
a capitalist culture by focusing on Max Weber's argument that it was a
distinctive form of *religious* thinking which led to the unique, and
uniquely successful, culture of capitalism which developed in the West.
Weber's approach provides a different methodology for analysing
culture, but there are significant links with Durkheim's, notably in
according religion a central role in determining cultural formation.

Finally, we shall examine the cultural changes associated with
industrialization, urbanization and secularization which emerged
towards the end of the nineteenth century. Analyses by Weber, Marx,
Freud and the Frankfurt School of social scientists all point to a growing
disillusion with this scientific and rationalist culture and further show
the significance of values and beliefs as constituents of culture. In
reading about the ways in which some of the greatest of sociologists have

set about classifying societies, and explaining cultural change, we learn something important. It is that, in attempting to analyse a pattern of behaviour in any given society, we are forced to reflect on how individuals *think,* communicate and attribute meaning to things. The attempt to relate individual experience to the wider social structure is the essence of sociology, and at its heart is the concept of culture.

2   DEFINING CULTURE

The meaning of the term 'culture' has changed over time, especially in the period of the transition from traditional social formations to modernity.

The **first** and earliest meaning of 'culture' can be found in writing of the fifteenth century, when the word was used to refer to the tending of crops (cultivation) or looking after animals. This meaning is retained in modern English in such words as 'agriculture' and 'horticulture'.

The **second** meaning developed in the early sixteenth century. It extended the idea of 'cultivation' from plants and animals to more abstract things, like the human mind. Francis Bacon, for example, wrote of 'the culture and manurance of minds' (1605) and Thomas Hobbes of 'a culture of their minds' (1651). There soon developed the idea that only some people — certain individuals, groups or classes — had 'cultured' or cultivated minds and manners; and that only some nations (mainly European ones) exhibited a high standard of culture or civilization.

By the eighteenth century, Raymond Williams observed, 'culture' had acquired distinct class overtones. Only the wealthy classes of Europe could aspire to such a high level of refinement. The modern meaning of the term 'culture', which associates it with 'the arts' is also closely related to this definition, since it refers not only to the actual work of artists and intellectuals, but to the general state of civilization associated with the pursuit of the arts by a cultivated élite. Raymond Williams commented that 'this seems often now the most widespread use: *culture* is music, literature, painting, and sculpture, theatre and film … sometimes with the addition of philosophy, scholarship and history' (Williams, 1983, p.87).

However, the notion of culture has been extended in the twentieth century to include the 'popular culture' of the working class and the lower middle class — a popular culture which is penetrated by, though not the same as, the contents of the mass media (film, television, sports, popular music, newspapers and magazines). Rather than this popular culture being an extension of the notion of the cultivated tastes of a 'cultured person', it is in tension with or can be said to have displaced it. There is often a sharp distinction drawn between 'high' and 'popular' culture, and the popular arts are sometimes seen as antagonistic to the fine arts.

Note that there is an interplay here between using such words as 'cultivated' and 'cultured' in a *descriptive* way (e.g. in characterizing the arts and artistic pursuits) and using them in an *evaluative* way which implies that some ways of life or some kinds of taste are of higher value than others. Much of what is sometimes called the 'cultural debate' about standards in the arts and the debasement of high culture by mass culture, stems from this ambiguity between the descriptive and the evaluative uses of the word 'culture'.

A **third** definition of 'culture', which has been most influential in the social sciences, stems from the Enlightenment. In the eighteenth century, writers used the word to refer to the general secular process of social development (as in 'European society and culture'). The Enlightenment view, common in Europe in the eighteenth century, was that there was a process of unilinear, historical self-development of humanity, which all societies would pass through, and in which Europe played the central, universal role because it was the highest point of civilization or cultured human development.

An important qualification in this usage was introduced by the German writer Herder in his book *Ideas on the Philosophy of the History of Mankind* (1784–91). Herder criticized this Eurocentric 'subjugation and domination of the four quarters of the globe'. 'The very thought of a superior European culture,' he wrote, 'is a blatant insult to the majesty of Nature.'

> It is necessary, Herder argued, in a decisive innovation, to speak of 'cultures' in the plural: the specific and variable cultures of social and economic groups within a nation [and between different nations]. This sense was widely developed, in the Romantic movement, as an alternative to the orthodox and dominant '*civilization*'. It was first used to emphasise national and traditional cultures, including the new concept of 'folk-culture'.
> (Williams, 1983, p.89)

Herder's innovation has proved highly significant for the social sciences, especially sociology and anthropology. In this **fourth** definition, the word 'cultures' (in the plural), refers to the distinctive ways of life, the shared values and meanings, common to different groups — nations, classes, sub-cultures (as, for example, in phrases like 'working-class culture' or 'bourgeois culture') — and historical periods. This is sometimes known as the 'anthropological' definition of culture.

Finally, a **fifth** meaning of the word 'culture' has emerged, which has had a considerable impact on all the social sciences and the humanities in general in recent years. It is derived from social anthropology, and like the fourth definition it refers to shared meanings within groups and nations. It differs in emphasis from the fourth definition, however, by concentrating more on the symbolic dimension, and on what culture *does* rather than on what culture *is*. It sees culture as a social practice rather than as a thing (the arts) or a state of being (civilization). This way of thinking about culture is grounded in the study of *language*, a practice which is seen as fundamental to the production of meaning. The anthropologist Lévi-Strauss, who did much to develop this approach, once described his own work as 'the study of the life of signs at the heart of social life'.

Those who adopt this fifth definition of culture argue that language is a fundamental social practice because it enables those people who share a common language system to communicate meaningfully with one another. Society, which arises through relations between individuals, would be impossible without this capacity to communicate — to exchange meanings and thus build up a shared culture. According to this view, things and events in the natural world exist, but have no intrinsic meaning. It is language — our capacity to communicate about them, using signs and symbols (like words or pictures) — which gives them meaning. When a group shares a culture, it shares a common set of meanings which are constructed and exchanged through the practice of using language. According to this definition, then, 'culture' is *the set of practices by which meanings are produced and exchanged within a group.*

It is important not to adopt too restricted a view of language. It is not only words which operate like a language. All sign and symbol systems work in this way. By language we mean any system of communication which uses signs as a way of referencing objects in the real world and it is this process of *symbolization* which enables us to communicate meaningfully about the world. Words create meaning because they function as symbols. Thus, the word 'dog' is the symbol or sign for the animal that barks. (We must not confuse the symbol for the real thing; as one linguist put it, a dog barks, but the word 'dog' cannot bark!) We could also represent, or 'say something meaningful' about the animal by a drawing, photograph, moving image, sculpture, cartoon or cave painting. So, when we say that language is fundamental to culture, we are referring to *all* the symbol and sign-systems through which meaning is produced and circulated in our culture.

Thus, even material objects can function as 'signs'. Two pieces of wood nailed together form the symbol of the Cross, which carries powerful meanings in Christian cultures. The crown is used as a symbol of secular or religious power and authority. Jeans and sweaters are signs of leisure and informality. There is a language of dress, of fashion, of appearance, of gestures, as there is a language for every other social activity. Each is a means of communicating meaning about this activity and the activity could not exist, as a social practice, outside of meaning. Thus every social activity has a *symbolic* dimension, and this dimension of symbolization and meaning is what we mean by 'culture'.

In this fifth definition, cultural practices are meaning-producing practices, practices which use signs and symbols to 'make meaning' — hence, they are often described as *signifying practices* (sign-ifying practices).

Let us summarize. We have identified five main definitions of the term 'culture':

1   Culture = cultivating the land, crops, animals.

2   Culture = the cultivation of the mind; the arts; civilization.

3   Culture = a general process of social development; culture as a universal process (the Enlightenment conception of culture).

4   Culture = the meanings, values, ways of life (cultures) shared by particular nations, groups, classes, periods (following Herder).

5   Culture = the practices which produce meaning; signifying practices.

None of these definitions has entirely disappeared. Each is still active in contemporary usage, as we shall discover as the argument of the chapter develops.

3   ANALYSING CULTURE

Now that we have a better idea of what culture is, how do we go about analysing it? This depends on which of the five definitions of 'culture' we are using. Take the fourth and fifth definitions, which have had the most impact on the social sciences. According to the fourth definition, we should analyse the beliefs, values and meanings — the powerful symbols — shared by a particular group, class, people or nation. In Section 4 of this chapter, when we discuss Weber and the transition from a religious to a secular culture, as Europe moved into the 'modern' period, we shall do exactly that. But let us stay for the moment with the fifth definition — culture as 'signifying practice' — in order to see what an analysis of culture using this definition looks like and how this method of analysis works.

The shift from the fourth definition (culture as shared meanings and ways of life) to the fifth definition (culture as the practices which produce meaning) marks a significant break in cultural analysis. Both definitions point to similar aspects of culture, but each focuses on very different things. The fourth concentrates on the meanings which groups share (e.g. religious beliefs); the fifth on the practices by which meanings are produced. Put another way, the fourth is concerned with the *contents* of a culture; the fifth with cultural *practices*. Also, the fourth focuses on culture as a whole way of life; the fifth concentrates on the interrelationships between the components that make up a particular cultural practice. One commentator has summed up this difference in approach as a movement 'from "what" to "how", from the substantive attitude to the adjectival attitude' (Poole, 1969, p.14). In looking, for example, at the totemic objects used in tribal cultures, anthropologists using the fourth definition would ask, 'What is totemism?', whereas analysts using the fifth definition would ask, 'How are totemic phenomena arranged?'

Arrangement is what the latter approach highlights. We can see what this means by taking an example. In analysing a ritual event, such as a wedding feast or reception in traditional societies, an analysis which uses the fifth definition would begin by looking at who sits next to the bride and groom at the main table. Decisions about who sits where at weddings have traditionally been made on the basis of who are the nearest relatives of the bride and groom. Usually these are the parents. Brothers, sisters, uncles, aunts and cousins are placed further away, in a clearly hierarchical seating arrangement. The seating arrangement — the way parents, siblings, aunts and uncles, etc., are placed in relation to one another — has a clear pattern or *structure*. It also carries a clear meaning or message. In kinship systems where uncles rank as 'closer' to children than their natural fathers, the position of honour next to the bride and groom would normally be occupied by the uncle, not the father.

Thus, to analyse the wedding feast as a meaningful cultural event, we must examine the practices and rules according to which different relations are seated, and the arrangement of seating positions which results from this practice. It is this 'structure' which 'tells us' something, which reveals the event's cultural meaning. Notice that each individual position at the table is less important than its relation to all the other positions. It is the *relation* to the others, not the position in itself, which carries meaning. The groom's father's place, for example, is important because it is close to where the bride and groom are sitting. The bride's father must be equally close, but on the other side, or else he will feel slighted by comparison with the groom's father.

To get the cultural meaning of the feast, we must analyse the structure and what it means. Each place in the structure functions as a sign. It symbolizes or stands for a particular relationship within the kinship system. To understand or 'decode' the meaning of this arrangement, we need access to the language or code within which these relationships make sense — the kinship system or language of kinship in that particular culture.

This approach to the analysis of culture looks for meaning in the arrangement, the pattern, the symbolic structure of an event. That is why it became known as *structuralism*. The advent of structuralism as a methodology or approach marked an intellectual revolution in the analysis of culture. It was pioneered by the French anthropologist Claude Lévi-Strauss (b. 1908), who built upon ideas developed for the study of language by the linguist, Ferdinand de Saussure (1857–1913). Lévi-Strauss was also influenced by the early founding figure of modern sociology, Émile Durkheim. (See *Penguin Dictionary of Sociology*: STRUCTURALISM.)

Structuralism, as we can see from the 'wedding feast' example, looks at the symbolic structure of an event in order to discover its cultural meaning. However, it has been extensively criticized for being unable to deal with social change, and therefore for being ahistorical. Also, unlike more conventional approaches in social science, it does not treat culture as 'reflecting' in some way the socio-economic structure of society (for example, the way the social class of the people getting married affects how much is spent on wedding receptions). In Section 4 of this chapter, we shall examine the role which culture played in the great historical transition from traditional or feudal society to early modern capitalism, and this analysis of culture and historical change (based largely on the work of another of sociology's founding figures, Max Weber) will draw more directly upon conventional sociological analyses of culture. However, my general argument is that there need not be a competition between the two approaches. It is possible to combine some of the advances of both structuralism and the sociological analysis of cultural change; and a non-dogmatic structuralist approach can throw interesting light on the analysis of cultural change.

To explain how the structuralist analysis of culture emerged entails adopting what might be called a 'structuralist' re-reading of a founding father of sociology, Émile Durkheim (1858–1917). I shall aim to show that Durkheim did work, and can be read, in a structuralist way. Why would anyone want to re-read Durkheim in this way? There are a number of reasons. One is that such a reading produces a reassessment of Durkheim's work. He has often been seen as having laid the foundations for a *positivistic* approach to sociology, as in his requirement (in *The Rules of Sociological Method* and in *Suicide: A Study in Sociology*) that social scientists treat 'social facts as things'. (See *Penguin Dictionary of Sociology*: DURKHEIM.) Seen in this light, however, it becomes difficult to place his last major text *The Elementary Forms of the Religious Life* (1912) — a text about Australian aborigines and Amer-Indian culture, not monks, nuns or priests!

This latter text of Durkheim's would seem to be of more interest to anthropologists who study pre-literate societies than to sociologists who study modern industrial societies. However, it is the *method* Durkheim uses in this text, and his claim that cultural elements are fundamental to understanding and analysing *all* social formations, which are important. The method and type of analysis which Durkheim used in *The Elementary Forms of the Religious Life* is one which can be seen as in broad respects 'structuralist'. To see what this claim entails, I want to discuss briefly the roots of structuralism in two other authors — Ferdinand de Saussure and Claude Lévi-Strauss. Their work affects how we might read Durkheim's *The Elementary Forms of the Religious Life* now, towards the end of the twentieth century.

Saussure introduced an important distinction in the way in which language could be studied and, by extension, the ways in which culture more broadly might be approached. He distinguished between two levels of language: language as a social institution, with its own structures, independent of the individual; and language as used and spoken by an individual user. He termed the social institution of language *langue*; that is, language as a collective system, with its own grammatical structure. Language in this sense is distinct from any single individual's use of his or her own language in everyday speech or writing, which Saussure termed *parole*. Saussure made the important point that language had to be seen as a social institution and as such was not the creation of an individual speaker. The structure, or system, of a language can also be studied outside of historical changes, for although vocabulary may change as new words are introduced and old ones die away, the grammar and structure of a language remains more stable and can be distinguished from such changes. Saussure called the kind of study of language which freezes change in order to look at structure the *synchronic* study of language, and he called the historical type of study of language *diachronic*. Synchronic means 'occurring at the same time'; diachronic means 'across time'. It is an important distinction of which to be aware in the analysis of culture as a whole, not only of language.

Lévi-Strauss argued that a culture operates 'like a language'. He took from Saussure the idea of language having a given structure; that is, a set of grammatical and other, deeper, rules about how to communicate, which lie below the consciousness of any individual speaker and which are not dependent on individual consciousness of them. Lévi-Strauss applied some of these ideas about language to other cultural items, such as myths, rituals and kinship structures, as we shall see in Section 3.3. There is an important methodological point or claim here — namely that the social scientist should analyse how a structure of any kind operates as a structure before he or she is in a position to know what counts as changes, or variations, *within* a structure and what counts as a change *of* a structure. (For example, a change from an elected Conservative to an elected Labour government would be a change *within* a political structure; a change to a fascist regime, with the abolition of elections, would be a change *of* the structure.)

Synchronic structuralist analysis concentrates in the first instance on change *within* a cultural system of some kind, whether it be a system of myth and ritual, of kinship, of food and cooking and eating patterns, or whatever. We shall turn to changes *of* structures (that is, *diachronic* analysis) in Section 4 of this chapter. In the rest of Section 3 we shall concentrate on the analysis of cultural structures, considered as operating independently of major historical changes.

The analysis which Durkheim provided in *The Elementary Forms of the Religious Life* was not explicitly structuralist — this terminology only entered the discourse of the social sciences after his death. However, the seeds of such an approach are to be found there. The common point of departure which Durkheim and the structuralists share is that both begin from the underlying framework, the classifying systems, the structures of a culture, and both start with an analysis of what Durkheim called 'collective representations'.

3.1 COLLECTIVE REPRESENTATIONS

During the eighteenth and nineteenth centuries, tradesmen and missionaries sent back reports to France, Britain, Germany and other European countries about the ways of life of other peoples in Asia, Africa, the Americas and Australasia (see Chapter 6). Many of these reports were not only descriptive accounts, but also contained the emotional and moral responses of the European travellers to these other ways of living. Social science analyses of such societies were not written until anthropologists began the more systematic approach of trying to grasp and describe a particular people's way of living in a more objective, non-judgemental, non-value-laden way.

Durkheim used these reports as a basis for his work. He did not visit the Australian aborigines or the Amer-Indian societies about which he wrote. However, the important claims which he made are not, as we shall see, dependent upon being proved right or wrong by empirical data. What his work provides are basic theoretical propositions which formed the foundations for later, more empirical, studies by other anthropologists and sociologists. The strength of Durkheim's analysis lies in the fact that he developed a whole new *approach* to the understanding of culture through his analysis of the religious beliefs and rituals in these societies.

Central to this approach was the concept of *collective representations*. By the term 'representations' Durkheim meant the cultural beliefs, moral values, symbols and ideas shared by any human group. Such cultural components serve as a way of representing the world meaningfully to members of a particular cultural group. It is not a question of asking what it is that such cultural items represent in the outside world, as though there could be true or false representations. Myths, which are literally false, have powerful meanings and real effects. Representations create a symbolic world of meanings within which a cultural group lives. For Durkheim this included such fundamental notions as the particular way time and space are perceived in a culture, as well as its moral and religious beliefs. This approach accepts that different people inhabit different cultures, or symbolic worlds of meaning. It avoids the question of how we, from our western cultural background, would judge which of a set of beliefs and ideas are 'true' or 'false', since this would only tell us what we find acceptable and congruent within our own cultural framework. The issue of the truth or falsehood of different cultural worlds is thus side-stepped by using the concept of 'representations' in a more relativistic, descriptive way.

The cultural values, beliefs, and symbols of a group (its representations) are produced and shared *collectively* by those who are members of the group. Like a language, they are not produced by individuals as a result of their own cultural initiative, as one might say. Indeed, in both pre-literate and modern societies, individuals who produce their own values, beliefs and symbol systems are frequently ostracized by others, treated with hostility, regarded as mad, or tolerated as interesting eccentrics. In any case, they are not treated as full members of the group, precisely because they do not share its cultural meanings. We learn our cultural group's language, values, beliefs and symbols as we are socialized. Even the basic layers of a person's sense of identity, of who he or she is, is produced by being a member of a specific ethnic, national, or tribal group.

In some pre-literate societies, particular symbols and rituals represent this group belongingness (much as the Union Jack, today, represents being 'British'). Among Australian aborigines and American indians, for example, the emblem of the collectivity may be an animal, bird or plant — what is called the *totem* of the group. Even today, at international sporting occasions, the flag of the country from which the winner comes is raised and its national anthem is played — a ritual which helps to establish and to produce a sense of collective ethnic identity among those who belong to the same group as the winners. Thus, national flags, like other totemic emblems, are major ways in which collectivities, tribes, ethnic groups, or nations represent for themselves and others a sense of their identity, of who they are, collectively. They are 'collective representations' — collectively shared elements of a culture which provide points of symbolic identification for a given group. They represent what the group shares in common; and they help to mark off one group from another.

A totem: a 'collective representation' of a totemic group

Durkheim's theory of culture starts from this claim that the major symbolic components of culture are *representations* which are *collectively* produced, reproduced, transmitted and transformed. The notion of collective representations is, therefore, the foundation of both Durkheim's approach to culture and the claim, made by structuralists, that cultural symbols are central to all sociology and social anthropology.

Durkheim included in his definition of collective representations even such general conceptions as time, space, personality and number. They provide the broad frameworks within which the social cultural life, the shared language and symbolic representations of human groups, are organized. Their existence does not require reference to some abstract cause such as 'reason' or 'God'. Durkheim argued that this insight into the necessarily *social* nature of meanings could dissolve, or resolve, the older problems which philosophy had encountered in trying to give a satisfactory account of how forms of knowledge arose. This important claim is made in the extract from *The Elementary Forms of Religious Life* which is reproduced as Reading A, 'Collective representations'.

ACTIVITY 1   You should now read **Reading A, 'Collective representations'**, by Émile Durkheim (which you will find at the end of this chapter). As you read, keep the following questions in mind:

1   What were the main examples of 'categories of understanding' which, according to Durkheim, philosophers since Aristotle have argued lie at the root of our intellectual life?

2   What are the two main doctrines which account for the 'categories of understanding'?

3   What is Durkheim's suggested solution to the problem of how we are to account for the 'categories of understanding'? Write down in a few words the main aspects of the solution Durkheim offers.

How did you get on? Durkheim is claiming here that even the most basic categories of thought, such as ideas of time, space, number and causation, are also collective representations — socially shared frameworks within which individual experience is classified. These social categories of thought form the backbone — the symbolic structures — of any culture. As Durkheim says: 'They are like the solid frame which encloses all thought.' Such frameworks have been accounted for by traditional philosophers as being *either* part of innate reason, in-built at birth, and known *a priori* or independently of experience (rationalism); *or* as something worked out by the individual from empirical observations (empiricism). Durkheim however argues that reason cannot be a purely individual construction, for then it could not provide a common standard of judgement. For Durkheim, the notion of 'reason' implies some socially shared standards of what is to count as a good, well-reasoned argument.

Durkheim rejects both the rationalist and the empiricist accounts of our basic categories of thought. He argues that the fundamental categories we need in order to think systematically and rationally are socially — that is, collectively — produced. Society is a reality of a unique kind, what Durkheim calls a reality '*sui generis*', and this enables groups to achieve more than individuals alone are able to accomplish.

Indeed, he maintains that it is necessary to assert the discontinuity between these two realms: the societal and the individual. Hence the importance of 'collective representations'. Collective representations enable individual people to think. But they are produced at the level of the collective. We learn them as we learn our group's language. Language is also inherently social, or collective — an idea Durkheim suggests elsewhere in *The Elementary Forms of the Religious Life,* though he did not develop it as fully as later linguistic philosophers did.

How does this idea of 'collective representations' work within a culture? Durkheim's answer is that they provide the categories, the basic frameworks, into which different items of a culture are classified. Classification schemes tell us which things belong together and which things are different. They help us to 'map out' or make sense of the world. Durkheim first studied this process of cultural classification in so-called 'primitive' societies.

3.2   PRIMITIVE CLASSIFICATION

Early in the twentieth century, anthropologists were struck by the way in which the cultures of pre-literate societies frequently contained complex systems for classifying animals, people, plants, and objects of many kinds. Within these classification systems, particular plants, animals, or objects (i.e. *totems*) were also associated with or used to represent particular groups, clans or tribes. The classification system thus showed which totem belonged with which group, and so helped to establish a collective sense of identity amongst all the members of a particular clan. It also served to establish the boundary between that group and other groups, represented by different totemic objects. Totems were thus a key part of classificatory systems in many primitive, or pre-literate, cultures. Totemic systems provided a sort of classificatory map of the society.

Such cultures were socially organized around complex patterns of kinship. Indeed, kinship was their principal form of social organization. Kinship told members of these societies who was related to whom, who they could and could not marry, who should inherit property, and who their 'enemies' were. Kinship in this context meant wider sets of relations than the immediate family of grandparents, parents, and children, which is how we classify kin relations in western societies. Kinship groups would certainly include not only aunts, uncles, cousins, brothers and sisters, but also people who in the West would not count as blood relations at all, and therefore would not be regarded as part of the kinship network.

These 'extra' members of kinship groups — extra that is from a western cultural perspective — were classified as being related because they were members of the same totemic group. Totemic group membership was created, in part, by taking part in a major ritual of some kind.

Classifying kinship according to a system had real consequences because it organized and regulated social behaviour. Table 5.1 shows the classificatory system printed in the old Church of England Prayer Book, which specifies where marriage is permitted, and where it is taboo, in relation to the kinship system. In pre-literate societies, such tables of kindred and affinity obviously could not be written down. Some people in the tribe or clan would retain this knowledge in their heads. Totemic emblems, and the complex classification patterns they involved, may therefore have acted as an *aides-mémoire* for those who had to remember whom a man or a woman were permitted to marry. These cultures contained no modern biological knowledge about human genetics, which we in the West sometimes imagine underpins our kinship system. Such controls over marriage partners pre-date modern medical and genetic knowledge. They are to do with something other than genetics.

Table 5.1   The 'Table of Kindred and Affinity' from the Church of England's Book of Common Prayer

A TABLE OF KINDRED AND AFFINITY
Wherein whosoever are related are forbidden by the Church of England to marry together

A Man may not marry his	*A Woman may not marry her*
Mother	Father
Daughter	Son
Father's mother	Father's father
Mother's mother	Mother's father
Son's daughter	Son's son
Daughter's daughter	Daughter's son
Sister	Brother
Father's daughter	Father's son
Mother's daughter	Mother's son
Wife's mother	Husband's father
Wife's daughter	Husband's son
Father's wife	Mother's husband
Son's wife	Daughter's husband
Father's father's wife	Father's mother's husband
Mother's father's wife	Mother's mother's husband
Wife's father's mother	Husband's father's father
Wife's mother's mother	Husband's mother's father
Wife's son's daughter	Husband's son's son
Son's son's wife	Husband's daughter's son
Daughter's son's wife	Son's daughter's husband
Father's sister	Daughter's daughter's husband
Mother's sister	Father's brother
Brother's daughter	Mother's brother
Sister's daughter	Brother's son
	Sister's son.

THE END

The analysis of classification systems, for Durkheim, like the analysis of symbolic structures for Lévi-Strauss, was fundamental to all cultural analysis. Lévi-Strauss argued that the process of classification replicated the way in which the human brain operates — in terms of pairs. Things arranged or divided into twos, or pairs, are easy for humans to remember. Lévi-Strauss pointed out that in pre-literate cultures, and we might add in modern cultures too, such pairs usually appear as opposed in some way to each other. Thus, we have oppositions such as the following: hot/cold; cooked/raw; sour/sweet; wet/dry; solid/liquid; earth/air; the city/the country, etc. You can see from this list how fundamental this division into 'binary opposites' is to meaning. We know what 'cooked' means because it is the opposite of 'raw'. The pairs work in relation to one another. One fundamental pair is male/female. This is fundamental in that it both operates as a basis for marriage and sexual reproduction and provides human cultures with a general model, based on sexual difference, for thinking in terms of pairs of differences. Some languages, such as French, have feminine and masculine words for objects in the world, for example.

However, not everything people experience or observe fits into the paired or opposed categories which a particular classification system provides: for example, fog or mist are neither earth nor air, but something 'in between'. Fog is neither solid nor fully liquid, neither fully dark nor fully light. It cross-cuts our categories, our classificatory system, at a number of points. This lack of fit may be why fog or mist can be used to suggest something spooky, eerie, mysterious, threatening — a quality which has been used in many novels, films and television programmes in our culture. Honey and other sticky, gooey substances also fail to fit into the categories of liquid or solid, as do some body fluids from the nose or throat. Phlegm, or mucus from the nose are substances which are difficult to classify as either hard or soft, solids or liquids, even as innocent or harmful.

Lévi-Strauss called this basic principle of paired oppositions which lies behind all classificatory systems *binary oppositions*. The term was derived from the basic way in which computer languages operate — either there is an electrical current flowing or there is not (which can be indicated by a plus or minus sign, or dots and dashes, long or short signals, etc.). The important point here for Lévi-Strauss is that this binary way of thinking is not only found in so-called primitive societies. What Lévi-Strauss called 'the savage mind' (i.e. thinking by classifying things into binary opposites) can also be found at the heart of the culture of modern, advanced societies.

There is one very fundamental binary opposition which is found in both pre-literate societies and, in a related but different form, in modern societies. Durkheim formulated it in *The Elementary Forms of the Religious Life* as a basic classification of all culture: the division of things into 'the sacred' and 'the profane'.

The sacred, as Durkheim defined it, is *not* based upon a belief in supernatural entities, which others had used as a definition of religion. Some sacred activities were not dependent on supernatural beliefs, he claimed, as for example in some forms of Buddhism. The central dichotomy in pre-literate cultures, Durkheim claimed, was to be understood as separating those things, times, places, persons, animals, birds, stones, trees, rivers, mountains, plants or liquids which were *set apart* (sacred) from *routine* (profane) uses in everyday activities. The sacred, he argued, is a fundamental category in such cultures. The distinction between the sacred and the profane involves both *beliefs*, which define what is classified as sacred in a culture, and *rituals* which actively *set apart* particular elements, times, people or places (the *negative* rites).

Negative rites, which set apart the sacred, can be actions, such as keeping vigil before a feast, being nude, being celibate, wearing special costumes, or using body-paint. Some are very severe, in the eyes of Western observers: examples include being buried under smouldering leaves overnight before young males are made full 'men' in a special ritual; circumcision; cuts on the face, or body; gashes on limbs; cutting veins; or being beaten by elders. All these are instances of often painful negative rituals which serve to set apart some time period, or some person or group, before being brought into positive contact with sacred things.

Positive rites, on the other hand, include any action which brings a person, or a group, into contact with sacred objects, places, people, spaces, animals or birds. They may involve the parading of the totemic emblem of a group (as in the example of the flags as emblems of national groups mentioned above). They may also involve eating or drinking some component from the totemic emblem — part of a bird or animal, or body substances from animals or people, such as blood, milk, urine or faeces. In later forms of cultural practices than those of totemism, these positive rituals may become more *symbolic*; as, for example, taking bread and wine symbolizes eating the flesh and blood of Jesus, in the communion rites of modern Christianity.

The experiences people have in their rituals are not based on something unreal, Durkheim argued, but upon a real force greater than, and operating outside of, the individual. But what is this force? Given the great variety of gods or spirits in which the members of different cultures have believed, it cannot simply be that they have all contacted the same god or spirit. Durkheim argued that, since 'the unanimous sentiment of the believers of all times cannot be purely illusory' (Durkheim, 1961, p.464), therefore the objective cause of the sensations of such people is not some supernatural being but *society* itself. In summarizing his long, complex argument on this point, Durkheim concluded *The Elementary Forms of the Religious Life* with the following statement of his sociological explanation for the existence, and indeed the persistence, of religions in human societies:

> ... we have seen that this reality, which mythologies have represented under so many different forms, but which is the universal and eternal objective cause of these sensations *sui generis* out of which religious experience is made, is society. ... society cannot make its influence felt unless it is in action, and it is not in action unless the individuals who compose it are assembled together and act in common. It is by common action that it takes consciousness of itself ...
> (Durkheim, 1961, pp.465–6)

This is how Durkheim formulates his major claim that religious experience is not based upon illusions, but upon concrete social, collective, ritual actions or practices. Participants in such rituals (a wedding ceremony, for instance) are involved in a set of practices, often including eating a ceremonial meal, which bind them together into a collective. The wider cultural group's *values* are also affirmed in such rituals — how a husband and wife should live and how they should raise their children are often explicitly, or implicitly, articulated in marriage rites in modern Christianity. The force which people feel in such circumstances is the moral pressure arising from this belongingness, or social solidarity.

Similar rituals are still found in modern industrial societies. But there are a multiplicity of ethnic groups, religious groups, and socio-economic classes in such societies who do not share a single set of meanings, values or beliefs. These kinds of societies have had to devise other rituals at the level of the nation-state in order to try to cement these divergent groups together. In Britain, the royal family, ceremonial occasions, even national emergencies like war, are major components in performing this task of binding diverse groups together into some sense of being part of a united society — with varying degrees of success.

The Cenotaph is a sacred place in the centre of London, used for the ritual commemorating of those killed in the wars

The distinction between the profane and the sacred was called by Durkheim an elementary form of 'primitive classification'. That means not only a classification which is found in pre-literate societies, but one which is fundamental, primal, basic, to all human cultures. All social formations will have some beliefs, values, symbols and rituals which are sacred or set apart from profane, everyday life. Even communist states in the twentieth century, whose regimes were explicitly against organized religion, nevertheless surrounded themselves with flags, parades, creeds and ceremonials — the symbols and rituals of rulers.

3.3   STRUCTURALIST DEVELOPMENTS

We have seen, then, how the structuralist's concern with analysing the symbolic structure of events was rooted in Durkheim's work on collective representations and primitive classification systems. (Durkheim had worked with the anthropologist Marcel Mauss in a study of *Primitive Classification* (1903).) Lévi-Strauss, the French anthropologist who worked in South America, applied the principle of binary opposites as a central feature of all classifying systems to a wide variety of cultural phenomena. He studied the *Elementary Structures of Kinship* (1949), the totemic systems of pre-literate societies (*Totemism, 1962)*, the myths of South American peoples (in *The Raw and the Cooked,* (1970), *Honey and Ashes* (1973)), and a variety of other anthropological phenomena (in *The Savage Mind* (1962) and *Structural Anthropology* (1958)). In all of these studies he applied the basic structuralist method of analysis. The object of analysis was, as it were, frozen in time (synchronic), so that its symbolic structure could be analysed. The structure was analysed in terms of how its different elements were classified and arranged, how the principle of 'binary opposition' (and the mediating categories which fitted neither sides of the binary) worked. What mattered was the *relations between* the different elements in the classifying system (remember the positions at the wedding feast?). The *meaning* of each pattern or structure was 'read' in terms of what it told us about the culture. The underlying 'code' (e.g. the kinship system) provided the analyst with a way of deciphering the phenomenon.

Such a structuralist method can be applied to any cultural pattern, regardless of the historical period in which it may be found. What we think of as 'primitive' ways of thinking may be found both among Australian aborigines and in modern cultures. A British anthropologist, Mary Douglas, writing in the 1960s, has used a structuralist method to analyse the rules governing pollution. In the extract in Reading B, she compares rules governing food in India with western ideas about hygiene.

ACTIVITY 2   Now read **Reading B, 'Hygiene and pollution'**, by Mary Douglas. You should note that the Havik are a group of Hindu Brahmins, priestly scholars, and as such are very high in the caste system.

As you read the extract from Mary Douglas, have a pen and paper to hand and try to answer the following questions:

1   What kinds of food can pass on pollution, according to Havik rules?

2   What is the key word Mary Douglas analyses from western culture to suggest the idea of pollution?

3   What are the two main differences between contemporary European ideas of pollution and those of primitive cultures?

4   How does Douglas use the ideas (derived from Durkheim and Lévi-Strauss) of *classification*?

Mary Douglas suggests that there are significant *continuities* in notions of pollution, taboo, and ritual rules, especially about food and drinks, body substances, and clothing, between traditional and modern cultures, in spite of the development of modern science. The reactions to AIDS among westerners, some newspapers labelling it the 'gay plague', illustrates that pollution ideas have not disappeared from modern cultures.

We have been looking at a particular method of analysis of culture. The method can be applied to a variety of components of a culture, from language to rituals, from cooking and types of food eaten to fundamental categories of thought, such as space, time and causation. All these diverse cultural phenomena can be analysed as structures, which arrange and order perceptions and regulate actions among those who share the same cultural frameworks, the same way of 'classifying' the world. The method is applicable in the broad area which may be termed 'the symbolic'. According to this conception of culture, tiny things — small differences between the way in which food is prepared and eaten, for instance — may be used to mark or symbolize a cultural difference between groups, between who is a member and who is an outsider. Different dietary habits, for example, mark major differences between national groups, and mobilize powerful feelings of solidarity or hostility, similarity and difference.

4   CULTURE AND SOCIAL CHANGE

So far we have been looking at culture in terms of a structural arrangement, which carries a cultural meaning or provides us with a clue as to the cultural codes and symbolic systems of classification which form the frameworks of meaning in a particular society. Essentially, as we have noted, this approach is *synchronic*. History, movement, action seem to be omitted. Thus, we know which objects in a society are classified 'sacred', which 'profane'. But this approach is not so good at telling us how changes in such cultural phenomena occur — for example, how the 'sacred' might decline, or change, when Christian missionaries arrive. On a larger canvas, it is not so good at the sort of *diachronic* analysis which would tell us, for example, what role culture played historically in the transition of European societies from feudalism to early capitalism, from a traditional to a modern form of society. And yet some of the great figures in classical sociology have argued that, contrary to conventional opinion, what we call *culture* did play an enormously significant role — even, perhaps, served as one of the main causal factors — in the historical transition to modernity. It is certainly the case that one of the principal ways of characterizing that transition is in terms of the move from a society in which religion pervaded every aspect of social life (a religious or 'sacred' culture, we might say) to the much more secular (or 'profane') culture, dominated by materialistic and technological values, which is to be found in modern, advanced industrial societies today. How are we to understand and analyse this process of *secularization* which is typical of the formation of modern culture?

This process of cultural change has been characterized by the German sociologist Norbert Elias (1897–1990) as *the civilizing process* (in two volumes published just before the Second World War called *The Civilizing Process* (1939)). This term takes us back to the second definition of culture discussed in Section 2. Elias attributes the process of pacification of medieval society to the development of individual, moral forms of restraint and control. He analyses these by studying the spread of social codes of behaviour, such as table manners and etiquette. Elias also points out how this process had been accompanied by the emergence of the state as a system of social regulation. The modern state assisted the development of *internal* peace through its monopoly control over the means of violence. Somewhat surprisingly, Elias sees the modern state's control over the means of violence in a given territory as also aiding the growth of 'civilization', which required a new individual sense of, and capacity for, self-restraint. Elias was drawing here upon the ideas of the German sociologist Max Weber (1864–1920) in developing his view of the conditions necessary for modern 'civilization'.

Max Weber had indeed emphasized the modern state's control over the means of violence, but his more significant contribution in this context was his extensive analysis of the role of cultural values and religious beliefs in the development of western capitalism. Weber was writing at about the same time as Durkheim wrote *The Elementary Forms of the Religious Life,* but his approach is very different, and provides us with a different methodology for analysing culture. Weber is much less concerned with the formal practices and rules of symbolic classification and much more concerned with the role which values play in major historical transitions. Above all, the question which preoccupied Weber was this: how did capitalism, the economic system which underpins 'modernity', arise and what part did religious values play in that evolution?

4.1 RELIGION AND THE RISE OF CAPITALISM

Weber was not a structuralist — indeed the method did not emerge in an explicit form in the social sciences in Weber's lifetime. Nevertheless, his work can also be seen to depend upon a series of binary oppositions which he used to *classify* types of capitalism and types of cultural symbols, though this has not often been remarked upon by contemporary sociologists. For example, Weber distinguished between what he called 'adventurer capitalism' and 'rational, peaceable, bourgeois capitalism'. 'Adventurer' capitalism was based upon the use of conquest and violence, to extract profits. This was the predominant form during the European acquisition of colonies in Africa, Asia and Latin America and the use of slavery in the Americas.

The second type, 'bourgeois capitalism', was based upon rational action, and non-violent means of exploiting labour. Weber argued that this new type of capitalism had emerged from a set of cultural values based on the notion of a vocation — that is, a calling from God. This was not like God's call to the Catholic priest to *leave* the world, but a calling which influenced behaviour *in* the world.

Monks had been *ascetics* but in roles *removed* from worldly affairs

Thus, as Weber wrote:

> One of the fundamental elements of the spirit of modern capitalism, and not only of that but of all modern culture: rational conduct on the basis of the idea of the calling, was born ... from the spirit of Christian asceticism. ...

> The Puritan wanted to work in a calling; we are forced to do so. For when asceticism was carried out of the monastic cells into everyday life, and began to dominate worldly morality, it did its part in building the tremendous cosmos of the modern economic order.
> (Weber, 1971, pp.180–1)

Why does Weber attribute the rise of capitalism to the spirit of Christian asceticism? To grasp Weber's argument, we must look, first, at the distinction he makes between these two types of capitalism, and then at the role which the concepts of 'rational' and 'asceticism' play in his analysis.

Capitalism, in the sense of profitable economic activity, had existed for a very long time, and in many different societies. But only in Western Europe, from about the sixteenth century, was capitalism in its rational, modern form to be found on any extended scale. Here, 'capitalism is identical with the pursuit of profit, and forever *renewed* by means of continuous, rational, capitalistic enterprise' (Weber, 1971, p.17).

What Weber called 'peaceable, bourgeois capitalism' is the predominant form which this development took in Europe (though exactly how 'peaceful' the transition to it was in reality has been a subject of debate amongst historians). It developed as conditions for peaceful trade and production, stimulated by profit, expanded. (Weber's analysis of the rise of capitalism was briefly discussed in Chapter 4.)

Now, an economic system driven by self-interest, the desire to maximize profit on a regular basis, to accumulate, invest and expand wealth, seems to require a very materialistic set of values — the very opposite of the religious culture which predated the rise of capitalism in Western Europe. Thus, we are not surprised to discover that, as capitalism developed and expanded, so cultural values became increasingly *secularized*: that is, more concerned with the material world and less with the spiritual world, more preoccupied with attaining wealth in *this* world than with salvation in the next. Religion of course remains an active cultural force in capitalist societies, but it is confined to a smaller area of social life and is more restricted in its appeal as compared with the cultural universe in the societies of feudal Europe dominated by the Catholic faith. Secularization appears to be the major process affecting culture in the transition to modern capitalist societies.

However, the paradox which Weber develops in his work (especially *The Protestant Ethic and The Spirit of Capitalism*) is that *religion* played an absolutely critical role in the formation of early capitalism. Modern rational capitalism could not have emerged, he argues, without the mediation of religious culture, especially that variant associated with the Calvinist puritan sects of the seventeenth century. It was the 'Protestant ethic' which helped to produce capitalism as a *distinctive* type of profit-making involving economic action based upon *sustained, systematic capital investment*, and employing *formally free labour* (not slavery). Weber wrote:

> ... the Occident [West] has developed capitalism both to a quantitative extent, and (carrying this quantitative development) in types, forms, and directions which have never existed elsewhere. All over the world there have been merchants, wholesale and retail, local and engaged in foreign trade. Loans of all kinds have been

made, and there have been banks with the most various functions, at least comparable to ours of, say, the sixteenth century. … This kind of entrepreneur, the capitalistic adventurer, has existed everywhere. With the exception of trade and credit and banking transactions, their activities were predominantly of an irrational and speculative character, or directed to acquisition by force, above all the acquisition of booty … by exploitation of subjects.

The capitalism of promoters, large-scale speculators, concession hunters, and much modern financial capitalism even in peace time, but, above all, the capitalism especially concerned with exploiting wars, bears this stamp even in modern Western countries, and some, but only some, parts of large-scale international trade are closely related to it, to-day as always.

But in modern times the Occident has developed, in addition to this, a very different form of capitalism which has appeared nowhere else: the rational capitalistic organization of (formally) free labour.
(Weber, 1971, pp.20–1)

Weber placed considerable emphasis on the role of *rationality* in the formation of early capitalism. What characterized 'bourgeois' capitalists was that they did not spend all the profits at once in immediate pleasures and luxurious living. Capitalists had learned the habits of thrift, of saving over a long period, so that they could (as in the parable of the talents in the Bible) put money to good use: in short they learned to accumulate and to invest. They also learned how to calculate whether their activities yielded a profit in the long run, or were making a loss, just as they constantly 'reckoned up' how well they were doing in the pursuit of salvation. In short, the capitalist learned to organize economic behaviour (like religious life) in regular, systematic, long-term, instrumental ways for the purpose of increasing wealth; that is, *rationally* maximizing profit. This adaption of means (of economic action) to secure certain ends (profits) represented, in essence, a *rationalization* of the whole sphere of economic behaviour, without which the sober, thrifty capitalist entrepreneur and the rationally-organized capitalist enterprise could never have come into existence.

But how did such a figure as the 'bourgeois capitalist' first arise? What inner compulsions converted the spendthrift feudal landlord into the sober, respectable capitalist? How were these new cultural values formed? How was a 'culture of capitalism' or 'capitalist spirit' created? Weber's surprising answer is that it was created through the compulsions of a certain type of *religious asceticism*. His argument was that some moral force had to compel the new capitalist entrepreneur to forego immediate pleasures and short-term gratifications in the interests of the *rational* pursuit of profitable enterprise in the long run. In other words, far from capitalism emerging because of a *loss* of religious values, the presence of a certain type of religious culture was *necessary to* its formation. But which type of religious culture best provided the

The Calvinist was an *ascetic* who worked *within* the world

seedbed for this new spirit of capitalist enterprise? Not Catholicism, Weber believed, since it allowed men and women to pursue pleasure, provided they confessed, repented and sought forgiveness from the Church. It did not create a tough enough personal inner conscience to drive the capitalist into sober, rational, entrepreneurial activity. So Weber turned to Protestantism.

There were basically two types of Protestantism: that which believed that a person could work for salvation by doing good deeds in the world; and that variant which believed that the decision as to who would be saved and who damned was God's alone and that people had to live their lives as spiritually as possible, watching their every action in the hope of salvation, but never knowing whether they were among God's 'elect' or not. It seems obvious that Weber would have chosen the version which stressed 'doing good in the world' as the seedbed of capitalist worldly activity. But in fact he chose the latter, the Calvinist Puritanism, which believed in predestination and the arbitrary will of God, as the most likely candidate. Why? Because, according to Calvinism, the individual could not depend on the Church for salvation but was constantly and directly under the stern eye of God. Not knowing whether 'he' (for most early capitalists were men) would be saved or not created:

1   a powerful inner compulsion (conscience) to order 'his' life in the rational pursuit of salvation; and

2   a permanent state of 'unsettledness', never knowing the outcome,
     which kept 'him' on the straight and narrow path, prevented any
     backsliding, and drove him forward relentlessly.

Calvinism, Weber argued, was the type of religious asceticism which
helped to form the inner character of the entrepreneurs who pioneered
the transition to early capitalism. This was the link which Weber
constructed between 'the Protestant ethic' and the 'spirit of capitalism'.

4.2   ORIENTATIONS OF THE WORLD RELIGIONS

To understand why Weber fastened on asceticism as a key component of
the Protestant ethic, we need to know something more about how he
classified or built a *typology* of the different world religions and the
cultures which they produced.

Weber's work on the world religions is pitched at a global and
comparative level of analysis. He wrote about Chinese, Indian and
Jewish cultures as well as the culture of Western Europe. Unfortunately,
he produced no full text on Islamic culture, but his writing on the
Middle East is extensive. Each of these cultures was based upon what
he called a 'world religion'.

Weber argued that the major world cultures and their religions can be
classified according to the main attitudes or orientations which each
fosters towards three aspects of the world:

1   The world of nature — soils, animals, plants, rivers, seas, fish, trees,
     etc.

2   Other people — who may be seen as sub-humans, inferiors, as
     slightly different, or as equals.

3   The body — the human body, a person's own body, which is not
     just another part of nature, but is usually seen as being 'special'.

Here, Weber can be seen using the method of classificatory systems and
binary oppositions as a way of contrasting the cultures generated by the
world religions. He contrasts Oriental (eastern) religions (Confucianism,
Hinduism, Taoism, and Buddhism) with Occidental (western) religions
(Judaism, Christianity and Islam). There was a major thrust in the
oriental cultures (in China and India especially) towards seeking
harmony with the natural world, other people, and the body. This set of
attitudes, or value-orientations, contrasts with those found in the
cultures of the 'Middle East', in Persia, Palestine, Arabia and North
Africa, where the main thrust of the religious culture was towards
seeking *mastery over* the world of nature, other people and the body.
The first type of orientation Weber called 'mysticism' (seeking *harmony*
with); the second 'asceticism' (seeking *mastery* over).

Weber also made use of another 'binary opposition' — that between
'inner-wordly' and 'other-wordly' religious orientations. What he had in
mind here were the specialist types of roles which developed for leaders
(or what he called the 'virtuosi') in different religions — those with a

special gift for practising the meditative techniques of religion and those who carried high social esteem, honour and prestige. Unfortunately the way Weber's terminology has been translated into English has proved very confusing. 'Inner-worldly' suggest turning away from the world and becoming preoccupied with one's inner spiritual life. For Weber, it meant exactly the opposite. It meant turning *in towards* the world. It is important to bear this point in mind. 'Other worldly' refers to those roles which are removed from everyday tasks — such as the monk, nun, priest, scholar, artist or intellectual. 'Inner-worldly' refers to those roles which carry high honour and esteem *in* the world: merchant, politician, ruler, army general or naval officer.

The two distinctions can be combined to produce four possible types of social role which may be given the highest social esteem within a specific society. The four types are shown in Table 5.2.

Table 5.2   Four types of religious orientation according to Weber

Direction of religion:	Orientations of esteemed roles:	
	Inner-worldly	Other-worldly or world-rejecting
Mysticism	1	2
Asceticism	3	4

By combining the two sets of distinctions, we can identify four positions or types of religious orientation.

Type 1   Inner-worldly mysticism — Hinduism; Taoism; Confucianism.

Type 2   Other-worldly mysticism — Buddhism; Sufism.

Type 3   Inner-worldly asceticism — Calvinism.

Type 4   Other-worldly asceticism — Catholicism; some popular forms of Islam; Orthodox Judaism.

The important example in the typology, so far as the transition to capitalism is concerned, is Type 3. 'Inner-worldly ascetic' religion produced a culture whose central values were:

1   seeking mastery over the natural world;
2   seeking mastery over other people who are seen as being prone to sinfulness, wickedness, sensuality and laziness;
3   seeking mastery over the self — by controlling impulses to the sensual enjoyment of bodily experiences arising from wearing fine clothes, make-up, or perfumes, consuming good food and wine, or other alcoholic drinks, and above all sexual pleasure, both inside and outside marriage.

Weber claimed that this set of cultural values had emerged *uniquely* from the later forms of Calvinism in the late 1500s and early 1600s, especially among Puritan groups in Britain, Holland and New England where early capitalism took firm root. The religious culture of inner-worldly asceticism had provided the seedbed for the formation the 'rational spirit' of modern capitalism.

Weber acknowledged that other material, technological, economic and financial conditions needed to be fulfilled for modern, rational, bourgeois capitalism to become a possibility. Many non-European civilizations had come close to producing these material factors — Chinese, Indian, and Arab civilizations for example, were highly developed technologically and economically, long before many parts of Europe. However, these other civilizations had not developed modern forms of capitalism, although they conducted trade for profit. Weber argued that the critical feature which these other cultures lacked was the cultural values which would have enabled rational capitalism to develop.

Many of the major world religions were not compatible with the way of life which rational capitalism imposed upon culture. Traditional religions were difficult or impossible to practise faithfully in the new conditions created by modern capitalism. On the other hand, Weber also became convinced that scientific and technological values, which increasingly dominated modern capitalism, could not resolve the problem of values — of *how* we ought to live.

Science, and modern capitalism, were both aspects of a long historical process which Weber claimed was going on in western culture. This was a process in which *rationality* — the instrumental adaptation of means to ends — came to dominate more and more areas of life in western cultures. We shall examine this process in Section 4.3 of this chapter.

4.3   WESTERN CULTURE, SCIENCE AND VALUES

Other world cultures — notably Chinese, Egyptian and Islamic cultures — had made notable scientific discoveries. But Western culture was unique in that it had developed modern science to an unprecedented degree. This process had begun in earnest with the Enlightenment, as you saw in Chapter 1. Weber wrote in his Introduction to *The Protestant Ethic and the Spirit of Capitalism*:

> A product of modern European civilization, studying any problem of universal history, is bound to ask himself to what combination of circumstances the fact should be attributed that in Western civilization, and in Western civilization only, cultural phenomena have appeared which (as we like to think) lie in a line of development having *universal* significance and value.
>
> Only in the West does a science exist at a stage of development which we recognize today as valid. Empirical knowledge, reflection on problems of the cosmos and of life, philosophical and theological wisdom of the most profound sort, are not confined to it, though in the case of the last the full development of a

> systematic theology must be credited to Christianity under the
> influence of Hellenism, since there were only fragments in Islam
> and in a few Indian sects.
> (Weber, 1971, p.13)

One of the major distinctive characteristics of modern western culture,
then, was its scientific character and the prestige it attached to 'the
scientific'. Other world cultures developed empirical knowledge, but
this is not the same thing as theoretically organized science. They also
contained complex philosophical and theological reflections, although
these, Weber claimed, reached a higher level of development in Ancient
Greece and in mediaeval Europe than elsewhere. Notice, however,
Weber's questioning attitude to the supposed 'universal significance and
value' of science in the above extract. Here is another formulation
which Weber gave to his concerns about science:

> Science has created a cosmos of natural causality and has seemed
> unable to answer with certainty the question of its own ultimate
> presuppositions. Nevertheless science, in the name of 'intellectual
> integrity', has come forward with the claim of representing the
> only possible form of a reasoned view of the world ... something
> has adhered to this cultural value which was bound to depreciate
> it with still greater finality, namely, senselessness ... all 'culture'
> appears as man's emancipation from the organically prescribed
> cycle of natural life. For this reason culture's every step forward
> seems condemned to lead to an ever more devastating
> senselessness. The advancement of cultural values, however,
> seems to become a senseless hustle in the service of worthless,
> moreover self-contradictory, and mutually antagonistic ends.
> (Weber, 1970, pp.355–7)

There is an even more questioning or pessimistic tone in this passage.
Developing scientific rationality, Weber seems to be saying, absorbing
more and more of social life into its domain, leads not to the
'emancipation' which the Enlightenment hoped for, but to 'a senseless
hustle in the service of worthless, ... self-contradictory, ... antagonistic
ends'.

During the period in which Weber was writing, this pessimistic
assessment of the Enlightenment faith in reason and science became
more widespread. The philosopher Nietzche (1844–1900), and the
nihilists, for example, began to argue that there were no grounds for
making claims for any moral or political values which everyone could
accept. By the late nineteenth century, many writers came to believe
that western civilization had fallen into a state of cultural crisis. It was a
'civilization' only in the sense of being technologically advanced,
especially in its industrial production processes. However, in the sphere
of moral philosophy and values, European 'civilization' had become
nihilistic — it had nothing positive to say.

This pessimistic analysis, and its implications, underpinned Weber's comparative sociology of the world cultures and their relation to political and economic change.

5   THE COSTS OF CIVILIZATION

Bryan Turner has recently argued that an essential feature of Weber's view of modernity is its ambiguity: 'Modernization brings with it the erosion of meaning, the endless conflict of polytheistic values, and the threat of the iron cage of bureaucracy. Rationalization makes the world orderly and reliable, but it cannot make the world meaningful' (Turner, 1990, p.6).

5.1   INCREASING RATIONALITY

The rise of science and technology, the growth of western capitalism as a 'rational' form of economic life, and of a political culture rooted in legal-rational laws or rules and procedure — all came to be seen as part of a wider process going on in western cultures: the process Weber called 'the increasing rationalization of more and more areas of life' (Weber, 1970). He made no distinction here between capitalism and socialism, both of which, he believed, led to an increasingly rational ordering of work, of the economic distribution of goods and services, and of social life in general. Both were in tension with more traditional cultures,where religion was the central component which formed ordinary people's attitudes and values.

The growth of bureaucracy as a form of organization in *both* capitalism and socialism was, for Weber, another source of evidence of the growing rationalization of modern culture. Bureaucracies were established as a means of achieving, in practice, values of *justice* (law courts) and *equality* (national insurance, for example). So modern cultures had derived considerable gains from the increasing rationality of social organization. But there were costs here too, when one compared modern societies with more traditional ones.

One strength of traditional cultures, as Weber saw it, lay in the fact that they offered people what he called 'a solution to the problem of theodicy' (Weber, 1970). That is to say, they provided ways of explaining and justifying the ways of God to man (theodicies). In particular, they provided an answer to one of the most perplexing of human dilemmas — the moral problem of suffering. Why is there so much suffering in the world? Why do children and other innocent people, who wish no harm to others, suffer? Weber argued that every culture should provide some answer or explanation to such existential questions. The role of culture was to give meaning to, or help people make sense of, life (Weber's whole sociological approach was directed towards the study of action which was 'meaningful', or to which meaning could be given). The persistence of traditional cultures, he thought, could be explained in this way: their religious dimension did offer some way of handling these deep questions of human existence.

In order to become established and to persist over time in a culture, theodicies had to make sense to two groups of people:

1   The intellectuals, and scholars, who could read or write in literate cultures, or who were the priests, medicine men, shamans, or witch doctors — the 'keepers of tribal and religious wisdom' — in pre-literate societies.

2   The main classes and strata in the rest of society — including the main property owners, small business and trading classes, farmers, herdsmen, warriors, peasants, artisans and the urban working class where this had emerged.

Some theodicies, developed by the intellectuals, were popularized by priests, preachers and teachers and, in that form, were picked up by and caught on among wider groups in society. This, Weber argued, is what had happened with Calvinism in the seventeenth century. It caught on among the newly emerging bourgeoisie during early capitalism, because its teaching and doctrine had an 'elective affinity' (i.e. made a neat fit) with the unique social, psychological and cultural needs of the rising class of early entrepreneurs. The term 'elective affinity' was Weber's way of explaining the 'fit' between a socio-economic group, such as a class (e.g. the rising bourgeoisie), its way of life (e.g. the new type of capitalist economic activity), and a specific set of cultural beliefs and values (e.g. Puritanism). The values and beliefs of the 'Protestant ethic' gave meaning to, and helped the early capitalists to make sense of, the new kinds of economic activity in which they were engaging.

One can think of other comparable historical examples. There was an 'elective affinity' between the early industrial working class in British nineteenth-century capitalist society and later versions of Calvinism, like Methodism, which offered the converted a role as the 'elect', the respectable, the chosen few, at a time when they were otherwise feeling excluded from society. Even today, in an advanced industrial capitalist society with a very materialist culture like the United States, about 50 per cent of the population still attend a church service once a month. American culture was deeply influenced by Protestantism, and there is a sizeable Catholic minority (a quarter to a third of all church attenders). So, one could say there is an 'elective affinity' between religion and being an American.

But what about *modern* culture — increasingly secular and materialistic in its values, instrumental rather than spiritual in its outlook and, as Weber said, dominated by scientific and technological rationality? What provides meaning in *this* culture? How do people find an answer to the fundamental problems of life?

The Enlightenment thinkers (as you may recall from Chapter 1) had hoped that science could *replace* religion as a basis for moral values, and thus provide the foundation for a new culture, a modern civilization. But Weber argued that the problem of meaning, of suffering and justice, *cannot* be satisfactorily addressed by science alone. However, given its relative decline, religion had ceased to provide meaningful solutions. Two areas, Weber believed, had taken on something of the function of religion in modern culture, as a source of meaning and values not yet wholly dominated by technical and scientific rationality: the spheres of the aesthetic and the erotic.

In some traditional cultures (e.g. Hinduism, Sufism and — though Weber did not study them — many African and native American cultures) the religious, the mystical and the erotic (especially in the form of dance and music) were deeply intertwined. However, in the West there has always been a tension between the erotic and religion — in both the Catholic and the Protestant faiths. Catholicism found aesthetic forms more acceptable, but Protestantism in general, and Puritanism in particular, have always been profoundly suspicious of *both* the erotic and the aesthetic. On the other hand, this 'asceticism' (i.e. renunciation of pleasure) was precisely the element in Calvinism which had proved of value to the early capitalists. (The puritans objected to bear-bating, for example, not because of the pain it gave to the bear, but because of the pleasure it gave to the spectators.) It provided that taboo on 'pleasure and gratification' which, Weber argued, compelled capitalists to save, accumulate, and invest, and drove them to adopt a sober and frugal rather than a spendthrift style of life. However, once the 'spirit of capitalism' had developed fully, this 'taboo' on the erotic and the aesthetic created problems, because art and sexuality were two of the few remaining areas of modern culture which had to some extent resisted 'rationalization'.

Weber wrote that :

> … asceticism descended like a frost on the life of 'Merrie old England'. And not only worldly merriment felt its effect. The Puritan's ferocious hatred of everything which smacked of superstition, of all survivals of magical and sacramental salvation, applied to the Christmas festivities and the May Pole and all spontaneous art. … The Theatre was obnoxious to the Puritans, and with the strict exclusion of the erotic and of nudity from the realm of toleration, a radical view of either literature or art could not exist. (Weber, 1971, pp.168–9)

Incidentally, this suggests an interesting connection with the second definition of 'culture' (meaning 'the arts') which we discussed in Section 2. In the 1860s, in England, cultural critics like Matthew Arnold believed that, with the decline of religion, literature and art would increasingly play the role of providing the main source of values and standards of judgement, in part because they were somewhat distanced from the imperatives of money-making. In general, the arts celebrate the non-rational — even the irrational — aspects of life. They are not subject to the same rules of evidence and proof as science. Unlike technology, they lack practical application to 'real life'. They belong with the world of fiction, make-believe, pleasure and play. Though the arts have stood as a symbol of civilization, they have also long been regarded as 'effete' and over-refined (as in the stereotype 'the long-haired artist').

Sexuality and the erotic have something of the same status — both are areas of taboo, set aside from 'normal' daily life, not governed by instrumental calculation, where irrational impulses surface which, many believe, threaten the even tenor of everyday life. Especially outside conventional marriage, the erotic also marks the eruption of non-rational forces — the pleasures, desires and wishes of the body. Weber's argument, in his essay 'The aesthetic and the erotic spheres' (Weber, 1970), is that intellectuals and others caught up in modern rational work processes regard the aesthetic and erotic spheres as important spaces *set aside* (remember Durkheim's notion of 'the sacred'?) from 'normal life' for living for a short time in the non-rational. The underside of the increasing rationalization of life at work, and in organized leisure, is the heightened role of aesthetic and erotic pleasure in industrial, urban social formations. They become privileged zones, places specially charged with emotion and value, the only cultural spaces left where people are still in touch with 'natural forces', in contact with the 'real' — the body, the flesh, desire — and where one can be taken out of everyday, conscious concerns and anxieties. You can see how, paradoxically, according to Weber's argument, not only have the aesthetic and erotic spheres to some extent replaced the role of religion in modern culture; they have also acquired something of the character of what both Durkheim and Weber called 'the sacred'.

However, they could not compensate for the overwhelming tendency of modern culture. Though the values of Puritanism had helped to bring the 'spirit of capitalism' and the rational pursuit of capitalist enterprise into existence, the religious element had long since — in Weber's judgement — given way to a more secular, materialistic culture, in which the processes of rationalization exerted the dominant force. There is no mistaking the note of chilling pessimism in Weber's description of the later stages of this development.

ACTIVITY 3   Now read **Reading C, 'The iron cage'**, by Max Weber, which is the last few paragraphs from *The Protestant Ethic and the Spirit of Capitalism*. It begins by repeating a sentence quoted above in Section 4.1. (Baxter was a Puritan divine who wrote in the late 1670s. He was one of the main sources Weber used for 'the Protestant ethic'.)

After reading the extract, try to answer the following questions:

1   What does Weber mean by the phrase the 'iron cage'?

2   What motivates people to work in modern industrial societies, now that religious asceticism has ceased to do so?

3   Where does Weber identify any chances of escaping from the iron cage?

5.2   DISENCHANTMENT WITH THE MODERN WORLD

Weber's theme of the ever-increasing rationalization of modern life was part of a more general argument that the evolution of modern culture has not produced the increase in overall human happiness that many hoped for. The project, set in motion by the Enlightenment, of increasing progress, wealth and happiness through the application of science and technology, first to industry and then to social life as a whole, and the weakening of the hold of custom, magic, superstition and other supernatural taboos over which the *philosophes* rejoiced, has been put in question. In the traditional culture of Europe before the Protestant Reformation, religion provided the moral framework for everyone. Everyday life was punctuated by saints days, fairs, pilgrimages, festivals, seasons of feasting, atonement and celebration. The culture of ordinary people was saturated with folk customs, magical spells, rituals and religious occasions. Springs and wells provided healing waters, the relics of saints offered safe journeys or protection to relatives and friends.

The gradual disappearance of this culture, saturated with the religious and what would now be regarded as the irrational, and the transition to a world more and more of which could only be understood and explained though the application of rational forms of explanation, mastered and controlled through the application of instrumental reason, was described by Weber as a process of *de-magification.* (The German phrase Weber used, '*Entzauberung der Welt*', is sometimes translated as 'the disenchantment of the world'.) Both are aspects of that long cultural shift towards modernity which many sociologists call *secularization.*

Weber was by no means the only social scientist or social critic and philosopher to take an increasingly negative or pessimistic view of the 'costs', rather than the 'benefits', of modern civilization. In Britain, from the Romantic poets at the end of the eighteenth century onwards, a long line of writers and critics criticized the increasingly mechanistic character of modern industrial society and culture, and the dominance of a competitive and utilitarian ethos in it. 'Men', the poet Coleridge, once said, railing against industrialism, 'should be weighed, not counted'. These critics were protesting against the habits of mind, the culture, which modern capitalism and industry had brought to the fore. Raymond Williams, who charted this tradition of cultural criticism in *Culture and Society, 1780–1950* (1958), observed that 'culture' was one of the terms used to measure critically 'the great historical changes which the changes in industry, democracy and class, in their own way, represent, and to which the changes in art are a closely related response' (Williams, 1981, p.16).

The rise of capitalism and the impact of industrial work and the factory system on workers in the nineteenth century in Britain also led Karl Marx (1818–83) to develop a not dissimilar critique of industrial 'civilization' and its cultural and social impact. Capitalism, Marx argued, expropriated from the worker the fruits of his/her labour for sale in the market. But in addition, the conditions of labour in the modern industrial factory robbed the worker of a sense of self and of the capacity to be creative and to recognize the things produced as the fruit of creative activity. Marx called this cultural condition a process of 'estrangement', or alienation:

> What, then, constitutes the alienation of labour? First, the fact that labour is *external* to the worker, i.e., it does not belong to his essential being; that in his work, therefore, he does not affirm himself but denies himself, does not feel content but unhappy, does not develop freely his physical and mental energy but mortifies his body and ruins his mind. The worker therefore only feels himself outside his work, and in his work feels outside himself. He is at home when he is not working, and when he is working he is not at home. His labour is therefore not voluntary, but coerced; it is *forced labour*. It is therefore not the satisfaction of a need; it is merely a *means* to satisfy needs external to it. Its alien character emerges clearly in the fact that as soon as no physical or other compulsion exists, labour is shunned like the plague. External labour, labour in which man alienates himself, is a labour of self-sacrifice, of mortification. Lastly, the external character of labour for the worker appears in the fact that it is not his own, but someone else's, that it does not belong to him, that in it he belongs, not to himself, but to another. Just as in religion the spontaneous activity of the human imagination, of the human brain and the human heart, operates independently of the individual — that is, operates on him as an alien, divine or diabolical activity — in the same way the worker's activity is not his spontaneous activity. It belongs to another; it is the loss of his self.
>
> As a result, therefore, man (the worker) no longer feels himself to be freely active in any but his animal functions — eating, drinking, procreating, or at most in his dwelling and dressing-up etc; and in his human functions he no longer feels himself to be anything but an animal. What is animal becomes human and what is human becomes animal.
>
> Certainly eating, drinking, procreating, etc, are also genuinely human functions. But in the abstraction which separates them from the sphere of all other human activity and turns them into sole and ultimate ends, they are animal.
> (Marx, 1959, pp.72–3)

Marx is assuming here that working creatively on the external world, finding pleasure in working with other people, is an essential part of what it is to be 'human'. The labour process in industrial capitalism, he argues, destroys these relationships with other people and with nature, turning them into alienating, estranged relations. This alienation also produces an alienated form of culture, in everyday ways of living, and in religion. Alien beings seem to be dominant: in the form of an angry God who seeks obedience, and in the form of the employer who represents Capital.

Other social theorists and critics of the industrialization and urbanization processes of modern, technical 'civilization' have also argued that the change from rural and agricultural to industrial social formations has had very disturbing effects upon people's moral, religious and everyday patterns of living. Durkheim, whose ideas about collective representations were discussed in Section 3 above, also believed that these changes were profoundly unsettling. He argued that they lay behind increases in rates of mental illness, drug abuse, and suicide in western societies, especially among those groups whose way of life encouraged *individual* competition, achievement and a sense of inner isolation. Like Weber, Durkheim found that Protestants were more prone to this condition than Catholics or Jews, where a sense of collective belongingness was stronger, and that this in large part explained why their suicide rate was higher (see Durkheim, 1952).

Urbanization and industrialization broke down traditional ways of living, with their ideas and moral values about right and wrong. No new, clear set of values or norms developed in the new situation. Durkheim described this situation as one of *anomie (*meaning literally 'without norms') — that is, a social condition where no clear, generally-accepted rules about how to live were shared among people. Individuals tried to invent their own ways of living, and many came unstuck in trying to do so.

We have already mentioned Nietzche and his philosophy of 'nihilism', which emerged in Germany towards the end of the nineteenth century, and whose pessimism about modern culture influenced Weber. One of Nietzche's arguments was that the values of western civilization, often represented as aspects of Truth and Beauty and Justice, were really simply 'masks' or 'fictions' used in a struggle for power — the 'will to power' — amongst the powerful, which dissolved any objective distinction between 'good' and 'evil'. This critique propagated a cynical or 'disenchanted' view of modern culture, and a cult of power and the irrational, which became increasingly influential in Western European culture during the late nineteenth and early twentieth centuries. The question of whether the values of technical and scientific reason could supply a moral centre to the cultural universe became a topic of widespread philosophical speculation amongst such philosophers as Husserl and Heidegger. In the social sciences, there was a parallel debate about whether science could provide the model for the construction of *positive* social laws (positivism). (Durkheim and Weber occupied leading, but contrasting, positions within this debate.)

In short, by the turn of the century, the evolution of modern culture, grounded on the domination of science and technology, scientific and technological reason, was being discussed everywhere in terms of a 'crisis'. This cultural 'crisis' occurred at the same time as, and came increasingly to be expressed in, those movements in modern culture, painting and the arts which came to be called 'modernism'.

Two of the most important critiques of modern, 'rationalized' culture deserve special mention because they pick up directly on themes discussed earlier. The first is the critique developed by Sigmund Freud, and the second is that of the group of German social theorists and cultural critics, Adorno, Horkheimer and Marcuse, who belonged to the 'Frankfurt School'.

5.3 CIVILIZATION AND ITS DISCONTENTS

Freud's (1856–1939) work was produced in two main periods: before the 1914–18 War, when Europeans were more self-confident about their civilization, despite the wars of the nineteenth century; and after the trench warfare of the First World War. Freud's work during this second period reflected the impact of war, both because some of his patients were soldiers suffering from what were called at the time 'war neurosis', and because he wished to take account of the massive implications of the fact of a total and destructive war between 'civilized' nations such as Germany, France, and Britain. In *Civilization and its Discontents*, first published in 1930, he wrote about the hostility people feel towards this modern civilization.

ACTIVITY 4   You should now read **Reading D, 'Civilization and its Discontents',** by Sigmund Freud. As you read, make brief notes on the aspects of modern civilization Freud thought produced neuroses.

Freud wrestles here with the dilemma of the lack of the expected gains from technological advances in modern 'civilization'. Instead of increased happiness, there is an increase in neuroses — that is, forms of mental distress milder than that found in madness (psychoses) but producing unhappy states of mind or of the body. Europeans are no longer so prone to imagine that primitive peoples are as happy as they once believed, but nevertheless technological progress does not guarantee an increase in ordinary happiness. It places demands on people, which affect their everyday lives at work and in the home. There are echoes here of Marx's notion of alienation — estrangement from others and from the *self* also.

The concept of the *unconscious,* which Freud used and systematized in his writings and in his therapeutic work with the neurotics of modern urban life, captured the importance of the irrational. The two central components of unconscious desire — sexuality and destructive aggression — became important features of the work of a group of social scientists known as *the Frankfurt School,* or *critical theorists.* It is to their work that we turn briefly in the next section.

5.4 THE FRANKFURT SCHOOL

The social critics and philosophers who came to be known as the Frankfurt School also addressed some of the themes rehearsed by both Weber and Freud. Of particular relevance is the work which they produced in the 1930s, in the context of the rise of fascism in Germany (from which they were all obliged to flee) and the fearful holocaust which followed in Europe. These events led the Frankfurt School critics to ask how the promise of the Enlightenment could possibly have led to such a 'barbarous' result. This was especially difficult to explain in Germany, which had come to pride itself on the 'civilizing process', as Norbert Elias called it — the long process of cultural refinement culminating in a high state of cultural achievement. The high standard of manners and etiquette of the French, English and German aristocracies, Elias argued, had been imitated by the new urban bourgeoisie. Gradually, the lower middle and the respectable working classes of Europe began to borrow and imitate these standards of behaviour. The new mass circulation press, and later radio, operated as the main vehicles for the expansion of this civilizing process. What, then, had gone wrong? How had this civilizing process produced the monstrosity of fascism with its doctrines of racial purity?

An Open Air Banquet in the Garden of Love: this sixteenth-century tapestry indicates how table manners slowly 'trickled down' from the aristocracy

The Frankfurt critics argued that, far from being a departure from the Enlightenment, these developments were its 'dark side' — as much part of its project as its dream of progress and emancipation. What in the Enlightenment had given rise to this apparent contradiction of all it appeared to stand for? The answer which they gave to this question was clearly related to Weber's. It was the domination of modern society and culture by what they called 'technical reason', the spread of bureaucratic and instrumental rationality to every sphere of life, producing what they called the 'totally administered' society — the society of totalitarianism — which had crippled and distorted the 'promise of Enlightenment'. The Enlightenment could only be, as it were, saved from itself by exposing this remorseless process of 'rationalization' to a ruthless philosophical critique. Such a critique would aim to show that *technical forms of reason* had subverted and eclipsed *critical* reasoning about moral and political values. This latter concept of *critical rationality* had become lost by confusing it with scientific forms of reasoning, a process which had begun in the Enlightenment. Hope lay in recovering this form of substantive reasoning, a form inaugurated in the West by the Ancient Greek philosophers, in which moral and political values were established by public, reasoned debate, not by force.

The Frankfurt School did not accept that 'reason' should be restricted to scientific and technological ways of thinking, for these excluded rational reflection upon social, political, cultural, and moral values. It was partly the value-neutrality of so many academics, the Frankfurt School argued, which had allowed fascism and Nazism to develop. For if academics, philosophers and social scientists say nothing about values, in a falsely modest eschewing of value-judgements, then no-one should be surprised if the moral vacuum thereby created is filled by irrational political movements. The error the modern West had made had been in thinking that science and technology could provide values, or even that societies did not need fundamental values. Since the Enlightenment, both these errors had become dominant among different élite groups in western societies. The results were nihilism, fascism, disenchantment, and unhappiness. The solution lay, the Frankfurt School thought, in reconnecting with earlier ways of thinking about society and its relations with nature — both external nature, the environment, and nature in the human body. 'Reason' could and should include such *ethical* thought. Value-neutrality was a dangerous illusion, a chimera, something to be avoided, not to be treated as a guarantee of academic respectability.

6 CONCLUSION

We have travelled a considerable distance in the course of this chapter. We began by considering definitions of culture, and two emerged as being particularly important for sociology: first, culture as the meanings, values, and ways of life shared by particular nations, groups, classes or historical periods; second, culture as the practices which produce meaning—signifying practices. The latter idea has been important in the approach called 'structuralism', a method which emphasises the *interrelations* between component parts in a wider system or *structure* of relations. Languages, not just verbal language but other sets of symbols, such as those found in pre-literate cultures (totemism) or rituals (including social practices such as marriage rules, kinship rules, and wedding feasts), can be analysed in terms of their meaning, using a structuralist method. Durkheim's work on the elementary forms of religion was discussed in the light of such an approach.

The concepts of *collective representations* and systems of *primitive classification* were highlighted as being especially important in reading Durkheim in a structuralist way. The idea of binary oppositions (from Lévi-Strauss), and of categories which do not fit into a particular classificatory scheme, producing, in turn, notions of the eerie, the spooky, or the weird, was used in relation to Durkheim's sacred–profane distinction. An example of the structuralist method of analysis was provided by Mary Douglas's work on modern ideas of pollution and *dirt*.

This type of structuralist analysis is *synchronic;* that is, it is concerned with the *workings* of a structure frozen in time. We moved on to consider *diachronic* changes, changes *of* structures across historical time, by examining Weber's claims about the role of religion (Calvinism) in the development of modern, rational capitalism. Weber's analysis of Calvinism was placed in the wider context of his analysis of other cultures, centred upon different orientations to the natural world, other people, and the human body from those found in Protestantism. Weber used two binary oppositions, in this work: 'mysticism' and 'asceticism'; and 'inner-worldly' and 'other-worldly'. Combining these produced four possible types of religious ethic. Calvinism was *the* unique example of one of these four types: an inner-worldly ascetic ethic. This cultural value system had been the absolutely necessary, though not the sufficient, condition for the development of modern rational capitalism, according to Weber's analysis.

Finally, the *costs* of the part played by culture in the formation of modern capitalism were addressed. Weber, although explicit about the benefits of some aspects of modernity (the gains in justice and equality from modern bureaucracy), was nevertheless haunted by the costs. The loss of a sense of *shared* meaning, and the sense of disenchantment in modern culture were, perhaps, the major disadvantages in Weber's view. Others, such as Marx and Freud, saw similar costs in modern capitalism. Marx spoke of a sense of *alienation* from others, from nature, and even from self. Freud developed the ideas of loss of meaning, of estrangement, in a way which focused upon the pains and discontents of modern *individuals*. (Weber had seen individualism as another product of Protestant culture.) The ideas of Marx, Weber and Freud provided a basis for the Frankfurt School's critique of modern culture, which they saw as dominated by a one-dimensional form of technical reason. They saw academic neutrality as having allowed fascism to develop — if reason is not used to provide collective purposes and to criticize existing assumptions then, in their view, unreason takes over.

This last point, about value-judgements, is an important one. When making a social scientific analysis of our own or other cultures, we must attempt to set aside our prejudices and preconceptions, to describe and not to judge. And yet we need to remain morally vigilant. Although value-neutrality is a necessary methodological stance for sociologists, or anthropologists, initially, it is never enough on its own. Someone must continue to think about, and write about, human life — there must be someone to weigh up questions of value and the ultimate purpose of existing values, and to debate how we ought to live and how we ought to try to arrange our collective lives together. Who else will take responsibility for this if not intellectuals?

REFERENCES

Abercrombie, N., Hill, S. and Turner, B.S. (eds) (1988) *The Penguin Dictionary of Sociology*, 2nd edn, Harmondsworth, Penguin.

Douglas, M. (1966) *Purity and Danger: An Analysis of Concepts of Pollution and Taboo*, London, Routledge and Kegan Paul.

Durkheim, E. (1952) *Suicide: A Study in Sociology* (trans. by J. Spaulding and G. Simpson), London, Routledge and Kegan Paul.

Durkheim, E. (1961) *The Elementary Forms of the Religious Life* (trans. by J.W. Swain), New York, Collier Books.

Elias, N. (1978) *The Civilizing Process. Vol.1: The History of Manners* (trans. by E. Jephcott), Oxford, Basil Blackwell.

Elias, N. (1982) *The Civilizing Process. Vol.2: State Formations and Civilization,* Oxford, Basil Blackwell.

Freud, S. (1963) *Civilization and its Discontents* (trans. by J. Riviere; ed. by J. Strachey), London, Hogarth Press.

Lévi-Strauss, C. (1966) *The Savage Mind,* London, Weidenfeld and Nicolson.

Lévi-Strauss, C. (1969) *Totemism*, Harmondsworth, Penguin Books.

Marx, K. (1959) *Economic and Philosophical Manuscripts of 1844,* London, Lawrence and Wishart.

Penguin Dictionary of Sociology: See Abercrombie *et al.* (1988).

Poole, R. (1969) 'Introduction' in Lévi-Strauss, C., *Totemism,* Harmondsworth, Penguin Books.

Turner, B. (ed.) (1990) *Theories of Modernity and Post-Modernity*, London, Sage.

Weber, M. (1970) *From Max Weber: Essays in Sociology* (trans. and ed. by H. Gerth and C. W. Mills), London, Routledge and Kegan Paul.

Weber, M. (1971) *The Protestant Ethic and the Spirit of Capitalism* (trans. by T. Parsons), London, Unwin University Books.

Williams, R. (1983) *Keywords*, London, Fontana.

Williams, R. (1981) *Culture and Society, 1780–1950,* London, Fontana.

READING A   COLLECTIVE REPRESENTATIONS

Émile Durkheim

At the root of all our judgements there are a certain number of essential ideas which dominate our intellectual life; they are what philosophers since Aristotle have called the categories of the understanding: ideas of time, space, ... number, cause, substance, personality, etc. They correspond to the most universal properties of things. They are like the solid frame which encloses all thought; this does not seem to be able to liberate itself from them without destroying itself, for it seems that we cannot think of objects that are not in time and space, which have no number, etc. Other ideas are contingent and unsteady; we can conceive of their being unknown to a man, a society or an epoch; but these others appear to be nearly inseparable from the normal working of the intellect. They are like the framework of the intelligence. Now when primitive religious beliefs are systematically analysed, the principal categories are naturally found. They are born in religion and of religion; they are a product of religious thought. ...

Up to the present there have been only two doctrines in the field. For some, the categories cannot be derived from experience: they are logically prior to it and condition it. They are represented as so many simple and irreducible data, imminent in the human mind by virtue of its inborn constitution. For this reason they are said to be *a priori*. Others, however, hold that they are constructed and made up of pieces and bits, and that the individual is the artisan of this construction.

But each solution raises grave difficulties. ...

... If reason is only a form of individual experience, it no longer exists. On the other hand, if the powers which it has are recognized but not accounted for, it seems to be set outside the confines of nature and science. In the face of these two opposed objections the mind remains uncertain. But if the social origin of the categories is admitted, a new attitude becomes possible, which we believe will enable us to escape both of the opposed difficulties.

... If ... the categories are, as we believe they are, essentially collective representations, before all else, they should show the mental states of the group; they should depend upon the way in which this is founded and organized, upon its morphology, upon its religious, moral and economic institutions, etc. ... there is all the difference ... between the individual and the social, and one can no more derive the second from the first than he can deduce society from the individual, the whole from the part, the complex from the simple. Society is a reality *sui generis;* it has its own peculiar characteristics, which are not found elsewhere and which are not met with again in the same form in all the rest of the universe. The representations which express it have a wholly different contents from

Source: Durkheim, É. (1961) *The Elementary Forms of the Religious Life*, New York, Collier Books, pp.21–9 (first published in 1912).

purely individual ones and we may rest assured in advance that the first add something to the second.

Even the manner in which the two are formed results in differentiating them. Collective representations are the result of an immense co-operation, which stretches out not only into space but into time as well; to make them, a multitude of minds have associated, united and combined their ideas and sentiments; for them, long generations have accumulated their experience and their knowledge. A special intellectual activity is therefore concentrated in them which is infinitely richer and complexer than that of the individual.

READING B   HYGIENE AND POLLUTION

Mary Douglas

A distinction is made between cooked and uncooked food as carriers of pollution. Cooked food is liable to pass on pollution, while uncooked food is not. So uncooked foods may be received from or handled by members of any caste — a necessary rule from the practical point of view in a society where the division of labour is correlated with degrees of inherited purity. Fruit and nuts, as long as they are whole, are not subject to ritual defilement, but once a coconut is broken or a plantain cut, a Havik cannot accept it from a member of a lower caste. ...

... Food which can be tossed into the mouth is less liable to convey saliva pollution to the eater than food which is bitten into. A cook may not taste the food she is preparing, as by touching her fingers to her lips she would lose the condition of purity required for protecting food from pollution. While eating, a person is in the middle state of purity and if by accident he should touch the server's hand or spoon, the server becomes impure and should at least change clothes before serving more food. Since pollution is transmitted by sitting in the same row at a meal, when someone of another caste is entertained he is normally seated separately. A Havik in a condition of grave impurity should be fed outside the house, and he is expected himself to remove the leaf-plate he fed from. No one else can touch it without being defiled. The only person who is not defiled by touch and by eating from the leaf of another is the wife who thus ... expresses her personal relation to her husband. And so the rules multiply. They discriminate in ever finer and finer divisions, prescribing ritual behaviour concerning menstruation, childbirth and death. All bodily emissions, even blood or pus from a wound, are sources of impurity. Water, not paper, must be used for washing after defaecating, and this is done only with the left hand, while food may be eaten only with the right hand. To step on animal faeces causes impurity. Contact with leather causes impurity. If leather sandals are worn they should not be touched with the hands, and should be removed and the feet be washed before a temple or house is entered. ...

Source: Douglas, M. (1966) *Purity and Danger: An Analysis of Concepts of Pollution and Taboo*, London, Routledge and Kegan Paul, pp.33–6.

... The more deeply we go into this and similar rules, the more obvious it becomes that we are studying symbolic systems. Is this then really the difference between ritual pollution and our ideas of dirt: are our ideas hygienic where theirs are symbolic? Not a bit of it: I am going to argue that our ideas of dirt also express symbolic systems and that the difference between pollution behaviour in one part of the world and another is only a matter of detail.

Before we start to think about ritual pollution we must go down in sack-cloth and ashes and scrupulously re-examine our own ideas of dirt. Dividing them into their parts, we should distinguish any elements which we know to be the result of our recent history.

There are two notable differences between our contemporary European ideas of defilement and those, say, of primitive cultures. One is that dirt avoidance for us is a matter of hygiene or aesthetics and is not related to our religion. ... The second difference is that our idea of dirt is dominated by the knowledge of pathogenic organisms. The bacterial transmission of disease was a great nineteenth century discovery. It produced the most radical revolution in the history of medicine. So much has it transformed our lives that it is difficult to think of dirt except in the context of pathogenicity. Yet obviously our ideas of dirt are not so recent. We must be able to make the effort to think back beyond the last 100 years and to analyse the bases of dirt-avoidance, before it was transformed by bacteriology; for example, before spitting deftly into a spittoon was counted unhygienic.

If we can abstract pathogenicity and hygiene from our notion of dirt, we are left with the old definition of dirt as matter out of place. This is a very suggestive approach. It implies two conditions: a set of ordered relations and a contravention of that order. Dirt, then, is never a unique, isolated event. Where there is dirt there is system. Dirt is the by-product of a systematic ordering and classification of matter, in so far as ordering involves rejecting inappropriate elements. This idea of dirt takes us straight into the field of symbolism and promises a link-up with more obviously symbolic systems of purity.

We can recognise in our own notions of dirt that we are using a kind of omnibus compendium which includes all the rejected elements of ordered systems. It is a relative idea. Shoes are not dirty in themselves, but it is dirty to place them on the dining-table; food is not dirty in itself, but it is dirty to leave cooking utensils in the bedroom, or food bespattered on clothing; similarly, bathroom equipment in the drawing room; clothing lying on chairs; out-door things in-doors; upstairs things downstairs; under-clothing appearing where over-clothing should be, and so on. In short, our pollution behaviour is the reaction which condemns any object or idea likely to confuse or contradict cherished classifications.

READING C THE IRON CAGE

Max Weber

The Puritan wanted to work in a calling; we are forced to do so. For when asceticism was carried out of monastic cells into everyday life, and began to dominate worldly morality, it did its part in building the tremendous cosmos of the modern economic order. This order is now bound to the technical and economic conditions of machine production which today determine the lives of all the individuals who are born into this mechanism, not only those directly concerned with economic acquisition, with irresistible force. Perhaps it will so determine them until the last ton of fossilized coal is burnt. In Baxter's view the care for external goods should only lie on the shoulders of the 'saint like a light cloak, which can be thrown aside at any moment'. But fate decreed that the cloak should become an iron cage.

Since asceticism undertook to remodel the world and to work out its ideals in the world, material goods have gained an increasing and finally an inexorable power over the lives of men as at no previous period in history. Today the spirit of religious asceticism — whether finally, who knows? — has escaped from the cage. But victorious capitalism, since it rests on mechanical foundations, needs its support no longer. The rosy blush of its laughing heir, the Enlightenment, seems also to be irretrievably fading, and the idea of duty in one's calling prowls about in our lives like the ghost of dead religious beliefs. Where the fulfilment of the calling cannot directly be related to the highest spiritual and cultural values, or when, on the other hand, it need not be felt simply as economic compulsion, the individual generally abandons the attempt to justify it at all. In the field of its highest development, in the United States, the pursuit of wealth, stripped of its religious and ethical meaning, tends to become associated with purely mundane passions, which often actually give it the character of sport.

No one knows who will live in this cage in the future, or whether at the end of this tremendous development entirely new prophets will arise, or there will be a great rebirth of old ideas and ideals, or, if neither, mechanized petrification, embellished with a sort of convulsive self-importance. For of the last stage of this cultural development, it might well be truly said: 'Specialists without spirit, sensualists without heart; this nullity imagines that it has attained a level of civilization never before achieved.'

But this brings us to the world of judgements of value and of faith, with which this purely historical discussion need not be burdened. The next task would be rather to show the significance of ascetic rationalism, which has only been touched in the foregoing sketch, for the content of practical social ethics, thus for the types of organization and the functions of social

Source: Weber, M. (1971) *The Protestant Ethic and the Spirit of Capitalism*, London, Unwin University Books, pp.181–3 (first published in 1904–5).

groups from the conventicle to the State. Then its relations to humanistic rationalism, its ideals of life and cultural influence; further to the development of philosophical and scientific empiricism, to technical development and to spiritual ideals would have to be analysed. Then its historical development from the mediaeval beginnings of worldly asceticism to its dissolution into pure utilitarianism would have to be traced out through all the areas of ascetic religion. Only then could the quantitative cultural significance of ascetic Protestantism in its relation to the other plastic elements of modern culture be estimated.

Here we have only attempted to trace the fact and the direction of its influence to their motives in one, though a very important point. But it would also further be necessary to investigate how Protestant Asceticism was in turn influenced in its development and its character by the totality of social conditions, especially economic. The modern man is in general, even with the best will, unable to give religious ideas a significance for culture and national character which they deserve. But it is, of course, not my aim to substitute for a one-sided materialistic an equally one-sided spiritualistic causal interpretation of culture and of history. Each is equally possible, but each, if it does not serve as the preparation, but as the conclusion of an investigation, accomplishes equally little in the interest of historical truth.

READING D CIVILIZATION AND ITS DISCONTENTS

Sigmund Freud

How has it happened that so many people have come to take up this strange attitude of hostility to civilization? I believe that the basis of it was a deep and long-standing dissatisfaction with the then existing state of civilization and that on that basis a condemnation of it was built up, occasioned by certain specific historical events. I think I know what the last and the last but one of those occasions were. I am not learned enough to trace the chain of them far back enough in the history of the human species; but a factor of this kind hostile to civilization must already have been at work in the victory of Christendom over the heathen religions. For it was very closely related to the low estimation put upon earthly life by the Christian doctrine. The last but one of these occasions was when the progress of voyages of discovery led to contact with primitive peoples and races. In consequence of insufficient observation and a mistaken view of their manners and customs, they appeared to Europeans to be leading a simple, happy life with few wants, a life such as was unattainable by their visitors with their superior civilization. Later experience has corrected some of those judgements. In many cases the observers had wrongly attributed to the absence of complicated cultural demands what was in fact due to the bounty of nature and the ease with which the major human needs were satisfied. The last occasion is especially familiar to us. It arose

Source: Freud, S. (1963) *Civilization and its Discontents*, London, The Hogarth Press, pp.24–5 (first published in 1930).

when people came to know about the mechanism of the neuroses, which threaten to undermine the modicum of happiness enjoyed by civilized men. It was discovered that a person becomes neurotic because he cannot tolerate the amount of frustration which society imposes on him in the service of its cultural ideals, and it was inferred from this that the abolition or reduction of those demands would result in a return to possibilities of happiness.

There is also an added factor of disappointment. During the last few generations mankind has made an extraordinary advance in the natural sciences and in their technical application and has established his control over nature in a way never before imagined. The single steps of this advance are common knowledge and it is unnecessary to enumerate them. Men are proud of those achievements, and have a right to be. But they seem to have observed that this newly-won power over space and time, this subjugation of the forces of nature, which is the fulfilment of a longing that goes back thousands of years, has not increased the amount of pleasurable satisfaction which they may expect from life and has not made them feel happier. From the recognition of this fact we ought to be content to conclude that power over nature is not the *only* precondition of human happiness, just as it is not the *only* goal of cultural endeavour; we ought not to infer from it that technical progress is without value for the economics of our happiness.

CHAPTER 6 THE WEST AND THE REST: DISCOURSE AND POWER

Stuart Hall

CONTENTS

1   INTRODUCTION

The first five chapters of this book examine the long historical processes through which a new type of society — advanced, developed and industrial — emerged. They chart in broad outline the paths by which this society reached what is now called 'modernity'. This chapter explores the role which societies *outside* Europe played in this process. It examines how an idea of 'the West and the Rest' was constituted; how relations between western and non-western societies came to be represented. We refer to this as the formation of the 'discourse' of 'the West and the Rest'.

1.1   WHERE AND WHAT IS 'THE WEST' ?

This question puzzled Christopher Columbus and remains puzzling today. Nowadays, many societies aspire to become 'western' — at least in terms of achieving western standards of living. But in Columbus's day (the end of the fifteenth century) going West was important mainly because it was believed to be the quickest route to the fabulous wealth of the East. Indeed, even though it should have become clear to Columbus that the New World he had found was *not* the East, he never ceased to believe that it was, and even spiced his reports with outlandish claims: on his fourth voyage, he still insisted that he was close to Quinsay (the Chinese city now called Hangchow), where the Great Khan lived, and probably approaching the source of the Four Rivers of Paradise! Our ideas of 'East' and 'West' have never been free of myth and fantasy, and even to this day they are not primarily ideas about place and geography.

We have to use short-hand generalizations, like 'West' and 'western', but we need to remember that they represent very complex ideas and have no simple or single meaning. At first sight, these words may seem to be about matters of geography and location. But even this, on inspection, is not straightforward since we also use the same words to refer to a type of society, a level of development, and so on. It's true that what we call 'the West', in this second sense, *did* first emerge in western Europe. But 'the West' is no longer only in Europe, and not all of Europe is in 'the West'. The historian John Roberts has remarked that, 'Europeans have long been unsure about where Europe "ends" in the east. In the west and to the south, the sea provides a splendid marker ... but to the east the plains roll on and on and the horizon is awfully remote.' (Roberts, 1985, p.149.) Eastern Europe doesn't (doesn't yet? never did?) belong properly to 'the West'; whereas the United States, which is not in Europe, definitely does. These days, technologically speaking, Japan, is 'western', though on our mental map it is about as far 'East' as you can get. By comparison, much of Latin America, which is in the western hemisphere, belongs economically to the Third World, which is struggling — not very successfully — to catch up with 'the West'. What are these different societies 'east' and 'west' of, exactly? Clearly, 'the West' is as much an idea as a fact of geography.

The underlying premise of this chapter is that 'the West' is a *historical,* not a geographical, construct. By 'western' we mean the type of society discussed in this series: a society that is developed, industrialized, urbanized, capitalist, secular, and modern. Such societies arose at a particular historical period — roughly, during the sixteenth century, after the Middle Ages and the break-up of feudalism. They were the result of a specific set of historical processes — economic, political, social and cultural. Nowadays, any society, wherever it exists on a geographical map, which shares these characteristics, can be said to belong to 'the West'. The meaning of this term is therefore virtually identical to that of the word 'modern'. Its 'formations' are what we have been tracing in the earlier chapters in this book. This chapter builds on that earlier story.

'The West' is therefore also an idea, a concept — and this is what interests us most in this chapter. How did the idea, the language, of 'the West' arise, and what have been its effects? What do we mean by calling it a *concept?*

The concept or idea of 'the West' can be seen to function in the following ways:

First, it allows us to characterize and classify societies into different categories — i.e. 'western', 'non-western'. It is a tool to think with. It sets a certain structure of thought and knowledge in motion.

Secondly, it is an image, or set of images. It condenses a number of different characteristics into one picture. It calls up in our mind's eye — it *represents* in verbal and visual language — a composite picture of what different societies, cultures, peoples and places are like. It functions as part of a language, a 'system of representation'. (I say 'system' because it doesn't stand on its own, but works in conjunction with other images and ideas with which it forms a set: for example, 'western' = urban = developed; or 'non-western' = non-industrial = rural = agricultural = under-developed.)

Thirdly, it provides a standard or model of comparison. It allows us to compare to what extent different societies resemble, or differ from, one another. Non-western societies can accordingly be said to be 'close to' or 'far away from' or 'catching up with' the West. It helps to explain *difference.*

Fourthly, it provides criteria of evaluation against which other societies are ranked and around which powerful positive and negative feelings cluster. (For example, 'the West' = developed = *good* = desirable; or the 'non-West' = under-developed = *bad* = undesirable.) It produces a certain kind of *knowledge* about a subject and certain attitudes towards it. In short, it functions as an *ideology.*

This chapter will discuss all these aspects of the idea of 'the West'.

We know that the West itself was produced by certain historical processes operating in a particular place in unique (and perhaps unrepeatable) historical circumstances. Clearly, we must also think of the *idea* of 'the West' as having been produced in a similar way. These two aspects are in fact deeply connected, though exactly how is one of the big puzzles in sociology. We cannot attempt to resolve here the age-old sociological debate as to which came first: the idea of 'the West', or western societies. What we can say is that, as these societies emerged, so a concept and language of 'the West' crystallized. And yet, we can be certain that the idea of 'the West' did not simply reflect an already-established western society: rather, it was essential to the very formation of that society.

What is more, the idea of 'the West', once produced, became productive in its turn. It had real effects: it enabled people to know or speak of certain things in certain ways. It produced knowledge. It became *both* the organizing factor in a system of global power relations *and* the organizing concept or term in a whole way of thinking and speaking.

The central concern of this chapter is to analyse the formation of a particular pattern of thought and language, a 'system of representation', which has the concepts of 'the West' and 'the Rest' at its centre.

The emergence of an idea of 'the West' was central to the Enlightenment', which was discussed at length in Chapter 1. The Enlightenment was a very European affair. European society, it assumed, was the most advanced type of society on earth, European man (*sic*) the pinnacle of human achievement. It treated the West as the result of forces largely *internal* to Europe's history and formation.

However, in this chapter we argue that the rise of the West is also a *global* story. As Roberts observes, '"Modern" history can be defined as the approach march to the age dominated by the West' (Roberts, 1985, p.41). The West and the Rest became two sides of a single coin. What each now is, and what the terms we use to describe them mean, depend on the relations which were established between them long ago. The so-called uniqueness of the West was, in part, produced by Europe's contact and self-comparison with other, non-western, societies (the Rest), very different in their histories, ecologies, patterns of development and cultures from the European model. The difference of these other societies and cultures from the West was the standard against which the West's achievement was measured. It is within the context of these relationships that the idea of 'the West' took on shape and meaning.

The importance of such perceived difference needs itself to be understood. Some modern theorists of language have argued that *meaning* always depends on the relations that exist between the different terms or words within a meaning system (see Chapter 5). Accordingly, we know what 'night' means because it is different from — in fact, opposite to — 'day'. The French linguist who most influenced this approach to meaning, Ferdinand de Saussure (1857–1912), argued that the words 'night' and 'day' on their own can't mean anything; it is the *difference* between 'night' and 'day' which enables these words to carry meaning (to signify).

Likewise, many psychologists and psychoanalysts argue that an infant first learns to think of itself as a separate and unique 'self' by recognizing its separation — its difference — from others (principally, of course, its mother). By analogy, national cultures acquire their strong sense of identity by contrasting themselves with other cultures. Thus, we argue, the West's sense of itself — its identity — was formed, not only by the internal processes that gradually moulded Western European countries into a distinct type of society, but also through Europe's sense of difference from other worlds — how it came to represent itself in relation to these 'others'. In reality, differences often shade imperceptibly into each other. (When exactly does 'night' become 'day'? Where exactly does 'being English' end and 'being Scottish' begin?). But, in order to function at all, we seem to need distinct, positive concepts many of which are sharply polarized towards each other. As Chapter 5 argues, such 'binary oppositions' seem to be fundamental to all linguistic and symbolic systems and to the production of meaning itself.

This chapter, then, is about the role which 'the Rest' played in the formation of the idea of 'the West' and a 'western' sense of identity. At a certain moment, the fates of what had been, for many centuries, separate and distinct worlds became — some would say, fatally — harnessed together in the same historical time-frame. They became related elements in the same *discourse*, or way of speaking. They became different parts of one global social, economic and cultural system, one interdependent world, one language.

A word of warning must be entered here. In order to bring out the distinctiveness of this 'West and the Rest' discourse, I have been obliged to be selective and to simplify my representation of the West, and you should bear this in mind as you read. Terms like 'the West' and 'the Rest' are historical and linguistic constructs whose meanings change over time. More importantly, there are many different discourses, or ways in which the West came to speak of and represent other cultures. Some, like 'the West and the Rest', were very western-centered, or Eurocentric. Others, however, which I do not have space to discuss here, were much more culturally relativistic. I have elected to focus on what I call the discourse of 'the West and the Rest' because it became a very common and influential discourse, helping to shape public perceptions and attitudes down to the present.

Another qualification concerns the very term 'the West', which makes the West appear unified and homogeneous — essentially one place, with one view about other cultures and one way of speaking about them. Of course, this is not the case. The West has always contained many internal differences — between different nations, between Eastern and Western Europe, between the Germanic Northern and the Latin Southern cultures, between the Nordic, Iberian and Mediterranean peoples, and so on. Attitudes towards other cultures within the West varied widely, as they still do between, for example, the British, the Spanish, the French and the German.

It is also important to remember that, as well as treating non-European cultures as different and inferior, the West had its own *internal* 'others'. Jews, in particular, though close to western religious traditions, were frequently excluded and ostracized. West Europeans often regarded Eastern Europeans as 'barbaric', and, throughout the West, western women were represented as inferior to western men.

The same necessary simplification is true of my references to 'the Rest'. This term also covers enormous historical, cultural and economic distinctions — for example, between the Middle East, the Far East, Africa, Latin America, indigenous North America and Australasia. It can equally encompass the simple societies of some North American Indians and the developed civilizations of China, Egypt or Islam.

These extensive differences must be borne in mind as you study the analysis of the discourse of 'the West and the Rest' in this chapter. However, we can actually use this simplification to make a point about discourse. For simplification is precisely what this discourse itself *does*. It represents what are in fact very differentiated (the different European cultures) as homogeneous (the West). And it asserts that these different cultures are united by one thing: the fact that *they are all different from the Rest*. Similarly, the Rest, though different among themselves, are represented as the same in the sense that *they are all different from the West*. In short, the discourse, as a 'system of representation', *represents* the world as divided according to a simple dichotomy — the West/the Rest. That is what makes the discourse of 'the West and the Rest' so destructive — it draws crude and simplistic distinctions and constructs an over-simplified conception of 'difference'.

2   EUROPE BREAKS OUT

In what follows, you should bear in mind the evolution of the system of European nation-states discussed in Chapter 2. 'The voyages of discovery were the beginning of a new era, one of world-wide expansion by Europeans, leading in due course to an outright, if temporary, European ... domination of the globe.' (Roberts, 1985, p.175.) In this section we offer a broad sketch of the early stages of this process of expansion. When did it begin? What were its main phases? What did it 'break out' from? Why did it occur?

2.1   WHEN AND HOW DID EXPANSION BEGIN?

Long historical processes have no exact beginning or end, and are difficult to date precisely. You will remember the argument in Chapter 2 that a particular historical pattern is the result of the interplay between a number of different causal processes. In order to describe them, we are forced to work within very rough-and-ready chronologies and to use *historical generalizations* which cover long periods and pick out the broad patterns, but leave much of the detail aside. There is nothing wrong with this — historical sociology would be impossible without it — provided we know at what level of generality our argument is working. For example, if we are answering the question, 'When did western Europe first industrialize?', it may be sufficient to say, 'During the second half of the eighteenth century'. However, a close study of the origins of industrialization in, say, Lancashire, would require a more refined time-scale. (For further discussion of this point, see the Introduction to this volume.)

We can date the onset of the expansion process roughly in relation to two key events:

1   The early Portuguese explorations of the African coast (1430–1498), and

2   Columbus's voyages to the New World (1492–1502).

Broadly speaking, European expansion coincides with the end of what we call 'the Middle Ages' and the beginning of the 'modern age'. Feudalism was already in decline in western Europe, while trade, commerce and the market were expanding. The centralized monarchies of France, England and Spain were emerging (see Chapter 2). Europe was on the threshold of a long, secular boom in productivity, improving standards of living, rapid population growth and that explosion in art, learning, science, scholarship and knowledge known as the Renaissance. (Leonardo had designed flying machines and submarines prior to 1519; Michelangelo started work on the Sistine Chapel in 1508; Thomas Moore's *Utopia* appeared in 1516). For much of the Middle Ages, the arts of civilization had been more developed in China and the Islamic world than in Europe. Many historians would agree with Michael Mann that, 'the point at which Europe "overtook" Asia must have been about 1450, the period of European naval expansion and the Galilean revolution in science'; though as Mann also argues, many of the processes which made this possible had earlier origins (Mann, 1988, p.7). We will return to this question at the end of the section.

2.2   FIVE MAIN PHASES

The process of expansion can be divided, broadly, into five main phases:

1   The period of exploration, when Europe 'discovered' many of the 'new worlds' for itself for the first time (they all, of course, already existed).

2   The period of early contact, conquest, settlement and colonization, when large parts of these 'new worlds' were first annexed to Europe as possessions, or harnessed through trade.

3   The time during which the shape of permanent European settlement, colonization or exploitation was established (e.g. plantation societies in North America and the Caribbean; mining and ranching in Latin America; the rubber and tea plantations of India, Ceylon and the East Indies). Capitalism now emerged as a global market.

4   The phase when the scramble for colonies, markets and raw materials reached its climax. This was the 'high noon of Imperialism', and led into the First World War and the twentieth century.

5   The present, when much of the world is economically dependent on the West, even when formally independent and decolonized.

There are no neat divisions between these phases, which often overlapped. For example, although the main explorations of Australia occurred in our first phase, the continent's shape was not finally known until after Cook's voyages in the eighteenth century. Similarly, the Portuguese first circumnavigated Africa in the fifteenth century, yet the exploration of the African interior below the Sahara and the scramble for African colonies is really a nineteenth-century story.

Since we are focusing on 'formations', this chapter concentrates on the first two phases — those involving early exploration, encounter, contact and conquest — in order to trace how 'the West and the Rest' as a 'system of representation' was formed.

2.3   THE AGE OF EXPLORATION

This began with Portugal, after the Moors (the Islamic peoples who had conquered Spain) had finally been expelled from the Iberian peninsula. Prince Henry 'The Navigator', the pioneer of Portuguese exploration, was himself a Crusader who fought the Moors at the battle of Ceuta (North Africa; 1415) and helped to disperse the Moorish pirates who lurked at the entrance to the Mediterranean. As Eric Newby explains:

> With the pirates under control there was a real possibility that the Portuguese might be able to take over the caravan trade — an important part of which was in gold dust — that Ceuta enjoyed with the African interior. In the event, the attempt to capture this trade failed ... . And so there emerged another purpose. This was to discover from which parts of Africa the merchandise, particularly the gold dust, emanated and, having done so, to contrive to have it re-routed ... to stations on the Atlantic coast in which the inhabitants would already have been converted to Christianity and of which the King of Portugal would be the ruler.
> (Newby, 1975, p.62)

This comment pinpoints the complex factors — economic, political and spiritual — which motivated Portuguese expansion. Why, then, hadn't they simply sailed southwards before? One answer is that they thought their ships were not sufficiently robust to endure the fierce currents and contrary winds to be encountered around the curve of the North African coastline. Another equally powerful factor was what is called the 'Great Barrier of Fear' — evident, for example, in the belief that beyond Cape Bojador lay the mouth of Hell, where the seas boiled and people turned black because of the intense heat. The late-mediaeval European conception of the world constituted as much of a barrier to expansion as technological and navigational factors.

In 1430, the Portuguese sailed down the west coast of Africa, hoping to find not only the sources of the African gold, ivory, spice and slave trades, but also the legendary black Christian ruler, 'Prester John'. In stages (each consolidated by Papal decree giving Portugal a monopoly 'in the Ocean Sea ... lying southward and eastward'), the Portuguese pushed down the African coast, and past the 'Great Barrier Of Fear'. In 1441, the first cargo of African slaves captured by Europeans arrived in Portugal — thereby beginning a new era of slave-trading.

In 1487/8 Bartolomeo Dias rounded the Cape of Good Hope and Pedro da Covilhão, taking the caravan route overland, reached the Sudan from where he sailed to India (1488). Later, Vasco da Gama sailed around Africa and then, with the aid of a Muslim pilot, across the Indian ocean to the city of Calicut (1497–8). Within ten years Portugal had established the foundations of a naval and commercial empire. Displacing the Arab traders who had long plied the Red Sea and Indian Ocean, they established a chain of ports to Goa, the East Indies, the Moluccas and Timor. In 1514, a Portuguese mission reached Canton (China), and in 1542 the first contact was made with Japan.

By comparison, the exploration of the New World (America) was at first largely a Spanish affair. After long pleading, Columbus, the Genoese navigator, finally persuaded King Ferdinand and Queen Isabella of Spain to support his 'western Enterprise' to find a westerly route to the treasures of the East. Deliberately underestimating the distance of Asia from Europe (he chose the shortest of a number of guesses on offer from mediaeval and classical sources) he sailed into the 'Green Sea Of Darkness' in 1492. In four remarkable voyages he became the first European to land on most of the islands of the Caribbean and on the Central American mainland. He never relinquished his belief that 'I am before Zaiton (Japan) and Quinsay (China), a hundred leagues, a little more or less' (Columbus, 1969, p.26). The misnamed 'West Indies' are a permanent reminder that the Old World 'discovered' the New by accident. But Columbus opened up a whole continent to Spanish expansion, founded on the drive for gold and the Catholic dream of converting the world to the Christian faith. Shortly afterwards, Amerigo Vespucci (to whom the American continents owe their name) sailed north to Carolina, and south along the coast of Brazil to Rio, Patagonia and the Falkland Islands.

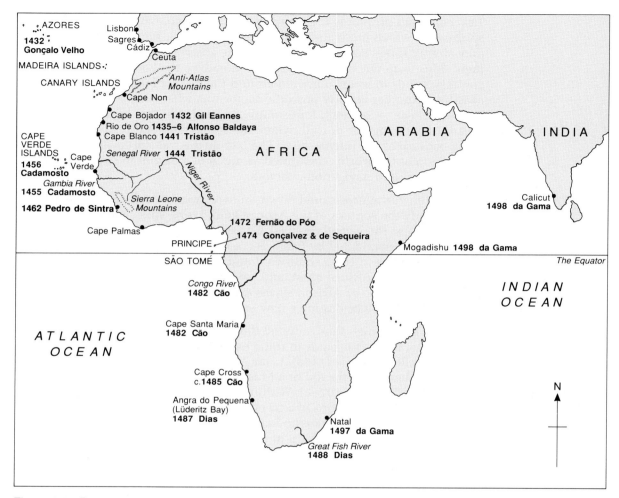

Figure 6.1   Portuguese expansion

In 1500 a Portuguese called Pedro Cabral, sailing to India, was blown out into the Atlantic and landed fortuitously on the coast of Brazil, giving Portugal her first foothold in what was to become Latin America. The threatened Spanish–Portuguese rivalry was aggravated by papal decrees favouring the Spanish, but was finally settled by the Treaty of Tordesillas (1494), which divided the 'unknown world' between the Spanish and the Portuguese along a line of longitude running about 1500 miles west of the Azores. This line was subsequently revised many times and other nations, like Spain's arch enemy and Protestant rival, England, greedy to partake of the riches of the New World, soon made nonsense of it with their buccaneering exploits and raids along the Spanish Main. 'Nevertheless', as John Roberts observes of the treaty,

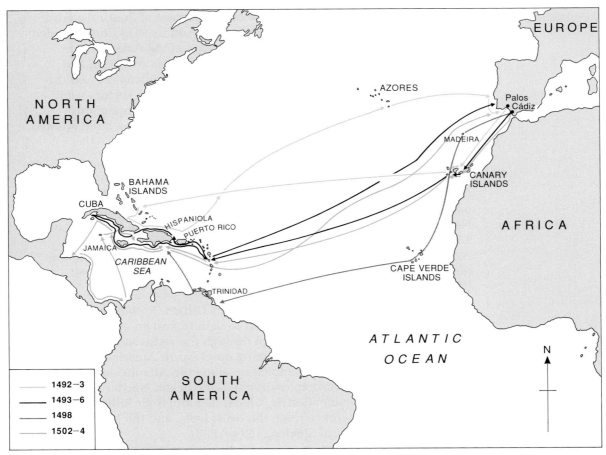

Figure 6.2 The voyages of Christopher Columbus

... it is a landmark of great psychological and political importance: Europeans, who by then had not even gone round the globe, had decided to divide between themselves all its undiscovered and unappropriated lands and peoples. The potential implications were vast ... The conquest of the high seas was the first and greatest of all the triumphs over natural forces which were to lead to domination by western civilisation of the whole globe. Knowledge is power, and the knowledge won by the first systematic explorers ... had opened the way to the age of western world hegemony.
(Roberts, 1985, p.194)

In 1519–22, a Portuguese expedition led by Magellan, circumnavigated the globe, and Sir Francis Drake repeated this feat in 1577–80.

The early Spanish explorers of the New World opened the way to that ruthless band of soldier-adventurers, the Conquistadors, who completed the conquest of Central and South America, effecting the transition from exploration to conquest and colonization.

In 1513 Balboa, having explored the northern coast of South America, crossed the Isthmus of Darien to the Pacific. And in 1519 Cortés landed in Mexico and carried through the destruction of the Aztec empire. Pizarro pushed south through Ecuador to the Andes and Peru, and destroyed the Inca empire (1531–4), after which Orellana crossed the continent by way of the Amazon (1541–4). The Conquistadors were driven by the prospect of vast, unlimited fortunes. 'We Spaniards', Cortés confessed, 'suffer from a disease that only gold can cure' (quoted in Hale, 1966, p.105).

The Spanish proceeded to push up into what is now New Mexico, Arizona, Florida, and Arkansas (1528–42). Meanwhile, further north, other nations were also busy exploring. John Cabot, a Venetian sailing under English patronage, landed at Nova Scotia, Newfoundland, and New England (1497–8). In 1500–1, the Portuguese Corte Real, and in 1524 the Italian Verrazano explored the Atlantic seaboard of North America. They were followed in 1585–7 by Sir Walter Raleigh, and a number of British colonies were soon established: Newfoundland (1583), Roanoke (1585), and Jamestown (1607).

Yet further north, British explorers such as Gilbert, Frobisher, Davis, Hudson and Baffin (1576–1616) tried in vain to find an alternative route to the East via a north-west passage through the arctic seas. This quest was partly responsible for the opening up of North America, and Dutch, French and English colonies sprang up along the Atlantic seaboard. Nevertheless, the serious exploration of Canada and North America was led largely by the French: Cartier, Champlain and their followers exploring the St. Lawrence river, the Great Lake, and the Mississippi river down to the Gulf of Mexico (1534–1682).

The Spanish and Portuguese established an early presence in the Far East, and soon the Spanish were exploring the Pacific, colonizing islands, and even commuting out of Manilla in the Philippines to the west coast of America (1565–1605). But the Dutch and the English set out to flout the Spanish and Portuguese commercial monopolies. The British East India Company was founded in 1599, the Dutch East India Company in 1602. After their independence from Spain in 1584, the Dutch became one of the most powerful commercial nations, their East Indies trade laying the basis for the flourishing of Dutch *bourgeois* culture (Schama, 1977). From a base in the old spice empire, the Dutch reached Fiji, the East Indies, Polynesia, Tasmania, New Zealand, and in 1606 were the first Europeans to catch sight of Australia. Over the next 30 years they gradually pieced together the Australian jigsaw-puzzle, though the Australian coast was not completely mapped until after Cook's famous voyages (1768–79) to Tahiti, the South Pacific and the Antarctic.

By the eighteenth century, then, the main European world-players — Portugal, Spain, England, France and Holland — were all in place. The serious business of bringing the far-flung civilizations they had discovered into the orbit of western trade and commerce, and exploiting their wealth, land, labour and natural resources for European development had become a major enterprise. (China and India remained closed for longer, except for trading along their coasts and the efforts of Jesuit missionaries.) Europe began to imprint its culture and customs on the new worlds. European rivalries were constantly fought out and settled in the colonial theatres. The colonies became the 'jewels in the crown' of the new European empires. Through trade monopolies and the mercantilist commercial system, each of these Empires tried to secure exclusive control of the flow of trade for its own enrichment. The wealth began to flow in: in 1554 America yielded eleven per cent of the Spanish Crown's income; in 1590, fifty per cent.

2.4 BREAKING THE FRAME

Towards the end of the fifteenth century, then, Europe broke out of its long confinement. What had bottled it up for so long? This is a difficult question to answer, but we can identify two sets of factors — the first, material, the second cultural.

Physical barriers to the East

The Middle Ages represented an actual *loss* of contact with and knowledge of the outside world. Alexander the Great's conquests (336–323 BC) had taken the Macedonian–Greek armies as far east as the Himalayas. Only his troops' reluctance prevented him from reaching what he believed to be the limits of the inhabited world. The Roman Empire stretched from Britain to the Arabian deserts. But in the Middle Ages Europe closed in on itself. It retained some knowledge of India (especially among Venetian traders), but beyond that lay unknown territory. Though every port and trade route on the Mediterranean was mapped, the basic contours of other seas and continents were shrouded in mystery. For example, though Europe bought great quantities of Chinese silk, transported by caravan across Central Asia, it took little interest in the great civilization from which the silk came.

A key factor in this was that, after the seventh century AD, 'sea-routes and land-routes alike were barred by the meteoric rise of Islam, which interposed its iron curtain between West and East' (Latham, 1958, p.8). It was Arab middlemen who brought eastern goods to the European sea-ports of the Mediterranean and Black Sea to sell. The Crusades (1095–1291) were the long, and for a time unsuccessful, struggle of Christian Europe to roll back this 'infidel threat'. But just when, at last, Europe seemed to be winning, a thunderbolt struck from a quarter unexpected by both Islam and Christendom: the invasions of the Mongol and Tartar nomads from the Central Asian steppes (1206–60), which left a trail of devastation in their wake. However, Islam suffered even more than Christendom from the Tartar invasions and, in the thirteenth century, the eastern curtain lifted briefly.

During this interval, the Venetian Marco Polo and other members of his family undertook their famous travels to the court of the Great Khan, China and Japan (1255–95).

Marco Polo's *Travels* with its tales of the fabulous wealth of the East played a decisive role in stimulating the European imagination to search for a westerly route to the East, a search that became increasingly important. For soon the eastern opening became blocked again by the rise of a new Islamic power, the Ottoman Empire, and China, under the Ming dynasty, once more turned inwards.

This had profound effects. It stimulated expansion westwards, favouring the European powers of the Atlantic seaboard (Spain, Portugal, Britain, Holland and France). It also tended to isolate Western from Eastern Europe — a process reinforced by the growing split between Western (Catholic) and Eastern (Orthodox) Churches. From this point onwards, the patterns of development within Western and Eastern Europe sharply diverged.

The barriers in the mind

A second major obstacle to the East lay in the mind — consisting not of only the sketchy knowledge that Europeans had of the outside world, but of the way they conceptualized and imagined it. To the north, they believed, there was 'nothing — or worse...barbarian peoples who, until

Figure 6.3   A mediaeval world map from a thirteenth-century psalter

civilized by the church, were only a menace' (Roberts, 1985, p.117). To the east, across the plains, there were barbarians on horseback: Huns, Mongols and Tartars. To the south lay the shifting empires of Islam, which, despite their early tolerance of Christianity and of the Jews, had advanced deep into Europe — to Poitiers and Constantinople, across North Africa and into Spain, Portugal and Southern Italy. The cradle of European civilization and trade was the Mediterranean. In the eastern Mediterranean, there was Byzantium — a civilization which was part of Christendom. But, as we said, the Catholic and Orthodox churches were drawing farther apart as the centuries passed.

For what lay beyond, Europe relied on other sources of knowledge — classical, Biblical, legendary and mythological. Asia remained largely a world of elephants and other wonders almost as remote as sub-Saharan Africa. There were four continents — Europe, Africa, Asia and 'Terra Australis Incognita' ('The Unknown Southern Land') — the way to the latter being judged impassable. On mediaeval maps, the land mass crowded out the oceans: there was no Pacific and the Atlantic was a narrow, and extremely dangerous, waterway. The world was often represented as a wheel, superimposed on the body of Christ, with Jerusalem at its hub (see Figure 6.3). This conception of the world did not encourage free and wide-ranging travel.

2.5   THE CONSEQUENCES OF EXPANSION FOR THE IDEA OF 'THE WEST'

Gradually, despite their many internal differences, the countries of western Europe began to conceive of themselves as part of a single family or civilization — 'the West'. The challenge from Islam was an important factor in hammering Western Europe and the idea of 'the West' into shape. Roberts notes that, 'The word "Europeans" seems to appear for the first time in an eighth-century reference to Charles Martel's victory [over Islamic forces] at Tours. All collectivities become more self-aware in the presence of an external challenge, and self-awareness promotes cohesiveness.' (Roberts, 1985, p.122.) And Hulme speaks of '... the consolidation of an ideological identity through the testing of [Europe's] Eastern frontiers prior to the adventure of Atlantic exploration. ... A symbolic end to that process could be considered Pius III's 1458 identification of Europe with Christendom.' (Hulme, 1986, p.84.)

But in the Age of Exploration and Conquest, Europe began to define itself in relation to a new idea — the existence of many new 'worlds', profoundly different from itself. The two processes — growing internal cohesion and the conflicts and contrasts with external worlds — reinforced each other, helping to forge that new sense of identity that we call 'the West'. Reading A and Reading B attempt to trace both these processes at work.

ACTIVITY 1

You should read now **Reading A, 'Explaining European development'**, by Michael Mann, which you will find at the end of this chapter.

As you read, you should bear the following points in mind:

1   Michael Mann offers an explanation of European development by making a series of historical generalizations about the main factors. At this stage, the details matter less than the broad notions offered by Mann. The question is: Why did Europe integrate and begin to 'take off' economically?

2   Mann's first argument relates to the main economic factors (land, capital, labour and markets). What does he say about them? What type of economic explanation is he using?

3   His second argument relates to the emergence of a common set of norms and values regulating behaviour ('normative regulation'). What fulfilled this role in Europe?

4   Which two factors does Mann say competition requires? (Note that, by 'multiple acephalous federation' he means that European societies had a small, localized, cell-like — rather than centralized — structure.)

5   What role, according to Mann, did Christianity play?

When you've completed the reading, try writing a *short paragraph* (300 words) summarizing Mann's argument.

Mann discusses both long-term socio-economic and religious factors. The next reading, by contrast, brings cultural and ideological aspects to the fore.

ACTIVITY 2

You should now read **Reading B, 'The idea of "Europe"'**, by John Roberts.

As you read, make a list of what you think are the *main points* in Robert's argument. When you have finished, *compare* your list with the points which I pick out, below. Did you miss something important? Have I left out something you thought important?

Robert's first point — that maps are 'fictions' which 'reflect changes in our pictures of reality' — provides a framework for the rest of the passage. His main argument concerns the centrality of Christianity to the idea of 'Europe.' For centuries, the concepts 'Europe' and 'Christendom' were virtually identical. Europe's cultural identity — what made its civilization distinct and unique — was, in the first instance, essentially religious and Christian. Eventually, the idea of 'Europe' acquired a sharper geographical, political and economic definition. This brought it closer to the modern, secular concept of 'the West'. However, the West has never entirely lost touch with its Christian roots. The encounter with the new worlds — with *difference* — actually reinforced this new identity. It promoted that 'growing sense of superiority', which Roberts calls a 'Eurocentric' view of the world.

3 DISCOURSE AND POWER

We have looked at the historical process by which an idea of 'the West' emerged from Europe's growing internal cohesion and its changing relations to non-Western societies. We turn, next, to the formation of the languages or 'discourses' in which Europe began to describe and represent the *difference* between itself and these 'others' it encountered in the course of its expansion. We are now beginning to sketch the formation of the 'discourse' of 'the West and the Rest'. However, we need first to understand what we mean by the term 'discourse'.

3.1 WHAT IS A 'DISCOURSE'?

In common-sense language, a **discourse** is simply 'a coherent or rational body of speech or writing; a speech, or a sermon'. But here the term is being used in a more specialized way (see *Penguin Dictionary of Sociology*: DISCOURSE). By 'discourse', we mean a particular way of *representing* 'the West', 'the Rest' and the relations between them. A discourse is a group of statements which provide a language for talking about — i.e. a way of representing — a particular kind of knowledge about a topic. When statements about a topic are made within a particular discourse, the discourse makes it possible to construct the topic in a certain way. It also limits the other ways in which the topic can be constructed.

A discourse does not consist of one statement, but of several statements working together to form what the French social theorist, Michel Foucault (1926–1984) calls a **'discursive formation'**. (See *Penguin Dictionary of Sociology*: FOUCAULT) The statements fit together because any one statement implies a relation to all the others: 'They refer to the same object, share the same style and support "a strategy ...a common institutional ...or political drift or pattern"' (Cousins and Hussain, 1984, pp.84–5).

One important point about this notion of discourse is that it is not based on the conventional distinction between thought and action, language and practice. Discourse is about the production of knowledge through language. But it is itself produced by a practice: 'discursive practice' — the practice of producing meaning. Since all social practices entail *meaning*, all practices have a discursive aspect. So discourse enters into and influences all social practices. Foucault would argue that the discourse of the West about the Rest was deeply implicated in practice — i.e. in how the West behaved towards the Rest.

To get a fuller sense of Foucault's theory of discourse, we must bear the following points in mind.

1   A discourse can be produced by many individuals in different institutional settings (like families, prisons, hospitals and asylums). Its integrity or 'coherence' does not depend on whether or not it issues from one place or from a single speaker or 'subject'. Nevertheless, every discourse constructs positions from which alone it makes sense. Anyone deploying a discourse must position themselves *as if* they were the subject of the discourse. For example, we may not ourselves believe in the natural superiority of the West. But if we use the discourse of 'the West and the Rest' we will necessarily find ourselves speaking from a position that holds that the West is a superior civilization. As Foucault puts it, 'To describe a ... statement does not consist in analysing the relations between the author and what he [*sic*] says ...; but in determining what position can and must be occupied by any individual if he is to be the subject of it [the statement]' (Foucault, 1972, pp.95–6).

2   Discourses are not closed systems. A discourse draws on elements in other discourses, binding them into its own network of meanings. Thus, as we saw in the preceding section, the discourse of 'Europe' drew on the earlier discourse of 'Christendom', altering or translating its meaning. Traces of past discourses remain embedded in more recent discourses of 'the West'.

3   The statements within a discursive formation need not all be the same. But the relationships and differences between them must be regular and systematic, not random. Foucault calls this a 'system of dispersion': 'Whenever one can describe, between a number of statements, such a system of dispersion, whenever ... one can define a regularity ... [then] we will say ... that we are dealing with a *discursive formation*' (Foucault, 1972, p.38).

These points will become clearer when we apply them to particular examples, as we do later in this chapter.

3.2   DISCOURSE AND IDEOLOGY

A discourse is similar to what sociologists call an 'ideology': a set of statements or beliefs which produce knowledge that serves the interests of a particular group or class. Why, then, use 'discourse' rather than 'ideology'?

One reason which Foucault gives is that ideology is based on a distinction between *true* statements about the world (science) and *false* statements (ideology), and the belief that the facts about the world help us to decide between true and false statements. But Foucault argues that statements about the social, political or moral world are rarely ever simply true or false; and 'the facts' do not enable us to decide definitively about their truth or falsehood, partly because 'facts' can be construed in different ways. The very language we use to describe the so-called facts interferes in this process of finally deciding what is true, and what false.

For example, Palestinians fighting to regain land on the West Bank from Israel may be described either as 'freedom fighters' or as 'terrorists'. It is a fact that they are fighting; but what does the fighting *mean*? The facts alone cannot decide. And the very language we use — 'freedom fighters/terrorists' — is part of the difficulty. Moreover, certain descriptions, even if they appear false to us, can be *made* 'true' because people act on them believing that they are true, and so their actions have real consequences. Whether the Palestinians are terrorists or not, if we think they are, and act on that 'knowledge', they in effect become terrorists because we treat them as such. The language (discourse) has real effects in practice: the description becomes 'true'.

Foucault's use of 'discourse', then, is an attempt to side-step what seems an unresolvable dilemma — deciding which social discourses are true or scientific, and which false or ideological. Most social scientists now accept that our values enter into all our descriptions of the social world, and therefore most of our statements, however factual, have an ideological dimension. What Foucault would say is that knowledge of the Palestinian problem is produced by competing discourses — those, of 'freedom-fighter' and 'terrorist' — and that each is linked to a contestation over power. It is the outcome of *this* struggle which will decide the 'truth' of the situation.

You can see, then, that although the concept of 'discourse' side-steps the problem of truth/falsehood in ideology, it does *not* evade the issue of power. Indeed, it gives considerable weight to questions of power since it is power, rather than the facts about reality, which make things 'true': 'We should admit that power produces knowledge ... . That power and knowledge directly imply one another; that there is no power relation without the correlative constitution of a field of knowledge, nor any knowledge that does not presuppose and constitute ... power relations' (Foucault, 1980, p.27).

3.3   CAN A DISCOURSE BE 'INNOCENT'?

Could the discourse which developed in the West for talking about the Rest operate outside power? Could it be, in that sense, purely scientific — i.e. ideologically innocent? Or was it influenced by particular class interests?

Foucault is very reluctant to *reduce* discourse to statements that simply mirror the interests of a particular class. The same discourse can be used by groups with different, even contradictory, class interests. But this does *not* mean that discourse is ideologically neutral or 'innocent'. Take for example, the encounter between the West and the New World. There are several reasons why this encounter could not be innocent, and therefore why the discourse which emerged in the Old World about the Rest could not be innocent either.

First, Europe brought its own cultural categories, languages, images and ideas to the New World in order to describe and represent it. It tried to fit the New World into existing conceptual frameworks, classifying it according to its own norms, and absorbing it into western traditions of representation. This is hardly surprising: we often draw on what we already know about the world in order to explain and describe something novel. It was never a simple matter of the West just looking, seeing and describing the New World/the Rest without preconceptions.

Secondly, Europe had certain definite purposes, aims, objectives, motives, interests and strategies in setting out to discover what lay across the 'Green Sea of Darkness'. These motives and interests were mixed. The Spanish, for example, wanted to:

(a) get their hands on gold and silver,

(b) claim the land for Their Catholic Majesties, and

(c) convert the heathen to Christianity.

These interests often contradicted one another. But we must not suppose that what Europeans said about the New World was simply a cynical mask for their own self-interest. When King Manuel of Portugal wrote to Ferdinand and Isabella of Spain that, 'the principal motive of this enterprise [da Gama's voyage to India] has been ... the service of God our Lord, and our own advantage' (quoted in Hale, 1966, p.38) — thereby neatly and conveniently bringing God and Mammon together into the same sentence — he probably saw no obvious contradiction between them. These fervently religious Catholic rulers fully believed what they were saying. To them, serving God and pursuing 'our advantage' were not necessarily at odds. They lived and fully believed their own ideology.

So, while it would be wrong to attempt to reduce their statements to naked self-interest, it is clear that their discourse was moulded and influenced by the play of motives and interests across their language. Of course, motives and interests are almost never wholly conscious or rational. The desires which drove the Europeans were powerful; but their power was not always subject to rational calculation. Marco Polo's 'treasures of the East' were tangible enough. But the seductive power which they exerted over generations of Europeans transformed them more and more into a myth. Similarly, the gold that Columbus kept asking the natives for very soon acquired a mystical, quasi-religious significance.

Finally, the discourse of 'the West and the Rest' could not be innocent because it did not represent an encounter between equals. The Europeans had outsailed, outshot and outwitted peoples who had no wish to be 'explored', no need to be 'discovered' and no desire to be 'exploited'. The Europeans stood, vis-a-vis the Others in positions of dominant power. This influenced what they saw and how they saw it, as well as what they did not see.

Foucault sums up these arguments as follows. Not only is discourse always implicated in *power*; discourse is one of the 'systems' through which power circulates. The knowledge which a discourse produces constitutes a kind of power, exercised over those who are 'known'. When that knowledge is exercised in practice, those who are 'known' in a particular way will be subject (i.e. subjected) to it. This is always a power-relation. (See Foucault, 1980, p.201.) Those who produce the discourse also have the power to *make it true* — i.e. to enforce its validity, its scientific status.

This leaves Foucault in a highly relativistic position with respect to questions of truth because his notion of discourse undermines the distinction between true and false statements — between science and ideology — to which many sociologists have subscribed. These epistemological issues (about the status of knowledge, truth and relativism) are too complex to take further here. (Some of them are addressed further in Book 4 (Hall *et al.*, 1992).) However, the important idea to grasp now is the deep and intimate relationship which Foucault establishes between discourse, knowledge and power. According to Foucault, when power operates so as to enforce the 'truth' of any set of statements, then such a discursive formation produces a 'regime of truth':

> Truth isn't outside power ... Truth is a thing of this world; it is produced only by virtue of multiple forms of constraint...And it induces regular effects of power. Each society has its regime of truth, its 'general politics' of truth; that is, the types of discourse which it accepts and makes function as true; the mechanisms and instances which enable one to distinguish 'true' and 'false' statements; the means by which each is sanctioned; and the techniques and procedures accorded value in the acquisition of truth; the status of those who are charged with saying what counts as true.
> (Foucault, 1980, p.131)

3.4   SUMMARY

Let us summarize the main points of this argument. Discourses are ways of talking, thinking or representing a particular subject or topic. They produce meaningful knowledge about that subject. This knowledge influences social practices, and so has real consequences and effects. Discourses are not reducible to class-interests, but always operate in relation to power — they are part of the way power circulates and is contested. The question of whether a discourse is true or false is less important than whether it is effective in practice. When it is effective — organizing and regulating relations of power (say, between the West and the Rest) — it is called a 'regime of truth'.

4   REPRESENTING 'THE OTHER'

So far, the discussion of discourse has been rather abstract and conceptual. The concept may be easier to understand in relation to an example. One of the best examples of what Foucault means by a 'regime of truth' is provided by Edward Said's study of **Orientalism**. In this section, I want to look briefly at this example and then see how far we can use the theory of discourse and the example of Orientalism to analyse the discourse of 'the West and the Rest'.

4.1   ORIENTALISM

In his book *Orientalism*, Edward Said analyses the various discourses and institutions which constructed and produced, as an object of knowledge, that entity called 'the Orient'. Said calls this discourse 'Orientalism'. Note that, though we tend to include the Far East (including China) in our use of the word 'Orient', Said refers mainly to the Middle East — the territory occupied principally by Islamic peoples. Also, his main focus is French writing about the Middle East. Here is Said's own summary of the project of his book:

> My contention is that, without examining Orientalism as a discourse, one cannot possibly understand the enormously systematic discipline by which European culture was able to manage — and even produce — the Orient politically, sociologically, militarily, ideologically, scientifically and imaginatively during the post-Enlightenment period. Moreover, so authoritative a position did Orientalism have that I believe no one writing, thinking, or acting on the Orient could do so without taking account of the limitations on thought and action imposed by Orientalism. In brief, because of Orientalism, the Orient was not (and is not) a free subject of thought and action. This is not to say that Orientalism unilaterally determines what can be said about the Orient, but that it is the whole network of interests inevitably brought to bear on (and therefore always involved in) any occasion when that peculiar entity 'the Orient' is in question. ... This book also tries to show that European culture gained in strength and identity by setting itself off against the Orient as a sort of surrogate and even underground self.
> (Said, 1985, p.3)

ACTIVITY 3   You should now read **Reading C, '"Orientalism": representing the Other'**, by Edward Said.

When you have finished, test your understanding of the reading by answering the following questions. If you're not happy with your answers, read the relevant paragraph again.

What does Said mean by the following:

1   European ideas about the Orient are 'hegemonic' (paragraph 1)?

2   Orientalism is governed by a 'battery of desires, repressions, investments and projections' (paragraph 2)?

3   Orientalism has an 'archive' (paragraph 4)?

4   Orientalism 'supplied Orientals with a mentality, a genealogy' (paragraph 4)?

5   Orientalism 'promoted the difference between "us" and "them"' (paragraph 5)?

We will now analyse the discourse of 'the West and the Rest', as it emerged between the end of the fifteenth and eighteenth centuries using Foucault's ideas about 'discourse' and Said's example of 'Orientalism'. How was this discourse formed? What were its main themes — its 'strategies' of representation?

4.2   THE 'ARCHIVE'

Said argues that, 'In a sense Orientalism was a library or archive of information commonly...held. What bound the archive together was a family of ideas and a unifying set of values proven in various ways to be effective. These ideas explained the behaviour of Orientals; they supplied Orientals with a mentality, a genealogy, an atmosphere; most important, they allowed Europeans to deal with and even to see Orientals as a phenomenon possessing regular characteristics.' (Said, 1985, pp.41–2.) What sources of common knowledge, what 'archive' of other discourses, did the discourse of 'the West and the Rest' draw on? We can identify four main sources:

1   **Classical knowledge:** This was a major source of information and images about 'other worlds'. Plato (c. 427–347 BC) described a string of legendary islands, among them Atlantis which many early explorers set out to find. Aristotle (384—322 BC) and Eratosthenes (c. 276–194 BC) both made remarkably accurate estimates of the circumference of the globe which were consulted by Columbus. Ptolemy's *Geographia* (2nd century AD) provided a model for map-makers more than a thousand years after it had been produced. Sixteenth-century explorers believed that in the outer world lay, not only Paradise, but that 'Golden Age', place of perfect happiness and 'springtime of the human race', of which the classical poets, including Horace (65–8 BC) and Ovid (43 BC–AD 17), had written.

The eighteenth century was still debating whether what they had discovered in the South Pacific was Paradise. In 1768 the French Pacific explorer Bougainville renamed Tahiti 'The New Cythera' after the island where, according to classical myth, Venus first appeared from the sea. At the opposite extreme, the descriptions by Herodotus (484–425 BC) and Pliny (AD 23–79) of the barbarous peoples who bordered Greece left many grotesque images of 'other' races which served as self-fulfilling prophecies for later explorers who found what legend said they would find. Paradoxically, much of this classical knowledge was lost in the Dark Ages and only later became available to the West via Islamic scholars, themselves part of that 'other' world.

2 **Religious and biblical sources:** These were another source of knowledge. The Middle Ages reinterpreted geography in terms of the Bible. Jerusalem was the centre of the earth because it was the Holy City. Asia was the home of the Three Wise Kings; Africa that of King Solomon. Columbus believed the Orinoco (in Venezuela) to be a sacred river flowing out of the Garden of Eden.

3 **Mythology:** It was difficult to tell where religious and classical discourses ended and those of myth and legend began. Mythology transformed the outer world into an enchanted garden, alive with misshapen peoples and monstrous oddities. In the sixteenth century Sir Walter Raleigh still believed he would find, in the Amazon rain-forests, the king 'El Dorado' ('The Gilded One') whose people were alleged to roll him in gold which they would then wash off in a sacred lake.

4 **Travellers' tales:** Perhaps the most fertile source of information was travellers' tales — a discourse where description faded imperceptibly into legend. The following fifteenth century German text summarizes more than a thousand years of travellers tales, which themselves often drew on religious and classical authority:

> In the land of Indian there are men with dogs' heads who talk by barking [and] ... feed by catching birds. ... Others again have only one eye in the forehead. ... In Libya many are born without heads and have a mouth and eyes. Many are of both sexes. ... Close to Paradise on the River Ganges live men who eat nothing. For ... they absorb liquid nourishment through a straw [and] ... live on the juice of flowers. ... Many have such large underlips that they can cover their whole faces with them. ... In the land of Ethiopia many people walk bent down like cattle, and many live four hundred years. Many have horns, long noses and goats' feet. ... In Ethiopia towards the west many have four eyes ... [and] in Eripia there live beautiful people with the necks and bills of cranes.
> (quoted in Newby, 1975, p.17)

A particularly rich repository was Sir John Mandeville's *Travels* — in fact, a compendium of fanciful stories by different hands. Marco Polo's *Travels* was generally more sober and factual, but nevertheless achieved mythological status. His text (embellished by Rusticello, a romance writer) was the most widely read of the travellers' accounts and was instrumental in creating the myth of 'Cathay' ('China' or the East generally), a dream that inspired Columbus and many others.

The point of recounting this astonishing mixture of fact and fantasy which constituted late mediaeval 'knowledge' of other worlds is not to poke fun at the ignorance of the Middle Ages. The point is: (a) to bring home how these very different discourses, with variable statuses as 'evidence', provided the cultural framework through which the peoples, places and things of the New World were seen, described and represented; and (b) to underline the conflation of fact and fantasy that constituted 'knowledge'. This can be seen especially in the use of analogy to describe first encounters with strange animals. Penguins and seals were described as being like geese and wolves respectively; the tapir as a bull with a trunk like an elephant, the opossum as half-fox, half-monkey.

4.3   A 'REGIME OF TRUTH'

Gradually, observation and description vastly improved in accuracy. The mediaeval habit of thinking in terms of analogies gave way to a more sober type of description of the fauna and flora, ways of life, customs, physical characteristics and social organization of native peoples. We can here begin to see the outlines of an early ethnography or anthropology.

But the shift into a more descriptive, factual discourse, with its claims to truth and scientific objectivity, provided no guarantees. A telling example of this is the case of the 'Patagonians'. Many myths and legends told of a race of giant people. And in the 1520s, Magellan's crew brought back stories of having encountered, in South America, such a race of giants whom they dubbed *patagones* (literally, 'big feet'). The area of the supposed encounter became known as 'Patagonia', and the notion became fixed in the popular imagination, even though two Englishmen who visited Patagonia in 1741 described its people as being of average size.

When Commodore John Byron landed in Patagonia in 1764, he encountered a formidable group of natives, broad-shouldered, stocky, and inches taller than the average European. They proved quite docile and friendly. However, the newspaper reports of his encounter wildly exaggerated the story, and Patagonians took on an even greater stature and more ferocious aspect. One engraving showed a sailor reaching only as high as the waist of a Patagonian giant, and The Royal Society elevated the topic to serious scientific status. 'The engravings took the explorers' raw material and shaped them into images familiar to Europeans.' (Withey, 1987, pp.1175–6.) Legend had taken a late revenge on science.

4.4   IDEALIZATION

'Orientalism', Said remarks, 'is the discipline by which the Orient was (and is) approached systematically, as a topic of learning, discovery and practice.' 'In addition', he adds, Orientalism 'designate[s] that collection of dreams, images and vocabularies available to anyone who has tried to talk about what lies east of the dividing line' (Said, 1985, p.73). Like the

Orient, the Rest quickly became the subject of the languages of dream and Utopia, the object of a powerful fantasy.

Between 1590 and 1634 the Flemish engraver Theodor de Bry published his *Historia Americae* in ten illustrated volumes. These were leading examples of a new popular literature about the New World and the discoveries there. De Bry's books contained elaborate engravings of life and customs of the New World. Here we see the New World reworked — re-presented — within European aesthetic conventions, Western 'ways of seeing'. Different images of America are superimposed on one another. De Bry, for example, transformed the simple, unpretentious sketches which John White had produced in 1587 of the Algonquian Indians he had observed in Virginia. Facial features were retouched, gestures adjusted and postures reworked according to more classical European styles. The effect overall, Hugh Honour observes, was 'to tame and civilize the people White had observed so freshly' (Honour, 1976, p.75). The same transformation can be seen in the three representations of the inhabitants of Tierra del Fuego (Figures 6.4a–c).

A major object of this process of idealization was Nature itself. The fertility of the Tropics was astonishing even to Mediterranean eyes. Few had ever seen landscapes like those of the Caribbean and Central America. However, the line between description and idealization is almost impossible to draw. In describing Cuba, for example, Columbus refers to 'trees of a thousand kinds ... so tall they seem to touch the sky', sierras and high mountains 'most beautiful and of a thousand shapes', nightingales and other birds, marvellous pine groves, fertile plains and varieties of fruit (quoted in Honour, 1976, p.5). Columbus's friend, Peter Martyr, later used his descriptions to express a set of rich themes which resound across the centuries:

> The inhabitants live in that Golden World of which old writers speak so much, wherein men lived simply and innocently, without enforcement of laws, without quarrelling, judges and libels, content only to satisfy Nature ... [There are] naked girls so beautiful that one might think he [*sic*] beheld those splendid naiads and nymphs of the fountains so much celebrated by the ancients.
> (quoted in Honour, 1978, p.6)

The key themes in this passage are worth identifying since they reappear in later variants of 'the West and the Rest':

(a) The Golden World; an Earthly Paradise;

(b) the simple, innocent life;

(c) the lack of developed social organization and civil society;

(d) people living in a pure state of Nature;

(e) the frank and open sexuality; the nakedness; the beauty of the women.

Figure 6.4a Inhabitants of Tierra del Fuego in their hut (Alexander Buchan, 1769)

Figure 6.4b A view of the Indians of Tierra del Fuego (Bartolozzi, 1773)

Figure 6.4c Natives of Tierra del Fuego (Read, 1843)

In these images and metaphors of the New World as an Earthly Paradise, a Golden Age, or Utopia, we can see a powerful European fantasy being constructed.

4.5 SEXUAL FANTASY

Sexuality was a powerful element in the fantasy which the West constructed, and the ideas of sexual innocence and experience, sexual domination and submissiveness, play out a complex dance in the discourse of 'the West and the Rest'.

When Captain Cook arrived in Tahiti in 1769, the same idyll of a sexual paradise was repeated all over again. The women were extremely beautiful, the vegetation lush and tropical, the life simple, innocent and free; Nature nourished the people without the apparent necessity to work or cultivate; the sexuality was open and unashamed — untroubled by the burden of European guilt. The naturalist on Bougainville's voyage to the Pacific said that the Tahitians were 'without vice, prejudice, needs or dissention and knew no other god but Love' (Moorhead, 1968, p.51). 'In short', Joseph Banks, the gentleman-scientist who accompanied Cook, observed, 'the scene that we saw was the truest picture of an Arcadia, of which we were going to be kings, that the imagination can form' (quoted in Moorhead, 1987, p.38). As Cook's biographer, J.C. Beaglehole, remarks, 'they were standing on the beach of the dream-world already, they walked straight into the Golden Age and embraced their nymphs' (quoted in Moorhead, 1968, p.66). The West's contemporary image of tropical paradise and exotic holidays still owes much to this fantasy.

Popular accounts by other explorers, such as Amerigo Vespucci (1451–1512), were explicit — where Columbus had been more reticent — about the sexual dimension. New World people, Vespucci said, 'lived according to Nature', and went naked and unashamed; 'the women ... remained attractive after childbirth, were libidinous, and enlarged the penises of their lovers with magic potions' (quoted in Honour, 1976, p.56).

The very language of exploration, conquest and domination was strongly marked by gender distinctions and drew much of its subconscious force from sexual imagery (see Figure 6.5).

ACTIVITY 4   Examine Figure 6.5, entitled 'Europe encounters America'. This is a famous engraving of Europe's first 'encounter' with the New World, by the Dutch engraver Jan van der Straet. It is a sort of allegory. Examine the details closely. Then write a short paragraph describing the engraving in relation to the following two questions:

1   In what ways does the engraving capture or embody the themes of 'innocence' and 'sexuality'?

2   How are relations between 'Europe' and 'America' represented?

Figure 6.5   Europe encounters America (van der Straet, c. 1600)

In Figure 6.5, 'Europe' (Amerigo Vespucci) stands bold and upright, a commanding male figure, his feet firmly planted on *terra firma*. Around him are the insignia of power: the standard of Their Catholic Majesties of Spain, surmounted by a cross; in his left hand, the astrolabe that guided him, the fruit of Western knowledge; behind him, the galleons, sails billowing. Vespucci presents an image of supreme mastery. Hulme comments that, 'In line with existing European conventions, the "new" continent was often allegorized as a woman' — here, naked, in a hammock, surrounded by the emblems of an exotic landscape: strange plants and animals and, above all, a cannibal feast (see Hulme, 1986, p.xii).

4.6   MIS-RECOGNIZING DIFFERENCE

Said says that 'the essence of Orientalism is the ineradicable distinction between Western superiority and Oriental inferiority' (Said, 1985, p.42). How was this strong marking of difference constructed?

Europeans were immediately struck by what they interpreted as the absence of government and civil society — the basis of all 'civilization' — among peoples of the New World. In fact these peoples did have several, very different, highly elaborated social structures. The New World the Europeans discovered was already home to millions of people who had lived there for centuries, whose ancestors had migrated to America from Asia across the neck of land which once connected the two continents. It is estimated that sixteen million people were living in the Western Hemisphere when the Spanish 'discovered' it. The highest concentration was in Mexico, while only about a million lived in North America. They had very different standards and styles of life. The Pueblo of Central America were village people. Others were hunter-gatherers on the plains and in the forests. The Arawaks of the Caribbean islands had a relatively simple type of society based on subsistence farming and fishing. Further North, the Iroquois of the Carolinas were fierce, nomadic hunters.

The high civilization of the Maya, with its dazzling white cities, was based on a developed agriculture; it was stable, literate and composed of a federation of nations, with a complex hierarchy of government. The civilizations of the Aztecs (Mexico) and the Inca (Peru) were both large, complex affairs, based on maize cultivation and with a richly developed art, culture and religion. Both had a complex social structure and a centralized administrative system, and both were capable of extraordinary engineering feats. Their temples outstripped in size anything in Europe, and the Royal Road of the Incas ran for nearly 2,000 miles through mountainous terrain — further than the extent of the Roman empire from York to Jerusalem. (See Newby, 1975, pp.95–7.)

These were functioning societies. What they were *not* was 'European'. What disturbed western expectations, what had to be negotiated and explained, was their *difference*. As the centuries passed, Europeans came to know more about the specific characteristics of different 'native American' peoples. Yet, in everyday terms, they persisted in describing them *all* as 'Indians', lumping all distinctions together and suppressing differences in one, inaccurate stereotype. (See Berkhofer, 1978.)

Another illustration of the inability to deal with difference is provided by Captain Cook's early experience of Tahiti (1769). The Englishmen knew that the Tahitians held property communally and that they were therefore unlikely to possess a European concept of 'theft'. In order to win over the natives, the crew showered them with gifts. Soon, however, the Tahitians began to help themselves. At first the pilfering amused the visitors. But when the natives snatched Banks's spyglass and snuff-box, he threatened them with his musket until they were returned. Cook's crew continued to be plagued by incidents like this. A similar misunderstanding was to lead to Cook's death at the hands of the Hawaiians, in 1779.

The first actual contact with local inhabitants was often through an exchange of gifts, quickly followed by a more regular system of trade. Eventually, of course, this trade was integrated into a whole commercial system organized by Europe. Many early illustrations represent the inauguration of these unequal exchanges (see Figure 6.6).

In Theodor de Bry's famous engraving of Columbus being greeted by the Indians (Figure 6.6), Columbus stands in exactly the same heroic pose as Vespucci ('Europe') in van der Straet's engraving. On the left, the Cross is being planted. The natives (looking rather European) come, bearing gifts and offering them in a gesture of welcome. As Columbus noted in his log-book, the natives were 'marvellously friendly towards

Figure 6.6   Columbus being greeted by the Indians (de Bry, 1590)

us'. 'In fact', he says, disarmingly, 'they very willingly traded everything they had' (Columbus, 1969, p.55). Subsequent illustrations showed the Indians labouring to produce gold and sugar (described by the caption as a 'gift') *for* the Spaniards.

The behaviour of the Europeans was governed by the complex understandings and norms which regulated their own systems of monetary exchange, trade and commerce. Europeans assumed that, since the natives did not have such an economic system, they therefore had no system at all and offered gifts as a friendly and suppliant gesture to visitors whose natural superiority they instantly recognized. The Europeans therefore felt free to organize the continuous supply of such 'gifts' for their own benefit. What the Europeans found difficult to comprehend was that the exchange of gifts was part of a highly complex, but different, set of social practices — the practices of reciprocity — which only had meaning within a certain cultural context. Caribbean practices were different from, though as intricate in their social meaning and effects as, the norms and practices of European exchange and commerce.

ACTIVITY 5   You should now read **Reading D, 'Reciprocity and exchange'**, by Peter
Hulme, keeping the following questions in mind as you read the
passage:

1   What, according to Hulme and Mauss, does the practice of
     reciprocity mean?

2   How does it differ from modern capitalist exchange, mediated by
     money?

Write a short paragraph summarizing this difference (250 words).

4.7   RITUALS OF DEGRADATION

The cannibal feast in the corner of the van der Straet engraving (Figure
6.5) was an intrusive detail. It points to a set of themes, evident from
the first contact, which were, in fact, the reverse side — the exact
opposites — of the themes of innocence, idyllic simplicity and
proximity to Nature discussed earlier. It was as if everything which
Europeans represented as attractive and enticing about the natives could
also be used to represent the exact opposite: their barbarous and
depraved character. One account of Vespucci's voyages brought these
two sides together in the same passage: 'The people are thus naked ...
well-formed in body, their heads, necks, arms, privy part, feet of women
and men slightly covered with feathers. No one owns anything but all
things are in common. ... The men have as wives those that please
them, be they mothers, sisters or friends ... They also fight with each
other. They also eat each other.' (Quoted in Honour, 1976, p.8).

There were disturbing reversals being executed in the discourse here.
The innocent, friendly people in their hammocks could also be
exceedingly unfriendly and hostile. Living close to Nature meant that
they had no developed culture — and were therefore 'uncivilized'.
Welcoming to visitors, they could also fiercely resist and had war-like
rivalries with other tribes. (The New World was no freer of rivalry,
competition, conflict, war and violence than the Old.) Beautiful nymphs
and naiads — could also be 'warlike and savage'. At a moment's notice,
Paradise could turn into 'barbarism'. Both versions of the discourse
operated simultaneously. They may seem to negate each other, but it is
more accurate to think of them as *mirror-images*. Both were
exaggerations, founded on stereotypes, feeding off each other. Each
required the other. They were in opposition, but systematically related:
part of what Foucault calls a 'system of dispersion'.

From the beginning, *some* people described the natives of the New World
as 'lacking both the power of reason and the knowledge of God'; as
'beasts in human form'. It is hard, they said, to believe God had created a
race so obstinate in its viciousness and bestiality. The sexuality which
fed the fantasies of some, outraged many others. The natives were more
addicted, it was said, to incest, sodomy and licentiousness than any other

race. They had no sense of justice, were bestial in their customs, inimical to religion. The characteristic which condensed all this into a single image was their (alleged) consumption of human flesh.

The question of cannibalism represents a puzzle which has never been resolved. Human sacrifice — which may have included cannibalism — was associated with some religious rituals. There may have been ritual sacrifice, involving some cannibalism, of captured enemies. But careful reviews of the relevant literature now suggest that the hard evidence is much sketchier and more ambiguous than has been assumed. The extent of any cannibalism was considerably exaggerated: it was frequently attributed by one tribe to 'other people' — who were rivals or enemies; much of what is offered as having been witnessed first-hand turns out to be second- or third-hand reports; the practice had usually just ended months before the European visitors arrived. The evidence that, as a normal matter of course, outside ritual occasions, New World Indians regularly sat down to an evening meal composed of juicy limbs of their fellow humans is extremely thin. (See, for example, the extensive analysis of the anthropological literature in Arens, 1978.)

Peter Hulme (1986) offers a convincing account of how cannibalism became the prime symbol or signifier of 'barbarism', thus helping to fix certain stereotypes. Columbus reported (13 January 1493) that in Hispaniola he met a warlike group, whom he judged 'must be one of the Caribs who eat men' (Columbus, 1969, p.40). The Spanish divided the natives into two distinct groupings: the 'peaceful' Arawaks and the 'warlike' Caribs. The latter were said to invade Arawak territory, steal their wives, resist conquest and be 'cannibals'. What started as a way of describing a social group turned out to be a way of 'establishing which Amerindians were prepared to accept the Spaniards on the latter's terms, and which were hostile, that is to say prepared to defend their territory and way of life' (Hulme, 1986, p.72).

In fact, so entrenched did the idea become that the 'fierce' Caribs were eaters of human flesh, that their ethnic name (Carib) came to be used to refer to anyone thought guilty of this behaviour. As a result, we today have the word 'cannibal', which is actually derived from the name 'Carib'.

4.8 SUMMARY: STEREOTYPES, DUALISM AND 'SPLITTING'

We can now try to draw together our sketch of the formation and modes of operation of this discourse or 'system of representation' we have called 'the West and the Rest'.

Hugh Honour, who studied European images of America from the period of discovery onwards, has remarked that 'Europeans increasingly tended to see in America an idealized or distorted image of their own countries, on to which they could project their own aspirations and fears, their self-confidence and...guilty despair' (Honour, 1976, p.3). We have identified some of these **discursive strategies** in this section. They are:

1 idealization;

2 the projection of fantasies of desire and degradation;

3 the failure to recognize and respect difference;

4 the tendency to impose European categories and norms, to see difference through the modes of perception and representation of the West.

These strategies were all underpinned by the process known as **stereotyping.** A stereotype is a one-sided description which results from the collapsing of complex differences into a simple 'cardboard cut-out'. (See *Penguin Dictionary of Sociology*: STEREOTYPES.) Different characteristics are run together or condensed into one. This exaggerated simplification is then attached to a subject or place. Its characteristics become the signs, the 'evidence', by which the subject is known. They define its being, its *essence*. Hulme noted that,

> As always, the stereotype operates principally through a judicious combination of adjectives, which establish [certain] characteristics as [if they were] eternal verities ['truths'], immune from the irrelevancies of the historical moment: [e.g.] 'ferocious', 'warlike', 'hostile', 'truculent and vindictive' — these are present as innate characteristics, irrespective of circumstances; ... [consequently, the Caribs] were locked as 'cannibals' into a realm of 'beingness' that lies beyond question. This stereotypical dualism has proved stubbornly immune to all kinds of contradictory evidence. (Hulme, 1986, pp.49–50)

By **'stereotypical dualism'** Hulme means that the stereotype is split into two opposing elements. These are two key features of the discourse of 'the Other':

1 First, several characteristics are collapsed into one simplified figure which stands for or represents the *essence* of the people; this is stereotyping.

2 Secondly, the stereotype is split into two halves — its 'good' and 'bad' sides; this is 'splitting' or *dualism*.

Far from the discourse of 'the West and the Rest' being unified and monolithic, 'splitting' is a regular feature of it. The world is first divided, symbolically, into good–bad, us–them, attractive–disgusting, civilized–uncivilized, the West–the Rest. All the other, many differences between and within these two halves are collapsed, simplified — i.e. stereotyped. By this strategy, the Rest becomes defined as everything that the West is not — its mirror image. It is represented as absolutely, essentially, different, *other*: the Other. This Other is then itself split into two 'camps': friendly–hostile, Arawak–Carib, innocent–depraved, noble–ignoble.

5   'IN THE BEGINNING ALL THE WORLD WAS AMERICA'

Writing about the use of stereotypes in the discourse of 'the Other', Sander Gilman argues that 'these systems are inherently bi-polar (i.e. polarized into two parts), generating pairs of antithetical signifiers (i.e. words with apparently opposing meanings). This is how the deep structure of the stereotype reflects the social and political ideologies of the time' (Gilman, 1985, p.27). He goes on to say:

> With the split of both the self and the world into 'good' and 'bad' objects, the 'bad' self is distanced and identified with the mental representation of the 'bad' object. This act of projection saves the self from any confrontation with the contradictions present in the necessary integration of 'bad' and 'good' aspects of the self. The deep structure of our own sense of self and the world is built upon the illusionary [*sic*] image of the world divided into two camps, 'us' and 'them'. 'They' are either 'good' or 'bad'.
> (Gilman, 1985, p.17)

The example Gilman gives is that of the 'noble' versus the 'ignoble savage'. In this section, we examine the 'career' of this stereotype. How did it function in the discourse of 'the West and the Rest'? What was its influence on the birth of modern social science?

5.1   ARE THEY 'TRUE MEN'?

The question of how the natives and nations of the New World should be treated in the evolving colonial system was directly linked to the question of what sort of people and societies they were — which in turn depended on the West's knowledge of them, on how they were represented. Where did the Indians stand in the order of the Creation? Where were their nations placed in the order of civilized societies? Were they 'true men' (*sic*)? Were they made in God's image? The point was vital because if they were 'true men' they could not be enslaved. The Greek philosophers argued that man (women rarely figured in these debates) was a special creation, endowed with the divine gift of reason; the Church taught that Man was receptive to divine grace. Did the Indians' way of life, their lack of 'civilization', mean that they were so low on the scale of humanity as to be incapable of reason and faith?

The debate raged for most of the fifteenth century. Ferdinand and Isabella issued decrees saying that 'a certain people called Cannibals' and 'any, whether called cannibals or not, who were not docile' could be enslaved. One view was that 'they probably descended from another Adam ... born after the deluge and ... perhaps have no souls' (see Honour, 1978, p.58). However, Bartolomé de Las Casas (1474–1566), the priest who made himself the champion of the Indians, protested vigorously at the brutality of the Spaniards in putting Indians to work as forced labour. Indians, he insisted, *did* have their own laws, customs, civilization, religion, and were 'true men' whose cannibalism was much exaggerated. 'All men', Las Casas claimed, 'however barbarous and bestial ... necessarily possess the faculty of Reason ...' (quoted by Honour, 1978, p.59). The issue was formally debated before Emperor Charles X at Vallodolid in 1550.

One paradoxical outcome of Las Casas' campaign was that he got Indian slavery outlawed, but was persuaded to accept the alternative of replacing Indians with African slaves, and so the door opened to the horrendous era of New World African slavery. A debate similar to that about the Indians was held about African slavery prior to Emancipation (1834). The charter of the Royal Africa Company, which organized the English slave trade, defined slaves as 'commodities'. As slavery expanded, a series of codes was constructed for the Spanish, French and English colonies governing the status and conduct of slaves. These codes defined the slave as a *chattel* — literally, 'a thing', not a person. This was a problem for some churches. But in the British colonies the Church of England, which was identified with the planters, accommodated itself to this definition without too much difficulty, and made little effort to convert slaves until the eighteenth century. Later, however, the Dissenters in the anti-slavery movement advocated abolition precisely because every slave *was* 'a man and brother' (see Hall, 1991).

5.2 'NOBLE' VS 'IGNOBLE SAVAGES'

Another variant of the same argument can be found in the debate about the 'noble' versus the 'ignoble savage'. The English poet John Dryden provides one of the famous images of the 'noble savage':

> I am as free as Nature first made man,
> E're the base Laws of Servitude began,
> When wild in woods the noble Savage ran.
> (*The Conquest of Granada*, I.I.i.207–9)

Earlier, the French philosopher Montaigne, in his essay *Des Cannibales* (1580), had placed his noble savage in America. The idea quickly took hold on the European imagination. The famous painting of 'The Different Nations of America' by Le Brun in Louis XIV's (1638–1715) Versailles Palace was dominated by a 'heroic' representation of an American Indian — grave, tall, proud, independent, statuesque, and naked (see Honour, 1978, p.118). Paintings and engravings of American Indians dressed like ancient Greeks or Romans became popular. Many paintings of Cook's death portrayed both Cook and the natives who killed him in 'heroic' mould. As Beaglehole explains, the Pacific voyages gave new life and impetus to the idealization of the 'noble savage', who 'entered the study and drawing room of Europe in naked majesty, to shake the preconceptions of morals and politics' (in Moorhead, 1987, p.62). Idealized 'savages' spoke on stage in ringing tones and exalted verse. The eponymous hero in Aphra Behn's novel *Oroonoko* (1688), was one of the few 'noble' Africans (as opposed to American Indians) in seventeenth century literature, and was fortunate enough to have 'long hair, a Roman nose and shapely mouth'.

'Heroic savages' have peopled adventure stories, Westerns, and other Hollywood and television films ever since, generating an unending series of images of 'the Noble Other'.

The 'noble savage' also acquired sociological status. In 1749, the French philosopher Rousseau produced an account of his ideal form of society: simple, unsophisticated man living in a state of Nature, unfettered by laws, government, property or social divisions. 'The savages of North America', he later said in *The Social Contract,* 'still retain today this method of government, and they are very well governed' (Rousseau, 1968, p.114). Tahiti was the perfect fulfilment of this preconceived idea — 'one of those unseen stars which eventually came to light after the astronomers have proved that it must exist' (Moorhead, 1987, p.62).

The French Pacific explorer Bougainville (1729–1811) had been captivated by the way of life on Tahiti. Diderot, the philosopher and editor of the *Encyclopédie* (see Chapter 1), wrote a famous *Supplement* about Bougainville's voyage, warning Tahitians against the West's intrusion into their innocent happiness. 'One day', he prophesied correctly, 'they [Europeans] will come, with crucifix in one hand and the dagger in the other to cut your throats or to force you to accept their customs and opinions' (quoted in Moorhead, 1987). Thus the 'noble savage' became the vehicle for a wide-ranging critique of the over-refinement, religious hypocrisy and divisions by social rank that existed in the West.

This was only one side of the story. For, at the same time, the opposite image — that of the 'ignoble savage' — was becoming the vehicle for a profound reflection in European intellectual circles on the nature of social development. Eighteenth century wits, like Horace Walpole, Edmund Burke and Dr Johnson, poured scorn on the idea of the noble savage. Ronald Meek has remarked that contemporary notions of savagery influenced eighteenth century social science by generating a critique of society through the idea of the *noble* savage; 'It is not quite so well known ... that they also stimulated the emergence of a new theory of the development of society through the idea of the *ignoble* savage.' (Meek, 1976, p.2.)

The questions which concerned the social philosophers were: What had led the West to its high point of refinement and civilization? Did the West evolve from the same simple beginnings as 'savage society' or were there different paths to 'civilization'?

Many of the precursors and leading figures of the Enlightenment participated in this debate. Thomas Hobbes, the political philosopher, argued in *Leviathan* (1651) that it was because of their lack of 'industry ... and consequently no culture of the earth, no navigation, nor use of commodities' that 'the savage people in many places of America ... live at this day in [their] brutish manner' (Hobbes, 1946, pp.82–3). The English satirist Bernard Mandeville, in his *Fable of the Bees* (1723), identified a series of 'steps' or stages in which economic factors like the division of labour, money and the invention of tools played the major part in the progress from 'savagery' to 'civilization'. The philosopher John Locke claimed that the New World provided a prism through which one could see 'a pattern of the first ages in Asia and Europe' — the origins from which Europe had developed. 'In the beginning', Locke said, 'all the World was America' (Locke, 1976, p.26). He meant by this that the world (i.e. the West) had evolved from a stage very much like that discovered in America — untilled, undeveloped and uncivilized. America was the 'childhood of mankind', Locke claimed, and Indians, should be classed with 'children, idiots and illiterates because of their inability to reason in abstract, speculative ... terms' (quoted in Marshall and Williams, 1982, p.192).

5.3   THE HISTORY OF 'RUDE' AND 'REFINED' NATIONS

The 'noble–ignoble' and the 'rude–refined' oppositions belonged to the same discursive formation. This 'West and the Rest' discourse greatly influenced Enlightenment thinking. It provided the framework of images in which Enlightenment social philosophy matured. Enlightenment thinkers believed that there was *one* path to civilization and social development, and that all societies could be ranked or placed early or late, lower or higher, on the same scale. The emerging 'science of society' was the study of the forces which had propelled all societies, by stages, along this single path of development, leaving some, regrettably, at its 'lowest' stage — represented by the American savage — while others advanced to the summit of civilized development — represented by the West.

This idea of a universal criterion of progress modelled on the West became a feature of the new 'social science' to which the Enlightenment gave birth. For example, when Edmund Burke wrote to the Scottish Enlightenment historian William Robertson on the publication of his *History of America* (1777), he said that 'the great map of Mankind is unrolled at once, and there is no state or gradation of barbarism, and no mode of refinement which we have not at the same moment under our view; the very different civility of Europe and China; the barbarism of Persia and of Abyssinia; the erratic manners of Tartary and of Arabia; the savage state of North America and of New Zealand' (quoted by Meek, 1976, p.173). Enlightenment social science reproduced within its own conceptual framework many of the preconceptions and stereotypes of the discourse of 'the West and the Rest'.

The examples are too voluminous to refer to in detail. Meek argues that, 'No one who reads the work of the French and Scottish pioneers [of social science] of the 1750s can fail to notice that all of them, without exception, were very familiar with the contemporary studies of the

Americans; that most of them had evidently pondered deeply about their significance and that some were almost obsessed by them. ... The studies of Americans provided the new social scientists with a plausible working hypothesis about the basic characteristics of the 'first' or 'earliest' stage of socio-economic development.' (Meek, 1976, p.128.) Many of the leading names of the French Enlightenment — Diderot, Montesquieu, Voltaire, Turgot, Rousseau — used the studies of early American Indians in this way.

This is also the case with the Scottish Enlightenment. In Adam Smith's *Theory of the Moral Sentiments* (1759), American Indians are used as the pivot for elaborate contrasts between 'civilized nations' and 'savages and barbarians'. They are also pivotal in Henry Kames's *Sketches of the History of Man* (1774), John Millar's *Origin of the Distinction of Ranks* (1771), and Adam Ferguson's *Essay on the History of Civil Society* (1767).

The contribution which this debate about 'rude–refined nations' made to social science was not simply descriptive. It formed part of a larger theoretical framework, about which the following should be noted:

1   It represented a decisive movement away from mythological, religious and other 'causes' of social evolution to what are clearly recognizable as material causes — sociological, economic, environmental, etc.

2   It produced the idea that the history of 'mankind' (*sic*) occurred along a single continuum, divided into a series of stages.

3   Writers differed over precisely *which* material or sociological factors they believed played the key role in propelling societies through these stages. But one factor assumed increasing importance — the 'mode of subsistence':

> In its most specific form, the theory was that society had 'naturally' or 'normally' progressed over time through four more or less distinct and consecutive stages, each corresponding to a different mode of subsistence, these stages being defined as hunting, pasturage, agriculture and commerce. To each of these modes of subsistence ... there corresponded different sets of ideas and institutions relating to law, property, and government and also different sets of customs, manners and morals.
> (Meek, 1976, p.2)

Here, then, is a surprising twist. The Enlightenment aspired to being a 'science of man'. It was the matrix of modern social science. It provided the language in which 'modernity' first came to be defined. In Enlightenment discourse, the West was the model, the prototype and the measure of social progress. It was *western* progress, civilization, rationality and development that were celebrated. And yet, all this depended on the discursive figures of the 'noble vs ignoble savage', and of 'rude and refined nations' which had been formulated in the discourse of 'the West and the Rest'. So the Rest was critical for the formation of western Enlightenment — and therefore for modern social science. Without the Rest (or its own internal 'others'), the West would not have been able to recognize and represent itself as the summit of human history. The figure of 'the Other', banished to the edge of the conceptual world and constructed as the absolute opposite, the negation, of everything which the West stood for, reappeared at the very centre of the discourse of civilization, refinement, modernity and development in the West. 'The Other' was the 'dark' side — forgotten, repressed and denied; the reverse image of enlightenment and modernity.

6   FROM 'THE WEST AND THE REST' TO MODERN SOCIOLOGY

In response to this argument, you may find yourself saying — 'Yes, perhaps the early stages of the "science of man" *were* influenced by the discourse of "the West and the Rest". But all that was a long time ago. Since then, social science has become more empirical, more "scientific". Sociology today is, surely, free of such "loaded images"?' But this is not necessarily the case. Discourses don't stop abruptly. They go on unfolding, changing shape, as they make sense of new circumstances. They often carry many of the same unconscious premises and unexamined assumptions in their blood-stream.

For example, some of you may have recognized in the Enlightenment concept of 'modes of subsistence' the outline of an idea which Karl Marx (1818–83), a 'founding father' of modern sociology, was subsequently to develop into one of the most powerful sociological tools: his theory that society is propelled forward by the class struggle; that it progresses through a series of stages marked by different modes of production, the critical one for capitalism being the transition from feudalism to capitalism. Of course, there is considerable divergance between the Enlightenment's 'four stages of subsistence' and Marx's 'modes of production'. But there are also some surprising similarities. In his *Grundrisse*, Marx speaks in broad outlines of the Asiatic, ancient, feudal and capitalist or bourgeois modes of production. He argues that each is dominated by a particular social class which expropriates the economic surplus through a specific set of social relations. The Asiatic mode (which is only sketchily developed), is that to which, in Marx's view, countries such as China, India and those of Islam belong. It is characterized by: (a) stagnation, (b) an absence of dynamic class struggle, and (c) the dominance of a swollen state acting as a sort of universal landlord. The conditions for capitalist development are here absent. Marx hated the capitalist system; nevertheless, he saw it, in contrast with the Asiatic mode, as progressive and dynamic, sweeping old structures aside, driving social development forward.

There are some interesting parallels here with Max Weber (1864–1920), another of sociology's founding fathers. Weber used a very dualistic model which contrasted Islam with Western Europe in terms of modern social development. For Weber, the essential conditions for the transition to capitalism and modernity are: (a) ascetic forms of religion, (b) rational forms of law, (c) free labour, and (d) the growth of cities (see Chapter 5 above). All these, in his view, were missing from Islam, which he represented as a 'mosaic' of tribes and groups, never cohering into a proper social system, but existing under a despotic rule which absorbed social conflicts in an endlessly repeating cycle of factional struggles, with Islam as its monolithic religion. Power and privilege, Weber believed, had been kept within, and rotated between, the ruling Islamic families, who merely syphoned off the wealth through taxation. He called this a 'patrimonial' or 'prebendary' form of authority. Unlike feudalism, it did not provide the preconditions for capitalist accumulation and growth.

These are, of course, some of the most complex and sophisticated models in sociology. The question of the causes and preconditions for the development of capitalism in the West have preoccupied historians and social scientists for centuries.

However, it has been argued by some social scientists that *both* Marx's notion of 'Asiatic' mode of production and Weber's 'patrimonial' form of domination contain traces of, or have been deeply penetrated by, 'Orientalist' assumptions. Or, to put it in our terms, both models provide evidence that the discourse of 'the West and the Rest' is still at work in some of the conceptual categories, the stark oppositions and the theoretical dualisms of modern sociology.

In his studies of *Weber and Islam* (1974) and *Marx and the End of Orientalism* (1978), Bryan Turner has argued that both sociology and Marxism have been unduly influenced by 'Orientalist' categories, or, if you lift the argument out of its Middle Eastern and Asian context, by the discourse of 'the West and the Rest':

> This can be seen…in Weber's arguments about the decline of Islam, its despotic political structure and the absence of autonomous cities. … Weber employs a basic dichotomy between the feudal economies of the West and the prebendal/patrimonial political economies of the East.…[He] overlays this discussion…with two additional components which have become the staples of the *internalist* version of development — the 'Islamic ethic' and the absence of an entrepreneurial urban bourgeoisie.
> (Turner, 1978, pp.7, 45–6)

Marx's explanation of the lack of capitalist development in the East is very different from Weber's. But his notion that this was due to the 'Asiatic mode of production' takes a similar path. Turner summarizes Marx's argument thus:

Societies dominated by the 'Asiatic' mode of production have no internal class conflicts and are consequently trapped within a static social context. The social system lacks a basic ingredient of social change, namely class struggle between landlords and an exploited peasantry ... [For example] 'Indian society has no history at all.' (Turner, 1978, pp.26–7)

ACTIVITY 6   Before reading on, look over the above quotations from Turner and answer the following questions:

1   What are the main differences between Weber's and Marx's arguments, as Turner summarizes them?

2   What are the main similarities?

3   Why does Turner call Weber's explanation 'internalist'?

4   Is Marx's 'Asiatic mode' an 'internalist' explanation too?

Despite their differences, both Weber and Marx organize their arguments in terms of broad, simple, contrasting oppositions which mirror quite closely the West–Rest, civilized–rude, developed–backward oppositions of 'the West and the Rest' discourse. Weber's is an 'internalist' type of explanation because 'he treats the main problems of "backward societies" as a question of certain characteristics *internal* to societies, considered in isolation from any international societal context' (Turner, 1978, p.10). Marx's explanation also looks like an 'internalist' one. But he adds certain 'externalist' features. By 'externalist' we mean 'relating to a theory of development which identifies the main problems facing "developing" societies as external to the society itself, which is treated as a unit located within a structured international context.' (See Turner, 1978, p.11.) In this chapter, we have adopted an 'externalist' or 'global' rather than a purely 'internalist' account of the rise of the idea of the West.

However these additional features of Marx's argument lead his explanation in a very surprising direction. 'Asiatic'-type societies, he argues, cannot develop into modern ones because they lack certain pre-conditions. Therefore, 'only the introduction of dynamic elements of western capitalism' can trigger development. This makes 'capitalist colonialism' a (regrettable) historical necessity for these societies, since it alone can 'destroy the pre-capitalist modes which prevent them from entering a progressive historical path'. Capitalism, Marx argues, must expand to survive, drawing the whole world progressively into its net; and it is this expansion which 'revolutionizes and undermines pre-capitalist modes of production at the periphery of the capitalist world'. (Turner, 1978, p.11.) Many classical marxists have indeed argued that, however stunting and destructive it may have been, the expansion of western capitalism through conquest and colonization was historically inevitable and would have long-term progressive outcomes for 'the Rest'.

Earlier, we discussed some of the forces which pushed a developing western Europe to expand outwards into 'new worlds'. But whether this was inevitable, whether its effects have been socially progressive, and whether this was the only possible path to 'modernity' are subjects increasingly debated in the social sciences today (as is discussed in Book 4 (Hall *et al.*, 1992)). In many parts of the world, the expansion of western colonization has *not* destroyed the pre-capitalist barriers to development. It has conserved and reinforced them. Colonization and imperialism have *not* promoted economic and social development in these societies, most of which remain profoundly under-developed. Where development has taken place, it has often been of the 'dependent' variety.

The destruction of alternative ways of life has *not* ushered in a new social order in these societies. Many remain in the grip of feudal ruling families, religious elites, military cliques and dictators who govern societies beset by endemic poverty. The destruction of indigenous cultural life by western culture is, for most of them, a very mixed blessing. And as the human, cultural and ecological consequences of this form of 'western development' become more obvious, the question of whether there is only one path to modernity is being debated with increasing urgency. The historically inevitable and necessarily progressive character of the West's expansion into the Rest is no longer as obvious as perhaps it once seemed to western scholars.

We must leave these issues as open questions at this stage. However, this is a useful point to summarize the main thrust of the argument of this chapter.

7 CONCLUSION

In the early chapters of this book, we looked at how the distinctive form of society which we call 'modern' emerged, and the major processes which led to its formation. We also looked at the emergence of the distinctive form of knowledge which accompanied that society's formation — at what the Enlightenment called the 'sciences of man', which provided the framework within which modern social science and the idea of 'modernity' were formulated. On the whole, the emphasis in those chapters was 'internalist'. Though the treatment was comparative — acknowledging differences between different societies, histories and tempos of development — the story was largely framed from within western Europe (the West) where these processes of formation first emerged.

This chapter reminds us that this formation was also a 'global' process. It had crucial 'externalist' features — aspects which could not be explained without taking into account the rest of the world, where these processes were not at work and where these kinds of society did not emerge. This is a huge topic in its own right and we could tell only a small part of the story here. We could have focussed on the economic, political and social consequences of the global expansion of the West; instead, we briefly sketched the outline history of that expansion, up to roughly the eighteenth century. We also wanted to show the *cultural* and *ideological* dimensions of the West's expansion. For if the Rest was necessary for the political, economic and social formation of the West, it was also essential to the West's formation both of its own sense of itself — a 'western identity' — and of western forms of knowledge.

This is where the notion of 'discourse' came in. A discourse is a way of talking about or representing something. It produces knowledge that shapes perceptions and practice. It is part of the way in which power operates. Therefore, it has consequences for both those who employ it and those who are 'subjected' to it. The West produced many different ways of talking about itself and 'the Others'. But what we have called the discourse of 'the West and the Rest' became one of the most powerful and formative of these discourses. It became the dominant way in which, for many decades, the West represented itself and its relation to 'the Other'. In this chapter, we have traced how this discourse was formed and how it worked. We analysed it as a 'system of representation' — a 'regime of truth'. It was as formative for the West and 'modern societies' as the secular state, capitalist economies, the modern class, race and gender systems, and modern, individualist, secular culture — the four main 'processes' of our formation story.

Finally, we suggest that, in transformed and reworked forms, this discourse continues to inflect the language of the West, its image of itself and 'others', its sense of 'us' and 'them', its practices and relations of power towards the Rest. It is especially important for the languages of racial inferiority and ethnic superiority which still operate so powerfully across the globe today. So, far from being a 'formation' of the past, and of only historical interest, the discourse of 'the West and the Rest' is alive and well in the modern world. And one of the surprising places where its effects can still be seen is in the language, theoretical models and hidden assumptions of modern sociology itself.

REFERENCES

Abercrombie, N., Hill, S. and Turner, B.S. (eds) (1988) *The Penguin Dictionary of Sociology*, 2nd edn, Harmondsworth, Penguin.

Arens, W. (1977) *The Man-Eating Myth: Anthropology and Anthropophagy*, New York, Oxford University Press.

Asad, T. (1973) *Anthropology and the Colonial Encounter*, London, Ithaca Press.

Barker, A. J. (1978) *The African Link: British Attitudes to the Negro in the Era of the Atlantic Slave Trade, 1550–1807*, London, Frank Cass.

Beaglehole, J.C. (ed.) (1961) *The Journals of Captain Cook on his Voyages of Discovery* (vol. 2 of 3), Cambridge, Cambridge University Press.

Baudet, H. (1963) *Paradise on Earth: European Images of Non-European Man,* New Haven, Yale University Press.

Berkhofer, R. (1978) *The White Man's Indian: Images of the American Indian from Columbus to the Present,* New York, Knopf.

Chiappelli, F. (ed.) (1978) *First Images of America: The Impact of the New World* (2 vols) Berkeley, University of California Press.

Cousins, M. and Hussain, A. (1984) *Michel Foucault,* London, Macmillan.

Columbus, C. (1969) *The Four Voyages of Christopher Columbus* (ed. J. M. Cohen), Harmondsworth, Penguin.

Dryden, J. (1978) *The Works of John Dryden* (vol. 11), Berkeley, University of California Press.

Fairchild, H. (1961) *The Noble Savage: A Study in Romantic Naturalism,* New York, Russell & Russell.

Foucault, M. (1972) *The Archeology of Knowledge*, London, Tavistock.

Foucault, M. (1980) *Power/Knowledge,* Brighton, Harvester.

Gilman, S. (1985) *Difference and Pathology: Stereotypes of Sexuality, Race, and Madness*, Ithaca, Cornell University Press.

Hakluyt, R. (1972) *Voyages and Discoveries*, Harmondsworth, Penguin.

Hale, J.R. *et al.* (1966) *Age of Exploration,* Netherlands, Time-Life International.

Hall, C. (1991) 'Missionary positions', in Grossberg, L. and Nelson, C. (eds) *Cultural Studies Now and in the Future*, London, Routledge.

Hall, S., Held, D. and McGrew, A. (eds) (1992) *Modernity and its Futures*, Cambridge, Polity Press.

Harris, M. (1977) *Cannibals and Kings: The Origins of Cultures*, New York, Random House.

Hobbes, T. (1946) *Leviathan*, Oxford, Blackwell.

Honour, H. (1976) *The New Golden Land: European Images of America*, London, Allen Lane.

Smith, B. (1988) *European Vision and the South Pacific*, New Haven,

Hulme, P. (1986) *Colonial Encounters: Europe and the Native Caribbean, 1492–1797,* London, Methuen.

Jennings, F. (1976) *The Invasion of America: Indians, Colonialism, and the Cant of Conquest*, New York, Norton.

Joppien, R. and Smith, B. (1985) *The Art of Captain Cook's Voyages* (2 vols), New Haven, Yale University Press.

Latham, R. (ed.) (1958) *Marco Polo: The Travels*, Harmondsworth, Penguin.

Léon-Portilla, M. (1962) *The Broken Spears: the Aztec Account of the Conquest of Mexico*, London, Constable.

Locke, J. (1976) *The Second Treatise on Government*, Oxford, Basil Blackwell.

Mandeville, B. (1924) *The Fable of the Bees*, Oxford, Clarendon Press.

Mandeville, Sir J. (1964) *The Travels,* New York, Dover.

Mann, M. (1988) 'European development: approaching a historical explanation', in Baechler, J. *et al.* (eds), *Europe and the Rise of Capitalism*, Oxford, Blackwells.

Marshall, P. and Williams, G. (1982) *The Great Map of Mankind: British Perceptions of the World in the Age of the Enlightenment,* London, Dent.

Marx, K. (1964) *Precapitalist Economic Formations* (ed. E.J. Hobsbawm), London, Lawrence & Wishart.

Marx, K. (1973) *Grundrisse*, Harmondsworth, Pelican.

Meek, R. (1976) *Social Science and the Ignoble Savage*, Cambridge, Cambridge University Press.

Montaigne, M. (1964) *Selected Essays*, Boston, Houghton Mifflin.

Moorhead, A. (1987) *The Fatal Impact: An Account of the Invasion of the South Pacific, 1767–1840*, Harmondsworth, Penguin

Newby, E. (1975) *The Mitchell Beazley World Atlas of Exploration,* London, Mitchell Beazley.

Parry J.H. (ed.) (1968) *The European Reconnaissance: Selected Documents,*New York, Harper & Row.

Parry, J.H. (1971) *Trade and Dominion: The European Oversea Empires in the Eighteenth Century*, London, Weidenfeld & Nicolson.

Penguin Dictionary of Sociology: see Abercrombie *et al.* (1988).

Roberts, J.M. (1985) *The Triumph Of The West*, London, British Broadcasting Corporation.

Rousseau, J.-J. (1968) *The Social Contract*, Harmondsworth, Penguin.

Said, E. W. (1985) *Orientalism: Western Concepts of the Orient,* Harmondsworth, Penguin.

Sale, K. (1991) *The Conquest of Paradise: Christopher Columbus and the Columbian Legacy*, London, Hodder & Stoughton.

Schama, S. (1977) *The Embarrassment of Riches: An Interpretation of Dutch Culture*, New York, Knopf. Yale University Press.

Turner, B.S. (1974) *Weber and Islam*, London, Routledge.

Turner, B.S. (1978) *Marx and the End of Orientalism*, London, Allen & Unwin.

Wallace, W.M. (1959) *Sir Walter Raleigh,* Princeton, Princeton University Press.

Withey, L. (1987) *Voyages of Discovery: Captain Cook and the Exploration of the Pacific,* London, Hutchinson.

Williams, E.E. (1970) *From Columbus to Castro: The History of the Caribbean, 1492–1969*, London, Andre Deutsch.

READING A   EXPLAINING EUROPEAN DEVELOPMENT

Michael Mann

The conventional wisdom of our age ... purports to give us a clear answer [about European development] in terms of neoclassical economics. Land, capital and labour interact as factors of production on competitive markets across given ecologies. As Jones (1981) argues, part of 'the European miracle' when compared to Asia resides in its ecological contrasts. This produces a 'dispersed portfolio of resources' whereby bulk ... goods — such as grains, meat, fruit, olives, wine, salt, metals, wood, animal skins and furs — were exchanged right across the continent. The high proportion of coastlines and navigable rivers kept transport costs low. Then, Jones continues, consequences flow from economic rationality: states had no interest in pillaging ['looting'] bulk subsistence goods traded as commodities, only in taxing them; in return, states would provide basic social order. Europe avoided the state 'plunder machine', hence economic development. As a neoclassical economist who believes that markets are 'natural', Jones paraphrases his mentor, Adam Smith — if you have peace, easy taxes and a tolerable administration of justice, then the rest is brought about by 'the natural course of things' (Jones, 1981, pp.90-6, 232-7).

But such a model has essential preconditions whose emergence we must explain. Why is 'Europe' to be regarded as a continent in the first place? This is not an ecological but a social fact. It had not been a continent hitherto: it was now created by the fusion of the Germanic barbarians and the north-western parts of the Roman Empire, and the blocking presence of Islam to the south and east. Its continental identity was primarily Christian, for its name was Christendom more often than it was Europe.

Europe was undoubtedly a place where competition flourished, but why? It is not 'natural'. ... In fact, competition presupposes two further forms of social organization. First, autonomous actors must be empowered to dispose of privately owned resources without hindrance from anyone else. These actors need not be individuals, or even individual households, enjoying what in capitalist societies we call 'private property'. ... But collective institutions also qualify, as long as they have a responsible authority structure empowered to dispose of its resources for economic advantage, without interference from others, or from custom — then the laws of neoclassical economics can begin to operate. ...

Second, competition among actors on a market [basis] requires normative regulation. They must trust one another to honour their word. They must also trust each other's essential rationality. These normative understandings must apply not only in direct interaction but right across complex, continental chains of production, distribution and exchange. ...

Source: Mann, M. (1988) 'European development: approaching a historical explanation', in Baechler, J. *et al.* (eds) *Europe and the Rise of Capitalism*, Oxford, Blackwells, pp.10–15.

European social structure supplied these requirements. The social structure which stabilized in Europe after the ending of the barbarian migrations and invasions (that is, by AD 1000) was a multiple acephalous federation. Europe had no head, no centre, yet it was an entity composed of a number of small, cross-cutting interaction networks. These, based on economic, military and ideological power, each differed in their geographical and social space and none was itself unitary in nature. Consequently no single power agency controlled a clear-cut territory or the people within it. As a result most social relationships were extremely localized, intensely focused upon one or more of a number of cell-like communities — the monastery, the village, the manor, the castle, the town, the guild, the brotherhood and so on. These collectivities has a power autonomy guaranteed by law or custom, an exclusivity of control over 'their' resources. They qualify, therefore, as 'private' property owners.

In agriculture the two main actors were the village community and the manor. Thus monopolistic power organizations rarely existed in the local economy. Formidable as were the powers of the lord, they were usually restrained by the fact that even the serf could find support from the village community and from customary law. The two power networks were also interpenetrating — peasant and lord were partly independent of one another, partly implicated in each other's organization, as the distribution of their strips of land reveals. Interpenetration was most pronounced along the old Roman frontier provinces where the German free village and the Roman estate mixed — in England, the Low Countries, northern and central France, West Germany, and eastern and northern England. But a similar balance between organized collectivities existed in the political, military and religious realms. No one ruled Europe.

Whatever this extraordinary multiple, acephalous federation would achieve, it was unlikely to be organized stagnation. Historians over and over again use the word *restless* to characterize the essence of medieval culture. As McNeill puts it, 'it is not any particular set of institutions, ideas or technologies that mark out the West but its inability to come to a rest. No other civilized society has ever approached such restless instability. ... In this ... lies the true uniqueness of Western civilization' (McNeill, 1963, p.539). But such a spirit need not induce social development. Might it not induce other forms of stagnation: anarchy, the Hobbesian war of all against all, or *anomie* where the absence of social control and direction leads to aimlessness and despair? We can marry the insights of two great sociologists to guess why social development, not anarchy or *anomie*, may have resulted.

First Max Weber, who in noting the peculiar restlessness of Europe, always added another word: *rational*. 'Rational restlessness' was the psychological make-up of Europe, the opposite of what he found in the main religions of Asia ... . Weber located rational restlessness especially in Puritanism. But Puritanism emphasized strands of the Christian psyche which had been traditionally present. ... Christianity encouraged a drive for moral and social improvement even against worldly authority. Though much of medieval Christianity was piously masking brutal repression, its currents of dissatisfaction always ran strong. We can read an enormous literature of social criticism, visionary, moralistic, satirical, cynical. Some is laboured and repetitious, but its peak includes some of the greatest works of the age — in English: Langland and Chaucer. It is pervaded by the kind of psychological quality identified by Weber.

But to put this rational restlessness in the service of social improvement probably also required a mechanism identified by another sociologist: Emile Durkheim. Not anarchy or *anomie* but normative regulation was provided at first primarily by Christendom. Political and class struggles, economic life and even wars were, to a degree, regulated by an unseen hand, not Adam Smith's but Jesus Christ's. ... The community depended on the general recognition of norms regarding property rights and free exchange. These were guaranteed by a mixture of local customs and privileges, some judicial regulation by weak states, but above all by the common social identity provided by Christendom.

Let us try a little hypothetical reconstruction of the case of England. If we were able to travel back to England around 1150, armed with questionnaires, tape-recorders and the necessary linguistic skills, to ask a sample of the population with all due circumspection to what social group they belonged, we would get rather complex answers. The majority would not be able to give one sole identity. The lords, whom we would interview in Norman French (though we could try Latin), might indicate that they were gentlefolk — Christians, of course; they might elaborate a genealogy indicating also that they were of Norman descent but linked closely to the Angevin king of England and to the English baronage. They would think that, on balance, their interests lay with the lords of the kingdom of England (perhaps including its French possessions, perhaps not) rather than with, say, the lords of the kingdom of France. I am not sure where they would place 'the people' — Christians, but barbarous, unlettered rustics — in their normative map. The merchants, whom we would interview in a diversity of languages, might say that they were English or citizens of towns from the Baltic coast to Lombardy; if they were English they would probably show more anti-foreigner 'nationalism' than anyone else, out of sectional interest; they would naturally say that they were Christians; and their interest lay in a combination of guild autonomy and alliance with the English crown. The higher clergy, whom we would interview in Latin, would say Christians first and foremost. But we would then usually find both a clear, kin-based, class solidarity with the lords, and an overlapping identity with some lords and merchants, but definitely excluding the people, centred on the possession of literacy. The parish priest, with whom we could try Latin — or failing that, Middle English — might say Christian and English. ... The peasants, the vast majority of our sample, we would interview in the various Middle English dialects and amalgams of Saxon, Danish, Celtic and Norman French (of which we only have the vaguest outlines). They were *illiterati* ['illiterates'], an abusive term denoting exclusion, not membership of a community. They would say Christian, and then they might say English, or they might say they were Essex or Northumbrian or Cornish folk. Their allegiances were mixed: to their local lord (temporal or spiritual), to their local village or other kin network and (if they were freemen) to their king.

The main conclusion is unmistakable. The most powerful and extensive sense of social identity was Christian, though this was both a unifying transcendent identity and an identity divided by the overlapping barriers of class and literacy. Cross-cutting all these were commitments to England, but these were variable and, in any case, included less extensive dynastic connections and obligations. Thus, Christian identity provided both a common humanity and a framework for common divisions among Europeans. ...

I use the term 'transcendence' for this identity quite deliberately, for I wish to suggest that it was capable of conquering geographical distance. Apart from trading activities, the most frequent type of movement around Europe was probably religious in nature. Clerics travelled greatly, but so too did lay people on pilgrimage. Pilgrimage has been called 'the therapy of distance'. ... But Europe was [also] integrated by the scattering [of holy relics], the constant journeying and the carefully cultivated, culminating experience of *praesentia*, the supposed physical presence of Christ or saint at the shrine (Brown, 1981). At the ethical level, the church also preached consideration, decency and charity towards all Christians: basic normative pacification, a substitute for costly coercive pacification normally required in extensive societies. The main sanction the church could provide was not physical force, but exclusion from the community, in the last resort, excommunication. ...

If we wished to eye this community more materialistically or cynically, then we would add two qualifications. First, the *ecumene* was infrastructure as well as superstructure. Until the thirteenth century it monopolized education and written communication and provided the *lingua franca*: Latin. Thus state bureaucracies, manorial estates and trading associations had access to generally useful knowledge through Church infrastructures. The network of churches, abbeys, monasteries and shrines also provided the major staging-posts of extensive communication and many of the most technologically advanced agrarian economies. Second, the church also led the nastier side of medieval society. The darker side of normative pacification was the savage treatment meted out to those outside the *ecumene*, to schismatics, heretics, Jews, Muhammadans or pagans. Indeed, let us not look at this religious community in modern, pious terms at all. It was also bawdy folklore, satirizing the common religion, carried by travelling players and mendicants whose plays and sermons would strike modern church congregations as blasphemous, as in parodies of all the major religious rituals. Preachers drawing audiences of thousands were conscious of their tricks-of-the-trade. ... But in all of this — ritual, ethics, technology, barbarity and the grotesque — the common culture *was* Christianity. ...

The Christian achievement was the creation of a minimal normative society across state, ethnic, class and gender boundaries. It did not in any significant sense include the Eastern Byzantine Church. It did, however, integrate the two major geographical areas of 'Europe', the Mediterranean lands with their cultural heritage, their historic and predominantly *extensive* power techniques — literacy, coinage, agricultural estates and trading networks — and north-western Europe with its more *intensive* power techniques — deep ploughing, village and kin solidarities and locally organized warfare. If the two could be kept in a single community, then European development was a possible consequence of their creative interchange.

References

Brown, P. (1981) *The Cult of the Saints,* London, SCM Press.

Jones, E. L. (1981) *The European Miracle,* Cambridge, Cambridge University Press.

McNeill, W. (1963) *The Rise of the West: A History of the Human Community*, Chicago, Chicago University Press.

MacFarlane, A. (1978) *The Origins of English Individualism,* Oxford, Oxford University Press.

READING B   THE IDEA OF 'EUROPE'

John Roberts

Europeans … now [took] a new view of themselves and their relation to the other peoples of the globe. Maps are the best clue to this change … . They are always more than mere factual statements. They are translations of reality into forms we can master; they are fictions and acts of imagination communicating more than scientific data. So they reflect changes in our pictures of reality. The world is not only what exists 'out there'; it is also the picture we have of it in our minds which enables us to take a grip on material actuality. In taking that grip, our apprehension of that actuality changes — and so does a wide range of our assumptions and beliefs.

One crucial mental change was the final emergence of the notion of Europe from the idea of Christendom. Maps show the difference between the two. After the age of discovery, Jerusalem, where the founder of Christianity had taught and died, could no longer be treated as the centre of the world — where it appeared on many medieval maps. Soon it was Europe which stood at the centre of Europeans' maps. The final key to a new mental picture was provided by the discovery of the Americas. Somewhere about 1500 European map-makers had established the broad layout of the world map with which we are familiar. In the fifteenth century, Europe had usually been placed in the top left-hand corner of attempts to lay out the known world, with the large masses of Asia and Africa sprawled across the rest of the surface. The natural centre of such maps might be in any of several places. Then the American discoveries slowly began to effect a shift in the conventional arrangement; more and more

Source: Roberts, J.M. (1985) *The Triumph of the West,* London, British Broadcasting Corporation, pp.194–202.

space had to be given to the land masses of North and South America as their true extent became better known. Juan de la Cosa, who had sailed with Columbus on his second voyage, was the first man to incorporate knowledge of his discoveries (as well as those of John Cabot's voyage of 1497) in a world map he made in 1500 which already shows the shift of Europe towards a world-central position. ...

By the middle of the century the new geographical view of the world had come to be taken for granted. It was given its canonical expression in the work of Mercator ... . Mercator's new 'projection', first used in a map in 1568, ... drove home the idea that the land surface of the globe was naturally grouped about a European centre. So Europe came to stand in some men's minds at the centre of the world. No doubt this led Europeans for centuries to absorb unconsciously from their atlases the idea that this was somehow the natural order of things. It did not often occur to them that you could have centred Mercator's projection in, say, China, or even Hawaii, and that Europeans might then have felt very different. The idea still hangs about, even today. Most people like to think of themselves at the centre of things. ... Mercator helped his own civilisation to take what is now called a 'Eurocentric' view of the world. ...

The ultimate origins of a change in men's minds, though, lie deeper than maps. They can be traced at least to the thirteenth and fourteenth centuries (Hay, 1957, p.58). Even then, to a few people, the European continent was beginning to be clearly identifiable as an area to all intents and purposes identical with Christendom, and so (though no one had the concept to hand) the seat of a distinctive civilisation. ... Meanwhile Christianity had been extended to every corner of Europe. The Christian churches of Asia, though, had been the victims of Muslim response to the crusaders' brutality, and then of the rise of the Ottoman Turks and the destruction of the Byzantine empire. Non-European Christianity had therefore never looked less impressive than at the beginning of the sixteenth century, and that gave even more importance to its Catholic and west European form. Finally, Europe's economic life, growing richer in these centuries, was giving the continent a new sort of homogeneity.

All these facts meant that fifteenth-century Europe was a unity in quite a new way. Some churchmen, statesmen and polemicists began to work out and make suggestions about the implications of this. They were not always fully aware of what they were doing. But 'Europe' slowly became inter-changeable with the concept 'Christendom', and 'European' with 'Christian'. In common parlance, Christendom no longer extended to the Christians under Ottoman rule, who were not regarded as Europeans. Maps, which had begun in the fourteenth century to distinguish symbolically between political authorities in different places, began in the next [century] to mark off a Christendom confined to Europe, from the area dominated by Islam.

With a growing self-consciousness went a growing sense of superiority. New knowledge of other continents seemed to bear this out, and ancient conceptions began to stir and to be given new applications. The old antithesis of civilised and barbarian rooted in Greek origin had never quite disappeared. … An Englishman, Purchas, writing in 1625, gave a remarkable expression to a new European confidence:

> Europe is taught the way to scale heaven not by mathematical principles, but by divine verity. Jesus Christ is their way, their truth, their life; who hath long been given a bill of divorce to ungrateful Asia, where He was born, and Africa, the place of his flight and refuge, and is become almost wholly and only European. For little do we find of this name in Asia, less in Africa, and nothing at all in America, but later European gleanings.
> (Purchas, 1905–7, p.251)

The sense of identity, of a special nature, derived from religion, was by then no longer new. It was reflected in the transition from the idea of Christendom to that of Europe. What is new in such a statement is the confidence it shows at a moral and mythical level, and its attachment to place and people, to Europe and Europeans. It shows Europeans who are beginning to feel they have little to learn from the rest of the world. …

The cultivated European's view of universal history at about the same time might be found in the work of a French clergyman, Jacques Bénigne Bossuet, bishop of Meaux, … [and] tutor to the king's son, the dauphin, [from] 1670. … During that time, one of he books he wrote for his pupil's instruction was a *Discourse on Universal History* (Bossuet, 1691). … [Yet] not the least interesting feature of [this] book is the fact that the history of most of the world finds no place in it.

It is focused on the tradition which Europe inherits — the tradition which leads to Bossuet and his master, Louis XIV — the Judaeo-Roman tradition. We learn from Bossuet much of the kings of Israel and the great days of Rome, something, even, of Assyria, Persia and Egypt, whose histories impinge on those of the Jews and Greeks, but nothing, for instance, of China, whose empire was already nearly two thousand years old when he wrote. Yet Bossuet was the dauphin's tutor when Louis XIV solemnly received the first ambassadors to Europe from Siam, a tributary state of the Chinese empire. He must have known of the avidly studied Jesuit missionaries' reports from the Chinese imperial court and may, perhaps, have heard of the concessions in behaviour and dress which some of those Jesuits were making to a civilisation they had learned to admire. Why does he show so little concern for its role in the story of mankind, then? The reasons must be a reflection of the emotional and logical self-sufficiency already achieved by European culture. The essential meaning of history, for Bossuet and his contemporaries, was to be found in the Christian story, which culminated in the Europe of his day and perhaps even in a Catholic monarch who saw himself as the 'Sun King' — *le roi soleil*. Only a little while before this had men learned that they lived in a heliocentric universe, that the planets revolved about the sun, which now stood at the centre of the celestial map in as unquestioned way as Europe stood at the centre of Mercator's. Now a king, the most powerful in Europe, could accept the theory as an image of his own position.

Nowadays, people have come to use a specially minted word to summarise this state of mind — 'Eurocentrism'. It means 'putting Europe at the centre of things' and its usual implication is that to do so is wrong. But, of course, if we are merely talking about facts, about what happened, and not about value we place on them, then it is quite correct to put Europe at the centre of the story in modern times. From the age of discovery onwards, Europe, and those countries which are descended from the European stocks, have been the mainspring of history, and to that extent (and no further) Purchas, Bossuet and others were sensing the truth. It was from Europe that the discoverers, *conquistadores*, settlers and traders had gone *out*: they created a world of which Europe was the centre, the Americas and Asia the periphery. Eurocentrism, nevertheless, at an early date went revealingly beyond the mere facts of power and influence (which, in any case, were only just beginning to show themselves). What Purchas and the rest felt was a qualitative superiority.

References

Bossuet, J.B. (1691) *Discours sur l'histoire universelle*, Paris.

Hay, D. (1957) *Europe: The Emergence of an Idea*, Edinburgh, Edinburgh University Press.

Purchas, S. (1905–7) *Hakluytus posthumus or Purchas his Pilgrimes*, Glasgow, Hakluyt Society.

READING C   'ORIENTALISM': REPRESENTING THE OTHER
Edward Said

Orientalism is never far from what Denys Hay has called the idea of Europe, a collective notion identifying 'us' Europeans as against all 'those' non-Europeans, and indeed it can be argued that the major component in European culture is precisely what made that culture hegemonic both in and outside Europe: the idea of European identity as a superior one in comparison with all the non-European peoples and cultures. There is in addition the hegemony of European ideas about the Orient, themselves reiterating European superiority over Oriental backwardness. ...

In a quite constant way, Orientalism depends for its strategy on this flexible *positional* superiority, which puts the Westerner in a whole series of possible relationships with the Orient without ever losing him the relative upper hand. ... Under the general heading of knowledge of the Orient, and within the umbrella of Western hegemony over the Orient during the period from the end of the eighteenth century, there emerged a complex Orient suitable for study in the academy, for display in the museum, for reconstruction in the colonial office, for theoretical illustration in anthropological, biological, linguistic, racial, and historical theses about mankind and the universe, for instances of economic and sociological theories

Source: Said, E.W. (1978) *Orientalism: Western Concepts of the Orient*, Harmondsworth, Penguin, pp.7–8, 20, 41–2, 44–5.

of development, revolution, cultural personality, national or religious character. Additionally, the imaginative examination of things Oriental was based more or less exclusively upon a sovereign Western consciousness out of whose unchallenged centrality an Oriental world emerged, first according to general ideas about who or what was an Oriental, then according to a detailed logic governed not simply by empirical reality but by a battery of desires, repressions, investments, and projections. ...

The period of immense advance in the institutions and content of Orientalism coincides exactly with the period of unparalleled European expansion; from 1815 to 1914 European direct colonial dominion expanded from about 35 percent of the earth's surface to about 85 percent of it. Every continent was affected, none more so than Africa and Asia. The two greatest empires were the British and the French; allies and partners in some things, in others they were hostile rivals. ...

What they shared, however, was not only land or profit or rule; it was the kind of intellectual power I have been calling Orientalism. In a sense Orientalism was a library or archive of information commonly and, in some of its aspects, unanimously held. What bound the archive together was a family of ideas and a unifying set of values proven in various ways to be effective. These ideas explained the behaviour of Orientals; they supplied Orientals with a mentality, a genealogy, an atmosphere; most important, they allowed Europeans to deal with and even to see Orientals as a phenomenon possessing regular characteristics. But like any set of durable ideas, Orientalist notions influenced the people who were called Orientals as well as those called Occidental, European, or Western; in short, Orientalism is better grasped as a set of constraints upon and limitations of thought than it is simply as a positive doctrine. If the essence of Orientalism is the ineradicable distinction between Western superiority and Oriental inferiority, then we must be prepared to note how in its development and subsequent history Orientalism deepened and even hardened the distinction. ...

Orientalism was ultimately a political vision of reality whose structure promoted the difference between the familiar (Europe, the West, 'us') and the strange (the Orient, the East, 'them'). This vision in a sense created and then served the two worlds thus conceived. Orientals lived in their world, 'we' lived in ours. The vision and material reality propped each other up, kept each other going. A certain freedom of intercourse was always the Westerner's privilege; because his was the stronger culture, he could penetrate, he could wrestle with, he could give shape and meaning to the great Asiatic mystery, as Disraeli once called it.

READING D RECIPROCITY AND EXCHANGE
Peter Hulme

What was the fundamental difference between Algonquian [a New World Indian] and English cultures? Inasmuch as a large and single answer to this question can be risked, it could be claimed that the native American cultures ... acted according to norms of *reciprocity*; and that the European cultures did not. ...

The classic study of reciprocity is Marcel Mauss's *Essai sur le don* (1925), where it denotes the complex system of exchanges between individuals and villages by means of which undivided (i.e. pre-state) societies function: 'The gift is the primitive way of achieving the peace that in civil society is secured by the State' (Sahlins, 1974, p.169). Divided societies are, by definition, no longer reciprocal, although the ideology of reciprocity has a long and continuing history. ... Only under the fetishized social relations of capitalism does reciprocity disappear altogether, however loudly its presence is trumpeted: 'a fair day's work for a fair day's pay'.

Reciprocity itself refers to a series of practices distinctly unamenable to breakdown into the economic, social, political and ideological. This is the gist of Mauss's argument:

> In tribal feasts, in ceremonies of rivals clans, allied families or those that assist at each other's initiation, groups visit each other; and with the development of the law of hospitality in more advanced societies, the rules of friendship and contract are present — along with the gods — to ensure the peace of markets and villages; at these times men meet in a curious frame of mind with exaggerated fear and an equally exaggerated generosity which appear stupid in no one's eyes but our own. In these primitive and archaic societies there is no middle path. There is either complete trust or mistrust. ...
>
> But then they had no choice in the matter. When two groups of men meet they may move away or in case of mistrust or defiance they may resort to arms; or else they can come to terms. Business has always been done with foreigners, although these might have been allies ... . It is by opposing reason to emotion and setting up the will for peace against rash follies ... that peoples succeed in substituting alliance, gift and commerce for war, isolation and stagnation.
> (Mauss, 1970, pp.78–80)

This is probably as accurate a brief account as could be given of how the native American societies of the extended Caribbean functioned in the centuries before the arrival of the Europeans. It is particularly useful for the emphasis placed on the vital importance, yet constant tentativeness, of

Source: Hulme, P. (1986) *Colonial Encounters: Europe and the Native Caribbean, 1492–1797*, London, Methuen, pp.147-52.

that nexus of relationships between selves and others. Without the authority of a state all intercourse would teeter between alliance and hostility. To treat with others was the indispensable requirement for life, yet it entailed a constant risk of death. Mauss's account highlights too the importance of ritual as a way of attempting to control these risky encounters. Boundaries, whether physical or social, are places of danger. Strangers are to be feared. Fear is coped with by ritual. Hospitality dissolves the category of stranger, resolving it into either alliance or hostility.

In stateless societies these categories are a matter of constant lived experience: they make up the very fabric of economic, social, political and cultural life. ...

[In] the Caribbean and Virgins ... strangers were dealt with hospitably, fed and honoured, until their intentions could be assessed. Transients and traders would be welcomed and, if appropriate, alliances entered into. Settlers, rivals for limited resources, would be sent on their way or killed. European transients and traders benefited greatly from this attitude. ... [However,] misunderstanding ... was rife: the English clearly had as little notion of Amerindian ideas of communal property rights as the Algonquians had of English ideas of private property.

References

Mauss, M. (1970) *The Gift: Forms and Functions of Exchange in Archaic Societies* (*Essai sur le don*), Routledge, London.

Sahlins, M.D. (1974) *Stone Age Economics*, London, Tavistock.

ACKNOWLEDGEMENTS

Grateful acknowledgement is made to the following sources for permission to reproduce material in this book:

Chapter 1

Text

Reading A: Anderson, B.S. and Zinsser, J.P. (1989) *A History of Their Own*, Penguin Books, copyright © Bonnie S. Anderson and J.P. Zinsser 1988. Reproduced by permission of Penguin Books; *Reading B:* Gay P. (1969) *The Enlightenment: An Interpretation,* Vol. 2, George Weidenfeld & Nicolson Ltd. Also reproduced by permission of Alfred A. Knopf & Sons Inc.

Illustrations

p.19 (left): Photo Giraudon; *p.19 (right):* Hulton Deutsch Collection; *p.23:* Mary Evans Picture Library; *p.28:* Diderot, *Encyclopédie Planches*, Volume 12; *p.31:* Mary Evans Picture Library; *p.33:* Bibliothèque Nationale; *p.35:* Mary Evans Picture Library; *p.38:* Mansell Collection; *p.39:* Hulton Deutsch Collection; *p.46:* Mary Evans Picture Library; *p.53 (left):* Mary Evans Picture Library; *p.53 (right):* Maison d'Auguste Comte, Paris.

Chapter 2

Text

Reading B: from *The Social Contract* (1968) Penguin Books Ltd, trans. Maurice Cranston. Reprinted by permission of the Peters, Fraser and Dunlop Group Ltd. First published in 1762.

Tables

Tables 2.2 and 2.3: Mann, M. (1986) *The Social Sources of Power*, Cambridge University Press.

Figures

Figures 2.1, 2.2 and 2.3: McEvedy, C. (1961) *The Penguin Atlas of Medieval History,* pp.17, 53 and 85, Penguin Books, copyright © Colin McEvedy 1961. Reproduced by permission of Penguin Books Ltd; *Figure 2.4:* McEvedy, C. (1982) *The Penguin Atlas of Recent History,* p.89, Penguin Books, copyright © Colin McEvedy 1982. Reproduced by permission of Penguin Books Ltd; *Figure 2.6:* Mann, M. (1986) *The Sources of Social Power*, Cambridge University Press.

Chapter 3

Text

Readings A and B: Porter, R. (1990) *English Society in the Eighteenth Century*, Penguin Books, copyright © Roy Porter 1990. Reproduced by permission of Penguin Books Ltd.

Routledge; *Reading C:* Weber, M. (1930, 1971) *The Protestant Ethic and the Spirit of Capitalism,* Routledge; *Reading D:* Sigmund Freud Copyrights, The Institute of Psycho-Analysis and the Hogarth Press for permission to quote from *The Standard Edition of The Complete Psychological Works of Sigmund Freud* and the translator. Reprinted from *Civilization and its Discontents* by Sigmund Freud, translated and edited by James Strachey. Used with the permission of W.W. Norton and Company, Inc. Copyright © 1961 by James Strachey. Copyright renewed 1989.

Illustrations

p.239: Canada House; *p.245:* Barnabys/Tony Parry; *p.249:* Mansell Collection; *p.252:* Private Collection; *p.265: An Open Air Banquet in the Garden of Love,* The Burrell Collection, Glasgow Museums and Art Galleries.

Chapter 6

Text

Reading A: Mann, M. (1988) 'European development: approaching a historical explanation', in Baechler, J. *et al.* (eds) *Europe and the Rise of Capitalism,* Basil Blackwell Ltd; *Reading B:* Roberts, J.M. (1985) *The Triumph of the West*, reproduced by permission of BBC Enterprises Ltd; *Reading D:* Hulme, P. (1986) *Colonial Encounters: Europe and the Native Caribbean*, 1492–1797, Methuen, London.

Figures

Figures 6.4a and 6.5: British Museum, London; *Figures 6.3, 6.4b and 6.6:* British Library, London.

INDEX